09

R. Dennis Ricks, Jr.

Map of
Milton's
universe.
page 223

C. H. E. L.
Cambridge History
of English Literature

A

MILTON HANDBOOK

6:45

MILTON AT THE AGE OF 10
(*From the painting in The Pierpont Morgan Library*)

A MILTON HANDBOOK

FOURTH EDITION

BY

JAMES HOLLY HANFORD

PROFESSOR OF ENGLISH
WESTERN RESERVE UNIVERSITY

APPLETON-CENTURY-CROFTS, INC.
NEW YORK

MANUFACTURED IN THE UNITED STATES OF AMERICA
BY VAIL-BALLOU PRESS, INC., BINGHAMTON, N. Y.

(indexed at the end of the volume) which will enable the student to pursue the subject further at any point. I have necessarily left to the editors and to the various special dictionaries of Milton's language and allusions (listed in the general bibliography) the task of supplying a detailed interpretation of the texts. Discussion of purely critical problems is also omitted, though the general course of Miltonic opinion is sketched in the final chapter. The first process in the study of Milton should be interpretation rather than judgment, and it is to this end that the materials given in the present volume are aimed. In view, finally, of the ready accessibility in cyclopedias and elsewhere of summary statements of the outward events of Milton's life, and because I am convinced of the superior value of the documents themselves over any modern digest of them, I have substituted for the usual biography the statements of Milton himself and those who knew him, arranged according to the accepted periods of his career.

Of the inadequacy of this handbook to represent the field in which it enters, I am well aware. Miltonic scholarship and interpretation, in distinction from purely aesthetic criticism, have made great strides of late. The discussions are complex and their full results as yet unmeasured. But it is quite certain that the present generation, in discarding many traditional presuppositions and prejudices, and in bringing to bear new data of importance, is in the way of attaining a sounder conception of Milton's essential quality and significance. Interest in him has been wider in the past, but it was never more vital than it is today. The glory of his utterance is as highly valued as ever, the power of his poetic and philosophic thought, as contrasted with the dogmatic aspects of his inherited theology, much more so. His personality, seen in the light of modern psychological knowledge, is no longer to be envisaged, whether with enthusiasm or dislike, in the simple terms of Puritanism, but rather as a complex of emotions and restraints which constitutes one of the most curious phenomena in the annals of poetic genius.

The present volume deals with these matters all too briefly. It will, however, at least guide the reader to the most important of them and it will be justified if it assists him to see Milton in clearer focus as the great figure in whom the intellectual and aesthetic enthusiasms of the Renaissance, the moral forces of the Reformation, and the fervor of a patriotic love of liberty met at their height and dwelt together for a moment, not inharmoniously.

My obligations to authorities, particularly to the more recent ones, are pretty well indicated in the footnotes. But I have omitted specific references to the authority to whom I owe the most—David Masson. His work is thoroughly indexed, and it may be assumed to be my general source for all biographical and historical data where no other is mentioned.

PREFACE TO THE FOURTH EDITION

It has been impossible to do justice to the "flowery crop of knowledge" about Milton which has sprung up since the publication of this handbook in its original form and in its earlier editions. The war interrupted some kinds of scholarly activity, but interest in the Puritan poet and his age persisted and even received additional stimulation. To some extent current Milton and seventeenth century scholarship is the result of mere momentum. Points which are perennially at issue, and projects enthusiastically begun in peace time continued to receive attention *inter arma* from those who had leisure and could keep at least a corner of their minds undisturbed. But the study of Milton has also responded to the great emotional and intellectual experiences of the present world. Not only such a book as Knight's *Chariot of Wrath,* in which Milton is made the spokesman of a Messiah nation, but many more profound and intricate studies reveal by their intensity that the author is concerned with something far more important in his mind than historic truth. It is still possible for men to disagree about Milton in a way in which they do not disagree about Chaucer or even Shakespeare.

Many recent works on Milton have dealt with his political and theological ideas and with the cultural backgrounds of both the poetry and the prose. Such studies tend to emphasize the position which he holds as the representative of Christian humanism in its English manifestation in a period of conflict and upheaval. It is clear that he was both a great conservative and a great reformer. If he appears less as an originator either of myth or of idea, he is more conclusively than ever the interpreter of a great and varied human heritage. He put his stamp on what were indeed the commonplaces of his age and in so doing he at once enhanced their value and conveyed them to the future. Seventeenth century studies have a way of taking off from or coming back to Milton. This is true of the work of Woodhouse, Barker, Fink, Haller, and others, who have made notable contributions to our general understanding of Puritan thought. It is true also of the studies of Whiting, McColley, Svendsen, and Arnold Williams, who have explored the

CONTENTS

xi

A MILTON HANDBOOK

CHAPTER I

MATERIALS FOR MILTON'S BIOGRAPHY

THE life of Milton is known to us in far more full-ness of detail than that of any other major English poet before the eighteenth century. The reasons for this fact are various. In the first place, he was in his own time a public figure, concerned in political events of a sensational character. His pamphlets in defense of liberty made his name one of which, to use his own extravagant but not wholly unjustifiable phrase, "all Europe talked from side to side." His service as Latin Secretary to the Council of State for eleven momentous years entitled him to the attention, favorable and unfavorable, which was accorded to the other members of the Commonwealth government. Then, too, he was a scholar in the days when scholarship was still held in high esteem. As such he was in communication with many distinguished men at home and on the Continent and was noticed as he never would have been in the capacity of a mere man of letters. Yet Milton also laid claim to the attention of his contemporaries as a poet. Although the seventeenth century possessed no such curiosity in literary biography as we have to-day, the modern interest in such matters was beginning to develop, and before the generation of those who had known Milton personally had passed away it was thought worth while to set down regarding him many of those intimate details of personality and habit which we wish for in vain in the case of Chaucer, Spenser, or Shakespeare.

Finally, and this perhaps is most important of all, Milton was intensely concerned to have his own image stand in the public eye as he himself conceived it. He inherited the Renaissance thirst for enduring fame and he combined with this desire an enthusiasm for self-portraiture akin to that of the romantic poets of modern times. He often had occasion to justify himself in his controversial writings against attacks upon his private life and he did so with the greatest gusto. Like many other humanists he preserved and published a number of his private letters. Carrying, finally, the same conscious interest in his own personality into the field of creative art, he made his poetry as well as his prose an intimate though dignified record of his own experience.

We have, then, the material for a life of Milton, as abundant in its detail of his outward career as it is vital in its human interest. There remain, of course, problems of interpretation. Everyone agrees that Milton was no ordinary person; but the judgments that have been passed on his personality and character have varied with the political sympathies, the moral attitude, and the personal temperament of each biographer. Every age, and, indeed, every individual, will, in a measure, have his own Milton, and since this is so it is desirable to have before us the actual materials, in the words of Milton himself and those who knew him, on which our estimates are based. The most important of these, excepting the poetry itself, are given as fully as possible in the ensuing pages.

Of the individual documents from which citation has been made, Milton's *Second Defense of the English People* contains the fullest statement he ever made of the facts of his private and public career. The general credibility of this and other utterances about himself cannot be questioned. It has been argued [1] that his remark in *Areopagitica* about visiting Galileo in Italy must be a fabrication, since Galileo was at that time sick and forbidden all communication with foreigners by the Inquisition. But the evidence is too inconclusive to stand against Milton's express statement.

With the interpretation of motive, on the other hand, the case is different. It was not given to Milton to see himself with dispassionate objectivity, and the reasons he gives for doing thus and thus are often questionable, though it would be a bold man who would undertake to determine the exact degree to which, in any given instance, he deceived himself. Was Milton really reluctant to exchange the "quiet and still air of delightful studies" for the stormy life of public service? Did he care as little as he pretends for the wide acclaim of his contemporaries? Did he abandon his intention of entering the church because of the ecclesiastical tyranny? Did he plan his major prose works beforehand as systematic contributions to the cause of liberty in its various aspects? In general, the answer to these questions is that human motives are always mixed, and that Milton was as adept as any man in rationalizing his actions. It will not do to take his interpretation of his own personality at its face value; neither will it do to reject it, for John

[1] Liljegren, *Studies in Milton*.

Milton was nothing if not sincere. We must remember, also, that Milton intended his life to be edifying. The personal passages were designed to exhibit the works of God in John Milton—to proclaim the fruits of faith, "his own faith not another's," in order that believers everywhere might be strengthened. The writing of this sort of spiritual autobiography, widely practiced among the Puritans, was the obligation of every man who felt conviction within himself, though ordinarily the record is less complicated by the secular and humanistic factors which are so strong in Milton. This motivation, while it does nothing to authenticate the poet's self-portraiture as an objective and complete analysis like the essays of Montaigne, at least explains and justifies its bias.[2]

The most complete of the contemporary biographies is that of Edward Phillips, first printed as an introduction to a translation of Milton's *State Letters* in 1694. Phillips was Milton's nephew and pupil. As an actual intimate of his uncle's household during his boyhood and a frequent visitor till Milton's death, his opportunity for knowing the circumstances of his public and domestic life was practically unlimited. Yet we must remember, in reading, for example,

[2] On the subject of Milton's spiritual autobiography, see Haller, *The Rise of Puritanism,* especially chapter VII. Haller has gone further than any previous scholar in the elucidation of Milton's relationship to the Puritan tradition, as represented by the voluminous body of sermons, personal testimonies, doctrinal expositions, and manuals of behaviour, now unread, but then an inescapable heritage of every person of Milton's temperament and upbringing. Haller points out the fact that humanistic learning is a strong ingredient in the writing of such Puritans as John Goodwin. With the more ardent sectaries—Lilburne, the Quakers, and later Bunyan—it is, of course, much less so. Milton himself gives as his reason for entering the controversy the fact that the ministers were unable to compete with the prelates in erudition.

his detailed account of Milton's first marriage, that he was a boy of twelve when these events took place. He was, moreover, obviously a person of smaller mould, proud of Milton but incapable of comprehending his greatness, and he was rather inclined to gossip. In spite of occasional romancing, however, his narrative is authentic.

Almost equally valuable is the so-called *Anonymous Biography* discovered in 1889 among the papers of Anthony Wood and first published by Parsons in 1902 under the title of *The Earliest Life of Milton*. It may, as the original editor suggests, have been the work of Milton's friend and physician, Dr. Paget, or, as the late John Smart believed, of Cyriack Skinner. A more recent view, based on the evidence of the handwriting and of certain characteristic spellings in the text, is that it was written by Milton's younger nephew John Phillips.[3] Whoever the author is he writes from an intimate and sympathetic understanding, sharing or at least fully understanding Milton's political and religious ideas and seeming particularly well informed about such matters as his literary habits and his use of amanuenses. The exactness with which he describes Milton's disease of the eyes and the scene of his deathbed shows that he must have been very close to him. This biography, which, by the way, was not used by Masson, supplies comparatively few facts unknown from other sources; but it is important as furnishing a systematic account of Milton, parallel to, and independent of, that of Edward Phillips.

[3] See Darbishire, *The Manuscript of Milton's "Paradise Lost,"* 73 f.; and *The Early Lives of Milton*. Parsons has undertaken to refute Miss Darbishire's ascription, as well as the recent attempt of Bundy to show that the Life postdates Wood.

Still further firsthand material is given by John Aubrey in the notes which he collected for Anthony Wood's use in his *Athenae* and *Fasti Oxonienses*. Aubrey had not only known Milton himself but had inquired diligently about him from his widow, from his brother Christopher Milton, from Edward Phillips, and from others. In many cases he gives the sources of his information. Though much of it is gossip, it is just such gossip as we wish to have, and it appears to be, on the whole, trustworthy. His notes on Milton were published by William Godwin in his *Life of E. and J. Phillips* and subsequently by Andrew Clark in his edition of Aubrey's *Brief Lives*. Anthony Wood himself based his *Life of Milton* in the *Fasti Oxonienses* (1692) chiefly on the material furnished by Aubrey and on the manuscript of the anonymous biographer. He, therefore, does not rank as a firsthand witness.

Of the later biographers two, John Toland and Jonathan Richardson, contribute some new items. With them, except for a few recollections of his granddaughter recorded by Birch and Newton, the direct tradition ends. There remain, however, the various records—entries of the births, marriages, and deaths of the Milton family; transfers of property, minutes of the Council of State, etc., which give documentary information on essential points. Much of this was brought to light in the eighteenth century and is contained in Todd's edition, but the great work of collecting and weighing it was done by David Masson. The materials discovered since his time, however, have been considerable.[4]

---

[4] A list of special articles written since 1800 and dealing with various biographical points will be found in Stevens' *Reference Guide*, pp. 165 ff. For supplementary bibliography see Fletcher's *Contributions* and the annual bibliography of the Renaissance pub-

There is finally a goodly amount of manuscript in Milton's hand or in that of his amanuenses, including, besides the text of his minor poems, a Commonplace Book made up of citations from his reading, his literary plans, marginalia in books from his library, a few of his letters, etc. This material was minutely described by the bookseller Sotheby in his bulky *Ramblings in Elucidation of the Autograph of Milton,* and the most important items are noted in their proper connection in this volume.

Since Milton and his early biographers are often incomplete, and sometimes inaccurate, in their statements, it will be well to give here a chronological summary of the most important facts of his outward life and of the chief historical events by which he was affected. Fuller detail regarding the composition, publication, and reception of his works will be found in later chapters, and three passages of importance as revelations of his inner life and thought about himself are quoted in the Appendix.

1608.   John Milton born, December 9.

1620?   Entered St. Paul's School; graduated 1624
             or 1625.

1625.   Enrolled as a lesser pensioner of Christ's Col-
             lege, Cambridge, February 12; matriculated
             and probably took up residence, April 9.

             Charles I acceded to the throne, March.

lished in the April issues of *Studies in Philology.* The latest documentary additions are to be found in *The Columbia Milton.*

1628.   The Petition of Right.

1629.   Took degree of B.A., March 26.
               Nativity Ode, December 25.

1632.   Took degree of M.A., July 3.
               Settled at Horton.

1633.   Laud became Primate.

1634.   *Comus* performed, September 29.

1637.   *Lycidas,* November.

1638–39.   Continental tour: Paris, Florence, Rome,
               Naples, Geneva. Returned to England, Au-
               gust, 1639. Took lodgings in St. Bride's
               Churchyard, London, but soon removed to
               Aldersgate Street.

1639.   War with Scotland (First Bishops' War,
               March).

1640.   Began to teach his two nephews, John and
               Edward Phillips.
               Short Parliament. Second Bishops' War.
               Long Parliament summoned.
               Laud and Strafford impeached.

1641–42.   The anti-prelatical pamphlets.

1641. Execution of Strafford.
       Irish Rebellion.
       Grand Remonstrance.

1642. Married Mary Powell, of Cavalier back-
       ground, who left him shortly.
       Took more pupils into his household.
       Attempted impeachment of the Five Members
       of Parliament.
       Preparations for civil war. Edgehill, Octo-
       ber 23.
       London theatres closed.

1643-45. The divorce tracts.

1644. *Of Education,* June.
       Areopagitica, November.
       Battles of Marston Moor and Newbury.

1645. Reconcilation with wife, July or August.
       Moved to larger house in Barbican.
       Battle of Naseby; victory of Cromwell and
       his New Model Army, June.

1645-46. First volume of poems published.

1646. First child, Anne, born, July 29.
       Powell family took refuge with the Miltons
       for a short time.
       Surrender of Oxford.

1647.	John Milton, Sr. died, March 15.
	Gave up teaching and moved to a smaller house in High Holborn.
	Charles' flight to Carisbrooke, November. Army occupied London.
1648.	Second child, Mary, born, October 25.
1649–53.	The Commonwealth.
1649.	Execution of Charles I, January.
	Tenure of Kings and Magistrates, February.
	Appointed Latin Secretary to Council of State in March, at an annual salary of £289 14s 4½d. Allowed chambers in Whitehall.
	Eikonoklastes, October.
1651.	Third child, John, who died in infancy, born, March 16.
	Defensio pro Populo Anglicano, February.
	Deprived of Whitehall lodgings; moved to a house in Petty France, Westminster.
	Total blindness; granted assistance in office.
1652.	Daughter, Deborah, born, May 2.
	Mary Powell died, May 5.
1653–58.	Cromwell's coup d'état; the Protectorate.
1654.	*Defensio Secunda.*

1655.   *Defensio pro Se.*
            Salary reduced.

1656.   Married Katharine Woodcock, November 12.

1657.   Daughter born, October 19.

1658.   Katharine Woodcock and infant daughter
            died, February and March.
            Cromwell died, September.

1659.   Two tracts against church establishment.
            Abdication of Richard Cromwell; Rump re-
            stored, May.

1660.   *The Ready and Easy Way to Establish a Free
            Commonwealth,* March.
            The Restoration, May. Act of Oblivion.
            Dismissed from office; took refuge in Bartholo-
            omew Close.
            Arrested, but released on payment of fees.

1663.   Married Elizabeth Minshull, February 24.
            Moved to a house in Artillery Walk, Bunhill
            Fields.

1665.   Resided at Chalfont St. Giles, Buckingham-
            shire, for a short time during the plague.

1666.   Great Fire of London.

1667.   *Paradise Lost* published.

1671.   *Paradise Regained* and *Samson Agonistes* published.

1673.   Enlarged and second edition of early poems issued.
           Private Letters and Academic Prolusions published.

1674.   Second edition of *Paradise Lost* published.
           Milton died of gout, November 8; buried in St. Giles, Cripplegate. Milton's three daughters and his widow survived him, the latter dying in 1727. The last of his known descendants, Elizabeth Foster, daughter of Deborah Milton, died in 1754.

HOME ENVIRONMENT AND EARLY SCHOOLING
(1608–1625)

Milton's Statement. I will now mention who and whence I am. I was born at London, of an honest family; my father was distinguished by the undeviating integrity of his life; my mother, by the esteem in which she was held, and the alms which she bestowed. My father destined me from a child to the pursuits of literature; and my appetite for knowledge was so voracious, that, from twelve years of age, I hardly ever left my studies, or went to bed before midnight. This primarily led to my loss of sight. My eyes were naturally weak, and I was subject to frequent headaches; which, however, could not chill the ardour of my curiosity, or retard the progress of my improvement. My father had me daily instructed in the grammar-school, and by other masters at home. He then, after I had acquired a proficiency in various languages, and had made a considerable progress in philosophy, sent me to the University of Cambridge.—*Second Defense of the English People.*

EDWARD PHILLIPS' ACCOUNT. He was born in London, in a house in Bread Street, the lease whereof, as I take it—but for certain it was a house in Bread Street—became in time part of his estate, in the year of our Lord 1606.[5] His father John Milton, an honest, worthy, and substantial citizen of London, by profession a scrivener;[6] to which profession he voluntarily betook himself, by the advice and assistance of an intimate friend of his, eminent in that calling, upon his being cast out by his father, a bigoted Roman Catholic, for embracing, when young, the protestant faith, and abjuring the popish tenets. For he is said to have been descended of an ancient family of the Miltons, of Milton near Abingdon in Oxfordshire,[7] where they had been a long time seated, as appears by the monuments still to be seen in Milton church; till one of the family having taken the wrong side, in the contest between the Houses of York and

[5] Error for 1608. The house was marked by the sign of the spread eagle. Milton's family seal bore the same device.

[6] Scriveners were originally writers of any kind of document. Later they combined the functions of attorney and law stationer. John Milton, Sr. was admitted to the company of Scriveners in 1600. In 1634 he was chosen master but declined. His fortune was made largely by moneylending. A clear picture of his activities as a broker is to be derived from J. Milton French's *Milton in Chancery.* See also Parker, "John Milton, Scrivener, 1590–1632."

[7] Milton's immediate ancestors lived at Stanton St. John, Oxfordshire.

Lancaster, was sequestered of all his estate, but what he held by his wife. However, certain it is, that this vocation he followed for many years, at his said house in Bread Street, with success suitable to his industry and prudent conduct of his affairs. Yet he did not so far quit his own generous and ingenious inclinations, as to make himself wholly a slave to the world; for he sometimes found vacant hours to the study (which he made his recreation) of the noble science of music, in which he advanced to that perfection, that as I have been told, and as I take it by our author himself, he composed an *In Nomine* of forty parts; for which he was rewarded with a gold medal and chain by a Polish prince, to whom he presented it. However, this is a truth not to be denied, that for several songs of his composition, after the way of these times (three or four of which are still to be seen in old Wilby's set of Airs, besides some compositions of his in Ravencroft's Psalms),[8] he gained the reputation of a considerable master in this most charming of all the liberal sciences. Yet all this while, he managed his grand affair of this world with such prudence and diligence, that by the assistance of divine Providence favoring his honest endeavors, he gained a competent estate, whereby he was enabled to make a handsome provision both for the education and maintenance of his children; for three he had, and no more, all by one wife, Sarah, of the family of the

[8] For a comprehensive survey of the musical activities of Milton's father, see Brennecke, *John Milton the Elder and his Music*. The list of his extant compositions (twenty-one in all) begins with his contribution to *The Triumphs of Oriana* in 1601, the only secular composition, and ends with "Three Fantasias for 5 Viols" in 1621. Nothing is known of any work for Wilby, but the editorship of the *Triumphs,* really Morley's, was often spoken of as Wilby's. The Polish prince was probably Albertus Alasco, who was honored at Oxford in 1583 when the elder Milton was twenty years old.

Castons,[9] derived originally from Wales, a woman of incomparable virtue and goodness: John the eldest, the subject of our present work; Christopher; and an only daughter Ann.[10] . . .

But to hasten back to our matter in hand. John, our author, who was destined to be the ornament and glory of his country, was sent, together with his brother, to Paul's school, whereof Dr. Gill [11] the elder was then chief master; where he was entered into the first rudiments of learning, and advanced therein with that admirable success, not more by the discipline of the school and good instructions of his masters (for that he had another master, possibly at his father's house, appears by the *Fourth Elegy* of his Latin poems written in his 18th year to Thomas Young, pastor of the English Company of Merchants at Hamburg, wherein he owns and styles him his master), than by his own happy genius, prompt wit and apprehension, and insuperable industry: for he generally sat up half the night, as well in voluntary improvements of his own choice, as the exact perfecting of his school exercises.

So that at the age of 15 he was full ripe for academic learning, and accordingly was sent to the University of Cambridge.—*Life of Milton.*

CAMBRIDGE (1625–1632)

MILTON'S STATEMENT. Here I passed seven years in the usual course of instruction and study, with the ap-

[9] Her last name was probably Jeffreys.

[10] Anne was actually the eldest child. Christopher was seven years younger than John.

[11] Alexander Gill, author of *Logonomia* (1619), a book of English grammar, rhetoric, and poetics.

probation of the good, and without any stain upon my character, till I took the degree of Master of Arts. After this I did not, as this miscreant feigns, run away into Italy, but of my own accord retired to my father's house, whither I was accompanied by the regrets of most of the fellows of the college, who showed me uncommon marks of friendship and esteem.—*Second Defense of the English People.*

ITEMS FROM AUBREY. Was a very hard student in the university, and performed all his exercises there with very good applause. His first tutor there was Mr. Chappell,[12] from whom receiving some unkindness [whipped him],[13] he was afterwards (though it seemed opposite to the rules of the college), transferred to the tuition of one Mr. Tovell [Tovey], who died parson of Lutterworth. . . .

He was scarce so tall as I am—quaere, quot feet I am high: resp. of middle stature— He had auburn hair. His complexion exceeding fair—he was so fair that they called him the Lady of Christ's College—. Oval face, his eye a dark gray. . . . His widow has his picture drawn very well and like when a Cambridge scholar. She has his picture when a Cambridge scholar, which ought to be engraven; for the pictures before his books are not at all like him.—*Collections for the Life of Milton.*

ILLUSTRATIONS OF MILTON'S RELATIONS TO THE UNIVERSITY AND OF HIS ATTITUDE IN STUDY. . . . I am housed in the city which the Thames washes with its refluent waves and am well content to be in my dear native town. No longer am I interested in returning to the Cam and its reeds, nor am I tormented with longing for my

[12] William Chappell, a well-known tutor, distinguished for his skill as a logician.
[13] These words are inserted in Aubrey's MS.

room there from which I have long been debarred. Those bare fields that grant no pleasant shade do not attract me (How ill does that place beseem the votaries of Phoebus!), nor am I disposed to continue to endure the threats of the stern Master and the other incidents to which my nature cannot submit. If this be exile, to be again in my father's home and, without a care, to follow the pleasant suggestions of leisure, then I reject neither the name nor the lot of a rusticated man, but rather am happy in the terms of my exile. *Elegy I. McCrea's Translation.*

. . . Among us, as far as I know, there are only two or three who without any acquaintance with criticism or philosophy, do not instantly engage with raw and untutored judgments in the study of theology; and of this they acquire only a slender smattering, not more than sufficient to enable them to patch together a sermon with scraps pilfered, with little discrimination, from this author and from that. Hence I fear lest our clergy should relapse into the sacerdotal ignorance of a former age. Since I find so few associates in study here, I should instantly direct my steps to London, if I had not determined to spend the summer vacation in the depths of literary solitude, and, as it were, hide myself in the chamber of the Muses.—*Letter to Alexander Gill, July 2, 1628.*[14]

[14] This is the younger Gill, who was tutor at St. Paul's under his father. Eleven years older than Milton, he had distinguished himself in the writing of Greek and Latin verse. Three months after the date of this letter Gill was censured in the Court of Star Chamber for drinking the health of Felton, assassin of the Duke of Buckingham, and barely escaped more serious consequences. It seems reasonable to suppose that his personal influence was strong in determining Milton's attitudes.

Of so much efficacy in producing private grudges is the rivalry even in schools of those who follow different studies or different principles in the same studies. . . . Nevertheless, that I may not wholly despond, I do, unless I am mistaken, see here and there some, who, even by their silent aspect, signify not obscurely how well they wish me; by whom, however few they may be, I, for my part, would rather be approved than by numberless hundreds of those unskilled ones in whom there is no mind, no right reason, no sound judgment, but only pride in a certain overboiling and truly laughable foam of words; from whom if you strip the rags they have borrowed from new-fangled authors, then, immortal God! how much barer than my nail you would behold them, and, reduced to dumbness by the exhaustion of their empty stock of words and little aphorisms. . . . *Prolusiones Oratoriae I, Masson's Translation.*

It was Aristotle, the rival and constant calumniator of Pythagoras and Plato, who, desiring to strew his own way to glory with the wrecks of the opinions of those great men, attributed to Pythagoras the notion of this unheard symphony of the heavens, this music of the spheres. But, if either fate or chance had so allowed it, Father Pythagoras, that thy soul had passed into me, there would then not be wanting one to defend thee, however long labouring under heavy obloquy. And, truly, why should not the heavenly bodies, in those perennial circuits of theirs, produce musical sounds? Does it not seem just to you, Aristotle? On my word, I should hardly believe that your own intelligences could have endured that sedentary labour of rolling the heaven for so many ages, unless that unspeakable melody of the stars had kept them from leaving their places, and persuaded them to stay by the charm of music. And, if you take from space those fine sensations, you give up your ministering deities also to a bridewell, and condemn them to a treadmill. . . .

If *we* carried pure and chaste and snow-clean hearts, as did Pythagoras of old, then should *our* ears resound and be filled with that sweetest music of the over-wheeling stars, and all things should on the instant return as to the golden age, and thus, free at last from misery, we should lead a life of easy blessedness, enviable even by the gods. *Prolusiones Oratoriae II, Masson's Translation.*

I shall produce abundant active effect at present if I can induce you, my auditors, to turn over seldomer those huge and almost monstrous volumes of the subtle doctors, as they are called, and to indulge a little less in the warty controversies of the sophists. . . .

Often, my hearers, when there chanced to be imposed upon me now and then the necessity of investigating these subtle trivialities, after blunting both my mind and my eye-sight with a day's reading,—often, I say, I have stopped to take breath, and thereupon, measuring the task with my eyes, I have sought a wretched relief from my fatigue; but, as I always saw more remaining than I had got through in my reading, I have wished again and again that, instead of these enforced vanities, there had been assigned me the task of a recleansing of the Augean cowhouse, and have called Hercules a happy fellow, to whom Juno in her good nature had never commanded the endurance of this kind of toil. Nor is this nerveless, languid, and earthy matter elevated or dignified by any beauty of style. . . . I think there never can have been any place for these studies on Parnassus, unless perhaps some uncultivated nook at the foot of the hill, unlovely, rough and horrid with brambles and thorns, overgrown with thistles and thick nettles, far removed from the dance and company of the goddesses, producing neither laurel nor flowers, and never reached by the sound of Apollo's lyre. . . .

By these two things in chief have I perceived a country to be advanced and adorned—either noble speaking or brave action; but this litigious battling of discordant opinions seems unable either to qualify for eloquence, or to instruct in prudence, or to incite to brave deeds. . . . How much better would it be, Academicians, and how much more worthy of your reputation, to walk as it were with the eyes over the universe of earth as it is portrayed in the map, to see places trodden by the ancient heroes, to traverse regions ennobled by wars, triumphs, and even the fables of illustrious poets,—now to cross the stormy Adriatic, now to approach safely the flame-emitting Ætna; furthermore to observe the manners of men and the fairly ordered states in which nations have arranged themselves, and then to investigate and study the natures of all living things, and from these again to direct the mind downward to the secret virtues of stones and plants! Nor hesitate, my hearers, even to soar into the heavens, and there contemplate the multiform shows of the clouds, and the collected power of the snow, and whence those morning tears, and then look into the coffers of the hail, and survey the magazines of the lightnings; nor let there be hidden from you what either Jupiter or Nature means when a dreadful and vast comet menaces the heaven with conflagration; nor let even the minutest little stars, in all their number, as they are scattered between the two poles, escape your notice; nay, follow the wandering sun as his companions, and call time itself to a reckoning, and demand an account of its eternal march. But let not your mind suffer itself to be contained and circumscribed within the same limits as the world, but let it stray even beyond the boundaries of the universe; and let it finally learn (which is yet the highest matter) to know itself, and at the same time those holy minds and intelligences with whom hereafter it is to enter into everlasting companionship. *Prolusiones Oratoriae III, Masson's Translation.*

When lately, Academicians, I returned hither from that city which is the head of cities (i. e. London), filled, even to repletion, with all the delights with which that place overflows, I hoped to have again for some time that literary leisure in which as a mode of life I believe that even celestial souls rejoice, and it was quite my intention to shut myself up in literature and apply myself to sweetest philosophy day and night; for the change from work to pleasure always removes the fatigue of satiety, and causes tasks left unfinished to be sought again with more alacrity. But, just as I was getting into a glow, this almost annual celebration of a very old custom has suddenly called me and dragged me from these studies, and I am ordered to transfer to trifles and the excogitation of new frivolities those pains which I had first destined for the acquisition of wisdom. As if, forsooth, all the world were not at this moment full of fools; as if that illustrious Ship of Fools, no less celebrated in song than the Argo, had gone to wreck; as if, finally, matter for laughter were now wanting to Democritus himself! *Prolusiones Oratoriae VI, Masson's Translation.*

By some of you [i. e. his auditors, the students] I used lately to be nicknamed *The Lady*.

Why seem I to them too little of a man? Is there no regard for Priscian? Do pert grammaticasters thus attribute the *propria quae maribus* to the feminine gender? Is it because I have never been able to quaff huge tankards lustily, or because my hands have not grown hard by holding the plough, or because I have never, like a seven years' herdsman, laid myself down and snored at midday; in fine, perchance, because I have never proved my manhood in the same way as those debauched blackguards? I would they could as easily doff the ass as I can whatever of the woman is in me. But see how absurdly and unreflectingly they have upbraided me with that which I on the best of grounds will turn to my glory. For Demosthenes himself was also called too little of a man by his rivals and adversaries. Quintus Hortensius, too, the most renowned of all orators after M. Tullius, was nicknamed "a Dionysiac singing-woman" by Lucius Torquatus. *Prolusiones Oratoriae VI, Masson's Translation.*

HORTON (1632–1638)

MILTON'S STATEMENT. On my father's estate, where he had determined to pass the remainder of his days, I enjoyed an interval of uninterrupted leisure, which I entirely devoted to the perusal of Greek and Latin authors; though I occasionally visited the metropolis, either for the sake of purchasing books, or of learning something new in mathematics or in music, in which I, at that time, found a source of pleasure and amusement. In this manner I spent five

consider that, if it were no more but the mere love of learning, whether it proceed from a principle bad, good, or natural, it could not have held out thus long against so strong opposition on the other side of every kind. For, if it be bad, why should not all the fond hopes that forward youth and vanity are fledge with, together with gain, pride, and ambition, call me forward more powerfully than a poor, regardless, and unprofitable sin of curiosity should be able to withhold me; whereby a man cuts himself off from all action, and becomes the most helpless, pusillanimous, and unweaponed creature in the world, the most unfit and unable to do that which all mortals most aspire to, either to be useful to his friends or to offend his enemies? Or, if it be thought a natural proneness, there is against that a much more potent and inbred inclination which about this time of a man's life solicits most—the desire of house and family of his own; to which nothing is esteemed more helpful than the early entering into credible employment, and nothing more hindering than this affected solitariness. And, though this were enough, yet there is to this another act, if not of pure, yet of refined, nature, no less available to dissuade prolonged obscurity—a desire of honor and repute and immortal fame, seated in the breast of every true scholar; which all make haste to by the readiest ways of publishing and divulging conceived merits—as well those that shall, as those that never shall, obtain it. Nature, therefore, would presently work the more prevalent way, if there were nothing but this inferior bent of herself to restrain her. Lastly, the love of learning, as it is the pursuit of something good, it would sooner follow the more excellent and supreme good known and presented, and so be quickly diverted from the empty and fantastic chase of shadows and notions, to the solid good flowing from due and timely obedience to that command in the Gospel set out by the terrible seasing of him that hid the talent.

It is more probable, therefore, that not the endless night of speculation, but this very consideration of that great commandment, does not press forward, as soon as may be, to undergo, but keeps off, with a sacred reverence and religious advisement how *best* to undergo, not taking thought of being *late,* so it give advantage to be more *fit;* for those that were latest lost nothing when the master of the vineyard came to give each one his hire. And here I am come to a streamhead copious enough to disburden itself like Nilus at seven mouths into an ocean, but then I should also run into a reciprocal contradiction of ebbing and flowing at once and do that which I excuse myself for not doing—preach and not preach. Yet that you may see that I am something suspicious of myself, and do take notice of a certain belatedness in me, I am the bolder to send you some of my nightward thoughts some while since, because they come in not altogether unfitly made up in a Petrarchan stanza. [Sonnet VII, *How soon hath Time,* follows.]

FROM A LATIN LETTER TO CHARLES DIODATI, LONDON, SEPT. 23, 1637.[16] I was long kept waiting for a letter from you, which you had engaged to write; but when no letter

---

[16] Milton's friendship with Charles Diodati, a youth of Protestant Italian parentage, dates from their association at St. Paul's, where, though the two boys were of the same age, Diodati was two years ahead of him and evidently acted as his mentor. Milton writes affectionate verse letters to him in his early Cambridge years (Diodati had gone to Oxford), and addresses him in the Italian love sonnets and in Elegy VI (1629). The two letters of 1637, quoted here, suggest that Milton has been more eager to maintain the relationship than Diodati and that he has made his absent friend the symbol of his own ideals. This important emotional episode of Milton's youth closes with the

came my old regard for you suffered not, I can assure you, the smallest diminution, for I supposed that the same apology for remissness, which you had employed in the beginning of our correspondence, you would again employ. This was a supposition agreeable to truth and to the intimacy between us. For I do not think that true friendship consists in the frequency of letters or in professions of regard, which may be counterfeited; but it is so deeply rooted in the heart and affections, as to support itself against the rudest blast. . . . But now you have got possession of this despotic citadel of medicine, do not alarm me with the menace of being obliged to repay those six hundred healths which you have bestowed if I should, which God forbid, ever forfeit your friendship. Remove that formidable battery which you seem to have placed upon my breast to keep off all sickness but what comes by your permission. But that you may not indulge any excess of menace I must inform you that I cannot help loving you such as you are; for whatever the Deity may have bestowed upon me in other respects, he has certainly inspired me, if any ever were inspired, with a passion for the good and fair. Nor did Ceres, according to the fable, ever seek her daughter Proserpine with such unceasing solicitude, as I have sought this perfect model of the beautiful in all the forms and appearances of things (for many are the forms of the divinities). I am wont day and night to continue my search; and I follow in the way in which you go before. Hence I feel an irresistible impulse to cultivate the friendship of him who, despising the prejudices and false conceptions of the vulgar,

famous *Epitaph of Damon* in 1640, in which Diodati has evidently been fashioned by Milton's imagination into a very different kind of human being from what he actually was.

dares to think, speak, and be that which the highest wisdom has in every age taught to be the best. . . .

But now I am sure you wish me to gratify your curiosity, and to let you know what I am doing, or am meditating to do. Hear me, my Diodati, and suffer me to speak without blushing, in a more lofty strain. Do you ask what I am meditating? By the help of Heaven, an immortality of fame. But what am I doing? I am letting my wings grow and preparing to fly; but my Pegasus has not yet feathers enough to soar aloft in the fields of air. I will now tell you seriously what I design: to take chambers in one of the Inns of Court, where I may have the benefit of a pleasant and shady walk; and where I with a few associates may enjoy more comfort when I choose to stay at home and have a more elegant society when I choose to go abroad. In my present situation, you know in what obscurity I am buried and to what inconveniences I am exposed. You shall likewise have some information respecting my studies. I went through the perusal of the Greek authors [i. e. historians] to the time when they ceased to be Greeks; I was long employed in unraveling the obscure history of the Italians under the Lombards and the Franks and Germans, to the time when they received their liberty from Rudolphus, king of Germany. From that time it will be better to read separately the particular transactions of each state. . . . In the meantime, if you can do it without inconvenience, I will thank you to send me Giustiniani the Historian of Venice.

FROM A LETTER OF SIR HENRY WOTTON TO MILTON, APRIL 13, 1638.[17] Sir, It was a special favour when you

[17] Sir Henry Wotton, after a long life spent in ambassadorial service abroad, was now retired as Provost of Eton College. He was a

lately bestowed upon me here the first taste of your acquaintance, though no longer than to make me know that I wanted more time to value it and to enjoy it rightly; and, in truth, if I could then have imagined your further stay in these parts, which I understood afterwards by Mr. H., I would have been bold, in our vulgar phrase, to mend my draught (for you left me with an extreme thirst), and to have begged your conversation again, jointly with your said learned friend, at a poor meal or two, that we might have bandied together some good authors of the ancient time; among which I observe you to have been familiar.

Since your going, you have charged me with new obligations, both for a very kind letter from you dated the 6th of this month, and for a dainty piece of entertainment which came therewith. Wherein I should much commend the tragical part, if the lyrical did not ravish me with a certain Doric delicacy in your Songs and Odes, whereto I must confess to have seen yet nothing parallel in our language: *Ipsa molities*. But I must not omit to tell you that I now only owe you thanks for intimating unto me (how modestly soever) the true artificer. For the work itself I had viewed some good while before with singular delight; having received it from our common friend Mr. R., in the very close of the late R.'s poems, printed at Oxford: whereunto it was added

distinguished man, of broad culture and ripe experience, the finest type of Elizabethan gentleman and scholar, with an exquisite taste also for English literature. This letter is the first brilliant recognition of Milton's merits. It was published in the 1645 edition of the Poems and refers to the 1637 edition of *Comus,* a copy of which Milton had sent to his new friend. Mr. H. is probably John Hales of Eton. "The late R." is probably Thomas Randolph, though no copy of his poems bound with *Comus* is known. On the relationship between *Comus* and Randolph's *The Muses Looking Glass* see below, p. 160.

(as I now suppose) that the accessory might help out the principal, according to the art of Stationers, and to leave the reader *con la bocca dolce.* . . .

ITALY (1638–1639)

MILTON'S STATEMENT. I then became anxious to visit foreign parts, and particularly Italy. My father gave me his permission, and I left home with one servant. On my departure, the celebrated Henry Wotton, who had long been King James's ambassador at Venice, gave me a signal proof of his regard, in an elegant letter which he wrote, breathing not only the warmest friendship, but containing some maxims of conduct which I found very useful in my travels. The noble Thomas Scudamore, King Charles's ambassador, to whom I carried letters of recommendation, received me most courteously at Paris. His lordship gave me a card of introduction to the learned Hugo Grotius, at that time ambassador from the Queen of Sweden to the French court; whose acquaintance I anxiously desired, and to whose house I was accompanied by some of his lordship's friends. A few days after, when I set out for Italy, he gave me letters to the English merchants on my route, that they might show me any civilities in their power. Taking ship at Nice, I arrived at Genoa, and afterwards visited Leghorn, Pisa, and Florence.[18] In the latter city, which I have always more particularly esteemed for the elegance of its dialect, its genius, and its taste, I stopped about two months; when I contracted an intimacy with many persons of rank and learning; and was a constant attendant at their literary

[18] Milton reached Florence by September 10, 1638.

parties;[19] a practice which prevails there, and tends so much to the diffusion of knowledge, and the preservation of friendship. No time will ever abolish the agreeable recollections which I cherish of Jacobo Gaddi, Carlo Dati,[20] Frescobaldo, Coltellino, Bonmatthei,[21] Clementillo, Francini, and many others.[22] From Florence I went to Siena, thence to Rome,[23] where, after I had spent about two months in viewing the antiquities of that renowned city, where I experienced the most friendly attentions from Lukas Holsten,[24] and other learned and ingenious men, I continued my route to Naples. There I was introduced by a certain recluse, with whom I had travelled from Rome, to John Baptista Manso,[25] marquis of Villa, a nobleman of distin-

[19] A note in the minutes of the academy of the Svogliati records Milton's reading of a Latin poem at their meeting of September 16, 1638.

[20] Carlo Dati, a youth of nineteen years at the time of Milton's visit, was perhaps his closest friend among the Florentine intelligentsia. He corresponded with him as late as 1647.

[21] One of Milton's earliest acts in Florence was to write a letter to Benedetto Bonmatthei, exhorting him to finish a work on the Italian language which he was writing, and expressing his own enthusiasm for the Italian genius.

[22] These men represented the intellectual élite of Italy, such as it then was. For an account of them, see Masson. Milton fails to mention by name Antonio Malatesti, who dedicated a volume of sonnets to him. He also omits to record his visit to Galileo (mentioned in *Areopagitica*).

[23] The traveler's book of the English Jesuit college in Rome records the presence of Milton and his servant there for dinner October 30, 1638.

[24] Lukas Holsten, a learned Roman scholar of German birth, was a protégé of the Barberini family. Through his courtesy Milton was shown the manuscript treasures of the Vatican and invited to a musical entertainment at the Barberini palace.

[25] The visit to Manso was evidently the high point of Milton's Ital-

guished rank and authority, to whom Torquato Tasso, the illustrious poet, inscribed his book on friendship. During my stay, he gave me singular proofs of his regard: he himself conducted me round the city, and to the palace of the viceroy; and more than once paid me a visit at my lodgings. On my departure he gravely apologised for not having shown me more civility, which he said he had been restrained from doing, because I had spoken with so little reserve on matters of religion. When I was preparing to pass over into Sicily and Greece, the melancholy intelligence which I received of the civil commotions in England made me alter my purpose; for I thought it base to be travelling for amusement abroad, while my fellow-citizens were fighting for liberty at home.[26] While I was on my way back to Rome, some merchants informed me that the English Jesuits had formed a plot against me if I returned to Rome,[27] because I had spoken too freely on religion; for it was a rule which I laid down to myself in those places, never to be the first to begin any conversation on religion; but if any ques-

ian journey. The old nobleman presented him with copies of his poems and his philosophical dialogue on love and received in exchange the only considerable poem written by Milton in Italy, *Mansus*. See de Filippis, "Milton and Manso." Manso was actually something of a bigot, and Milton may have exaggerated the warmth of his hospitality.

[26] This would be in December, 1638. The civil war had not actually broken out in England but the significance of the Scottish rebellion against Charles I would have been clear enough to Milton. Some biographers have objected to Milton's representation of himself as answering the call of duty, in view of the leisurely character of his return north.

[27] Milton was apparently in Rome till the end of February, 1639. He wrote to Lukas Holsten from Florence, March 30, 1639. There are three more records of attendance at meetings of the Svogliati.

tions were put to me concerning my faith, to declare it
without any reserve or fear. I, nevertheless, returned to
Rome. I took no steps to conceal either my person or my
character; and for about the space of two months I again
openly defended, as I had done before, the reformed religion in the very metropolis of popery. By the favour of
God, I got safe back to Florence, where I was received with
as much affection as if I had returned to my native country.
There I stopped as many months as I had done before,
except that I made an excursion for a few days to Lucca; [28]
and, crossing the Apennines, passed through Bologna and
Ferrara to Venice. After I had spent a month in surveying
the curiosities of this city, and had put on board a ship the
books which I had collected in Italy, I proceeded through
Verona and Milan, and along the Leman lake to Geneva.
The mention of this city brings to my recollection the
slandering More, and makes me again call the Deity to
witness, that in all those places in which vice meets with so
little discouragement, and is practised with so little shame,
I never once deviated from the paths of integrity and virtue,
and perpetually reflected that, though my conduct might
escape the notice of men, it could not elude the inspection
of God. At Geneva I held daily conferences with John Diodati, the learned professor of Theology.[29] Then pursuing
my former route through France, I returned to my native
country, after an absence of one year and about three

[28] Lucca was the ancestral home of the Diodati family.

[29] Giovanni Diodati, an uncle of Milton's English friend, Charles,
was distinguished as a translator of the Bible into Italian. He enter-
tained young men of rank from various parts of Europe as pupils in
his house. On June 10, 1639, Milton wrote in the visitors' album of the
Cardogni, an Italian Protestant family at Geneva, his name, a Latin
motto, and the last two lines of *Comus*.

months;[30] at the time when Charles, having broken the peace, was renewing what is called the episcopal war with the Scots, in which the royalists being routed in the first encounter, and the English being universally and justly disaffected, the necessity of his affairs at last obliged him to convene a Parliament.—*Second Defense of the English People.*

But much latelier in the private academies of Italy, whither I was favoured to resort, perceiving that some trifles which I had in memory, composed at under twenty or thereabout, (for the manner is, that every one must give some proof of his wit and reading there), met with acceptance above what was looked for; and other things, which I had shifted in scarcity of books and conveniences to patch up amongst them, were received with written encomiums, which the Italian is not forward to bestow on men of this side the Alps; I began thus far to assent both to them and divers of my friends here at home, and not less to an inward prompting which now grew daily upon me,[31] that by labour and intent study (which I take to be my portion in this life) joined with the strong propensity of nature, I might perhaps leave something so written to aftertimes, as they should not willingly let it die.—*The Reason of Church Government.*

ENGLAND (1640–1649)

SCHOOL TEACHING—EDWARD PHILLIPS' ACCOUNT. Soon after his return, and visits paid to his father and

[30] This would be some time during the summer of 1639.

[31] Note once more how Milton insists on self-reliance rather than reliance on others' advice.

other friends, he took him a lodging in St. Bride's Church-yard, at the house of one Russel, a tailor, where he first undertook the education and instruction of his sister's two sons, the younger whereof had been wholly committed to his charge and care.

And here by the way, I judge it not impertinent to men-tion the many authors both of the Latin and Greek, which through his excellent judgment and way of teaching, far above the pedantry of common public schools (where such authors are scarce ever heard of), were run over within no greater compass of time, than from ten to fifteen or sixteen years of age. Of the Latin, the four grand authors *De Re Rustica,* Cato, Varro, Columella and Palladius; Cornelius Celsus, an ancient physician of the Romans; a great part of Pliny's *Natural History;* Vitruvius his *Archi-tecture;* Frontinus his *Stratagems;* with the two egregious poets, Lucretius and Manilius. Of the Greek, Hesiod, a poet equal with Homer; Aratus his *Phaenomena,* and *Diosemeia;* Dionysius Afer *De Situ Orbis;* Oppian's *Cyn-egetics* and *Halieutics;* Quintus Calaber his *Poem of the Trojan War* continued from Homer; Apollonius Rhodius his *Argonautics:* and in prose, Plutarch's *Placita Phi-losophorum,* and περὶ παιδῶν 'Αγωγίας; Geminus's *Astron-omy;* Xenophon's *Cyri Institutio,* and *Anabasis;* Ælian's *Tactics;* and Polyaenus his *Warlike Stratagems.* Thus by teaching, he in some measure increased his own knowledge, having the reading of all these authors as it were by proxy; and all this might possibly have conduced to the preserving of his eyesight, had he not moreover been perpetually busied in his own laborious undertakings of the book and pen.

Nor did the time thus studiously employed in conquering the Greek and Latin tongues hinder the attaining to the chief oriental languages, *viz.,* the Hebrew, Chaldee, and Syriac, so far as to go through the *Pentateuch,* or Five Books of Moses in Hebrew, to make a good entrance into the *Targum,* or Chaldee Paraphrase, and to understand several chapters of St. Matthew in the Syriac Testament: besides an introduction into several arts and sciences, by reading Urstisius his *Arithmetic,* Riff's *Geometry,* Petiscus his *Trigonometry,* Joannes de Sacrobosco *De Sphæra;* and into the Italian and French tongues, by reading in Italian Giovan Villani's *History of the Transactions between several petty States of Italy;* and in French a great part of Pierre Davity, the famous geographer of France in his time.

The Sunday's work was, for the most part, the reading each day a chapter of the Greek Testament, and hearing his learned exposition upon the same (and how this savored of atheism in him, I leave to the courteous backbiter to judge). The next work after this, was the writing from his own dictation, some part, from time to time, of a tractate which he thought fit to collect from the ablest of divines who had written of that subject: Amesius, Wollebius, &c., *viz., A Perfect System of Divinity,* of which more hereafter.—*Life of Milton.*

MARRIAGE—TWO VERSIONS. During the time also of his continuance in this house [in Aldersgate Street], there fell out several occasions of the increasing of his family. His father, who till the taking of Reading by the Earl of Essex his forces, had lived with his other son at his house there, was upon that son's dissettlement necessitated to betake himself to this his eldest son, with whom he lived for some years, even to his dying day. In the next place he had an addition of some scholars; to which may be added, his entering into matrimony; but he had his wife's company so small a time, that he may well be said to have become a single man again soon after.

About Whitsuntide it was, or a little after, that he took a journey into the country; nobody about him certainly knowing the reason, or that it was any more than a journey of recreation; after a month's stay, home he returns a married man, that went out a bachelor; his wife being Mary, the eldest daughter of Mr. Richard Powell, then a justice of peace, of Forest Hill, near Shotover in Oxfordshire; some few of her nearest relations accompanying the bride to her new habitation; which by reason the father nor any body else were yet come, was able to receive them; where the feasting held for some days in celebration of the nuptials, and for entertainment of the bride's friends. At length they took their leave, and returning to Forest Hill, left the sister behind; probably not much to her satisfaction, as appeared by the sequel. By that time she had for a month or thereabout led a philosophical life (after having been used to a great house, and much company and joviality), her friends, possibly incited by her own desire, made earnest suit by letter, to have her company the remaining part of the summer, which was granted, on condition of her return at the time appointed, Michaelmas, or thereabout. In the meantime came his father, and some of the forementioned disciples.

And now the studies went on with so much the more vigor, as there were more hands and heads employed; the old gentleman living wholly retired to his rest and devotion, without the least trouble imaginable. Our author, now as it were a single man again, made it his chief diversion now and then in an evening, to visit the lady Margaret Lee, daughter to the —— Lee, Earl of Marlborough, Lord High Treasurer of England, and President of the Privy Council, to King James the First. This lady being a woman of great wit and ingenuity, had a particular honor for him, and took much delight in his company, as likewise her husband Captain Hobson, a very accomplished gentleman; and what esteem he at the same time had for her, appears by a sonnet he made in praise of her, to be seen among his other *Sonnets* in his extant *Poems*.

Michaelmas being come, and no news of his wife's return, he sent for her by letter; and receiving no answer, sent several other letters, which were also unanswered; so that at last he dispatched down a foot messenger with a letter, desiring her return. But the messenger came back not only without an answer, at least a satisfactory one, but to the best of my remembrance, reported that he was dismissed with some sort of contempt. This proceeding, in all probability, was grounded upon no other cause but this, namely, that the family being generally addicted to the cavalier party, as they called it, and some of them possibly engaged in the King's service, who by this time had his headquarters at Oxford, and was in some prospect of success, they began to repent them of having matched the eldest daughter of the family to a person so contrary to them in opinion; and thought it would be a blot in their escutcheon, whenever that court should come to flourish again.

However, it so incensed our author, that he thought it would be dishonorable ever to receive her again, after such a repulse; so that he forthwith prepared to fortify himself with arguments for such a resolution, and accord-

ingly wrote two treatises, by which he undertook to maintain, that it was against reason, and the enjoinment of it
not provable by Scripture, for any married couple dis-
agreeable in humor and temper, or having an aversion to
each other, to be forced to live yoked together all their days.
The first was, his *Doctrine and Discipline of Divorce;* of
which there was printed a second edition, with some additions. The other in prosecution of the first, was styled
Tetrachordon. Then the better to confirm his own opinion
by the attestation of others, he set out a piece called *The
Judgment of Martin Bucer,* a protestant minister, being a
translation, out of that reverend divine, of some part of
his works, exactly agreeing with him in sentiment. Lastly,
he wrote in answer to a pragmatical clerk, who would
needs give himself the honor of writing against so great a
man, his *Colasterion,* or *Rod of Correction for a Saucy
Impertinent.*

Not very long after the setting forth of these treatises,
having application made to him by several gentlemen of
his acquaintance for the education of their sons, as understanding haply the progress he had infixed by his first
undertakings of that nature, he laid out for a larger house,
and soon found it out.

But in the interim before he removed, there fell out a
passage, which though it altered not the whole course he
was going to steer, yet it put a stop or rather an end to a
grand affair, which was more than probably thought to
be then in agitation; it was indeed a design of marrying
one of Dr. Davis's daughters, a very handsome and witty
gentlewoman, but averse, as it is said, to this motion. However, the intelligence hereof, and the then declining state
of the King's cause, and consequently of the circumstances

of Justice Powell's family, caused them to set all engines on work, to restore the late married woman to the station wherein they a little before had planted her. At last this device was pitched upon. There dwelt in the lane of St. Martin's-le-Grand, which was hard by, a relation of our author's, one Blackborough, whom it was known he often visited, and upon this occasion the visits were the more narrowly observed and possibly there might be a combination between both parties; the friends on both sides concentring in the same action, though on different behalfs. One time above the rest, he making his usual visit, the wife was ready in another room, and on a sudden he was surprised to see one whom he thought to have never seen more, making submission and begging pardon on her knees before him. He might probably at first make some show of aversion and rejection; but partly his own generous nature, more inclinable to reconciliation than to perseverance in anger and revenge, and partly the strong intercession of friends on both sides, soon brought him to an act of oblivion, and a firm league of peace for the future; and it was at length concluded, that she should remain at a friend's house, till such time as he was settled in his new house at Barbican, and all things for her reception in order; the place agreed on for her present abode, was the widow Webber's house in St. Clement's Church-yard, whose second daughter had been married to the other brother many years before. The first fruits of her return to her husband was a brave girl, born within a year after; though, whether by ill constitution or want of care, she grew more and more decrepit.

But it was not only by children that she increased the number of the family; for in no very long time after her coming, she had a great resort of her kindred with her in the house, *viz.* her father and mother, and several of her brothers and sisters, which were in all pretty numerous; who upon his father's sickening and dying soon after, went away.—Phillips' *Life of Milton.*

In this while, his manner of settlement fitting him for the reception of a wife, he in a month's time (according to his practice of not wasting that precious talent) courted, married, and brought home from Forresthall,[32] near Oxford, a daughter of Mr. Powell. But she, that was very young, and had been bred in a family of plenty and freedom, being not well pleased with his reserved manner of life, within a few days left him, and went back into the country with her mother. Nor though he sent several pressing invitations could he prevail with her to return, till about four years after, when Oxford was surrendered (the nighness of her father's house to that garrison having for the most part of the meantime hindered any communication between them), she of her own accord came, and submitted to him, pleading that her mother had been the inciter of her to that frowardness. He, in the interval, who had entered into that state for the end designed by God and nature, and was then in the full vigor of his manhood, could ill bear the disappointment he met with by her obstinate absenting; and, therefore, thought upon a divorce, that he might be free to marry another; concerning which he also was in treaty. The lawfulness and expedience of this, duly regulate in order to all those purposes for which marriage was at first instituted, had upon full consideration and reading good authors been formerly his opinion; and

[32] Error for Forest Hill.

the necessity of justifying himself now concurring with the opportunity, acceptable to him, of instructing others in a point of so great concern to the peace and preservation of families, and so likely to prevent temptations as well as mischiefs, he first writ *The Doctrine and Discipline of Divorce,* then *Colasterion,* and after *Tetrachordon.* In these he taught the right use and design of marriage; then the original and practice of divorces amongst the Jews, and showed that our Saviour, in those four places of the Evangelists, meant not the abrogating but rectifying the abuses of it; rendering to that purpose another sense of the word fornication (and which is also the opinion amongst others of Mr. Selden in his *Uxor Hebraea*) than what is commonly received. Martin Bucer's *Judgment* in this matter he likewise translated into English. The Assembly of Divines then sitting at Westminster, though formerly obliged by his learned pen in the defense of Smectymnuus, and other their controversies with the bishops, now impatient of having the clergies' jurisdiction, as they reckoned it, invaded, instead of answering, or disproving what those books had asserted, caused him to be summoned for them before the Lords. But that house, whether approving the doctrine, or not favoring his accusers, soon dismissed him.—*Anonymous Life of Milton.*

LITERARY ACTIVITY—MILTON'S STATEMENT. As soon as I was able, I hired a spacious house in the city for myself and my books; where I again with rapture renewed my literary pursuits, and where I calmly awaited the issue of the contest, which I trusted to the wise conduct of Providence, and to the courage of the people. The vigour of the Parliament had begun to humble the pride of the bishops. As long as the liberty of speech was no longer subject to control, all mouths began to be opened against the bishops; some complained of the vices of the individuals, other of those of the order. They said that it was unjust that they alone should differ from the model of other reformed churches; that the government of the Church should be according to the pattern of other churches, and particularly the Word of God. This awakened all my attention and my zeal. I saw that a way was opening for the establishment of real liberty; that the foundation was laying for the deliverance of man from the yoke of slavery and superstition; that the principles of religion, which were the first objects of our care, would exert a salutary influence on the manners and constitution of the republic; and as I had from my youth studied the distinctions between religious and civil rights, I perceived that if I ever wished to be of use, I ought at least not to be wanting to my country, to the Church, and to so many of my fellow-Christians, in a crisis of so much danger; I therefore determined to relinquish the other pursuits in which I was engaged, and to transfer the whole force of my talents and my industry to this one important object. I accordingly wrote two books to a friend concerning the reformation of the Church of England. Afterwards, when two bishops of superior distinction vindicated their privileges against some principal ministers, I thought that on those topics, to the consideration of which I was led solely by my love of truth, and my reverence for Christianity, I should not probably write worse than those who were contending only for their own emoluments and usurpations. I therefore answered the one in two books, of which the first is inscribed, "Concerning Prelatical Episcopacy" and the other "Concerning the Mode of Ecclesiastical Government"; and I replied to the other in some "Animadversions," and soon after in an "Apology." On this occasion it was supposed that I brought a timely succour to the ministers, who were hardly a match for the eloquence of their opponents; and from that time I was actively employed in refuting any answers that appeared. When the bishops could no longer resist the multitude of their assailants, I had leisure to turn my thoughts to other subjects; to the promotion of real and substantial liberty; which is rather to be sought from within than from without; and whose existence depends, not so much on the terror of the sword, as on sobriety of conduct and integrity of life. When, therefore, I perceived that there were three species of liberty which are essential to the happiness of social life —religious, domestic, and civil; and as I had already written concerning the first, and the magistrates were strenuously active in obtaining the third, I determined to turn my attention to the second, or the domestic species. As this seemed to involve three material questions, the conditions of the conjugal tie, the education of the children, and the free publication of the thoughts, I made them objects of distinct consideration. I explained my sentiments, not only concerning the solemnization of the marriage, but the dissolution, if circumstances rendered it necessary; and I drew my arguments from the divine law, which Christ did not abolish, or publish another more grievous than that of Moses. I stated my own opinions, and those of others, concerning the exclusive exception of fornication, which our illustrious Selden has since, in his *Hebrew Wife,* more copiously discussed; for he in vain makes a vaunt of liberty in the senate or in the forum, who languishes under the vilest servitude, to an inferior at home. On this subject, therefore, I published some books which were more particularly necessary at that time, when man and wife were often the most inveterate foes, when the man often stayed to take care of his children at home, while the mother of the family was seen in the camp of the enemy, threatening death and destruction to her husband. I then discussed the principles of education in a summary manner, but sufficiently copious for those who attend seriously to the subject; than which nothing can be more necessary to principle the minds of men in virtue, the only genuine source of political and individual liberty, the only true safeguard of states, the bulwark of their prosperity and renown. Lastly, I wrote my "Areopagitica," in order to deliver the press from the restraints with which it was encumbered; that the power of determining what was true and what was false, what ought to be published and what to be suppressed, might no longer be entrusted to a few illiterate and illiberal individuals, who refused their sanction to any work which contained views or sentiments at all above the level of the vulgar superstition. On the last species of civil liberty, I said nothing, because I saw that sufficient attention was paid to it by the magistrates; nor did I write anything on the prerogative of the crown, till the king, voted an enemy by the Parliament, and vanquished in the field, was summoned before the tribunal which condemned him to lose his head. But when, at length, some Presbyterian ministers, who had formerly been the most bitter enemies to Charles, became jealous of the growth of the Independents, and of their ascendency in the Parliament, most tumultuously clamoured against the sentence, and did all in their power to prevent the execution, though they were not angry, so much on account of the act itself, as because it was not the act of their party; and when they dared to affirm, that the doctrine of the Protestants, and of all the reformed churches, was abhorrent to such an atrocious proceeding against kings; I thought that it became me to oppose such a glaring falsehood; and accordingly, without any immediate or personal application to Charles, I showed, in an abstract consideration of the question, what might lawfully be done against tyrants; and in support of what I advanced, produced the opinions of the most celebrated divines; while I vehemently inveighed against the egregious ignorance or effrontery of men, who professed better things, and from whom better things might have been expected. That book did not make its appearance till after the death of Charles; and was written rather to reconcile the minds of the people to the event, than to discuss the legitimacy of that particular sentence which concerned the magistrates, and which was already executed. Such were the fruits of my private studies, which I gratuitously presented to the Church and to the State; and for which I was recompensed by nothing but impunity; though the actions themselves procured me peace of conscience, and the approbation of the good; while I exercised that freedom of discussion which I loved. Others, without labour or desert, got possession of honours and emoluments; but no one ever knew me either soliciting anything myself or through the medium of my friends, ever beheld me in a supplicating posture at the doors of the senate, or the levees of the great. I usually kept myself secluded at home, where my own property, part of which had been withheld during the civil commotions, and part of which had been absorbed in the oppressive contributions which I had to sustain, afforded me a scanty subsistence. When I was re-

the tintamar and hurry of public business) to take upon
him the office of Latin secretary to the Council of State
for all their letters to foreign princes and states; for
they stuck to this noble and generous resolution, not to
write to any, or receive answers from them, but in a language most proper to maintain a correspondence among
the learned of all nations in this part of the world; scorn-
ing to carry on their affairs in the wheedling, lisping jargon
of the cringing French, especially having a minister of
state able to cope with the ablest any prince or state could
employ, for the Latin tongue. And so well he acquitted
himself in this station, that he gained from abroad both
reputation to himself, and credit to the state that employed him.

And it was well the business of his office came not very
fast upon him; for he was scarce well warm in his secretaryship before other work flowed in upon him, which took
him up for some considerable time. In the first place there
came out a book said to have been written by the king, and
finished a little before his death, intituled εἰκὼν βασιλική,
that is, *The Royal Image;* a book highly cried up for its
smooth style, and pathetical composure; wherefore to ob-
viate the impression it was like to make among the many,
he was obliged to write an answer, which he intituled
εἰκονοκλάστης or *Image-Breaker.*

And upon the heels of that, out comes in public the great
kill-cow of Christendom, with his *Defensio Regis contra
Populum Anglicanum;* a man so famous and cried up for
his Plinian Exercitations, and other pieces of reputed
learning, that there could no where have been found a
champion that durst lift up the pen against so formidable
an adversary, had not our little English David had the

courage to undertake this great French Goliath. To whom he gave such a hit in the forehead, that he presently staggered, and soon after fell. For immediately upon the coming out of the answer, intituled, *Defensio Populi Anglicani contra Claudium Anonymum,* &c. he that till then had been chief minister and superintendent in the court of the learned Christina, Queen of Sweden, dwindled in esteem to that degree, that he at last vouchsafed to speak to the meanest servant. In short, he was dismissed with so cold and slighting an adieu, that after a faint dying reply, he was glad to have recourse to death, the remedy of evils, and ender of controversies.

And now I presume our author had some breathing space, but it was not long. For though Salmasius was departed, he left some stings behind; new enemies started up, barkers, though no great biters. Who the first asserter of Salmasius his cause was, is not certainly known, but variously conjectured at, some supposing it to be one Janus, a lawyer of Gray's Inn, some Dr. Bramhal, made by King Charles the Second, after his restoration, Archbishop of Armagh in Ireland; but whoever the author was, the book was thought fit to be taken into correction; and our author not thinking it worth his own undertaking, to the disturbing the progress of whatever more chosen work he had then in hand, committed this task to the youngest of his nephews; but with such exact amendations before it went to the press, that it might have very well passed for his, but that he was willing the person that took the pains to prepare it for his examination and polishment, should have the name and credit of being the author; so that it came forth under this title, *Joannis Philippi Angli Defensio pro Populo Anglicano contra,* &c.

During the writing and publishing of this book, he lodged at one Thomson's next door to the Bull-head tavern at Charing-Cross, opening into the Spring-Garden; which seems to have been only a lodging taken till his designed apartment in Scotland-Yard was prepared for him. For hither he soon removed from the aforesaid place; and here his third child, a son, was born, which through the ill usage, or bad constitution, of an ill-chosen nurse, died an infant.

From this apartment, whether he thought it not healthy, or otherwise convenient for his use, or whatever else was the reason, he soon after took a pretty garden-house in Petty-France in Westminster, next door to the Lord Scuda-more's, and opening into St. James's Park. Here he remained no less than eight years, namely, from the year 1652, till within a few weeks of King Charles the Second's restoration.

In this house his first wife dying in childbed, he married a second, who after a year's time died in childbed also. This second marriage was about two or three years after his being wholly deprived of sight, which was just going about the time of his answering Salmasius; where-upon his adversaries gladly take occasion of imputing his blindness as a judgment upon him for his answering the King's book, &c. whereas it is most certainly known, that his sight, what with his continual study, his being subject to the headache, and his perpetual tampering with physic to preserve it, had been decaying for above a dozen years before, and the sight of one [eye] for a long time clearly lost. Here he wrote, by his amanuensis, his two *Answers to Alexander More,* who upon the last answer quitted the field.—*Life of Milton.*

FROM THE ANONYMOUS BIOGRAPHER. While he was thus employed his eyesight totally failed him; not through any immediate or sudden judgment, as his adversaries insultingly affirmed, but from a weakness which his hard, nightly study in his youth had first occasioned, and which by degrees had for some time before deprived him of the use of one eye. And the issues and seatons, made use of to save or retrieve that, were thought by drawing away the spirits, which should have supplied the optic vessels, to have hastened the loss of the other. He was, indeed, advised by his physicians of the danger, in his condition, attending so great intentness as that work required. But he, who was resolute in going through with what upon good consideration he at any time designed, and to whom the love of truth and his country was dearer than all things, would not for any danger decline their defense.

Nor did his darkness discourage or disable him from prosecuting, with the help of amanuenses, the former design of his calmer studies.—*Anonymous Life of Milton.*

RETIREMENT, THE GREAT POEMS, LAST YEARS (1660–1674)

EDWARD PHILLIPS' ACCOUNT. So that being now quiet from state adversaries and public contests, he had leisure again for his own studies and private designs; which were his foresaid *History of England;* and a new *Thesaurus Linguae Latinae,* according to the manner of Stephanus, a work he had been long since collecting from his own reading, and still went on with it at times, even very near to his dying day; but the papers after his death were so discomposed and deficient that it could not be made fit for the press; however, what there was of it, was made use of for another dictionary.

But the height of his noble fancy and invention began now to be seriously and mainly employed in a subject worthy of such a Muse, *viz.* a heroic poem, entitled, *Paradise Lost;* the noblest in the general esteem of learned and judicious persons, of any yet written by any either ancient or modern. This subject was first designed a tragedy, and in the fourth book of the poem there are ten verses, which several years before the poem was begun, were shown to me and some others, as designed for the very beginning of the said tragedy. The verses are these:

> O thou that with surpassing glory crown'd!
> Look'st from thy sole dominion, like the god
> Of this new world; at whose sight all the stars
> Hide their diminish'd heads; to thee I call,
> But with no friendly voice; and add thy name,
> O Sun! to tell thee how I hate thy beams
> That bring to my remembrance, from what state
> I fell, how glorious once above thy sphere;
> Till pride and worse ambition threw me down,
> Warring in Heaven, against Heaven's glorious King.

There is another very remarkable passage in the composure of this poem, which I have a particular occasion to remember; for whereas I had the perusal of it from the very beginning, for some years, as I went from time to time to visit him, in a parcel of ten, twenty, or thirty verses at a time, which being written by whatever hand came next, might possibly want correction as to the orthography and pointing; having as the summer came on, not been showed any for a considerable while, and, desiring the reason thereof, was answered: that his vein never happily flowed but from the autumnal equinoctial to the vernal, and that whatever he attempted [otherwise] was never to his satisfaction, though he courted his fancy never so much, so that in all the years he was about this poem, he may be said to have spent but half his time therein.

It was but a little before the King's restoration that he wrote and published his book *In Defence of a Commonwealth;* so undaunted he was in declaring his true sentiments to the world; and not long before, his *Power of the Civil Magistrate in Ecclesiastical Affairs,* and his *Treatise against Hirelings,* just upon the King's coming over; having a little before been sequestered from his office of Latin secretary, and the salary thereunto belonging.

He was forced to leave his house also in Petty-France, where all the time of his abode there, which was eight years, as above-mentioned, he was frequently visited by persons of quality, particularly my Lady Ranalagh, whose son for some time he instructed; all learned foreigners of note, who could not part out of the city, without giving a visit to a person so eminent; and lastly, by particular friends that had a high esteem for him, *viz.* Mr. Andrew Marvel, young Lawrence (the son of him that was president of Oliver's council), to whom there is a sonnet among the rest, in his printed *Poems;* Mr. Marchamont Needham, the writer of *Politicus;* but above all, Mr. Cyriack Skinner whom he honored with two sonnets, one long since public among his *Poems,* the other but newly printed.

His next removal was, by the advice of those that wished him well, and had a concern for his preservation, into a place of retirement and abscondence, till such time as the current of affairs for the future should instruct him what farther course to take. It was a friend's house in Bartholomew Close, where he lived till the act of oblivion came forth; which it pleased God, proved as favorable to him as could be hoped or expected, through the intercession of some that stood his friends both in Council and Parliament; particularly in the House of Commons, Mr. Andrew Marvel, a member for Hull, acted vigorously in his behalf, and made a considerable party for him; so that, together with John Goodwin of Coleman Street, he was only so far excepted as not to bear any office in the Commonwealth.

Soon after appearing again in public, he took a house in Holborn near Red Lyon Fields; where he stayed not long, before his pardon having passed the seal, he removed to Jewin Street. There he lived when he married his 3d wife, recommended to him by his old friend Dr. Paget in Coleman Street.

But he stayed not long after his new marriage, ere he removed to a house in the Artillery-walk leading to Bunhill Fields. And this was his last stage in this world, but it was of many years continuance, more perhaps than he had had in any other place besides.

Here he finished his noble poem, and published it in the year 1666. The first edition was printed in quarto by one Simons, a printer in Aldersgate Street; the other in a large octavo, by Starky near Temple-Bar, amended, enlarged, and differently disposed as to the number of books by his own hand, that is by his own appointment; the last set forth, many years since his death, in a large folio, with cuts added, by Jacob Tonson.

Here it was also that he finished and published his

history of our nation till the Conquest, all complete so far as he went, some passages only excepted; which, being thought too sharp against the clergy, could not pass the hand of the licenser, were in the hands of the late Earl of Anglesey while he lived; where at present is uncertain.

It cannot be concluded when he wrote his excellent tragedy entitled *Samson Agonistes,* but sure enough it is that it came forth after his publication of *Paradise Lost,* together with his other poem called *Paradise Regained,* which doubtless was begun and finished and printed after the other was published, and that in a wonderful short space considering the sublimeness of it; however, it is generally censured to be much inferior to the other, though he could not hear with patience any such thing when related to him. Possibly the subject may not afford such variety of invention; but it is thought by the most judicious to be little or nothing inferior to the other for style and decorum.

The said Earl of Anglesey, whom he presented with a copy of the unlicensed papers of his history, came often here to visit him, as very much coveting his society and converse; as likewise others of the nobility, and many persons of eminent quality; nor were the visits of foreigners ever more frequent than in this place, almost to his dying day.

His treatise *Of True Religion, Heresy, Schism and Toleration,* &c. was doubtless the last thing of his writing that was published before his death. He had, as I remember, prepared for the press an answer to some little scribing quack in London, who had written a scurrilous libel against him; but whether by the dissuasion of friends, as thinking him a fellow not worth his notice, or for what other cause I know not, this answer was never published.

He died in the year 1673,[33] towards the latter end of the summer, and had a very decent interment according to his quality, in the church of St. Giles, Cripplegate, being attended from his house to the church by several gentlemen then in town, his principal well-wishers and admirers. —*Life of Milton.*

From a Latin Letter to Peter Heimbach. Aug. 15, 1666. It is not strange, as you write, that report should have induced you to believe that I had perished among the numbers of my countrymen who fell in a year so fatally visited by the ravages of the plague. If that rumor sprung, as it seems, out of solicitude for my safety, I consider it as no unpleasing indication of the esteem in which I am held among you. But by the goodness of God, who provided for me a place of refuge in the country, I yet enjoy both life and health; which so long as they continue I shall be happy to employ in any useful undertaking. It gives me pleasure to think that, after so long an interval, I have again occurred to your remembrance; though, owing to the luxuriance of your praise, you seem almost to lead me to suspect that you had quite forgotten one in whom you say that you admire the union of so many virtues; from such a union I might dread too numerous a progeny, if it were not evident that the virtues flourish most in penury and distress. But one of those virtues has made me but an ill return for her hospitable reception in my breast; for what you term policy, which I wish that you had rather called patriotic piety, has, if I may so say, almost left me, who was charmed with so sweet a sound, without a country. The other virtues harmoniously agree. Our country is wherever we are well off. I will conclude

[33] Error for 1674.

after first begging you if there be any errors in the diction or the punctuation, to impute it to the boy who wrote this, who is quite ignorant of Latin, and to whom I was, with no little vexation, obliged to dictate not the words, but, one by one, the letters of which they were composed.

FROM THOMAS ELLWOOD, THE QUAKER.[34] Some little time before I went to Alesbury Prison I was desired by my quondam Master Milton to take an house for him in the neighbourhood where I dwelt, that he might go out of the city for the safety of himself and his family, the pestilence then growing hot in London. I took a pretty box for him in Giles-Chalfont, a mile from me, of which I gave him notice, and intended to have waited on him and seen him well settled in it, but was prevented by that imprisonment.

But now being released and returned home, I soon made a visit to him to welcome him into the country.

After some common discourses had passed between us, he called for a manuscript of his; which being brought he delivered to me, bidding me take it home with me and read it at my leisure and when I had so done, return it to him with my judgment thereupon.

When I came home and had set my self to read it, I found it was that excellent poem which he entitled *Paradise Lost*. After I had with the best attention read it through, I made him another visit and returned him his book with

[34] Thomas Ellwood, who had become a Quaker in 1660 through the influence of the Penningtons and had already suffered persecution, was twenty-three years old at the time of his introduction to Milton. He continued with him for six weeks, left London on account of his health, and returned later in the year only to have his studies again interrupted, this time by imprisonment. From 1663 to 1669 he lived in Chalfont St. Peter's as tutor to the Pennington family. Milton was evidently fond of his simple-hearted admirer and showed him great kindness.

due acknowledgement of the favour he had done me in communicating it to me. He asked me how I liked it and what I thought of it, which I modestly but freely told him, and after some further discourse about it I pleasantly said to him, "Thou hast said much here of Paradise Lost, but what hast thou to say of Paradise Found?" He made me no answer but sat some time in a muse, then brake off that discourse and fell upon another subject.

After the sickness was over and the city well cleansed and become safely habitable again, he returned thither. And when afterwards I went to wait on him there (which I seldom failed of doing whenever my occasions drew me to London) he shewed me his second poem, called *Paradise Regained,* and in a pleasant tone said to me, "This is owing to you; for you put it into my head by the question you put to me at Chalfont, which before I had not thought of."

CONTEMPORARY TESTIMONY AS TO MILTON'S PERSONALITY, HABITS, ETC.

ITEMS FROM AUBREY. His harmonical and ingenious soul did lodge in a beautiful and well-proportioned body.
In toto nusquam corpore menda fuit—Ovid.
He had a very good memory; but I believe that his excellent method of thinking and disposing did much to help his memory.

Of a very cheerful humor. He would be cheerful even in his gout-fits, and sing.

Seldom took any physic, only sometimes he took manna [a mild drug used as a laxative].

He was very healthy, and free from all diseases, only

toward his later end, he was visited with the gout, spring and fall. . . .

He was an early riser, scil, at 4 o'clock manè, yea, after he lost his sight. He had a man read to him. The first thing he read was the Hebrew Bible, and that was at 4h. manè ½ h. + Then he contemplated. At 7 his man came to him again, and then read to him and wrote till dinner; the writing was as much as the reading. His 2d daughter, Deborah, could read to him Latin, Italian and French, and Greek. [She] married in Dublin to one Mr. Clarke (sells silk etc); very like her father. The other sister is Mary, more like her mother. After dinner he used to walk 3 or 4 hours at a time (he always had a garden where he lived): went to bed about 9. Temperate man, rarely drank between meals. Extreme pleasant in his conversation, and at dinner, supper, &c. but satirical. . . .

He pronounced the letter R very hard (*littera canina*). A certain sign of a satirical wit. From John Dryden. . . .

He had a delicate, tuneable voice, and had good skill. His father instructed him. He had an organ in his house; he played on that most. . . .

He was visited much by learned [men], more than he did desire. . . .

As he was severe on one hand, so he was most familiar and free in his conversation to those to whom most sour in his way of education. N. B. He made his nephews songsters, and sing, from the time they were with him. . . .

From Mr. E. Phillips:—All the time of writing his *Paradise Lost,* his vein began at the autumnal equinoctial, and ceased at the vernal, (or thereabouts, I believe about May), and this was 4 or 5 years of his doing it. He began about 2 years before the King came in, and finished about

3 years after the King's restoration.—*Collections for the Life of Milton.*

From Edward Phillips. And those [children] he had by the first [wife] he made serviceable to him in that very particular in which he most wanted their service, and supplied his want of eyesight by their eyes and tongue. For though he had daily about him one or other to read to him; some persons of man's estate, who of their own accord greedily catched at the opportunity of being his readers, that they might as well reap the benefit of what they read to him, as oblige him by the benefit of their reading; others of younger years sent by their parents to the same end; yet, excusing only the eldest daughter by reason of her bodily infirmity and difficult utterance of speech (which to say the truth I doubt was the principal cause of excusing her), the other two were condemned to the performance of reading, and exactly pronouncing of all the languages of whatever book he should at one time or other think fit to peruse; *viz.* the Hebrew (and I think the Syriac), the Greek, the Latin, the Italian, Spanish, and French. All which sorts of books to be confined to read, without understanding one word, must needs be a trial of patience almost beyond endurance; yet it was endured by both for a long time. Yet the irksomeness of this employment could not be always concealed, but broke out more and more into expressions of uneasiness; so that at length they were all (even the eldest also) sent out to learn some curious and ingenious sorts of manufacture, that are proper for women to learn, particularly embroideries in gold or silver. It had been happy indeed, if the daughters of such a person had been made in some measure inheritrixes of their father's learning; but since fate otherwise decreed, the greatest honor that can be ascribed to this now living (and so would have been to the others, had they lived) is to be daughter to a man of his extraordinary character.—*Life of Milton.*

FROM THE ANONYMOUS BIOGRAPHER. He had naturally a sharp wit, and steady judgment; which helps toward attaining learning he improved by an indefatigable attention to his study; and was supported in that by a temperance, always observed by him, but in his youth even with great nicety. Yet did he not reckon this talent but as entrusted with him; and therefore dedicated all his labors to the glory of God and some public good; neither binding himself to any of the gainful professions, nor having any worldly interest for aim in what he taught.

He was of a moderate stature, and well proportioned, of a ruddy complexion, light brown hair, and handsome features; save that his eyes were none of the quickest. But his blindness, which proceeded from a gutta serena, added no further blemish to them. His deportment was sweet and affable; and his gait erect and manly, bespeaking courage and undauntedness (or a *nil conscire*), on which account he wore a sword while he had his sight, and was skilled in using it. He had an excellent ear, and could bear a part both in vocal and instrumental music.

He rendered his studies and various works more easy and pleasant by allotting them their several portions of the day. Of these the time friendly to the Muses fell to his poetry; and he, waking early, (as is the use of temperate men) had commonly a good stock of verses ready against his amanuensis came; which if it happened to be later than ordinary, he would complain, saying *he wanted to be milked.* The evenings he likewise spent in reading some choice poets, by way of refreshment after the day's toil, and to store his fancy against morning. Besides his ordinary lectures out of the Bible and the best commentators on the week day, that was his sole subject on Sundays. And David's Psalms were in esteem with him above all poetry. The youths that he instructed from time to time served him often as amanuenses, and some elderly persons were glad for the benefit of his learned conversation, to perform that office. His first wife died a while after his blindness seized him, leaving him three daughters, that lived to be women. He married two more, whereof one survived him. He died in a fit of the gout, but with so little pain or emotion, that the tide of his expiring was not perceived by those in the room. And though he had been long troubled with that disease, insomuch that his knuckles were all callous, yet was he not ever observed to be very impatient. He had this elegy in common with the patriarchs and kings of Israel, that he was gathered to his people; for he happened to be buried in Cripplegate, where about thirty years before he had by chance also interred his father.—*Anonymous Life of Milton.*

From Thomas Ellwood the Quaker. This person, having filled a publick station in the former times, lived now a private and retired life in London; and, having wholly lost his sight, kept always a man to read to him, which usually was the son of some gentleman of his acquaintance, whom in kindness he took to improve in his learning.

Thus, by the mediation of my friend Isaac Pennington with Dr. Paget and of Dr. Paget with John Milton, was I admitted to come to him—not as a servant to him (which at that time he needed not) nor to be in the house with him, but only to have the liberty of coming to his house at certain hours when I would, and to read to him what books he should appoint me; which was all the favour I desired. . . .

He received me courteously, as well for the sake of Dr. Paget who introduced me, as of Isaac Pennington who recommended me, to both whom he bore a good respect. And having enquired divers things of me with respect to my former progression in learning, he dismist me, to provide myself of such accommodations as might be most suitable to my future studies.

I went therefore and took myself a lodging as near to his house (which was then in Jewen Street) as conveniently I could, and from thenceforward went every day in the afternoon (except on the first days of the week), and, sitting by him in his dining room, read to him in such books in the Latin tongue as he pleased to hear me read.

At my first sitting to read to him, observing that I used the English pronunciation, he told me, if I would have the benefit of the Latin tongue, not only to read and understand Latin authors but to converse with foreigners either abroad or at home, I must learn the foreign pronunciation. To this I consenting, he instructed me how to sound the vowels; so different from the common pronunciation used by the English, who speak Anglice their Latin, that (with some few other variations in sounding some consonants in particular cases, as "C" before "E" or "I" like "Ch", "Sc" before "I" like "Sh" etc.) the Latin thus spoken seemed as different from that which was delivered as the English generally speak it, as if it were another language. . . .

It was now harder to me to read than it was before to understand when read. But

Labor omnia vincit improbus.
Incessant pains the end obtains.

And so did I. Which made my reading the more acceptable to my master. He, on the other hand, perceiving with what earnest desire I pursued learning, gave me not only all the encouragement but all the help he could. For, having a curious ear, he understood by my tone when I understood what I read and when I did not, and accordingly would stop me, examine me, and open the most difficult passages to me.

FROM JONATHAN RICHARDSON. I have heard many years since that he used to sit in a grey coarse cloth coat at the door of his house, near Bunhill Fields, without Moorgate, in warm, sunny weather, to enjoy the fresh air, and so, as well as in his room, received the visits of people of distinguished parts, as well as quality; and very lately I had the good fortune to have another picture of him from an aged clergyman in Dorsetshire, Dr. Wright. He found him in a small house, he thinks but one room on a floor. In that, up one pair of stairs, which was hung with a rusty green, he found John Milton, sitting in an elbow chair, black clothes, and neat enough, pale but not cadaverous, his hands and fingers gouty and with chalk-stones. Among other discourse he expressed himself to this purpose: that, was he free from the pain this gave him, his blindness would be tolerable. . . .

In relation to his love of music and the effect it had upon his mind I remember a story I had from a friend I was happy in for many years, and who loved to talk of Milton as he often did. Milton hearing a lady sing finely, "Now I swear," says he, "this lady is handsome." His ears now were eyes to him. . . .

Milton had a servant who was a very honest silly fellow, and a zealous and constant follower of those teachers [i. e. non-conformists]. When he came from the meeting, his master would frequently ask him what he had heard, and divert himself with ridiculing their fooleries, or, it may be, the poor fellow's understanding : both one and t'other probably. However, this was so grievous to the good creature that he left his service upon it. . . .

As we are at a loss as to the particulars of the affair, what I have suggested will, I hope, be sufficient—only let me add, that that daughter, who was certainly one (if there was really more than one) that was thus serviceable to her excellent father in his distress, expressed no uneasiness that I ever heard of when she gave accounts of Milton's affairs to the many inquirers lately ; but, on the contrary, spoke of him with great tenderness. Particularly, I have been told, she said he was delightful company, the life of the conversation—and *that* on account of a flow of subject and an unaffected cheerfulness and civility. One instance of her tender remembrance of him I cannot forbear relating. The picture in crayons I have of him was shown her after several others, or which were pretended to be his. When those were shown and she was asked if she could recollect if she had ever seen such a face: "No, no." But when this was produced, in a transport: " 'Tis my Father! 'Tis my dear Father! I see him! 'Tis him!" And then she put her hands to several parts of her face, " 'Tis the very man! Here, here." . . .

Other stories I have heard concerning the posture he was usually in when he dictated: that he sat leaning backward obliquely in an easy chair, with his leg flung over the elbow of it; that he frequently composed lying in bed in the morning ('twas winter sure then).

One that had often seen him told me he used to come to a house where he lived, and he has also met him in the street, led by Millington (the same who was so famous as an auctioneer of books about the time of the Revolution and since). This man was then a seller of old books in Little Britain, and Milton lodged at his house. This was three or four years before he died. He then wore no sword that my informer remembers, though probably he did—at least 'twas his custom not long before to wear one with a small silver hilt, and in cold weather a grey camblet coat. His band was usually not of the sort as that in the print I have given; that is, as my original is, but like what are in the common prints of him, the band usually worn at that time. To have a more exact idea of his figure, let it be remembered that the fashion of the coat then was not much unlike what the Quakers wear now.—*Life of Milton.*

FROM THE COURT PROCEEDINGS RELATIVE TO MILTON'S WILL.[35] That on, or about the twentieth day of July, 1674, the day certain he now remembreth not, this deponent being a practicer in the Law, and a Bencher in the Inner Temple, but living in vacations at Ipswich, did usually at the end of the Term visit John Milton, his this deponent's brother the Testator articulate, deceased, before his going home; and so at the end of Midsummer Term last past, he this de-

---

[35] Milton's nuncupative or verbal will leaving all his property to his wife was contested by his daughters, Mary, Anne, and Deborah. The quotations are from the sworn testimony of Milton's brother and his servant, who appeared as witnesses for the widow. See Todd (1809 edition), vol. I, pp. 165 ff. Though the will was held invalid on technical grounds there can be little doubt of the reliability of the evidence.

ponent went to visit his said brother, and then found him in his chamber within his own house, situated on Bunhill within the parish of Saint Giles, Cripplegate, London. And at that time, he the said Testator, being not well, (and this deponent being then going into the country,) in a serious manner, with an intent, (as he believes,) that what he then spoke should be his will, if he died before his this deponent's coming the next time to London, declared his will in these very words as near as this deponent can now call to mind. Viz. "Brother, the portion due to me from Mr. Powell, my former first wife's father, I leave to the unkind children I had by her; but I have received no part of it, and my will and meaning is, they shall have no other benefit of my estate, than the said portion and what I have besides done for them; they having been very undutiful to me. And all the residue of my estate I leave to the disposal of Elizabeth my loving wife."—*Testimony of Christopher Milton.*

That this deponent was servant unto Mr. John Milton, the testator in this cause, deceased, for about a year before his death, who died upon a Sunday the fifteenth of November [36] last at night, and saith that on a day happening in the month of July last, the time more certainly she remembereth not, this deponent being then in the deceased's lodging chamber, he the said deceased, and the party producent in this cause his wife, being then also in the said chamber at dinner together, and the said Elizabeth Milton the party producent having provided something for the deceased's dinner which he very well liked, he the said deceased then spoke to his said wife these or the like words as near as this deponent can remember, *viz.* "God have mercy Betty, I see

[36] Error for November 8.

thou wilt perform according to thy promise in providing me such dishes as I think fit whilst I live, and when I die thou knowest that I have left thee all," there being nobody present in the said chamber with the said deceased and his wife but this deponent. And the said testator at that time was of perfect mind and memory, and talked and discoursed sensibly and well, but was then indisposed in his body by reason of the distemper of the gout, which he had then upon him. Further this deponent saith, that she hath several times heard the said deceased, since the time above deposed of, declare and say, that he had made provision for his children in his life-time, and had spent the greatest part of his estate in providing for them, and that he was resolved he would do no more for them living or dying. . . .

That this respondent hath heard the deceased declare his displeasure against the parties ministrant his children, and particularly the deceased declared to this respondent that, a little before he was married to Elizabeth Milton his now relict, a former maid servant of his told Mary one of the deceased's daughters and one of the ministrants, that she heard the deceased was to be married, to which the said Mary replied to the said maid servant, that that was no news to hear of his wedding, but if she could hear of his death that was something; and further told this respondent, that all his said children did combine together and counsel his maid servant to cheat him the deceased in her marketings, and that his said children had made away some of his books and would have sold the rest of his books to the dunghill women.—*Testimony of Elizabeth Fisher.*[37]

[37] For additional biographical data see Appendix. *The Columbia Milton,* Vol. XVIII, pp. 364 ff., contains a collection, made up from various sources, of Miltonic apothegmata.

CHAPTER II

THE PROSE WORKS

IT was not without reason that David Masson in his great biography of Milton felt compelled to narrate, beside the events of the poet's life, practically the whole political, ecclesiastical, and literary history of his times. Milton's career was not a private one, and a full understanding of his character and activity demands acquaintance with the entire series of historical events and changes from the beginnings of the great rebellion to the death of the Puritan movement in the Restoration. There are also the religious, cultural, and scholarly aspects of his age to take account of, for Milton, more perhaps than any other English literary man, received into himself the full intellectual inheritance of his own day. The best way to envisage Milton as a public figure, interpreting and moulding great events and being profoundly influenced by them in turn, the best way, also, to arrive at a comprehension of his wide ranging intellectual activity, to follow his developing thought and ideals, to witness the play of his character in action, is to make a careful study of his voluminous prose works.

Milton said that in writing prose he had the use, as it were, only of his left hand. But that left hand was a powerful one, whether in Latin or in English, and whenever he deals with matters of more than transitory significance (and it is characteristic of him to interpret particular issues at hand in accordance with large and enduring principles) his writings at their best constitute a vital and permanent contribution to literature and thought. Many passages have in them all the intensity of Milton's personality. The temperamental and passionate qualities which belonged to him as a poet, while they often prevent him from taking a calm and judicious view of his subject, fire his eloquence and make his work a personal record of the highest interest.

One element in the prose that has militated against its acceptability is the endless haggling over Scriptural and other authority. Milton does this because it seemed necessary and because he had not emancipated himself from the habits of his age. But it is, after all, a secondary and relatively insignificant part of his activity as a publicist and intellectual reformer. His initial thinking is independent, and the resort to authority is largely by way of defense. The workings of his mind in this regard are well illustrated by the first divorce tract, a document which, in its original form, contains a minimum of citation, but which, in the second edition, introduces many authors whom Milton had obviously consulted only after his fundamental argument was complete. This revision and the three later divorce tracts add practically nothing in the way of ideas to Milton's first statement; they are concerned mainly with rebuttal and the elaboration of authority. For this reason, they seem to the modern reader relatively ephemeral and worthless.

Even more offensive to some critics than Milton's textual quibbling is the savage joy with which he heaps on his opponents the language of ridicule and abuse. It is difficult to remain sympathetic with him when he resorts to personalities, and it will not quite do to say that Milton shares these practices with other controversialists in that bitter and hard-hitting epoch. We expect better things of one whose mood can at times be so serene and dignified. Milton might have won a crown of laurels even in the dust and heat of battle had he imitated the sweet reasonableness of Hooker or of some exceptional pamphleteers of his own day. William Walwyn, for example, can be much more damaging to the enemy than Milton without ever losing the temper of a Christian or the literary manners of a gentleman.[1]

It is, of course, useless to ask Milton for something he could not or did not choose to give. We must rather accept him for what he is and envisage him in the fierceness of the open conflict to which his temperament and his sense of duty drove him, as well as in the calm of contemplation which he affirms that he preferred. Even here we feel his versatility and power. Milton was, as Professor French maintains, a witty, effective satirist, not incapable of genuine though sardonic humor. He adopted the method consciously or at least knew how to justify his employment of it, and to that extent he worked as an artist.[2] "Now that the confutant may also know as he desires," he writes in the *Apology,* "what force of teaching there is sometimes in laughter, I shall return him, in short, that laughter . . . answering 'a fool according to his folly.'" And again, in *Animadversions,* "it will be nothing disagreeing from Christian meekness to handle such a one [as Bishop Hall] in a rougher accent, and to send home his haughtiness well be-spurted with his own holy water." He was familiar with the whole tradition of satire from Aristophanes to his own day,

[1] See for example *A Prediction of Mr. Edwards his Conversion.* Haller, *Tracts,* Vol. III, pp. 337 ff.

[2] French, *Milton as a Satirist,* and Whiting, *The Satire in "Eikono-klastes."*

and he apparently enjoyed trying to match it at its best and worst. French gives a picturesque list of "terms of endearment," many of them vulgar and colloquial, some coined for the purpose, which Milton bestows upon his enemies in one or another of his pamphlets: "Apostate, ague-cake, Babylonish merchants of souls, mammoc, quillets, scantling, slugs, hell-pestering rabble, Ephesian beasts, riff-raff of Sarum, hipshot grammarian, hoyden, brain-worm, phlegmy clod," etc., etc. He can do equally well in Latin. There are passages of irony, denunciation, or comic exaggeration in the prose as unforgettable as the parallel outbursts which occasionally found their way into the poetry, and they are an equally authentic expression of Milton's genius.

It remains true, however, that the controversial writing is most valuable when it is least controversial. And we may well doubt whether an earnest reformer can be called successful when he allows the savage joy of combat to get the better of his constructive purposes. Milton was, after all, born for higher things than to bandy epithets on the level of Martin Marprelate. The description in *Areopagitica* of "five imprimaturs, dialogue-wise, complimenting and ducking each to other with their shaven reverences, in the piazza of one title page," is Miltonic in its way and sufficiently amusing, but it cannot hold place beside utterances of another type:

A good book is the precious life-blood of a master spirit, embalmed and treasured up on purpose to a life beyond life.

or

God the son hath put all things under his feet, but his commandments he hath left all under the feet of charity.

One thing grows out of the personal emotions excited in Milton by opposition, which we could ill afford to miss. The prose works are interlarded with passages in which he pauses to take the reader into his confidence regarding his inmost thought, offering his own past life, his ideals, his hopes of future achievement, as the best defense he can make against those who violate his convictions and impugn his personality. These appeals for acceptance are touching and eloquent in themselves, and they constitute, as we have seen, an autobiographical record of great importance. Because Milton is first of all a man and a poet, they are the most permanently valuable portions of his prose.

ACADEMIC EXERCISES AND CORRESPONDENCE (1625–1666)

Milton's various rhetorical exercises, written in Latin for delivery on stated occasions in the college or university as a regular requirement of academic discipline, were preserved by him and published along with his personal Latin letters by Brabazon Aylmer in 1674 under the title *Johannis Miltoni Prolusiones quaedam Oratoriae*. These disputations or orations deal with such topics as "Whether day or night be the more excellent," "That occasional sportive exercises are not obstructive to philosophical studies," "That art is more conducive to human happiness than ignorance." They cover the entire period of Milton's residence at Cambridge from his sophomore year and constitute, in spite of their purely rhetorical character, an interesting record of a part of his intellectual activity as a student.[8] They show, in

[8] The Prolusions have recently been translated and studied by Tillyard, *Private Correspondence,* etc. See also Masson, Vol. I, pp. 140 ff. and 272 ff. for a discussion of the academic requirements under which they were composed and for an attempt to date them.

the first place, that Milton was skilled beyond his fellows in the elegance and ingenuity of his performance of these duties, being already a master of literary expression in the Latin tongue. They are full of a sportive but not always felicitous humor; they reveal also a strong consciousness of superiority and the tendency, so characteristic of the later Milton, to make his own personality an issue in the controversy in which he is engaged. In the sixth exercise he alludes to the epithet "Lady" [4] which had been applied to him and defends his ascetic way of life against the implications of his detractors, answering scorn for scorn. He shows himself already an adherent to the more progressive way of thought represented by Bacon and the humanists generally against the larger and more conservative group who still moved in the ruts of medieval scholasticism. This comes out in the second Prolusion, where Plato is exalted above Aristotle, and in the third, which contains an attack on scholastic philosophy. It is equally evident in two academic pieces included among Milton's Latin poems. In one of these, *De Idea Platonica quemadmodum Aristoteles intellexit,* Milton delicately satirizes the hard-headed attitude which denies the real existence of the ideas because they cannot be seen and touched. His sympathies are evidently on the side of the more imaginative Platonic mode of thought. The other, entitled *Naturam non pati Senium,* a defense of the continued vigor of the physical world in opposition to the discomforting idea that it is degenerating toward senility, goes with the utterances in the Prolusions as showing the hopeful philosophic position that Milton had already allied himself with and which he was never wholly to abandon even after the discouragements of his later life.

[4] Quoted above, p. 22.

The issue regarding the decay of nature was but one point
in a broad controversy which is fundamental in the thought
of the seventeenth century. This controversy had recently
been brought to a head by the publication of George Hakewill's important *Apology or Declaration of the Power and
Providence of God in the Government of the World,* which
denies not only the physical decline of nature, but also the
general thesis that modern civilization can never hope to
rival that of the early world. Milton's verses were written
for a Cambridge disputation on the subject of Hakewill's
book, and Milton must have been thoroughly conversant
with the whole argument. His ardent, reforming temperament forbade him to be anything but a modern, and despite
his theological presuppositions and his reverence for antiquity he instinctively championed the point of view which
lent encouragement to human effort.[5]

Milton's personal letters (*Epistolae Familiares*), thirty-
one in number, date from 1625 to 1666. The earlier ones
are addressed to his two tutors, Young and Gill, and to
his schoolboy friend, Charles Diodati. Most of those written
after the Horton period were sent to various Continental
correspondents, with some of whom he had become acquainted on his Italian journey. Milton took pains to make
these letters models of Latin epistolary art and published
them as works of literature. In this respect he is following
a tradition of the Renaissance humanists, who endeavored
in their correspondence to imitate the elegance of Cicero's
letters to Atticus and the members of his own family. They
contain, however, valuable personal data and are sometimes the expressions of his most intimate thought and feeling. Epistle VII gives full scope to the Platonic exaltation

[5] See Jones, *The Background of the Battle of the Books,* pp. 107 ff.

of his friendship with Diodati. A letter to the Athenian Philaras sets forth very minutely the symptoms of his blindness. Others tell of his sickness and domestic distresses. Throughout the series there is much interesting talk of books and book buying. In tone the letters are often light and bantering. There is in them a somewhat affected urbanity and a tendency toward self-depreciation which is hardly in accord with Milton's deep satisfaction with his own gifts and achievements. On the other hand, he addresses his friends in terms of admiration sometimes approximating flattery. All this and the occasional note of complaint find their precedent in humanistic correspondence generally, particularly in the letters of Erasmus.

In addition to this selection of personal letters published by Milton himself, there exists in manuscript a considerable correspondence between Milton and his friends or political associates, all of which is now collected in Volumes XII and XVIII of the Columbia Milton. There are, first of all, two interesting letters in Greek by Diodati (c. 1626), the first making an appointment for a holiday excursion, the second expressing longing for Milton's company in Cheshire and pleasantly chaffing him for his over-seriousness. Carolo Dati, the Florentine, writes at length in Italian asking Milton to honor a dead poet with some verses, discussing a passage in Catullus, and thanking him in flattering terms for copies of his poems. Leo van Aizema, who, as ambassador from the Hanse towns, had had official dealings with Milton, proposes to translate the *Doctrine and Discipline of Divorce* into Dutch; Peter Heimbach felicitates the poet in 1666 on his release from public affairs. There are also business letters in English from Milton to Whitlock and Bradshaw, a letter from Moses Wall in 1659, and a frag-

cluding the so-called Root and Branch Bill of June, 1641, which provided for the utter abolition of Archbishops, Bishops, and other ecclesiastical officers. The intention was to establish a synodical or Presbyterian form of church government analogous to that in Scotland. There was opposition by both the high and broad church parties, and a more moderate bill curtailing the powers of the Bishops but preserving the traditional system was proposed in the House of Lords.

The struggle in Parliament was prepared for and attended by a series of pamphlets on both sides of the question, the protagonist of the principle of episcopacy being Bishop Joseph Hall, who published a tract entitled *Episcopacy by Divine Right* in 1640 and another, *An Humble Remonstrance to the High Court of Parliament,* in January, 1641. In reply to this latter work, besides various tracts by Scottish Presbyterians in London, there appeared in March, 1641, a pamphlet entitled *An Answer to a Book entitled 'An Humble Remonstrance' in which the Originall of Liturgy and Episcopacy is Discussed.* This was written by a group of English Puritan ministers who signed themselves "Smectymnuus," a word composed of the initials of their various names. The leader of this group was Thomas Young, Milton's former tutor, and it is assumed by Masson that the poet himself may have assisted in its composition. The Smectymnuus pamphlet was followed in April by a reply of Bishop Hall and in May by one from the pen of the learned James Ussher, Bishop of Armagh. It was at about this point that Milton, putting aside his literary plans, intervened with his first ecclesiastical document, *Of Reformation touching Church Discipline*

in England and the Causes that hitherto have hindered it,
published anonymously.[6]

This is a rather temperate and carefully reasoned historical discussion, revealing close study of the progress of
the English church from the time of Henry VIII. Milton
endeavors, first, to show the reasons in the situation under
Henry, Edward, and Elizabeth why a compromise with
Catholicism rather than a complete Protestant reform came
to be adopted in the Anglican church. He then refutes
the arguments of those who contend for episcopacy on
grounds of antiquity,[7] showing that the system represented
a corruption of primitive Christianity. But primitive Christianity, in any case, is, he claims, not a model for later
times, since there is in the writings of the fathers and
historians of the church abundant evidence of depravity
and worldliness in the early centuries. Furthermore, the
ancient fathers disclaimed authority in the matter of church
government and deferred to scripture. At this point Milton waxes eloquent as he contrasts the transparent simplicity of truth as one finds it in the Gospel with the tangled
forest of theological argument and interpretation. In a
second book he assails the defense of an episcopal régime
as a form of church government naturally agreeing with
monarchy and necessarily implied by it. Finally, he denounces with vehemence the corruptions into which the
clergy have fallen, closing with a wonderful prayer for the

[6] It is impossible to determine the date exactly. The tract is mentioned by "Peloni Almoni" in a pamphlet dated May 31, 1641, but this
tract is actually an answer to Milton's second pamphlet. See below.
The best edition of *Of Reformation* is that edited by Hale.

[7] Professor George Whiting, *RES,* Oct., 1935, has shown that
Milton's arguments are directed against a speech of Lord Digby's
(1640), which, however, is not mentioned by name.

deliverance of the nation from this un-English tyranny and the completion of God's glorious work of religious reform.

It is interesting to note that in this work Milton's position is essentially that of Calvinism. He is primarily interested in getting rid of bishops and he does not elaborate a system of church government, but by suggesting that the English church should be "brought into unity with our neighbor reformed sister churches" he suggests that he has Scotch Presbyterianism in mind as his model. Later, in *The Reason of Church Government* (1642), he comes out openly in favor of that system. It is rather ironical that Milton should have been so blind to the possibility of a Presbyterian tyranny over free conscience that he actually mentions and brushes aside the argument of the "libertines" who claimed that the Presbyterian discipline would be more strict than that of Episcopacy and would establish "a Pope in every parish." Within a few years Milton was to feel the truth of this and rage against it. The fact is that he was already writing as a crusading propagandist rather than as a philosopher. His policies and specific points of view are formed in the heat of debate and therefore are subject to modification as the situation changes. Theologically Milton as yet shows no sign of heresy. He prays to the Trinity and speaks slightingly of Arianism. Politically he is still, with the majority of his countrymen, conservative, assuming the monarchical form of government as that to which the nation is permanently committed. But to say all this is not to deny that the fundamental trend of his inner thought was already set in the direction of individualism. He had made entries in the Commonplace Book indicating interest in the more radical ideas of the

Reformation and he was already a republican at heart. In only two places in this pamphlet does Milton show his deeper and more personal passion. At the beginning of the second book he describes in a glow of eloquence the ideal aim of the science of government, "to train up a nation in true wisdom and virtue, and that which springs from thence, magnanimity," and he decries the "masterpiece of the modern politician, how to qualify and mold the sufferance and subjection of the people to the length of the foot that is to tread upon their necks." At the end, in describing the hymns and hallelujahs which will greet the triumph of the church, he speaks of himself as one who may perhaps be heard among the others "offering at high strains in new and lofty measures."

The second tract is entitled *Of Prelatical Episcopacy, and whether it may be deduced from the Apostolical times by vertue of those testimonies which are alleged to that purpose in some late Treatises; one whereof goes under the name of James, Archbishop of Armagh.* This pamphlet, which appeared without Milton's name before May 31, 1641, is a brief point by point refutation, without any particular animus, of the Patristic authorities employed by Ussher in *The Judgment of Dr. Rainoldes touching the original of Episcopacy* to prove that the order of Bishops, superior to that of Presbyters, was an institution of the primitive church. Milton shows that the authorities alleged either do not justify the inferences or are themselves untrustworthy. In so doing he exhibits an intimate acquaintance with the church Fathers, an acquaintance the foundations of which we know to have been laid by a systematic study of their writings in the Horton period.[8]

[8] Hanford, *Chronology,* p. 291.

That study was, to a certain extent at least, impartial and discriminating, and Milton undoubtedly derived important materials for his own thought from the ancient writers of the church, but here, as in the other ecclesiastical pamphlets, his use of them is purely controversial and his attitude in general disparaging. "Whatsoever time, or the heedless hand of blind chance, hath drawn down from of old to this present in her huge drag-net, whether fish or seaweed, shells or shrubs, unpicked, unchosen, those are the fathers." In the course of the argument Milton condemns Tertullian for making the Son a derivation from and therefore inferior to the Father, precisely the point of view he was himself later to adopt. He ridicules the superstitious acceptance of such marvels as that of the seven sleepers of Cologne. In one passage he refers to the occasional necessity in state affairs of a strong leader, a Brutus or a Pericles, taking on the functions of a king, though without thereby acquiring at any time "more than a temporary and elective sway, which was in the will of the people when to abrogate." This is the earliest intimation of Milton's doctrine of popular sovereignty, his ideas being evidently based on the constitutions of Greece and Rome. He was evidently well prepared in mind for both the Commonwealth and the Protectorate. The pamphlet *Of Prelatical Episcopacy* did not fall entirely on deaf ears. It was answered immediately by a pseudonymous writer, Peloni Almoni; and some months later the arguments employed in it were of considerable influence in shaping Lord Brooke's more famous discourse against Episcopacy referred to in *Areopagitica*.[9]

[9] See Whiting, *A Pseudonymous Reply*. Hezekiah Woodward, who wrote nine pamphlets against episcopacy between 1643 and 1644,

The third tract, published almost simultaneously with the first and second, is directed against Bishop Hall, whose *Defense of the Humble Remonstrance against the frivolous and false exceptions of Smectymnuus,* had, as we have seen, appeared in April. Milton evidently believed in the principle "divide and conquer." His first tract had been an impersonal treatise setting forth the historical aspects of the problem; his second and third dealt severally with the two chief defenders of the Bishops. The title of this third pamphlet is *Animadversions upon the Remonstrant's Defense against Smectymnuus.* Like the others it was anonymous.

Milton's tone toward Hall is much more flippant and satirical than that which he had adopted in the refutation of Ussher. He reveals as yet no personal bitterness nor does he resort to slander but he does everything he can to throw ridicule and scorn upon his opponent's arguments. A reason for this is that Hall himself had made use of similar weapons in dealing with the Smectymnuans. Besides this, he found in Hall a cleverer and more popular controversialist, whose sallies naturally provoked rhetoric and satire rather than scholarship. His method is to quote verbatim Hall's more questionable statements and to append some sarcastic comment on each. He alludes to Hall's "toothless satires" in verse and makes merry with his satirical fiction *Mundus Alter et Idem.* Little material which is not already contained in the earlier tracts is added to the discussion except for one section concerning a matter on which Milton had deep and permanent convictions,—the question of the true nature of the office of minister of the

seems to owe a general debt to Milton's early tracts. See Whiting, *Woodward's Debt to Milton.*

gospel. To Milton the ministry was an inward calling, a labor of charity "next to that love which dwells in God to save souls." Ordination is a mere outward symbol which creates nothing and confers nothing. Those who enter the church for material reward of place or profit are no true ministers and it is unnecessary and harmful to hold out such rewards as is done in the Episcopal system. Neither here nor elsewhere does Milton meet the practical problem of how the unpaid clergy is to be recruited and to live, except to suggest that rich fathers will bestow exquisite education upon their children and so dedicate them to the service of the gospel, and that a true pastor, for greatest labors and greatest merits in the church, "requires either nothing, if he could so subsist, or a very common and reasonable supply of human necessaries." The conclusion is that we may leave this care to God. Milton's citation of a passage against hireling ministers from Spenser's *Shepheards Calendar* reveals one of the sources in his youthful reading of these convictions of his heart.

A period of some eight months elapsed between the publication of the third and the fourth and fifth tracts. During that interval the country was drifting rapidly toward civil war. Charles had been forced to yield on the church question and had signed the Bishops' Exclusion Bill in February, but the paper controversy over episcopacy continued furiously, the cause of the Bishops being again championed in a collection of tracts by various important divines. Milton's new work was an elaborately written treatise in two books entitled *The Reason of Church Government urg'd against Prelaty,* published, with the author's name, in February, 1642. This is the longest and most interesting of Milton's ecclesiastical tracts. Though pausing

occasionally to refute specific arguments in the collective
volume above-mentioned he proceeds on the whole in a
more philosophical manner, arguing systematically that the
Presbyterian rather than the Episcopal system is the one
prescribed in the gospel, and that Prelacy, in its external
lordliness, in its predilection for rites, symbolisms, and vest-
ments, and in its reliance on temporal authority in matters
which should be purely moral and spiritual, is foreign to
the spirit of Christianity. The last point, implying as it
does the separation of Church and State, represents Milton's profound conviction and is a principle from which
he never receded. He becomes eloquent also in opposition
to the idea of enforcing uniformity of belief. The multipli-
cation of sects and schisms, instead of frightening him as
it does others, is in his thought a wholesome sign that
the living work of reformation is going on. Diversity of
doctrine, even the wildest, is better than a stagnant uniformity secured by the forcible suppression of free thought.
The point of view looks forward to that of the *Areopagitica*
to be composed a year and a half later. Underlying all is
the essentially Protestant and Puritan feeling that religion
is an affair of the individual. No priest can mediate between the soul and God; faith is not real until it is discovered anew in personal experience; the private conscience is the sole judge of man's moral and spiritual duties.
Masson [10] quotes from the fourth pamphlet a noble passage
praising the self-confidence of the righteous man who has
learned to revere himself or rather the image of God within
himself and is, therefore, indifferent to the approval or
disapproval of others. How, Milton asks, can a man best
be led to this "hill-top of sanctity and goodness"? By being

[10] Vol. II, p. 374.

taught that he is himself appointed and ordained by God to a sacred calling as a member of the church. The Episcopal system "excludes Christ's people from the offices of holy discipline" and causes them "to have an unworthy and abject opinion of themselves, to approach to holy duties with a slavish fear, and to unholy things with a familiar boldness." The logic of this position, as Milton afterward found, leads through Presbyterianism to Independency and finally to pure individualism. But, however far in this direction his real opinions may already have gone, he allies himself in these pamphlets with the orthodox Presbyterian cause and he still speaks of the Scots in terms of friendly admiration. Particularly interesting and important is the long personal digression which forms the introduction to Book II. Milton has kept still about himself long enough. He expatiates in noble language upon the idealistic motives which have led him to abandon more pleasing tasks for the duty of playing a man's part in the work of purifying religion from its corruptions, and at the same time confides to the reader his personal ambition to write a lofty poem which the world will not willingly let die.[11] The concluding chapter is a denunciation of the mischief that Prelacy does in the state, another expanded prose rendering of the invective against the clergy in *Lycidas*. The general trend of Milton's argument in this as in his other pamphlets is toward liberty, but liberty with him was never license and he introduces his discussion with a philosophic discourse on discipline which contains ideas from which he never, in his hottest denunciations of the external restraints imposed by man-made laws, receded, and which anticipates in a most interesting way some of

[11] See Appendix B, pp. 373 ff.

the basic principles later to be embodied in *Paradise Lost*. "There is," he says, "not that thing in the world of more grave and urgent importance throughout the whole life of man, than is discipline." The flourishing and decay of all civil societies move upon its axis. It holds with its musical chords all the parts of this life together. "And certainly discipline is not only the removal of disorder; but if any visible shape can be given to divine things, the very visible shape and image of virtue, whereby she is not only seen in the regular gestures and motions of her heavenly paces as she walks but also makes her voice audible to mortal ears. Yea, the angels themselves, in whom no disorder is feared, as the apostle that saw them in his rapture describes, are distinguished and quaternioned into their celestial princedoms and satrapies, according as God himself has writ his imperial decrees through the great provinces of heaven." One wishes that Milton's controversial position had oftener allowed him thus to deploy his prose eloquence in the praise of order. The passage is worthy to stand beside the best of Hooker. It belongs with that cited above from *Of Reformation* regarding the science of government as indicating how deeply in accord Milton was with one of the central interests of the Renaissance. We learn from the Commonplace Book that Milton had studied Machiavelli, and with admiration, in spite of the divergence between their creeds.

In the last tract, *An Apology against a Pamphlet called "A Modest Confutation of the Animadversions of the Remonstrant against Smectymnuus,"* issued early in the year 1642, Milton again returns to the pettier and more personal phases of the controversy. Bishop Hall, aided now by his son, had at last swung his battery against Milton himself in the pamphlet to which Milton alludes in his title. Goaded by the scorn of Milton's third tract, the *Animadversions,* the Halls, besides endeavoring to confute his reasons item by item, had launched all manner of scurrilous and irresponsible charges against him in his private life. Milton takes these quite seriously and attends at length to the congenial work of self-vindication. He describes his honorable career at the University, from which the Halls had said he was "vomited" forth. He tells in what employments he actually spends the morning and afternoon hours which he was charged with giving to debauchery, and, finally, replying to the accusation of unchastity, he communicates to the reader his "inmost thoughts," tracing through his early life, the growth of an exceptionally idealistic attitude on this very subject.[12] These personal digressions Milton justifies as necessary. He also defends the violence of his invective and the use of undignified, even indecent, language, by adverting to the examples of Luther and of Christ himself. Having satisfied his readers, or at least himself, on these points, he returns to the onslaught against the remonstrances point by point. There is little sober reasoning, and Milton is more than once led in the heat of controversy to stultify his better judgment, as when he refuses to see any beauty or excellence in the English liturgy, but the object of leaving no word of his opponents without its retort and of holding the Halls personally up to ridicule is successfully achieved. They are, to use a phrase of Masson's, "gored and mangled" on every page. The pamphlet marks something of a turning point in Milton's history as a controversialist. Up to this time he has been simply a vigorous crusader for what seems to him the cause of truth

12 See Appendix B, pp. 365 ff.

and righteousness and an incidental pleader for attention to his own capacity for another and higher form of service when these disputes are at an end. Now that his own personality is at issue he becomes more deeply concerned. Henceforth the cause, whatever it may be, and the man, are one. We may expect as a consequence an intenser intellectual effort, the willingness to resort to baser weapons, also a profounder conviction, and at times the attainment of a loftier and more passionate eloquence.

THE DIVORCE TRACTS (1643–1645)

Milton's crusade against the divorce laws of his country followed almost immediately on the conclusion of the ecclesiastical controversy and continued to occupy him for nearly two years. *The Doctrine and Discipline of Divorce* was published before August 1, 1643. A second edition, much enlarged, appeared in February, 1644, a new pamphlet, *The Judgment of Martin Bucer concerning Divorce,* in July of the same year, and finally *Tetrachordon* and *Colasterion,* in March, 1645. Milton's active prosecution of this campaign was punctuated by the composition of the tracts *Of Education* and *Areopagitica.* The divorce treatises form, however, a closely knit series and should be considered as a unit.

The composition of the first divorce pamphlet is associated by all Milton's biographers with his own difficulties in his matrimonial venture with Mary Powell, and much pretty speculation as to the precise nature of his experience has been built on the interpretation of this document. The most authoritative statement appears to be that of the anonymous biographer [13] to the effect that Milton, practically deserted by his wife, was preparing for a second marriage and sought to justify himself by writing his first divorce tract. He adds, however, that the need of a more liberal divorce law "had upon full consideration and by reading good authors previously been his opinion." According to Milton's own statement the divorce campaign was a second impersonal step in the cause of liberty, following upon the successful war against the authority of the Bishops (see page 76). Phillips gives an account which agrees essentially with that of the anonymous biographer, and states that Milton's resentment and the consequent incubation of the first pamphlet followed his wife's failure to return to him at Michaelmas (i. e., September 29). This dating creates a problem, for we know that the tract was written and actually on sale by the date set for Mary Powell's return, assuming, as Masson does, that Milton was married in 1643. Some students, notably Chilton Powell, [14] have argued from this discrepancy that Milton's interest in divorce was entirely independent of his personal situation and desires. There is, however, reason to believe that the marriage may have taken place in 1642 rather than in 1643, in which case we can accept the theory of the anonymous biographer that the poet's thoughts were turned in the direction of divorce by [15]

[13] Quoted above, p. 40.

[14] *English Domestic Relations,* Appendix B.

[15] See the studies of Martin and of Wright (Bibliography). It is pointed out that political and military conditions in 1643 are against the probability of Milton's having married Mary Powell in that year. The king had set up his standard in Oxford in October, 1642; the place was wild with royalist enthusiasm thereafter; and communication with London was difficult. The fact that an unusually long gap in Milton's pamphleteering activities occurs between April, 1642, and

the failure of his wife to live up to her duties and his expectations. It is an open question how much further one can go in tracing the details of Milton's experience in the ostensibly impersonal discussion. Certain phrases sound very much like a reflection of his own bitterness and disillusionment. He says, however, very little about desertion as a ground of divorce, assuming that there would be general agreement on that point, though the canon laws which were still officially in force in England failed to recognize it. His main plea is that incompatibility of temper is a more vital impediment to the higher objects of marriage than any other and that the will of the parties should therefore be admitted as decisive for the continuance or dissolution of the bond. The function of the magistrate in the matter he would limit to the securing of conditions of divorce equitable for both parties. The principle is in perfect accord with Milton's whole philosophy. It was because he thought nobly of marriage as a spiritual rather than a merely physical union that he resented the common idea that it was dissoluble only on physical grounds. The idea of an external compulsion, binding two human beings together when mutual love and sympathy had departed, was repellent to his reason and excited him to eloquent and passionate denunciation. Milton reiterates this fundamental idea again and again, and it furnishes the one interesting and vital element in the whole voluminous debate. The attempt, which occupies him through many pages, to reconcile Scripture with his views has lost most of its significance for the modern reader. He explains Christ's answer to the Pharisees—"Moses, because of the hardness of your hearts, suffered you to put away your

August, 1643, adds to the probability that those months were the period of his domestic difficulties and subsequent mental distress.

wives"—as follows: Moses' law was a grave and prudent law, full of moral equity, and Jesus approved of it. But the Pharisees, in interpreting "uncleanness" to mean *every* cause of dissatisfaction, however trivial, have wrested it to suit their own bad purposes. Moses preferred to allow them in the hardness of their hearts so to abuse his doctrine "rather than that good men should lose their just and lawfull privilege of remedy." Jesus does not therefore intend to rescind the Mosaic law or to limit "uncleanness" to adultery but to administer a rebuke to the hypocritical Pharisees.

It is characteristic of Milton's temper and of his views as to the natural superiority of man to woman that he should speak oftenest of him as the injured party and should put the decision in favor of divorce chiefly in his hands. Yet he admits that the situation may sometimes be reversed, and he appears to make an effort to be just to the woman and to put her interests on an equal footing with those of her husband in the matter.[16] If either party is dissatisfied, incompatibility is established and the marriage *ipso facto* dissolved. It belongs to man as the natural head of the house ordinarily to discern the situation and pronounce the decree.

In the preface to the second edition of the first tract Milton gives the impression that he had arrived at his views about divorce solely as a result of his own reflection, and he speaks of himself as a pioneer in the attempt to free mankind from his domestic fetters. Yet the subject had been in almost continuous agitation since the Reformation, and Milton's ideas, though extreme, were not inconsistent with the general drift of Protestant opinion. Certain observations in the Commonplace Book, moreover, show that Milton had interested himself in the general philosophy of marriage as

[16] See Gilbert, *Milton on the Position of Woman*, pp. 11 ff.

early as the Horton period, and that his mind was already set toward liberal thought regarding it. He appears, however, to have been ignorant, when he began his tract, of the great body of Reformation discussion on divorce, for he there refers to none of the outstanding authorities. He must have studied them vigorously in the months immediately following the publication of his work, for the revised edition is interlarded with weighty opinions and reverend names. His greatest discovery in this research was the support lent to his ideas by the Protestant divine, Martin Bucer, who, in his *De Regno Christi,* written for Edward VI, had argued stoutly in favor of absolute divorce in place of the separation from bed and board allowed by canon law, and had also admitted incompatibility as a ground for the annulment of marriage. Milton excerpted and published the relevant chapters of Bucer's book as a second document in the case under the title *The Judgment of Martin Bucer concerning Divorce.* His third tract, *Tetrachordon,* [17] adds no new arguments but enters in more detail into the interpretation of the Scriptural passages, to satisfy, as there was grave need of doing, those who found his earlier explanations a bit too glib.

In the preface Milton alludes to the fact that Parliament had "been instigated to a hard censure of the former book," i. e., *The Doctrine and Discipline.* The reference is to the two petitions of the Stationers' Company for the punishment of Milton among other authors of scandalous volumes, one addressed to the Commons, another, later, to the

[17] Tetrachord is a technical term in music, referring to the succession of four notes represented by the strings of the Greek lyre. Tetrachordon is the four-stringed lyre itself. Milton's tract deals with the four chief scriptural passages on divorce.

Lords. Milton also inveighs briefly against the hostile mention of his "wicked book" by Mr. Herbert Palmer in a sermon before Parliament preached in August, 1644, and by Dr. Daniel Featley in his pamphlet *Dippers Dipt*. Ephraim Paget in his *Heresiography* had also alluded with horror to Milton's doctrine. The real work of refuting the opponents who had now sprung up against him and of overwhelming them forever with invective was reserved for the last pamphlet, *Colasterion. A Reply to a Nameless Answer against "The Doctrine and Discipline of Divorce," wherein the trivial Author of that Answer is discover'd, the Licencer conferr'd with, and the Opinion which they traduce defended. By the former author, J. M.* The "nameless answer" had been published in November, 1644, with a special note of approval prefixed to it by the licenser, Joseph Caryl. Milton had inquired into the origin of the document and had discovered that it was the work of a serving man turned solicitor. This wretch he belabors with personal abuse and insult, paying his compliments incidentally to William Prynne, who had stigmatized the monstrous heresy of "divorce at pleasure" in one of his recent pamphlets, and to the officious licenser himself. Milton answers the arguments, such as they are, by reiterating his former points, but he evidently relies chiefly on ridicule to dispose of his opponent. Outrageous and even gross as is the language he applies to his victim, there is no evidence that Milton is really angry. His fate, he says, in providing so silly an antagonist, extracts from him a "talent for sport." He promises on further provocation to deliver his answer in a satiric poem. Unfortunately no such occasion was given, and the divorce issue, so far as Milton was concerned, was closed. He did not change his ideas, for they are restated as a part of the program of Christian belief in the *De Doctrina Christiana* (Book I, Chapter X).

Milton's arguments fell in his own day on deaf ears and his more radical principles have never been embodied in English law or indeed in the law of any western country. The tendency, however, has been toward rather than away from them, and the latest British legislation, with its provision for divorce on grounds of desertion, cruelty, etc., goes much farther than would have once seemed believable toward the complete realization of Milton's idea of domestic liberty. An odd instance of the literary use of his ideas occurs in Farquhar's *The Beaux' Strategem,* where some of the material of the first pamphlet is reproduced in dialogue.[18]

OF EDUCATION (1644)

Milton's little tractate on education was anonymously published in June of the year 1644, just before the second divorce pamphlet. It is addressed as a letter to Samuel Hartlib, a public-spirited reformer who was interested in educational matters, particularly in the ideas of Comenius, and who had requested Milton to make a statement of his views on the subject. The treatise is the fruit of Milton's thoughtful experience of teaching and represents the program of humanistic education as it was conceived by the man who, of all scholars of his time, perhaps, best understood its meaning. The wisdom and modernity of many of the methods recommended, as, for example, the supplementing of textbook instruction by contact with men of practical experience, and by the observation of actual in-

[18] Larson, *The Influence of Milton's Divorce Tracts.*

stitutions and activities, has won the admiration of all thinkers on this subject. The goal of the discipline which Milton
outlines is the formation of the well-rounded scholarly gentleman, who shall also be well fitted for public leadership,
an ideal inherited from the early Renaissance. This is expressed in the famous definition of a complete and generous
education as one which "fits a man to perform justly, skill-
fully, and magnanimously all the offices, both public and
private, of peace and war." The way to this object is through
an understanding of the civilization of antiquity, not as a
dead or remote thing, but as an experience applicable at
every point to modern life. Milton insists that the Greek
and Latin languages should be studied not for themselves
but as tools for the acquisition of the "solid things in them."
The emphasis is from the first on the subject rather than the
expression. He is violently opposed to forcing children into
the composition of empty rhetorical and scholastic exercises
before they have anything to say. The program is a severe
one, including besides the reading of representative works
in almost the whole range of Greek and Latin literature and
the study in them of all the arts and sciences, the acquisition
of Italian, Hebrew, and even Syriac, and a full course in
military discipline. It is interesting to observe in Milton's
program a reflection and modification of the education
which he had himself received, partly from schools and
tutors, partly by his own independent effort. His model
school provides for the entire training of boys from the
ages of twelve to twenty-one, after which they may, as he
himself did, engage in foreign travel. Attendance at the
University, which Milton had found so unsatisfactory,[19] is
not contemplated in the plan. On the other hand, the liberal

[19] See Appendix A.

principles embodied in the tractate are those of the more enlightened humanist reformers generally and are ultimately based on the educational thought of the ancients—Cicero, Plato, Quintilian, etc. Milton says he will not specify his indebtedness to these "old renowned authors," nor search "what many modern Januas and Didactics, more than ever I shall read, have projected." This is a disparaging reference to the titles of two of Comenius' works. But Milton certainly owed many suggestions to his contemporaries and predecessors in educational theory. The Spaniard Vives, in his *De Tradendis Disciplinis,* has been mentioned as among the most important influences.[20]

It is also pointed out that *Of Education* does not adequately represent Milton's thought on education as a matter of public policy. The tractate offers an essentially aristocratic plan, designed for the training of the sons of gentlemen to leadership in war and peace. Elsewhere Milton advocates a system of state-supported universal instruction as necessary to the safety and welfare of a free commonwealth. No man ever believed in education more passionately than Milton or was himself more essentially a teacher.[21]

Of the practical working of his system as applied by Milton himself we have little evidence. The two Phillips boys, his nephews, who are the only individuals whom we know to have been subjected to the full weight of his pedagogical influence, proved weak vessels. John, the younger,

[20] Watson, *A Suggested Source of Milton's Tractate.* See also for discussion of Milton's ideas and their origin, Thompson, *Milton's "Of Education";* and Ainsworth, *Milton as a Writer on Education.*

[21] For a discussion of the reflections of Milton's pedagogic interests and philosophy in his poetry, see Bundy, *Milton's View of Education in "Paradise Lost."*

who was Milton's special charge from boyhood and became his assistant as Latin Secretary, rebelled against the serious and lofty tradition in which he had been nurtured, even before the fall of the Commonwealth régime. He paid his compliments to Puritanism in *A Satyr against Hypocrites,* ridiculed Cromwell and his colleagues in a burlesque romance, pandered to the sons of Belial by collaborating in a licentious publication, and ended his days as a general Restoration hack writer without principle or purpose. There is no doubt as to his ability and he did bear witness to his classical training by doing some translation, but Milton's idealism was evidently too much for him. His brother Edward was on the whole a good and dutiful product of Milton's teaching but an uninspired one. He was himself a schoolmaster on and off throughout his life, and he produced a really considerable amount of work in literary and philological scholarship, particularly an English dictionary, various lexicographical works on Latin, and a *Theatrum Poetarum,* or index of poets of all countries and ages. The introductory discourse on poetry in the last mentioned volume and several of the comments on individual writers seem to reflect Milton's own ideas and may well have been directly inspired by him.[22] The Latin dictionary is said by Wood to have been based upon his notes. As Milton's literary executor Phillips later translated into English the *Letters of State,* prefixing to the translation the biographical memoir from which quotation has been made in the first chapter of this Handbook. But this was when it was no longer dangerous to exhibit interest in the heroes of the good old cause. He had previously shown that he was no

---

[22] See Thompson, *Milton's Part in the Theatrum Poetarum;* also The Columbia Edition, XVIII, 460.

candidate for martyrdom by writing a Royalist continuation of Baker's chronicle through the Cromwellian period. If Milton ever seriously counted on either Phillips to exemplify the virtues of a "complete and generous education" he must certainly have been disappointed, but one feels that no inference can be drawn from this negative result either against the validity of the system or against Milton's personal ability to make it work.

AREOPAGITICA (1644)

Areopagitica, Milton's great defense of the freedom of the press, was the fourth and last of the prose works to be written and published in the industrious year 1644. It appeared in November. The ordinance of Parliament which had occasioned it, an act requiring, among other things, that all books be licensed by an official censor before publication, had been passed June 14, 1643. This act reflected the increasing determination of the Presbyterian party, now in control in Parliament, to reduce English religious practice and opinion to a new uniformity and to silence political opposition. It was recognized by Milton and other men of independent tendencies as a revival in another form of the tyranny of the Stuart régime and particularly of a decree of the court of Star Chamber concerning printing, issued in 1637. This earlier licensing act had fallen in 1640 with the abolition of the illegal court which made it, and for three years printing had been practically free, during which time a multitude of pamphlets had been published of every shade of religious and political opinion. To Milton this diversity of writing was a wholesome sign of free intellectual activity, a promise of progress and reform; to

the narrower Presbyterians it was a menace against orthodox Calvinistic thought and the stability of the new order.
The whole matter had a special significance for Milton
personally, since his own writings on divorce represented
exactly such publications as were likely to be suppressed by
the new law. *The Doctrine and Discipline* had, as we have
seen, been attacked in a sermon before Parliament by Mr.
Herbert Palmer. As a consequence, doubtless, of this Presbyterian wrath against it, the attention of the company of
Stationers had been drawn to the fact that both this document in its first and second editions and another heretical
work which Palmer had coupled with it were printed without being licensed under the new act. In reply to a petition
by this organization (whose commercial rights were injured by unlicensed publication) Parliament ordered the
printing committee to inquire out the authors of these
works. Though the matter went no further, Milton must
have felt in anticipation the injuries which he himself was
likely to be subjected to by the new decree. We know, however, from a passage [23] in the *Reason of Church Government* (1641), that his opinion regarding the liberty of the
press antedated both this personal incident and the ordinance of 1643 itself. His convictions in this matter were an
essential part of his general philosophy of freedom and a
product of his instincts as a scholar and a teacher.

The work is addressed to Parliament in the hope of
influencing its members to repeal a decree so inconsistent
with their own history and purposes as the restorers of
English liberties. After adroitly complimenting this body

[23] "For me, I have determined to lay up as the best treasure of a
good old age, if God vouchsafe it me, the honest liberty of a free
speech from my youth."

on its past achievements and excusing himself for venturing in a private capacity on this criticism of their recent act, Milton reviews the history of licensing from ancient times, showing that it has always been a concomitant of tyranny and associating its invention in its modern form with the reactionary Catholic Council of Trent. The aim is to prove the practice suspect in its origin and a product of the very forces which Parliament has overthrown. Secondly, Milton enters upon a noble defense of the benefit of books freely used, showing how necessary reading of every sort is to the attainment of knowledge and experience in a world where good and evil grow up indiscriminately together. Next, he deals with the impossibility of the attempt to make men virtuous by external restraint. Corrupting influences are present everywhere and can be met only by building up an inner discipline and the power of rational choosing. This is the fundamental tenet of Milton's ethical philosophy and in setting it forth he rises to great heights of eloquence. He goes on to argue more specifically that the present law will be ineffective even as applied to publication. *Areopagitica* itself, though he does not say so, being published in defiance of the law, is an instance of the impossibility of enforcing it. Finally, Milton attacks the order as a discouragement to intellectual activity and a hindrance to the cause of truth. The plea here is one of resolute faith in the competence of human nature and particularly of English nature to work out its own intellectual salvation; [24] in the

---

[24] Tillyard (*Milton*, p. 156) calls *Areopagitica* Milton's "chief song of hope." Events are already undermining his confidence in the sturdiness of revolutionary England, and the note of disillusionment is to become increasingly predominant in his writing. On this subject see also Grierson's *Milton and Wordsworth* and Haller, *The Rise of Puritanism*. Grierson feels that Milton was more truly a prophet in

divine property, also, of Truth itself, which is sure to prevail ultimately over error if the two are allowed to grapple.
Milton expresses with extraordinary forcefulness the resentment of the mature mind at being kept under watch and
ward; and vividly displays the results of such a policy, in
spiritual stagnation and a "starched conformity of opinion."
The very spirit of the English Protestant speaks through
him, but his principles are as vital and his warnings as necessary to-day as they ever were. The *Areopagitica* is Milton's greatest prose work; it is one of those few books which
are capable, as John Morley said of Mill's *Essay on Liberty,*
of adding a cubit to a man's intellectual stature.

Milton's plea for liberty failed in its purpose of bringing
about an immediate repeal of the licensing act, but it was
employed when the issue was raised again in 1679 and
1693;[25] it furnished Mirabeau with the substance of a
pamphlet on the freedom of the press in 1788; and it has
armed the minds of individuals in all times against the
ever-recurring attempt to silence thought.

In form the *Areopagitica* is a majestic example of the
classical oration. The title is that of a written speech of
Isocrates addressed, in a private capacity, to the Athenian
Court of the Areopagus. It conforms to all the principles
of oratory laid down by Quintilian and embodied in Demosthenes and Cicero. The speeches of the fallen angels
in the second book of *Paradise Lost,* the description of

---

his early prose works than in his poems. Haller shows that Milton's
utopianism was a transitory phenomenon shared by others at this
time.

[25] *A Just Vindication of Learning or an Humble Address to the
High Court of Parliament in behalf of Liberty of the Press,* London,
1679. *Reasons humbly offered for the Liberty of Unlicenced Printing,*
London, 1693. Both works are abridgments of *Areopagitica.*

Satan's address to Eve (*P. L.* IX, 670 ff.), and the characterization of the Athenian orators who "wielded at will that fierce democracy" in the days of a noble eloquence "since mute" (*P. R.* IV, 268 ff.) show how deeply Milton had studied and admired this branch of ancient literature. The general principle of toleration, applied especially to publication in *Areopagitica,* had been maintained before Milton's time against the prevailing doctrine by other Independents, including Roger Williams in his *Bloody Tenet of Persecution.*[26]

OF THE TENURE OF KINGS AND MAGISTRATES (1649)

A period of four years' respite from public controversy followed the publication of the last of the divorce tracts in March, 1645. Near the beginning of this interval Milton issued the first edition of his poems. Between 1645 and 1648 he composed six sonnets and translated eight Psalms. He also carried on his work of teaching, adding several pupils to the two Phillips boys who had been with him since 1642. The bulk of his time must, however, have been devoted to study in preparation for projected works, particularly *The History of Britain* and the treatise *Of Christian Doctrine.* It seems likely, also, that the composition of one or both of these works was actually begun in this period. Meanwhile he was silently watching public events, and the movement of his mind regarding them may be clearly traced in the sonnets above-mentioned. The reception of his divorce pamphlets had completed the work of turning him against the Presbyterian party and of aligning

[26] The most scholarly edition of *Areopagitica* is still that of Hales. For its background in contemporary thought see Haller, *Before Areopagitica* and *Tracts on Liberty.*

him with the Independents, who, in 1647, finally triumphed in Parliament and took possession of the government. He must also, in company with the rest of this group, have become increasingly republican in sentiment, as the impossibility of a compromise with Charles became more and more apparent. We know from an early entry in the Commonplace Book that he had long since privately nourished such thoughts even before the civil war began, but he allowed them to find no place in any of his published utterances thus far. By the time the second civil war was successfully concluded and the captive king brought to trial, Milton was quite ready to adhere to the Republic and to join the cry for the king's deposition and death.

The document in which he did so, the treatise *Of the Tenure of Kings and Magistrates*,[27] was, like his first contribution to the episcopal controversy, unsolicited. It was probably composed during the king's trial, certainly before his execution on January 30, 1649, and was designed to silence the opposition of the Presbyterians and others against extreme measures, also to reconcile the public mind to the event itself. The pamphlet appeared two weeks after Charles's death.

In it Milton makes no indictment of Charles, does not, in fact, even mention him by name. His argument is the abstract one, that men are by nature free, that their relation to their governors is one of voluntary contract which may be terminated at will. He assembles the authority of the Greeks and Romans, of the church Fathers, of modern political theorists, of the Reformation divines, and of Scripture itself to show that men have a right to depose a tyrant and even to put him to death. He cites many instances from

[27] An annotated edition with full introduction is that of Allison.

history of the exercise of this right. More specifically, he inveighs against the Presbyterian ministers, who, having in the beginning fostered the rebellion, now refuse to accept the logical consequences of their own action.

The underlying philosophy of the tract is in line with the main development of liberal political theory throughout the Middle Ages and the Renaissance, and Milton says nothing that had not been said a hundred times. In style the work is plain and unimpassioned. Milton takes the momentous step of writing himself regicide without the usual accompaniment of enthusiastic eloquence inspired by the contemplation of his own personality and his cause.

WORK FOR THE COUNCIL OF STATE. EIKONOKLASTES (1649)

As a result of the zeal for the Commonwealth displayed in the *Tenure of Kings and Magistrates* Milton received in March, 1649, an appointment to the office of Secretary for Foreign Tongues to the Council of State. He was immediately called to the performance of a series of exacting literary duties which took precedence of all other work and occupied him continuously for nearly ten years. These duties consisted in the translation of such documents in foreign tongues as were referred to him by the Council, the drafting of the Latin correspondence of state with foreign powers, and finally the composition to order of replies whether in Latin or English to various attacks leveled against the Commonwealth.

Milton's official correspondence or *Letters of State* are usually published among Milton's works and they constitute an interesting and important record of his public activity.

There are one hundred and fifty-six such letters in all—
about a third of them from the years 1649–1652, bearing the
signatures of the Speaker of Parliament, the President of
the Council, or some other official of the Commonwealth;
the rest from the period of the Protectorate (1652–1659)
under the name of Oliver Cromwell. Milton himself kept
copies, which were inherited and transcribed after his death
by Daniel Skinner. This MS., which Skinner was prevented
from publishing, was delivered to the Secretary of State
and is now in the Public Records Office. In 1676 a bookseller issued an incomplete edition which he had obtained
surreptitiously, under the title *Literae Pseudo-Senatus
Anglicani*. There was a better one in 1690 and an English
translation by Edward Phillips in 1694. The Columbia Edition prints the complete series; [28] Masson gives a careful
analysis of their contents, with quotations.

Though these letters are not Milton's in substance they
are so in expression, and the greatest of them bear unmis-
takably the stamp of his literary power. Masson believes
that they were often written first in English by Milton after
consultation with Cromwell or others, read and approved in
that form by Parliament or the Council, then translated into
Latin. He believes, also, that Cromwell used Milton especially for letters which he wanted written "in the highest
strain of his most characteristic passion," those, for example, in which the United Provinces of the Netherlands
are solemnly warned against quarreling with Sweden to the
advantage of the common enemy, or the Protestant cantons
of Switzerland heartened in their struggle against the Cath-

---

[28] From the edition of 1676 supplemented by the Skinner MS. and
the Columbia MS., which is the sole authority for six letters and
several other state papers hitherto unpublished. Vol. XIII, pp. 4–503.

olics. But the correspondence deals with every sort of issue which came up in England's vigorous foreign policy at that time. There are protests to France against the reception of English pirates in her ports, demands of redress from Spain for the murder of an English agent, appeals to Venice for the release of a captain imprisoned by the Turks, commendations of English agents and ambassadors, and negotiations for a league of the Protestant powers. The dispatches which came closest to Milton personally and which most profoundly inspired his Latin eloquence were undoubtedly the ones addressed to Louis XIV and other foreign sovereigns in protest against the massacre of the Waldensian Protestants by the Duke of Savoy. Milton shared to the full the indignation of his country at this crime, and the letters are the equally impassioned prose counterparts of the famous sonnet which he wrote in his private capacity of poet, "Avenge O Lord thy Slaughtered Saints."

Among the first of the more miscellaneous tasks assigned to him was to attack the peace which had been concluded with the Catholics in Ireland by Charles's representative, the Earl of Ormond, in 1648. In 1649 Milton printed the articles with the correspondence between Ormond and the Governor of Dublin, and a pronouncement by the Presbyterians of Belfast, appending thereto an original discussion entitled *Observations on the Articles of Peace with the Irish Rebels,* in which he denounces the Irish bitterly as enemies to religion, condemns the agreement whereby Ireland is in effect released from fealty to England, and answers the various accusations made by the Belfast Presbyterians against the acts of the republicans. This is Milton's contribution to the Irish question. It prepares the way for the merciless suppression of the rebellion a few months later by Cromwell.

The next commission given to Milton by the Council was far more momentous. It was that of writing a work to counteract the menacing effect on public opinion of the famous *Eikon Basilike* or King's Book, which had appeared almost immediately after the king's death (i. e., in February, 1649) and was achieving an enormous circulation. The *Eikon,* or, to employ its subtitle, *The True Portraiture of his Sacred Majesty in his Solitudes and Sufferings,* purports to be a private record of the self-communings of Charles through the last years, almost the last hours, of his life, revealing him as a model of conscientiousness and piety, tender of his family, solicitous for the good of his people, loyally Protestant, and given to earnest prayer. The book was suspected from the moment of its appearance and is now believed to be a pious fraud, the work not of Charles at all but of one of his adherents, Bishop Gauden, who took this means of winning public sympathy for the king's memory and cause by setting up his image as that of a martyred saint. This object it signally accomplished and the popularity of the work was rightly felt by the leaders of the Commonwealth to constitute a danger of the first magnitude.

Milton called his answer *Eikonoklastes* (i. e., the imagebreaker). It is a lengthy examination of the *Eikon,* chapter by chapter, as was the manner of seventeenth century controversy. He deprecates the idea of assailing the memory of one who has paid his debt to nature, but, accepting the necessity of meeting such a challenge, proceeds to demonstrate the worthlessness of Charles's defense of his conduct at every point. The personal indictment which he had

avoided making in the *Tenure of Kings and Magistrates*
is now drawn with a vengeance. The pious passages, which
constituted the most popular feature of the work, he assails as mere hypocrisy, instancing Shakespeare's Richard
III as an example of a tyrant who masked his evil purposes with religious cant. The most damaging point in the
entire statement was his demonstration that one of the
rhetorical prayers had been plagiarized word for word from
that "vain and amatorious poem," Sir Philip Sidney's *Ar-
cadia.* It was subsequently charged against Milton that he
himself, in collaboration with Bradshaw, had caused this
prayer to be inserted in some of the editions of the *Eikon*
for the purpose of discrediting the king's sincerity, and the
reliability of this charge has been vigorously maintained in
a recent study.[29] The balance of evidence is, however,
strongly against it.[30]

In writing *Eikonoklastes* Milton drew heavily on Thomas
May's *History of Parliament,* a work published by order
in 1647. He also used various official Parliamentary Decla-
rations. The comparison of his pamphlet with these documents shows him to have been no mere irresponsible controversialist but, to quote a recent investigator,[31] "a careful
(though a partisan) writer utilizing reputable parliamentary authorities, and striving painstakingly to establish his
foundation of fact, on which with the aid of his scorching
invective he might overwhelm the King's reputation and
so demolish the royalist faction." He was also apparently
acquainted with the *Eikon Alethine,* which had appeared
anonymously on or before August 26, 1649, and which as-

[29] Liljegren, *Studies in Milton.*

[30] The arguments of Smart in *Milton and the King's Prayer* appear
decisive against Liljegren's case.

[31] Whiting, *The Sources of Eikonoklastes.*

sailed among other things the genuineness of the royal authorship of the *Eikon Basilike*.[32] It is interesting that Milton should abandon this issue and attack the *Eikon Basilike* on the assumption that he had to deal with the King's own words.

POLITICAL TRACTS IN THE CONTROVERSY WITH SALMASIUS AND MORUS (1651–1655)

In 1650, the next year after the publication of *Eikonoklastes*, Milton began the last and greatest battle of his controversial career. Charles II, now in exile in France, had engaged Salmasius (Claude Saumaise), a French scholar resident in Holland, to prepare an elaborate Latin tract, addressed to the intellectual leaders of Europe and designed to hold up to public execration the men who had voted the death of the king. This work, which appeared in 1649 with the title *Defensio Regia pro Carolo I*, though less insidious in its effects in England than the *Eikon Basilike*, was even more dangerous to the Commonwealth in its international relations. It had the prestige of a great name behind it, for Salmasius was universally recognized as one of the foremost men of learning in an age in which scholarly distinction was still supposed to vouch for the validity of a public utterance of this sort.

Milton, in his official capacity and as the most learned and eloquent controversialist on the republican side, was ordered to compose the answer to this attack. The result

[32] See Loewenhaupt, *The Writing of Milton's Eikonoklastes*. The *Eikon Alethine* was itself a reply to a royalist book, *The Princely Pelican*, "containing satisfactory reasons that his sacred person was the sole author"; it was followed in turn by the royalist *Eikon Episte*, another argument to the same effect. Milton's tract was therefore the fifth in a controversial series.

was the longest of his prose works hitherto—the *Defense of the English People Against Salmasius* (*Ioannis Miltoni Angli Pro populo anglicano defensio contra Claudii anonymi, alias Salmasii, Defensionem regiam*). It was published by the printer Dugard in February, 1651. Since Milton's tract was addressed to a Continental rather than an English audience it was composed in Latin. Its author inevitably felt the thrill of this first appearance before the wider court of European opinion and he put into the work his maximum effort. Later he spoke with pride of his "noble task of which all Europe talks from side to side." Yet the *Defensio* can hardly be called to-day a noble work. It is filled from beginning to end with personalities, assailing in abusive phrase the scholarship, the mercenary motives, and the private character of Salmasius, as if to discredit him as a man and a grammarian were the best means of discrediting the cause which he was pleading. There is also argument in abundance, but Milton seldom rises to principles, confining himself rather to point by point replies to his opponent, demonstrating again and again that the action of the regicides was justified by English law, by ancient and modern learned authority, by the precedent of other peoples, by the tyrannical character of Charles, and by public necessity. The materials of the *Tenure of Kings and Magistrates* and of *Eikonoklastes* are repeated and elaborated. The Presbyterians are scored anew. Such eloquence as the piece can show is the eloquence of scorn. Above all Milton denounces the intrusion of a foreigner into the affairs of his countrymen and he shows at length the inconsistency of Salmasius' point of view with ideas expressed in his previous writings.

The *Defense of the English People* made such a stir

abroad as Milton could have wished.[33] Salmasius left the court of Queen Christina of Sweden, where he had been living in great honor, discredited and disgraced, according to report, by Milton's scathing treatment of his work and character. The reply to which he was goaded was written, but for some reason withheld from publication until 1660. He died in 1653. Meanwhile several minor Continental royalists entered the field, leveling their attack at Milton personally. It was not, however, until the appearance in 1652 of an anonymous answer of real power (*Regii Sanguinis Clamor ad Coelum adversus Parricidas Anglicanos, The Cry of the King's Blood to Heaven against the English Parricides*) that he undertook an answer. This new work, *The Second Defense of the English People by John Milton, Englishman, in reply to an Infamous Book entitled "Cry of the King's Blood,"* did not appear until the spring of 1654, though it had been ordered by the Council long before. Milton was waiting, he said, for the rumored reply of Salmasius. Besides this he was now blind, the complete ruin of his eyesight having followed in 1652 the composition of the *First Defense,* caused according to Milton's own statement by his unremitting application to that task.

The *Second Defense,* like the first, contains an abundance of virulent and undignified personalities, directed now against Alexander More or Morus, a Scottish-French scholar domiciled in Holland and closely associated with Salmasius. The actual author was Peter Du Moulin but

---

[33] The fullest record of foreign interest is to be found in the pages of *Mercurius Politicus* (which Milton licensed) for 1650 and 1652. See French, "Milton, Needham, and *Mercurius Politicus,*" pp. 246–253.

the more distinguished More had had a hand in the printing and circulation of the volume and had supplied a preface; he was widely believed in Holland to be its author, and reports to that effect, together with certain scandals regarding his relations with Bontia, a serving maid of Salmasius' wife, had reached Milton through the English press. Though Morus denied his responsibility for the work, and though Milton was officially urged by the Dutch ambassador in London to stay his hand, he remained unconvinced and proceeded to administer chastisement accordingly, making the most of the Bontia scandal and afterward regretting that he had not included other discreditable stories about More which reached him later.

Apart from these elements, which are excusable only in the light of the provocation given by the *Regii Sanguinis Clamor* with its personal abuse of Milton, and of the controversial practice of the times, the *Second Defense* is a much nobler and more interesting book than the first. It was designed not merely to be a crushing blow to the author of the *Clamor* but also a worthy celebration of the cause of the Commonwealth and its great leaders. This object is more nearly in accord with Milton's conception of the public function of the poet as stated in the *Reason of Church Government* than anything he had hitherto written. It is a genuine fruit of patriotic feeling and an enthusiastic love of liberty. These emotions Milton characteristically associates with his own personality, making himself not only the defender of a cause but also a portion of the cause. Such identification it is that rouses the poet in him and fires his noblest eloquence. Thus the passage which he devotes to an account of his life and services to liberty, written to clear his name from the slanders of his opponents, becomes a

by More himself under the title *Fides Publica* (i. e., Public
Testimony in his own behalf). This work, bound in a single
volume with a new edition of Milton's *Second Defense,* was
issued at The Hague in 1654 by the printer Ulac, who was
quite willing that his press should speak on both sides of the
question so long as sales continued good. Besides vigorously
denying responsibility for the *Clamor* and carefully docu-
menting his own honorable career in reply to the aspersions
of the *Defensio,* More very naturally censures Milton's injustice in attacking him, claiming that the English writer
had every opportunity of knowing that he was not the author of the work. With keen instinct he pitches upon the
evidences of Milton's excessive self-esteem, denouncing his
presumption in taking it upon himself to instruct Cromwell
in his duties. The *Fides Publica* was followed by a supplement in 1655. Milton's reply, the *Pro Se Defensio,* or, to
translate its full title, *The English John Milton's Defense
for himself, in reply to Alexander Morus, churchman,
rightly called author of the notorious book entitled "Cry of
the King's Blood,"* appeared in August of the same year.
This work attempts to establish if not the actual authorship
yet at least the full responsibility of Morus for the *Clamor*
and to discredit item by item his published testimonials.
The new scandals which had come to him too late for in-
clusion in the *Second Defense* are now rehearsed at length.
The work lacks entirely the higher qualities of the *Second
Defense* and is on the whole devoid of interest. It contains,
however, one of those curious passages in defense of the
use of gross language and personal vilification against the
enemies of righteousness which show how little at ease Milton really was about his own controversial practices. It is
only by convincing himself that, in prosecuting private

enmities, he is exposing and correcting public delinquencies,
that he is enabled to take that satisfaction in his achievement
which is for him a psychological necessity. The *Pro Se Defensio* is not included in the Bohn or Mitford editions of
Milton's works. It is, however, included in the Columbia
Milton together with the translation made by George Bur-
nett in 1808.

THE HISTORY OF BRITAIN (1646–1670)

The dust and turmoil of the Salmasius-Morus controversy was followed by a period in Milton's career of
comparative leisure. He had, since the beginning of his
blindness, been progressively less active in the Latin secretaryship. An assistant, Philip Meadows, had been appointed for him in 1653; his salary was reduced and com-
muted to a life pension in 1655, after which time, though
he nominally remained in office till the Restoration, and
though his state letters continue until 1659, he must have
been comparatively free from his official responsibilities.
The result was a renewed occupation with three works of
scholarship, begun before the execution of the king, but
interrupted by the call to public service. One of these, a
Latin Dictionary, was never completed and remained unpublished. The others were a *History of Britain* and the
Latin theological work, *Of Christian Doctrine,* both of
which appear to have been finished or practically so between
1655 and 1660.

The *History of Britain* may be regarded as a sort of
commutation of Milton's earlier projects for a drama or
an epic on a British legendary theme. He rejected the
Arthurian story in favor of the more significant and au-

thentic biblical theme, but his literary and patriotic interest in the materials continued keen and demanded expression.[34] More directly, the *History* is the fruit of the long course of historical reading recorded in the Commonplace Book. Milton reached in his program the British historians about 1641–2 and went carefully through Holinshed, Speed, Camden, Buchanan, together with a few of the older authorities like Gildas and Bede. His carefully annotated copy of Gildas has survived to show the closeness with which he studied his authorities.[35] His study apparently convinced him that the story of his country had never been worthily related. The credulity and garrulousness of men like Holinshed must have contrasted strongly in his mind with the dignified work of the Greek and Roman historians. His resolution to do something for the annals of his own people like what Tacitus and Sallust had done for Rome must have taken form shortly after, but the more pressing matters of the ecclesiastical and divorce controversies postponed the beginning of the work till about 1646. By March, 1649, he had, as he himself tells us, completed the first four books, bringing the story down to the union of England under Egbert. His secretaryship apparently interrupted further activity until 1655, when he added Books V and VI, containing the story of the Danish invasions and the Norman Conquest.

[34] It has recently been shown that the historicity of Arthur was a matter of political controversy in the seventeenth century as it had been in the early sixteenth. King James had emphasized his descent from Arthur and the fulfillment of British prophecy. The opponents of divine right were critical and made much of the Anglo-Saxon tradition against the British. See Brinkley, *Arthurian Legend in the Seventeenth Century*.

[35] See French, *Milton's Annotated Copy of Gildas*.

At this point he stopped, but the fact that the work remained unpublished until 1670 would seem to indicate that he continued to cherish his original idea of bringing it down to his own day. The *History* and the Latin dictionary represent perhaps Milton's only uncompleted projects.

In the composition of the work Milton aims at veracity, brevity, and readableness. Although Milton declares his intention of including "reputed tales" from the old chroniclers for the benefit of "our English poets who by their art will know how to use them judiciously," he does so, as French points out,[36] only grudgingly and with more evidence of disgust at the credulity which accepts them for truth than enthusiasm for their appeal to the imagination. He inveighs against Geoffrey's materials as "too palpably untrue to be worth rehearsing in the midst of truth," objects to Buchanan's taking on himself to relate the inroads of the Scots and Picts into Britain "as if they had but yesterday happened," calls the later Anglo-Saxon chroniclers "obscure and blockish," and condemns even Malmesbury and Huntington for their ambition to adorn history with surmises of their own. "Them rather than imitate," he says, "I shall choose to represent the truth naked, though as lean as a plain journal."

Though he is influenced by modern writers, particularly Holinshed, Camden, and Buchanan, he goes back to the original authorities—the Anglo-Saxon Chronicle and Laws, Bede, the medieval chroniclers, etc.—as no English historian had done before him, and exhibits a very modern sense of the need of weighing their respective values. His critical and scholarly point of view has won the admiration

[36] *Milton as a Historian.*

of such a distinguished contemporary historian as Sir Charles Firth,[87] who finds that Masson has greatly underestimated the originality of Milton's work.

But Milton, however critical he may be of others, could not himself write either history or poetry without a fundamentally ethical and philosophic bias. We accordingly find him emphasizing throughout the *History* the relation between national morality and national prosperity, as when he attributes the ease of the Norman conquest to the corruption of the English, which had "fitted them for servitude." He often has his eye on contemporary affairs as he analyzes the causes of failure or success in the past; to him a chief value of the study of history is to be found in the lessons which it holds for the modern statesman. As originally written, Book III of the *History* contained a long digression, apropos of the state of Britain when the Romans left it, on the parallel confusion which attended the close of the civil wars in 1648. This was excised by the censor and separately published in 1681 as *Mr. John Milton's Character of the Long Parliament and the Assembly of Divines*. Personal and political prejudice is revealed in his description of the warrior queen Boadicea as "a distracted woman with a mad crew at her heels," in his unsympathetic treatment of the evangelization of Britain under Augustine, and in his deliberate refusal to go into the details of ecclesiastical history.[38]

[87] *Milton as an Historian.*

[38] The original edition of 1670 was reprinted without change in 1677 and 1695. Toland's text, published in 1698, contained several insertions not found in the first three editions. He apparently used a copy of the 1670 volume annotated by Milton's hand. See Glicksman, *The Editions of Milton's "History of Britain."*

THE CHRISTIAN DOCTRINE (1655–1660?)

The details of the composition of Milton's great theological work, *De Doctrina Christiana,* are not so clear as in the case of the *History of Britain.* The statement of Phillips indicates that he returned to it in 1655; Milton himself describes in the preface the collection of the materials from Scripture of which it is composed and the reading of books of divinity in preparation for it as a work which began in his youth. There is, finally, evidence in the preserved manuscript (see below) that the work was complete by about 1661.

This manuscript came to light in 1823 and it was published for the first time in 1825. Its earlier history is most interesting. After Milton's death the document was in the hands of a young Oxford graduate, Daniel Skinner, who had served as the last of the poet's literary and scholarly assistants. Quite possibly Milton had himself delivered it with instructions for its publication. At any rate, Skinner recopied the first half of it and sent the whole to the Dutch publisher Elzevir to be printed. Being warned, however, that his responsibility for the publication of such a work would mean the death of his own political ambitions, Skinner had the document returned to him. It subsequently found its way into the Public Record Office where it lay forgotten until its discovery by the Keeper, Robert Lemon. The work of deciphering, translating, and editing it was entrusted by the command of George IV to Bishop Charles Sumner. Its appearance occasioned Macaulay's famous essay on Milton in 1825. The second half of the manuscript, which represents the original draft, is in the hand of one of Milton's amanuenses whose name we know [39] and whose work for the poet can be traced in every dictated document which has been preserved from the years 1657 to 1661. He was evidently a trained scribe whom Milton regularly employed until the fall of his fortunes at the Restoration compelled him to do with more casual assistance. This portion of the text contains corrections in various other scribal hands, indicating that Milton kept revising, perhaps until his death. These alterations afford a happy hunting ground for those students who suspect Milton's theological opinions of undergoing change.

It is easy to see why the work remained unpublished in Milton's lifetime. He had conceived it in the enthusiasm of the Commonwealth period, when religious belief was in a state of flux and there seemed to be a hope that mankind could be united in a program of liberal Christianity such as Milton desired. Propaganda was actually on foot in Europe, headed by Milton's friend John Durie, for bringing the Protestant sects together in a community of belief and action. The *De Doctrina*, written in Latin so that the leaders of European thought might read it and addressed to Christian churches everywhere, was perhaps intended to furnish the reasoned theological basis of this new religious unity. With the Restoration all immediate expectation of the fulfillment of the plan (at least so far as England was concerned) came to an end. There was, besides, the actual personal danger involved in publishing the work. Milton's hope of safety depended on his silence, and the *De Doctrina* was a piece of daring heresy. His maintenance of the conditional nature of God's decrees would not, to be

[39] It was Jeremie Picard. See Hanford, *The Rosenbach Milton Documents.*

sure, have hurt him after the passing of the Presbyterian régime, for Anglican theology had always inclined toward this Arminian modification of Calvinistic harshness, but his treatment of the second and third persons of the Trinity implied an attitude which was anathema to all the dominant Christian creeds. The repudiation, moreover, of all forms and organizations of worship except those simple ones prescribed by Scripture renewed the Puritan indictment against Anglicanism, now reëstablished and enforced as the state religion. As if to add gratuitously to the offenses of the work against established doctrine, Milton introduces a statement in favor of divorce and demonstrates that even polygamy is not prohibited by divine law.

The chief virtue of the work in Milton's eyes was that its principles were derived solely from Scripture. Its main bulk consists of quotations and references from the Bible, arranged under appropriate headings, with a generalized statement of the doctrine which each group of them supports. Of course Milton could not have arrived at these formulations without a wide acquaintance with the varieties of Christian thought, and he enters into elaborate discussions of many of the controverted points of theological history. He owes much, moreover, especially in Book II, to a Protestant compendium of theology by Wollebius, who is mentioned, along with Fisher Ames, as his model by Edward Phillips.[40] But his infallible test for the acceptance or rejection of a doctrine is its conformity with God's own word as recorded in the inspired writings of the Old and New Testaments.

[40] See Kelley, *Milton's Debt to Wolleb.* For a general discussion of the *De Doctrina* as a guide to Milton's changing theological ideas see Sewell, *A Study of Milton's Christian Doctrine.*

The peculiarities of Milton's theological ideas will be treated more fully in the discussion of the intellectual background of *Paradise Lost*. The *De Doctrina* reads like a doctrinal commentary on that work and can be ignored by no thorough student. Milton has, however, deliberately avoided in his poem, especially in the more dangerous issues, the clear and uncompromising precision of his statements in the prose. Or perhaps it was simply that these issues ceased to interest him when the doctrinal controversy became less a matter of public concern. The *De Doctrina* is written in a coldly intellectual style, terse and logical, without the slightest touch of eloquence. The document is the steely framework of Milton's intellectual system, deliberately stripped of all the elements of personality, color, and passion which invested his customary vision of the world. His rigid will and the years of logical training at Cambridge are responsible for his ability to accomplish such a result.

LATER ECCLESIASTICAL PAMPHLETS

The troublous times which followed the death of Cromwell in 1658 brought a renewal of pamphlet activity in Milton. Occupied though he was with calmer scholarly tasks and already launched on the composition of *Paradise Lost* he could not fail, now that public affairs were again in a state of flux, to endeavor to exert an influence. His method is the old one of memorials to Parliament in his private capacity of citizen.

Politically Milton had been, through the Protectorate, a staunch Cromwellian. But he never assented to Cromwell's policy of maintaining a modified church establishment with a committee empowered to settle the compensation of ministers and to solder the various denominations together in a loosely orthodox unity. From this unity the Catholics, the High Church and Arminian Episcopalians, the Quakers, and those sects which denied the divinity of Jesus Christ were excluded, and though Cromwell himself attempted to secure toleration even for Jews, he never became an open champion of that complete religious freedom for which Milton hoped. Under a new Protector and a new Parliament it seemed possible that these abuses might be remedied. Milton's convictions in the matter centered in two points: first, that the civil authorities had no right to exercise any compulsion whatsoever in matters of religious belief, and, second, that the system of tithes or taxes exacted by law for the support of the clergy was an abuse and should give way to voluntary contributions by individual congregations. He attacked these two problems separately, the first in a brief pamphlet entitled *A Treatise of Civil Power in Ecclesiastical Causes; Shewing that it is not lawful for any power on Earth to compel in matters of Religion,* published in February, 1659. The foundation of the argument is that, Scripture alone being the divine rule of belief and the interpretation thereof being an affair of private judgment, "no man or body of men in these times can be infallible judges or determiners in matters of religion to any other men's consciences but their own." Christ's kingdom, moreover, is purely spiritual and the attempt to regulate it by external force can only do harm. Milton's plea is, as it was in *Areopagitica,* for universal toleration, Papists only excepted, because they represent a political power dangerous to the safety of the state. Beyond this there is implied rather than clearly expressed the conviction that religion should be left entirely to itself without even such a tolerant state support as Cromwell wished to give it in his establishment. The argument is largely based on Scripture.

On May 25, 1659, Richard Cromwell was forced to abdicate and the original Rump Parliament, composed largely of republican members, restored to power. The question of disestablishment and the abolition of the tithe system was now actually brought before the house, and Milton accordingly launched in August his second pamphlet, *Considerations touching the likeliest means to remove Hirelings out of the Church. Wherein is also discoursed of Tithes, Church Fees, Church Revenues; and whether any maintenance of Ministers can be settled by law.* Milton hails the new Parliament with enthusiastic praise, implying that the true custodians of English liberty have returned to power. His thesis is that the mercenary spirit in the clergy has always been the most mischievous evil in the church, and that this spirit is encouraged and promoted by the present system of legally enforced contributions. His ideal is a clergy serving without any material reward at all, but he makes so much concession to the necessities of the case as to allow them compensation from the voluntary offerings of their parishioners. Poor congregations may be served by the occasional visits of missionaries supported by the wealthier parishes or even, if necessary, by subsidies out of public funds. In general, he believed that ministers should be content with scanty salaries, finding true reward in the fulfillment of their spiritual mission as preachers of the Word. He is convinced that if profits are cut off only such men as are really worthy will be drawn into the ministry. In the suggestion that preachers may support themselves by other occupations and in Milton's denial of the value for them of an elaborate education we see an inclination toward the idea of a lay ministry, which is the logical consequence of Milton's Protestantism and which was already in practice among the Quakers and other radical sects. Milton by no means stood alone in his opinions; but the majority was still against him, and Parliament refused to take the proposed action looking toward religious disestablishment.

TRACT ON A FREE COMMONWEALTH (1660)

Except for a brief interruption in 1659 the Rump Parliament continued in office until February, 1660. The burning question of the hour was no longer that of establishment or disestablishment, but what form of government would finally emerge from the anarchy into which England had increasingly fallen since the death of Cromwell. There was active discussion, in Parliament and out, of the best plan of establishing a republican government to meet the menace of the restoration of the monarchy for which the public was beginning to clamor with increasing insistency. At this stage of affairs Milton undertook again to exercise an influence on public opinion and on parliamentary action by making a final plea against bringing back the Stuarts and by recommending a constitutional scheme quite different from any that had been proposed. Before his pamphlet could be published, however, General Monk, in whom the real authority now rested, had turned against the Rump, canceled the writs which it had issued for a reëlection, and reconstituted the Long Parliament by restoring the members who had been secluded from it in 1648. This body promptly issued its own writs for the election of "a full and free Parliament." The likelihood of either the newly reconstituted Long Parliament or the people in their approaching choice of its successor listening to anything Milton had to say was very slim. He, nevertheless, issued the tract which he had composed, and, conscious of the fact that the word of General Monk would decide the future of the Commonwealth, sent it to him, with a letter giving its substance in briefer form.

The tract, which appeared in February or March, 1660, was entitled *The Ready and Easy Way to Establish a Free Commonwealth and the Excellence thereof with the Inconveniences and Dangers of Readmitting Kingship in this Nation.*[41] It opens with a review of the steps which had led to the establishment of the Commonwealth and a representation of the evils which would result from undoing the work of liberty by bringing back Charles's son. His constructive proposal is that sovereignty should henceforth be vested in a Grand or General Council chosen by a carefully sifted electorate and sitting in perpetuity. Such a body, Milton thinks, will give a stable government by the best men more effectively than successive parliaments. As a concession to the views of Harrington and his followers in the Rota Club, Milton reluctantly admits the principle of a partial rotation whereby a few members are retired each year and others chosen (apparently by the Council itself) to fill their places. To this body he adds a smaller council for executive action, elected by the General Council, and also a series of representative assemblies in every county, which shall have complete autonomy in local affairs. Milton's scheme is partly

[41] Milton wrote still a third appeal against the threatened restoration, the *Proposals of Certain Expedients for the Preventing of a Civil War now Feared and the Settling of a Firm Government,* published from the Columbia Manuscript in Vol. XVIII of *The Columbia Milton.* No contemporary issue of this pamphlet is known to exist. The best edition of *The Ready and Easy Way* is that of E. M. Clark.

modeled on the government of the Netherlands, partly on the ideal commonwealth of Plato, with its aristocratic rule by the guardian class. It expresses his lack of faith in a true democracy and yet avoids the equal evil of a one man power.

The Ready and Easy Way was eagerly read and it provoked immediate replies from the Royalist Group, who were becoming more and more outspoken. The "good old cause" was evidently lost, but Milton fought till the end. He published in April a brief reply to an open argument for the restoration by Charles I's former chaplain, Dr. Griffith,[42] and he reissued *The Ready and Easy Way* in a second, expanded edition, less than a month before the newly elected Parliament voted the Restoration. In this revision Milton no longer disguises from himself the fact that the event he dreads is practically inevitable. He intensifies the picture of the ruin and disgrace which will attend it and elaborates his scheme of a Grand Perpetual Council, but he knows that he is "exhorting a torrent." His pamphlet has become a final indulgence in free speech before the "long lent of servitude," his eloquence "the last words of our expiring liberty."

LAST PAMPHLETS (1673–1674)

The Restoration silenced Milton politically for many years. Even he realized the present uselessness and the danger of further pleas for liberty when there was none. Besides this, he was at last engaged on his great poetic enterprise. Yet it seems likely that he would unhesitatingly have laid *Paradise Lost* aside again and risked his personal

---

[42] *Brief Notes Upon a late Sermon, titl'd "The Fear of God and the King"* . . . *by Matthew Griffith, D.D.* This was answered in April by Roger L'Estrange in *No Blinde Guides*.

safety if occasion had presented itself in which to strike another real blow for liberty. Meanwhile he must have watched the progress of affairs almost as closely as before, and, when the three poems were written, he found a last opportunity to exercise in a limited way an influence on public opinion on one of the old issues with which he had been concerned. Charles II's Declaration of Indulgence, granting freedom of worship to the Non-Conformists, was issued in March, 1672. The evident fact that it was mainly intended as a relief for Catholics raised a cry against it from Dissenters and Anglicans alike, and it was rescinded by Parliament in the following year. The Non-Conformists hoped for the passage of an act which without benefiting the Papists would free themselves from their disabilities. Some of them advocated a recomprehension within the establishment. Milton's tract, published along with many others in 1673, was entitled *Of True Religion, Heresy, Toleration, and the growth of Popery*. It is an attempt to bring the Protestant sects together in mutual charity and to induce them to take a tolerant attitude toward differences in the nonessential points of doctrine. Any creed based on the word of God, however variously interpreted, is true religion. Heresy is a religion taken up and believed from the traditions of men. Catholicism, therefore, is the essential heresy, and it alone, though rather because of its political pretensions than of its doctrinal errors, is not to be allowed. Milton deprecates the exercise of violence even toward the Romanists, but is firm in advocating the suppression of their public worship. The pamphlet is, as Masson says, a rather tame one, compared with the two ecclesiastical tracts written in the last days of the Republic.

One further document remains. In the spring of 1674,

Milton wrote and published a translation from the Latin of a Polish manifesto entitled *A Declaration of the Election of this present King of Poland, John the III,* i. e., the national hero Sobieski, who had manfully defended his country against the Turks. Milton's interest in the event was because of the instance it afforded of the true ideal of monarchy, when a man universally acknowledged the strongest and most virtuous is elected king by the sovereign people. The implied contrast between the courageous patriot Sobieski and the traitorous idler Charles II was too sharp to be mistaken. With this final recommendation of right reason to his supine countrymen John Milton, weary with approaching death, laid down his pen.

MISCELLANEOUS ITEMS OF UNCERTAIN DATE

At some interval of leisure during the Commonwealth or early Protectorate, at any rate before his blindness, possibly even as early as the Horton period,[43] Milton composed a popular account of Russia—the land, the government, and the people—based on the stories of various explorers which had been printed in Hakluyt's *Voyages,* Purchas's *Pilgrimages* and elsewhere (a list of sources is appended by Milton himself). Such narratives were one of the favorite branches of Milton's reading and the subject of geography was full of appeal to his curiosity and his imagination. He speaks in his preface as though he had projected a series of descrip-

[43] See *Brief History of Moscovia,* Preface, which describes the work as composed "many years since," and which Prince Mirsky believes to have been itself written before the civil wars. G. B. Parks argues for Dec., or Jan., 1649/50, when the attitude of Russia was of concern to the Commonwealth and protest was being made by the Council of State against the banishment of the English merchants.

tions of various countries. As in the *History of Britain* he proposes to give a readable and veracious account in small compass, purged of "long stories of absurd superstition, ceremonies, quaint habits, and other petty circumstances little to the purpose." He condenses and paraphrases his originals, transforming into his own Latinized prose the plain or florid English of the Elizabethan navigators.[44] The work was published after his death in 1682. The poetic fruits of his study of the voyages had already been garnered in *Paradise Lost*. Two school textbooks—a Latin Grammar in English, and a treatise on logic in Latin—close the list of Milton's original prose works. The first of these, *Accedence Commenc't Grammar, Supply'd with sufficient Rules, For the use of such (Younger or Elder) as are desirous, without more trouble than needs to learn the Latin Tongue,* is a fruit of Milton's interest in pedagogy and of his conviction, expressed in the tractate *Of Education,* that an immense amount of time was wasted by the cumbersome methods of Latin instruction then in vogue. It was published in 1669. The *Artis Logicae Plenior Institutio,* published three years later, is an elaboration in the interest of clarity of the system of Peter Ramus which had been welcomed by the Protestant universities in opposition to the traditional logic of Aristotle, which was felt to be too much identified with Catholicism.[45] Both works were presumably written

---

[44] Parallels are given by Mirsky. Gilbert's *Geographical Dictionary* contains many references to Milton's readings in the voyagers and geographers. See also Thompson, *Milton's Knowledge of Geography.*

[45] Moore-Smith notes that the *Logic* must have been written or revised after Milton had abandoned the orthodox view of the Trinity. He cites interesting doctrinal parallels with *Paradise Lost.* See *A Note on Milton's "Art of Logic."*

in the days when Milton was occupied with the practical work of education.

In 1658 Milton published the first edition of a work on government by Sir Walter Raleigh entitled *The Cabinet Council; containing The Chief Arts of Empire and Mysteries of State*. The manuscript, he says in a foreword, had been given to him by a learned man at his death and had been in his hands many years. Milton was keenly interested in the principles and maxims of civic leadership, as set forth by the statesmen of the Rennaissance; witness his careful study of Machiavelli.[46]

There are other records of Milton's intellectual activities in the form of annotations to volumes which have been preserved from his library, some of them perhaps designed as materials for scholarly editions. We have also his Commonplace Book, consisting of quotations and references from his reading in the fields chiefly of political and ecclesiastical history, arranged under appropriate headings. These notes were, of course, intended for his own use only. The manuscript was discovered in 1874 and published in 1876.[47] The entries, which range in date from the Horton period to some time after Milton had become blind, are an interesting index of his changing interests and opinions. When arranged chronologically they show him to have been following a consistent program of historical study from the fall of Rome to his own day.[48]

[46] Recorded in the Commonplace Book.
[47] By A. J. Horwood. A new edition of the text, with a translation, is included in *The Columbia Edition*, Vol. XVIII. The editors have added a fragmentary legal index from the Columbia Manuscript, a collection of documents which includes a series of transcripts of Milton's State Letters, together with other materials said to have been prepared for him in connection with his official work. See above, p. 105.
[48] Hanford, *Chronology*.

CHAPTER III

THE MINOR POEMS

MILTON'S minor poems in English, Latin, and Italian cover a period of his life from the last year of his attendance at St. Paul's School to the moment at which he undertook the actual composition of *Paradise Lost* (i. e., circa 1655). We are told by Aubrey that he was already a poet at the age of ten, but the earliest verses which have been preserved are two Psalm paraphrases done when he was fifteen years old.

The total body of this work is not large; to Milton himself, who felt, with his contemporaries, that tragedy and epic were the great literary forms, and who deliberately shaped his life toward the highest poetic achievement, this experimental and occasional verse was probably trifling. He cherished it sufficiently, however, to publish the bulk of it in an independent volume in 1645, as an evidence of his youthful poetic promise, with the sense, perhaps, that now in his thirty-sixth year, the reconciliation with his wife accomplished, he was about to enter on a new and maturer phase of his life activity. A second edition, which appeared in 1673, contained a few additional early pieces and the subsequently composed translations and sonnets.

Though this part of Milton's poetical activity is fairly continuous for the period which it covers, we may observe that there are in it some especially prolific years and some rather notable gaps. Thus, in his eighteenth year, his second at the University, Milton gave himself eagerly to the composition of Latin verse, writing not less than six poems in this medium. Again in 1629–31, near the end of his residence in Cambridge, he appears to have begun composing in English with a new enthusiasm. At Horton he wrote *Comus* in 1634, and then, except for *Lycidas* in 1637, nothing until his return from Italy, a period of seven years. The more abundant moments of his later life are 1644–46 (six sonnets), April, 1648 (nine Psalms), 1653 (eight Psalms), and 1655–56 (four sonnets).

In the following discussion the poems are arranged chronologically, except that the two early Psalm paraphrases are considered with the translations, most of which belong to the period after 1640, and the few Latin poems of the Horton epoch and later with those written at the University. The two groups of English sonnets are also, for convenience, treated in a section by themselves.

THE LATIN AND ITALIAN POEMS

Milton divided the Latin poems which he published in the 1645 volume into poems in elegiac meter including eight of his epigrams (*Elegiarum Liber*), and poems in miscellaneous meters (*Sylvarum Liber*). Three epigrams were added in the 1673 edition to the first group and an ode, *Ad Ioannem Rousium,* to the second. In either publication Milton arranges the pieces in an approximately chronological order and he carefully dates many of them, especially those which belong to his earlier college years. These dates are not, however, wholly to be trusted. Elegies

II, III,[1] and the poem, *In Obitum Praesulis Eliensis,* which are headed *anno aetatis 17,* can be shown to have been written in 1626, when Milton was in his eighteenth, not his seventeenth year. It is probable that the poet was using the Latin phrase regularly in this sense.[2] There is, however, one case (the poem on the death of Gostlin) where Milton's date is two years out of the way, and the precise fixing of the chronology of those poems regarding which we have no evidence other than the poet's statement is conjectural. There are, moreover, a number, notably *Ad Patrem*[3] and the *Epitaphium Damonis,* to which as works of greater maturity, he assigned no dates.

Even with this uncertainty the Latin poems constitute an immensely important year-by-year record of Milton's thoughts, feelings, and literary development in the University and Horton periods. Most interesting are the three poems (*Elegies I, V,* and *VII*) in which Milton gives rein to his delight in sensuous beauty and dallies with the thought of love. They should be read in connection with

[1] The date of Elegy IV, regarding which there has been dispute, is apparently fixed by the allusion to the siege of Hamburg, begun by Wallenstein early in the year 1627. Rumor of this event has evidently just reached him. Two summers, two autumns and three springs have passed, he says, since Young left England. He must then be writing in the summer of 1627, i. e., in his nineteenth year. The poem is, however, headed *anno aetatis 18.*

[2] This inference receives additional support from the English prose. In the *History of Britain* he translates "completis annis vitae suae 142," "the 142 year of his age." See Parker, *Some Problems.*

[3] This poem has usually been assigned to the first years of the Horton period because it, like the letter which accompanies the sonnet *How soon hath time,* has to do with Milton's unwillingness to take up a profession, but Tillyard and Grierson argue that it more plausibly belongs after *Comus,* on the ground that only then would such an apology for poetry be appropriate.

a passage in the *Apology for Smectymnuus*,[4] in which he tells how he was first roused to literary enthusiasm by the amatory poetry of the Roman elegists and inspired to imitate them. Besides the amatory motive these poems contain suggestions of his personal loyalty to his boyhood tutor, Young (*Elegy IV*), his discomfort in the atmosphere of the University and his enthusiasm for the life of cultured and studious leisure (*Elegy I*), his gratitude to his father for providing him with generous opportunities to indulge such tastes (*Ad Patrem*), his pride in his association with a famous Italian patron of the arts (*Manso*). Such works as the poem on the Gunpowder Plot (*In Quintum Novembris*) and the elegies commemorating the deaths of University dignitaries are impersonal academic exercises, done, however, with a zealous enthusiasm for the art of modern Latin composition and often revealing much of Milton's intellectual habit and of the sources of his literary culture. *In Quintum Novembris,* the most ambitious of these efforts, is an epic narrative of two hundred and twenty-six lines describing the attempt of Satan to punish England for its rebellion to his rule by instigating the Pope to frame the plot against King James. It expresses the violent Protestant patriotism of the Fifth of November tradition and has as its model Phineas Fletcher's *Locustae,* a Latin poem on the same theme. If this poem and the five others (*Elegies I, II, III, In Obitum Praesulis Eliensis,* and *In Obitum Procancellarii Medici*) all belong, as they are commonly supposed to, to Milton's eighteenth year (in the fall of 1626), they constitute evidence of an extraordinary poetic outburst at that time. Since the first elegy, which records Milton's banishment from Cambridge as a consequence of

[4] Quoted and discussed in Appendix.

his quarrel with Chappell, is the earliest in the series we may perhaps credit the ambitious impulses of this creative time to some kind of stimulation resulting from his rustication and his change of tutors.

Two of the later poems are more deeply serious than anything which Milton had hitherto written. In *Elegy VI* (December, 1629), addressed to Diodati in reply to a letter describing his revels at the Christmas season, he expresses dissatisfaction with the trifling verse he has been composing, announces himself an epic poet, and expresses the resolve to live a life of lofty and ascetic consecration to that end. He describes at the close his first attempt at a kind of poetry worthy of himself, the poem *On the Morning of Christ's Nativity*. Finally, in the *Epitaphium Damonis* (1641), he pays a noble tribute in the form of a carefully wrought pastoral elegy to his friendship for Diodati, telling incidentally of his own over-ambitious poetic flights, now no longer to be shared with the beloved companion of his school and college days. This work, of which Milton printed some copies for private circulation, is incomparably the best of the Latin poems.[5] In the warmth and tenderness of its personal emotion it is superior to the parallel English elegy, *Lycidas*.

The whole body of Milton's Latin verse represents the finest achievement ever attained in this medium by an Englishman. A great classicist, Professor E. K. Rand,[6] finds it not unworthy of a place beside its ancient models. Milton is

[5] Tillyard (*Milton,* pp. 99 ff.) is of a different opinion. He says that the poem reveals a troubled, disunited mind, and begins to flag after line 124, as if Milton were "recalling with false ardor feelings which he has outgrown and which scarcely concern him now." Rand thinks *Ad Patrem* the finest of the Latin poems.

[6] *Milton in Rustication.*

at first a follower of the ornate and romantic style of Ovid; his later poems have more of the Virgilian dignity and restraint. He also reflects the work of the Renaissance humanists, particularly Buchanan, widely known as the most elegant Latin poet of his time. In pouring so much of his own poetic energy into an ancient tongue (to the extent that in his earlier University years he wrote scarcely anything in English) Milton was following the learned precedent of his age. He recognized, however, that English was to be his ultimate medium (witness the verses on his mother tongue inserted in the *Vacation Exercise* of 1628) and, from the point of view of his own loftier purposes, he probably regarded Latin composition largely as a way of disciplining his powers. The use of a learned language did, however, give him an opportunity to say some things in a more directly personal way and to indulge the sensuous side of his nature more freely than he would have felt suitable in undraped English.

The Italian sonnets represent a poetical excursion into yet another linguistic medium. There is every reason to believe them a product of Milton's university years and not, as Masson assumed, of his Italian journey. For it is evident from the poems themselves that Milton is writing in an English environment. He is attempting, he says (Sonnet III), to make the flower of a foreign speech grow in a climate not its own; and he pictures himself (Canzone) as surrounded by youths and maidens who expostulate with him for writing in an alien and unintelligible tongue (*lingua ignota e strana*). The poems are, moreover, closely associated in theme and attitude with the seventh elegy and they are, like it, addressed to Diodati. Milton tells how Cupid has punished him for his former stubbornness against love.

He reveals the name of the lady, Emilia, in riddling fashion in Sonnet I. She is a "type of foreign beauty," a singer and "adorned with more languages than one." Presumably she is someone whom he had met in the circle of the Diodati family in London. Milton assumes in declaring his passion for her the extravagant attitude of the sonneteer and makes liberal use of the conventional phraseology of Petrarch. The expression, though unoriginal, is full of grace and the language reasonably correct. It seems likely that the pieces are an outcome of Milton's dilettante enthusiasm for the newly discovered delights of the Petrarchan sonnet and a boyishly proud display of his mastery of the tongue best suited to the refinements of poetic love, rather than an expression of any profound personal emotion.

ENGLISH POEMS WRITTEN AT THE UNIVERSITY

"ON THE DEATH OF A FAIR INFANT DYING OF A COUGH." Except for the two psalm paraphrases (see below), which date from his school days, this is probably the earliest of Milton's English poems. Milton heads it *anno aetatis 17*, i. e.—1625 or 1626. Recent research by Professor Parker has, however, given good grounds for believing that it belongs to a later period, the year in which Milton wrote his *Vacation Exercise* and turned deliberately from Latin to English verse. The infant, according to Edward Phillips, was the daughter of his sister Anne, who had married Edward Phillips the Elder on November 22, 1623. An entry in the Parish Register of St. Martin-in-the-Fields gives the dates of baptism and burial of the first three children of this marriage as follows: John, January 16,

1625—March 15, 1629; Anne, January 12, 1626—January 22, 1628; Elizabeth, April 9, 1628—February 19, 1631. The first daughter, Anne, would therefore be the subject of Milton's elegy; the second, Elizabeth, may be the child whose birth he seems to predict in the last stanza. If this is the case, the elegy was written between January 22 and April 9, 1628.[7] Milton's failure to include it in the first edition of his poems seems to show that he thought it immature. Perhaps he unconsciously antedated the poem for the same reason. He need not have been ashamed of it even at the age of twenty, for despite its quaintly awkward title and the presence in it of strained images in the fashion of the day, it is a sincere and beautiful composition, springing from a mood of tender grief and rising in one stanza, where the poet touches the theme of immortality, to a genuine poetic fervor.

Milton employs in this poem a seven line stanza a b a b b c c with a final alexandrine. He perhaps derived it from Phineas Fletcher, who uses it commonly (with frequent double rhyme, a practice abandoned by Milton after the first stanza) in his *Poetical Miscellanies* and in *Eliza*.[8] Tillyard says that the poem is rather in the tradition of the Ovidizing Elizabethans than of the Spenserians and cites as a parallel to the opening,

> O fairest flower no sooner blown but blasted,
> Soft silken Primrose fading timesslie,

[7] See Parker, W. R., "Milton's *Fair Infant*," *TLS*, December 17, 1938. It is possible, but unlikely, that Edward Phillips was mistaken in connecting the elegy with his own family. The present writer is inclined to withdraw his own arguments for an earlier date as given in *The Review of English Studies*, IX (1935), 58 and 312–315.

[8] Published in 1633 but doubtless known to Milton in MS.

the following fragment from *The Passionate Pilgrim:*

> Sweet Rose, fair flower, untimely pluckt, soon faded,
> Pluckt in the bud, and faded in the spring.
> Bright orient pearl, alack too timely shaded,
> Fair creature killed too soon by Death's sharp sting.

"AT A VACATION EXERCISE IN THE COLLEGE, PART LATIN, PART ENGLISH." This piece was dated by Milton in the 1673 edition of the poems where it first appeared *"anno aetatis 19."* The Latin prolusion (see above, p. 73) with which it belongs is the sixth, where Milton appears as official spokesman in one of the periodic revels of the collegians either in the spring or summer recess. Masson ascribes it on the ground of Milton's heading (assuming as usual that *"anno aetatis 19"* means at the age of 19) and of references in the Latin portion to the year 1628. The Latin text (translated by Masson I, 292) gives the explanation of the last part, in which the poet masquerades as Ens or Being and designates certain of his fellow students as the Aristotelian categories, his sons. The chief significance of the poem is its expression of Milton's patriotic and aesthetic enthusiasm for the English tongue and his declaration of intention to write worthily in it on some lofty theme. In lines 19 ff. he gives his adverse reaction against the "late fantastics" in literature, thereby declaring his allegiance to the older and more richly poetic style of Spenser and the Elizabethans against that of some more fashionable group of his own contemporaries. It has been suggested that George Herbert might have been in Milton's mind as having in the era just before him at Cambridge represented the new modes of expression initiated by John Donne.

The meter is the heroic couplet, used loosely according

to the practice of such Elizabethans as Jonson. The description of the heavenly and heroic themes which he contemplates (suggestive of the subject matter of Du Bartas as well as of the ancient epic poets) has the true Miltonic ring. In the description of the rivers Milton imitates Spenser and Browne, as he was later to do in the poem *On the Nativity,* in some far-fetched metaphors of the sort he seems to be condemning.

"ON THE MORNING OF CHRIST'S NATIVITY" and "THE PASSION." Milton printed the great nativity ode, the first serious and lofty work of his genius, as the opening poem in the 1645 edition with the date 1629. We learn from the close of *Elegy VI* that it was begun before daylight on Christmas morning, "as a birthday gift to Christ." The deeply religious mood in which it was undertaken marks, as we have seen (above, p. 136), not only a feeling appropriate to the season, but a definite abandonment of literary trifling and a consecration of himself to a way of life in harmony with the most serious kind of poetic inspiration. It is to be remembered that the poet had come of age on the 9th of December in the same year.

The subject is a very common one in sixteenth and seventeenth century English poetry. Among the more important of Milton's immediate predecessors who had written of the nativity in independent odes are Jonson, Drummond, Beaumont, Southwell, Sylvester. The theme appears also in Giles Fletcher's *Christ's Victory and Triumph* and, indeed, throughout the religious poetry of the period.

The main features of Milton's treatment of the subject naturally find abundant precedent in this literature, but the only parallel of significance is with a nativity poem in Tasso's *Rime Sacre,* in which the cessation of the oracles

and the overthrow of the Pagan deities of Greece and Egypt
are described in a manner very similar to Milton's. Less
specific but equally important is the influence of Virgil's
fourth eclogue, prophesying the golden age which was to
follow upon the birth of a son to Pollio, a poem universally
interpreted as an allegory of the birth of Christ. Milton appears to have regarded the entire body of his youthful work
as belonging roughly to the pastoral genre; and the poem
On the Nativity is, as Professor Rand remarks,[9] "an attempt to match the Pagan Messianic prophecy in a pastoral
Birth Song for the real Messiah, in which Christian purity
and truth dispense with the gaudy trim of Pagan imagery."

Yet Milton does not escape from the Renaissance habit
of employing classical modes of conception for his Christian
theme. Christ is for him not the suffering Saviour but the
mighty Pan, kindly come to dwell among men. The sweetness of the manger scene, so beautifully imaged in Crashaw's
nativity ode and in the Christmas carols, gives way to the
picture of an infant Hercules who "can in swaddling bands
control the damnèd crew" of Satan. Theologically Milton
accepts at this time the orthodox doctrine of the Trinity.
His true theme, however, is the moral significance of Christ,
as a symbol of ethical and religious truth, which in its pure
simplicity banishes the multiformity of error, typified in the
welter of Pagan divinities. Milton is adoring an idea rather
than a person. His poem is Protestant and humanistic rather
than Catholic in feeling.

In both meter and style *On the Morning of Christ's
Nativity* reflects the Spenserian tradition of Milton's prin-
cipal masters at this time in the art of poetry, Giles and
Phineas Fletcher. The introductory stanzas are in the seven

[9] *Milton in Rustication.*

line rhyme of the earlier piece, *On the Death of a Fair Infant*. The Hymn itself employs a form apparently original with Milton, but bearing in the final alexandrine the mark of its ultimate origin in Spenser. The scheme is a6, a6, b10, c6, c6, b10, d8, d12. The style is elaborate and somewhat diffuse. Milton indulges occasionally in the exercise of poetic ingenuity.[10] These tricks of thought and expression are Milton's legacy from fashion in a period of his development before he had found his own majestic poetic idiom or even, as he was shortly afterward to do, felt the superiority of the more classical lyric style of the followers of Jonson. The poem is, however, full of preludings of the great Miltonic tone, as in the line "The wakeful trump of doom must thunder through the deep." His later fondness for the resonance and suggestiveness of strange names is also evident (cf. stanzas XXI ff.).

Professor Tillyard, in noting these traits of style in the ode, describes it as a poem of wholly un-Miltonic inspiration and of a unique charm. Its essence, he says, is not stateliness excusing conceits, but homeliness, quaintness, tenderness, extravagance, and sublimity, harmonized by a pervading youthful candor and ordered by a commanding architectonic grasp. "When Milton wrote the nativity ode he seemed to write with a pulse beating quicker, with a mind more alert, more varied, more susceptible to fancy as well as to imagination, less censorious, tenderer, less egotistical, than when he wrote any other poem before or since." These remarks and what Tillyard says further in analysis of the complex mood out of which the poem sprang,

[10] His conceits here and elsewhere are those rather of the Elizabethan sonneteers and of Giles Fletcher than of the metaphysical school. See Potter, *Milton's Early Poems*.

raise interesting critical and psychological questions concerning the unfolding of Milton's genius at this turning point in his career.

There are, finally, in the poem important anticipations of motives later to be employed in *Paradise Lost*. Thus the idea that the Pagan divinities are in reality demons, suggested in stanzas XXIV–XXV, is the basic principle of the representation of the fallen angels. The conception was a familiar one in Patristic writers. The idea of the death of Pan and the cessation of oracles is the subject of a long gloss in Spenser's "Shepherd's Calendar" (May) and of an essay of Plutarch. Milton's knowledge of Egyptian divinities comes in part from Plutarch's *Of Osiris,* etc. He knew also Eusebius's *Praeparatio Evangelorum,* which is full of interesting material concerning the Phoenician and Egyptian gods. Finally, Milton's introduction of the personifications, Peace, Justice, Truth, and Mercy, shows his familiarity with the allegory of the four daughters of God as developed by medieval writers and revived by Giles Fletcher in *Christ's Victory in Heaven,* whence Milton derived it.[11] The material of this allegory, stripped of its metaphorical element, is embodied in the debate in Heaven (*Paradise Lost,* Book III).[12]

The Passion immediately follows *On the Morning of Christ's Nativity* in the 1645 edition and apparently belongs to the following Easter (i. e., April, 1630). It is bound to the preceding work by allusions in the opening lines and by the use of a meter identical with that employed in the introductory portion of the other. The poem represents an

[11] See below, p. 264.
[12] For the most learned commentary on the *Nativity* see Cook's *Notes.*

attempt to continue the lofty religious vein which Milton
had entered upon in earnest of his new consecration in 1629.
Quite possibly he projected such a series of commemora-
tions of the divine events at their appropriate anniversaries
in the Church calendar as are to be found among the works
of Herbert and Donne. The poem *Upon the Circumcision,*
discussed in the next section, constitutes a third member of
the group. *The Passion* contains a specific reference to Vida's
Latin poem, *The Christiad,* which, with Giles Fletcher's
Christ's Victory and the religious verse of his brother
Phineas and of Sylvester, must be counted among the
sources of Milton's devotional poetic mood at this period.
The Passion, however, remained unfinished and Milton
appended a note to the effect that he found it "above the
years he had when he wrote it." The truth is that the
crucifixion was not a congenial theme to him at any time.
Even thus early he seems to have felt instinctively that
man's salvation depends upon himself and that he needs
Christ as a guide and model rather than as a redeemer. His
lack of inspiration in *The Passion* is very evident. Both the
emotion and the style are forced, and Milton seems unable
to pass beyond the process of introduction into the theme
itself.

"SONG ON MAY MORNING." The only evidence for the
date of this lovely lyric is its position in the 1645 volume
among the university poems. Milton had grouped his more
serious religious pieces, including several written in the
Horton period, together at the beginning. The lighter verse
follows, arranged apparently in chronological order, with
this poem at its head. Had it not been composed before the
epigram *On Shakespeare* and the two pieces on the *University Carrier* I think he would have placed it after them,

with *L'Allegro* and *Il Penseroso*. Its purer lyric style, free
from conceit and verbal curiosity, is a result of Milton's
writing for the moment in the classic Jonsonian rather than
in the Fletcherian tradition. He was evidently at this time
and for several years to come an eclectic follower of many
masters. The return to lighter themes may be a reaction
from his failure to complete *The Passion*. It is natural
enough that he should not have maintained consistently the
mood of high seriousness which he had proclaimed in *Elegy
VI* and illustrated in the poem *On the Nativity*.

"ON SHAKESPEARE." This sixteen line epigram in heroic
couplets was first printed among other commendatory
verses prefixed to the second folio of Shakespeare's works
in 1632 with the title "An Epitaph on the Admirable Dra-
matick Poet, W. Shakespeare." It is, however, dated 1630
by Milton himself in the 1645 edition. Since it was very
probably written to order for the folio, I should assume that
Milton's date is, as frequently, a little too early. The idea
which Milton elaborates is that of Jonson in his lines on
Shakespeare in the first folio—"Thou art a monument
without a tomb—" but the conceit that Shakespeare, by
turning his readers to stone, creates for himself a monument was perhaps suggested by the second stanza of the
elegy of William Browne on the Countess of Pembroke.[13]
The phrase, "star-ypointing pyramid" is echoed from an
epitaph on Sir Edward Standly which was attributed to

[13] Originally published in Camden's *Remains,* 1629, p. 336, in the
following form :

> Marble piles let no man raise
> To her name; for after days
> Some kind woman, born as she,
> Reading this, like Niobe,
> Shall turn marble, and become
> Both her mourner and her tomb.

Shakespeare.[14] Significant verbal parallels have also been pointed out between Milton's poem and two Elizabethan plays: Massinger's *The Fatal Dowry* and Thomkis's *Albumazar*.[15] These indications reveal Milton's close familiarity with the English literature of his own and the preceding age and also his capacity for assimilating the phrase and thought of other men. Milton's admiration for Shakespeare is sincere, in spite of the implied reservations of other passages in his works. Like every critic for over a century after Shakespeare's death, he praises him as a spontaneous genius rather than as a conscious artist. (Cf. *L'Allegro,* lines 133–134.)

"ON THE UNIVERSITY CARRIER." The date of composition of the two poems on this subject is fixed by the death of old Hobson, the carrier, January 1, 1631. They belong with the poem *On Shakespeare* metrically and as examples of the seventeenth century punning and conceited epigram, and they seem to have enjoyed some contemporary popularity in university circles.[16] Milton's attitude, jocose but not unkindly, is similar to that which he had previously taken in the second Latin elegy on the death of the University Beadle. It is characteristic of undergraduate feeling toward those minor academic functionaries who are made butts of ridicule during their careers and offices only to have it faintly remembered at their passing that they were human.

[14] See Spencer, *Shakespeare and Milton.* The poem begins:

> Not monumentall stones praeserves our Fame;
> Nor sky-aspiring Piramides our name.

[15] Garrod, *Milton's Lines on Shakespeare.*

[16] See Parker, *Milton's Hobson Poems,* and Evans, *Two New MS Versions of Milton's Hobson Poems.* Many other poems were written on Hobson. One epigram, which appeared with Milton's in *A Banquet of Jests,* 1640, may also be from his pen. See Columbia Edition, XVIII, 359.

This is one of the few places in his work in which Milton exhibits humor unmixed with moroseness.

"AN EPITAPH ON THE MARCHIONESS OF WINCHESTER." The Lady Jane, wife of John Paulet, fifth Marquis of Winchester, died in childbirth, April 15, 1631. The event was celebrated by Ben Jonson, then Poet Laureate, as well as in this lovely elegy of Milton's. It is natural to suppose that the poet was socially acquainted with her family. The poem follows the pure style of the school of Jonson, contrasting sharply in its sweet simplicity of manner with the earlier elegy *On the Death of a Fair Infant*. The opening lines echo Browne's famous epitaph on the Countess of Pembroke. The piece is written in the octosyllabic couplet of *L'Allegro* and *Il Penseroso*.[17]

POEMS OF UNCERTAIN DATE, 1629–1634

"L'ALLEGRO" and "IL PENSEROSO." The date of this famous pair of lyrics is purely conjectural. Though formerly ascribed to the beginning of the Horton period, they more probably belong to some vacation interval in the last years of Milton's University life. We know that Milton had already fallen under the sway of the Jonsonian lyric tradition and had experimented in the octosyllabic couplet. His capacity for a refinement of poetic feeling and expression as exquisite as that found in these poems and his possession of their mood and temper are also confirmed for the University epoch. The motive, a record of aesthetic pleasures, is identi-

---

[17] To complete the list of English poems written before Milton's retirement at Horton we must add, besides some of those listed as doubtful, the paraphrases on Psalms 114 and 136 (discussed below) and the two sonnets *To the Nightingale* and *On His Being Arrived to the Age of Twenty-Three* (below, p. 171).

cal with that of *Elegy I,* though in that poem Milton's objectivity was disturbed by sensations only faintly traceable in the companion pieces. Finally *L'Allegro* and *Il Penseroso* are not included in the Cambridge MS., a document in which Milton set down practically everything he wrote from the Horton period on. On the other hand, the maturity of style in these poems and the evidence they contain of leisurely reading and enjoyment may be taken as an argument for a later date.

An interesting new suggestion has recently been made by Tillyard,[18] who, finding many parallels with the first Prolusion, "Whether Day or Night is the more Excellent," thinks that the pieces are a poetical exercise on practically the same theme (though with both sides represented), and that they were intended for recitation before an academic audience. The openings, he thinks, are humorous and the social tone of the poems as a whole more appropriate to Cambridge than to Horton. He dates them in the long vacation of 1631, by which time Milton felt or professed himself to feel more happy in his relations to the student body than he had been earlier.

However this may be, *L'Allegro* and *Il Penseroso* are the finest expressions of Milton's joyous and sensitive poetic nature at a moment of his life when he could still indulge a dilettante enthusiasm for beauty in nature and the manifold delights of music, books, society, and self-pleasing reverie without the intrusion either of his moral idealism or of his intense personal passion. They represent also, in their delicate and flawless lyric technique, the utmost perfection of his youthful art. Milton has worked in a purely objective spirit, composing the materials of his aesthetic life into

[18] *The Miltonic Setting,* pp. 1–28.

parallel pictures of contrasting moods. The idea of two persons, the gay and the pensive man, is, of course, a mere device. A catholic artistic taste does not prefer tragedy to comedy, or a somber to a laughing landscape, or society to solitude. It takes its suggestion, rather, from the object and is equally responsive to beauty in its bright and in its sober guise. Such, surely, is Milton's temper, and it seems idle to discuss which poem best represents his nature or to regard them as though the contradiction pretended in them were real. The truer interpretation is that which considers the two lyrics as the contrasting movements in a musical composition, and the titles, suggesting, as they do, the terminology of musical directions,[19] justify a parallel with the sister art which the poet knew so well.

On the other hand it may be and has been argued that Milton himself did not view the poems in quite this light. We know that he was much given to weighing and considering the choices which lay before him with reference to the fulfillment of his hopes and expectations of himself. In the sixth elegy he considers the claims of poetry born of two different inspirations, a gayer and more trivial, on the one hand, a soberer and more purposeful, on the other. He there declares his allegiance to the latter and proposes for himself a severe life of self-denial in preparation for it. This is essentially an ethical resolution, but it implies also a choice of customary aesthetic occupation, and *L'Allegro* and *Il Penseroso* may represent a somewhat lighter balancing of a similar issue. The solitary, reflective life of study was certainly more in accord with Milton's idea of his own future activity than the social, and though L'Allegro is sometimes

---

[19] For a survey of Milton's employment throughout his works of the technical language of music see Spaeth.

alone in his enjoyment he is not generally so. *Il Penseroso,* therefore, may be said to represent Milton's temperamental preference and the program which he expected to adopt, though without complete suppression of the other. To say this is not to agree with the extreme statement of W. V. Moody [20] who describes *Il Penseroso* as representing the choice which circumstances were soon to thrust on Milton "in the shape of a life lived for ideal ends through days of dusty publicity." For the pursuits of Il Penseroso, no less than those of L'Allegro, are engaged in for delight, rather than under the rod of duty, and these pursuits do not lead in the direction of dusty publicity. The idea of Darnell that Milton might have been thinking of Diodati's temperament in comparison with his own is not without plausibility. The case would then be, however, that Diodati besides representing the gay and social mood himself, called it forth also in Milton, leaving him the choice of which one chiefly to cultivate. Mr. D. C. Dorian,[21] in pleading for the autobiographical significance of the companion poems, points out the relevant fact that they describe not merely ideal days but customary occupations, as is indicated by such expressions as "oft," "never," "sometimes," by the mixture of seasons, and finally by such contradictory proposals as that in *L'Allegro* of spending the evening in upland hamlets or in populous cities.

The tradition in which Milton writes is that of the Elizabethan lyric, and several definite poems may be indicated as having almost certainly furnished him with suggestions. Chief among these is the piece prefixed to Burton's *Anatomy of Melancholy,* entitled *A Dialogue between Pleasure*

[20] *Poems,* p. 24.
[21] In *Modern Philology,* 1933, pp. 177–182.

and Pain. Here, to be sure, the contrasted objects are the painful and the pleasurable types of melancholy; but some of the detail is so similar to Milton's as to make it seem plausible that Burton's poem afforded the initial suggestion for his own. The opening of *Il Penseroso* is plainly reminiscent of a song in Beaumont and Fletcher's *Nice Valour,* in which "vain delights" are banished and "lovely melancholy" welcomed in a formula identical with Milton's. One of Nicholas Breton's lyrics has also been mentioned as resembling *L'Allegro* and *Il Penseroso* and appears to have been in the poet's memory as he wrote.[22] All three of the lyrics mentioned use the dancing octosyllabic measure of Milton's poems. There is no precedent, however, for the precision and comprehensiveness with which Milton marshals his delights, or for the intricate and artful manner in which each detail in one poem is counterpoised in the other. The general tradition of the ideal day of pastoral delight goes back to Virgil's *Georgics,* and it was, as Miss Sara Watson demonstrates, the totality of this tradition which mainly influenced Milton.

L'Allegro and *Il Penseroso* have always been among the best loved of Milton's poems. Modern critics have united in praising the perfection of their workmanship and the sweetness of temper revealed in them, which contrasts sharply with the Puritan severity of Milton's later life and work. But they represent, after all, only a holiday moment in a life already deeply serious, and to this kind of holiday Milton could always in some degree return. The record

[22] See Lowes, *"L'Allegro" and "The Passionate Shepheard."* For another related lyric see Padelford, *An Unnoted Source of "L'Allegro."* Damon, *Milton and Marston,* thinks the opening lines of *L'Allegro* to be imitative of the beginning of Marston, *The Scourge of Villanie,* another proof of the range of his Elizabethan reading.

which they embody of the poet's youthful culture is complete on one side only. Thus he represents himself in *Il Penseroso* as witnessing tragedy, whether on the stage or in his mind's eye only, as a spectacle of solemn beauty, and as reading Plato in the indulgence of the speculative fancy. But we know that the Greek tragedians were for him first of all "teachers of moral wisdom" and that Plato was already one of his great guides toward truth. It is with a deliberate consistency that he excludes from focus everything which could not be brought within the limits of a fine amateurism. He did so once and once only in these poems.

"AT A SOLEMN MUSIC," "ON TIME," "UPON THE CIRCUMCISION." With these poems we reach the body of material which Milton set down in the manuscript volume now preserved at Trinity College, Cambridge. The order in which the various compositions stand in that document affords some indication of their relative dates, though by no means a complete or certain one. We have also the fact that he arranged the poems in the 1645 edition with some regard to their chronological order; but here, again, the situation is not wholly clear, since he occasionally adopted another principle of arrangement. The earlier items in the MS. are as follows: *Arcades, At a Solemn Music* in three drafts, a prose letter to a friend (see above, p. 23), *On Time, Upon the Circumcision,* three sonnets of later date, copied on a page which had been left blank, *Comus, Lycidas. Comus* is dated 1634. The prose letter contains the sonnet, *How soon hath time,* described as "my nightward thoughts some time since." The letter itself is apparently a first draft, like *At a Solemn Music. On Time* and *Upon the Circumcision* are clean copies. They stand after *The Passion* and before *At a Solemn Music* in the 1645 edition. *Arcades,* which, though

much corrected in the autograph, hardly looks like a first
attempt, is grouped in the edition with *Lycidas* and *Comus*,
presumably because of its pastoral character. It is safe to
say that no one will succeed in dating precisely the pieces
which precede *Comus* in the manuscript; but we are on
sure enough ground in ascribing them all to the close of
Milton's University career or the beginning of his sojourn
at Horton.[23]

With regard to the literary qualities of the three lyrics
little need be said. They are in the form of odes or canzoni
with irregular rhyme and line length, a unique experiment
with Milton except for the approach to it in *Lycidas*. In
his mind they evidently constituted one group with the
poems on Christ's birth and death, a body of sacred or at
least solemn verse by which he wished his early earnestness
to be judged. Though less interesting intrinsically than *On
the Morning of Christ's Nativity* they are works of a sincere inspiration, in the best vein of seventeenth century
meditative poetry. *On Time* has the character of an inscription, as is suggested by its canceled manuscript title "Set
on a Clock Case." *At a Solemn Music* bears witness to Milton's enthusiasm for the "sphere-born harmonious sisters
voice and verse," and in its mystical and Christian interpretation of the Platonic idea of the music of the spheres is
deeply characteristic of Milton's thought.[24] Both pieces
conclude with the contemplation of Heaven and immortality, a theme much in Milton's thoughts throughout his early
life. *Upon the Circumcision* is relatively unattractive. Milton seems to be rather forcing himself to meditate on the

[23] See Parker, *Some Problems* and Woodhouse, *Notes on Milton's
Early Development*.
[24] See Tillyard, *Milton*, Appendix C. and Barker, *The Pattern of
Milton's Nativity Ode*.

significance of an event which has for him little more than
a conventional appeal. Here, as in *The Passion,* he shows
unconsciously his remoteness from the emotion of religious
sorrow.

"ARCADES." This short masque, consisting of three songs
and a recitation in pentameter couplets, follows the ten
sonnets in the 1645 edition and is, as we have seen, the first
item in the Cambridge manuscript. These facts and the
evident connection of the piece with *Comus* are the sole
basis for the date of composition, which is given by Masson
as 1633 or possibly 1634, but by Grierson as 1630 or 1632.
According to Milton's own note in the 1645 edition it was
"part of an entertainment presented to the Countess Dow-
ager of Derby at Harefield by some noble persons of her
family." These noble persons presumably include the family
of Sir John Egerton, Earl of Bridgewater, her stepson, for
whom Milton wrote *Comus* in 1634. It is probable that
Henry Lawes, then musical tutor in the Egerton family,
who later superintended the production of *Comus,* was also
the deviser of this masque. Lawes's friendship with Milton
is established by the sonnet addressed to him in 1646. No
great degree of intimacy between Milton and the distinguished circle of the Countess of Derby is necessarily implied by his having been engaged to furnish the words for
these masques, yet Harefield is but a dozen miles from Horton and some acquaintance may have existed. The Countess
of Derby, a daughter of Sir John Spencer of Althorpe, had
married Ferdinando Stanley, Lord Strange. To her Ed-
mund Spenser, who counted himself of the same family, had
dedicated the *Tears of the Muses* in 1591. By a second marriage in 1600 she had become the wife of Sir Thomas Egerton, Lord Keeper of the Seal. The Countess was already
in her 70's when Milton moved to Horton. Her birthday,

which possibly occurred on May 4, would have been an appropriate occasion for the masque.

Milton's verses present a situation rather than a plot. A group of shepherds have been searching for their Arcadian queen and, finding her in the person of the great lady in whose honor the entertainment is given, they sing her a song of compliment. The Genius of the Wood, a part probably taken by Lawes, enters and addresses her. The conception of such a figure is a familiar one in the masque and is repeated in the Attendant Spirit in *Comus*. In the beautiful song "O'er the smooth enamelled green" he brings the Arcadians to the lady. A dance and a concluding lyric follow. One notable passage describes the music of the spheres, an idea which appealed powerfully to Milton's imagination and is employed also in the *Nativity* and in the poem *At a Solemn Music* (see p. 154). The whole is done in the purest and most delicate Elizabethan vein. The tone is that of the Jonsonian masque, but no specific influences are traceable in Milton's work. On the basis of Milton's statement, *Arcades* is usually described as a fragment, but there is nothing in the piece itself to indicate incompleteness. Of the character of the rest of the entertainment we know nothing.

ENGLISH POEMS WRITTEN AT HORTON (1632–1638)

"COMUS." *Comus*, entitled by Milton simply *A Maske*, is dated 1634 in the Cambridge manuscript and in the editions. In 1637 Henry Lawes had the work printed to save the trouble of making transcripts for the many persons who requested copies.[25] Except for the lines to Shakespeare this

[25] Reproduced in facsimile in Dodd, Mead & Company's *Facsimile Reprints of Rare Books,* 1903. The divergences from the 1645 edition and the Cambridge MS. are interesting. We have in these three ver-

Comus is, in point of time, one of the last representatives of the tradition of the English masque, a type of courtly entertainment introduced from Italy in simple form as early as the time of Henry VIII and developed to its highest point of elaboration by Ben Jonson in the reign of James. The masque is essentially a private entertainment, performed, in part at least, by members of society, and depending for its effect largely on music, pageantry, and dance. The courtly dance is, indeed, the essential and original feature. It had become the custom also to introduce a set of comic or grotesque characters, the parts being more often taken by professionals, and to assign them one or more dances of a burlesque character. This humorous element was known as the antimasque. It is represented in *Comus* by the crew of man-monsters who have been transformed by the enchanter, and again by the countrymen who do a rural turn at the close. The subject matter of the masque is almost always a combination of mythology and allegory, adapted in the Elizabethan manner to the social occasion for which the masque is written. In the composition of masques delicacy and prettiness rather than dramatic effect are sought for. The poetry, even in the dialogue, has commonly a lyric quality. Milton had plenty of opportunity to see masques, and it is reasonable to suppose that he would have taken a particular interest in them. He shows close familiarity with the tradition, and *Comus* illustrates every one of the points made in the above description. There are, however, important differences between *Comus* and the typical masque of the period, differences which spring largely from the strongly individual temper of its author, though some of them are to be found also in the masque-like plays or morals of James Shirley. Milton minimizes

Renaissance ideal: Goodness, Beauty, Truth

the element of pageantry and dance; he substitutes an out-door scene for the ordinary setting of the banquet hall; he expands the dialogue portion of the piece far beyond its usual limits and injects into it an earnestness of meaning quite foreign to the tradition. The fable of the masque is characteristically designed to illustrate the triumph of some moral ideal, but usually this is merely conventional. Milton, on the other hand, besides achieving the most exquisite poetic beauty and fulfilling very gracefully all the courtly and complimentary purposes of the masque, succeeds in expressing a serious ethical philosophy.

His theme is the unassailable security of the virtuous mind amid every circumstance of violence and wrong. Specifically he exalts the virtue of chastity, an ideal which, as we know from many sources, was passionately dear to him in his youth. The Lady is little more than a personification of purity; Thyrsis represents the divine protection which surrounds the good; Comus is vice in its seductive form; his monsters, vice in its true brutishness; the Elder Brother is the youth who by the study of philosophy has become secure in his understanding of these truths; the Younger Brother is a neophyte who has not yet acquired a complete faith. The Platonic doctrine that the condition of the soul reflects itself in the outward form—creates, indeed, the body which is its temple—is implied throughout and specifically set forth in the famous passage beginning with line 453. In the Spirit's epilogue Milton introduces in Pagan terms but with a Christian meaning the idea of a mystic marriage of the soul with God, the heavenly compensation for a life of chastity on earth. An interesting piece of symbolism is introduced in the passage concerning the magic herb Haemony (lines 618 ff.), which Thyrsis gives to the

(Spenser's "Fairie Queen")

"Younger brother"—"wandering between 2 worlds"—Arnold

brothers as a protection against the spells of Comus. Its use was taught him by "a certain Shepherd Lad of small regard to see to, yet well-skilled." The shepherd lad is probably Milton himself, and the plant represents the lofty moral wisdom which he possessed, more specifically, perhaps, the Platonic doctrine, in which he was wont to instruct his friend Lawes in requital for his songs, or poetry embodying such doctrine. There may also be an association with αἷμα, the blood of Christ, as Le Comte has recently argued.

Certainly *Comus* expresses some of Milton's most passionately held convictions. Having chosen for himself the way of chastity, he must proclaim it to the world. The issue undoubtedly goes back in his thought to his Cambridge days, when he defended the traits which had won him the name of "Lady" against the habits of those who maintained their manhood by gross debauchery (see above, p. 22). The debate of principles between Comus and The Lady (lines 710–742) suggests that he may have had in mind the Cyrenaic arguments of a specific fellow student, Thomas Randolph, in *The Muses Looking Glass,* a drama which was perhaps acted in Cambridge when Milton was there.[29]

The question of Milton's literary sources in *Comus* is a particularly interesting one. It so happens that we can trace with more of certainty than in the case of *Paradise Lost* the varied elements, ancient and modern, which his extraordinarily assimilative mind converted to its uses. Such a study serves to illustrate Milton's culture, and also to throw into relief the highly individual quality which his

[29] See G. C. Moore Smith, *TLS,* January 19, 1922, p. 44. Sensabaugh, "The Milieu of Comus," suggests that Milton is providing an antidote against the talk of "Platonic love" current in the queen's coterie at court. Milton's masque and Randolph's poems were bound together in Sir Henry Wotton's copy. See above, p. 28.

imagination imparts to his materials. For Milton's borrowings, here and elsewhere, are never literal. Even when we are reasonably sure of his indebtedness, the relation is apt to be so distant and intangible that one feels that his recollection must have been an unconscious one.

The mythological groundwork of Milton's story is of course the Circe episode in the *Odyssey* (Book X). In giving an allegorical interpretation to this myth Milton had a precedent in the Platonizing mythographer, Heraclides Ponticus, of whose *Allegoriae* he is known to have owned a copy.[30] A more immediate suggestion came to him, however, from Spenser, whose Bower of Bliss (*Faerie Queene*, Book II, Canto xii) is presided over by the enchantress Acrasia, a Circe-like figure, the symbol of intemperance, and surrounded by creatures who have been transformed to beasts. That Milton had paid especial attention to the ethical meaning of this passage we know from *Areopagitica*. William Browne's *Inner Temple Masque*, acted about 1620, deals with Circe and Ulysses, and, like *Comus*, employs an antimasque of men transformed to monsters.

Comus himself derives originally from a personification of the Greek common noun κῶμος (revelry), which had already taken place in antiquity. But Milton must have been familiar with the conception from more modern sources. In Ben Jonson's masque, *Pleasure Reconciled to Virtue* (1619), Comus appears as a glutton. In a neo-Latin play,[31] the *Comus* of Erycius Puteanus (Hendrik van der Putten), he is an embodiment of a more refined sensuality and, as

[30] Sotheby, *Ramblings*, p. 125. For a full discussion of Milton's use of classical myth in *Comus* see Bush, *Mythology and the Renaissance Tradition*, pp. 248 ff.

[31] First published at Louvain in 1608, reprinted 1611, 1613, 1615, and at Oxford in 1634.

with Milton, a magician. The resemblances between Milton's *Comus* and this document are too striking to be the result of accident. The author sees in vision a riotous banquet in which Comus, an embodiment of intemperate pleasure, has as his guests various personified pleasures and passions. An old man declaims against the various vices and attacks the ideals held by the revelers. Some specific parallels in the speeches of *Comus* are pointed out by Todd. But whatever precedents Milton may have had for his chief character, he is apparently original in making Comus a son of Circe and Bacchus.

The central fiction of the masque, the abduction and rescue of the Lady, has many analogues. The closest is George Peele's *Old Wives Tale,* where two brothers go in search of their sister, Delia, who has been imprisoned by an enchanter. He gives her a magic potion causing her to forget her brothers and rather feebly endeavors to win her to his lust. They meet an old man who knows the arts of magic and enlist his aid, but are themselves enthralled and goaded to labor by their enchanted sister. The release of all three comes when the magician's glass containing a light is broken by the wife of the old man and his wreath and sword possessed by a dead man, Jack. A dance of harvestmen and an echo dialogue offer slight parallels to incidents in *Comus.* The main action of the play is much obscured by the introduction of various unrelated episodes. Milton very probably took the suggestion for his plot situation from Peele's play.[82] Here again, however, his elaboration of the material was partly determined by his beloved author Spenser.

---

[82] See Badt, *Milton's "Comus."* There is similar material in Drury's *Alvredus,* 1619, which has also been claimed as a Miltonic source (see Hall, *Comus,* etc.), and in *The Valiant Welshman,* by

In *The Faerie Queene* (Book III, Canto xii), the chaste Amoret is imprisoned by a magician in a castle symbolizing lust. She stands chained before Busyrane, her captor, who endeavors to force her to do his will. Her rescuer, breaking in, compels the enchanter to release her by saying his charms backward. Cf. *Comus,* lines 815–817:

> Without his rod revers't,
> And backward mutters of dissevering power,
> We cannot free the Lady that sits here.

Another practically certain influence is Fletcher's *The Faithful Shepherdess,* a pastoral drama with a decidedly masque-like tone.[33] If, however, in moulding his drama, Milton is mainly under the sway of the Elizabethans, his classical predilections lead him to make it conform, wherever possible, to classical precedent. Clear traces of ancient dramatic practice are to be found in the Euripidean prologue, in the somewhat riddling dialogue in which each speech is exactly a line's length (stichomythia) in lines 277–290, and in the deliberate use of irony in lines 657–658.[34]

When all these relationships (and others less tangible might be mentioned) are taken into account, the paramount influence remains, I believe, that of Spenser. Besides the points already mentioned there is a clear relation between Spenser's Garden of Adonis (*Faerie Queene,* III, vi) and the description of the paradise of heavenly love at the close of *Comus.* For one episode, that of Sabrina, Milton directly

---

"R. A., Gent.," published in 1615. The story of Child Rowland is a remoter folklore analogue. See Brie, *Das Märchen von Childe Rowland und sein Nachleben.*

[33] See Axon, *"Comus" and Fletcher's "Faithful Shepherdess."*

[34] For further parallels with Euripides see Sandys' edition of the *Bacchae,* notes to lines 188, 234, 314.

refers to Spenser as his source (cf. *Faerie Queene*, Book II, Canto x), though, of course, he knew it also in Geoffrey of Monmouth's *British History*. His use in this connection of the pastoral name Meliboeus is analogous to Spenser's own praise of Chaucer as Tityrus and suggests that Milton recognized a kindred discipleship.[35] He later told Dryden that Spenser was his original. We know from other evidence that this discipleship was in 1634 a rather recent thing, partly superseding Milton's earlier literary devotion to the Fletchers. It seems quite clear that Spenser was of the greatest value to Milton at this time in helping him interpret his genius to himself, in fostering his poetical idealism and his enthusiasm for purity, in teaching him how to give concrete literary embodiment to Platonism, and, specifically, in furnishing him with no small part of the substance of *Comus*. The passage already referred to in *Areopagitica* in which he calls "our sage and serious Spenser" a "better teacher than Scotus or Aquinas" shows that he chiefly valued him for his power of giving beauty and concreteness by the aid of poetry to spiritual and philosophic truth. The same attitude is reflected in the reference in *Il Penseroso:*

> Or if aught els great Bards beside
> In *sage and solemn* tune have sung.

In the account of his developing personal ideals in the *Apology for Smectymnuus* Milton says that the solemn cantos of the fables and romances of knighthood (by which he evidently means chiefly the *Faerie Queene*) taught him the beauty of the virtue of chastity.[36] All of which instructs

[35] See Bense, *"Meliboeus old" in Milton's "Comus"* for proof of the identification with Spenser.
[36] See Appendix B.

us to look to Spenser as one of the greatest moulding influences in Milton's youthful experience, and a chief inspirer of his poetry in the Horton period and thereafter— and this in spite of the fact that Milton's taste was leading him more and more away from the somewhat exuberant manner of expression which Spenser employed and passed on to his successors. The style of *Comus,* like that of *L'Allegro* and *Il Penseroso,* has its affinities with the Elizabethan and Jonsonian lyric and masque. It is not, save in a passage or two, Miltonic in the later sense, yet, with all its grace and delicacy, it has a quality of logical exactness and a condensation which are a fruit of Milton's classical self-discipline. Tillyard has analyzed the mixture of manners in *Comus,* pointing out that the masque begins with a Euripidean prologue, passes into vigorous dramatic dialogue, changes to pure poetry in the Lady's soliloquy, to the formulae of Greek dialogue in the stichomythy between Comus and the Lady, to the vein of *Midsummer Night's Dream* in Comus' speech beginning

> I know each lane and every alley green.

And so throughout.

The motto which appears on the flyleaf of Lawes's edition, and which must have been selected by Milton, is suggestive not so much of a consciousness of imperfection as of Milton's general sensitiveness to possible lack of sympathy:

> Eheu quid volui misero mihi! floribus austrum
> Perditus [et liquidis immisi fontibus apros.]

What, alas, did I purpose to my own destruction, wretched man that I am, when I let the south wind blow upon my flowers and the wild boars trample my clear springs?

The motto selected for the 1645 volume bears witness to the same sentiment:

Baccare frontem
Cingite, ne vati noceat mala lingua futuro.

Crown my brow with ivy and let no hostile tongue do injury to the destined poet.

"LYCIDAS." The exact date of the composition of *Lycidas* is fixed by the canceled superscription in the Cambridge manuscript, "November, 1637." Edward King, the alumnus of Christ's College in whose memory the poem was written, had been drowned in the Irish sea on August 10 of the same year. *Lycidas* was first printed with the initials J. M. as the last poem in a collection of memorial verses, Latin, Greek, and English, entitled *Obsequies to the Memory of Mr. Edward King, Anno Dom. 1638*. Milton republished it with minor alterations in the volume of 1645. The manuscript contains, beside the record of these later changes, many revisions made during the process of composition, material of the keenest interest to the student of the poetic art. We learn, for example, that the flower passage was an afterthought and we can trace the phrasing of many another passage through various stages on the way to its final perfection.[37] A few corrections are inserted in Milton's hand in a copy of the 1638 edition. One of these, "he well knew" for "he knew," in line 10, failed to get into the 1645 text, but it is confirmed by the manuscript and should probably be incorporated in modern editions.

In form *Lycidas* is a pastoral elegy, embodying a set of

[37] For a study of the alterations see Lockwood, *Milton's Corrections to the Minor Poems*.

conventions [38] which had gradually become fixed in poetic usage from antiquity. Chief among these are the fiction that all nature mourns the dead shepherd's loss, the question "where were ye, Nymphs," the procession of appropriate mourners, each uttering his grief, the pastoral consolation or change of tone from sadness to joy in the thought of the dead shepherd's immortality. Most of these features are embodied also in the parallel elegy, *Epitaphium Damonis.* Their ultimate classical origins may be sought in the second Idyll of Theocritus, Moschus' *Elegy on Bion,* Bion's own *Lament for Adonis,* and the fifth and tenth eclogues in Virgil's *Bucolics.* To these conventions the Renaissance added the representation of the association between the poet and his friend as a companionship of shepherds feeding their flocks, and the tendency to introduce allegorically an attack on the corruptions of the Church. Milton probably knew, among the multitude of pastorals written in his own age, those of Petrarch, in which this material is prominent; he certainly knew the *Shepherd's Calendar* of Spenser, where, besides much ecclesiastical allegory, there is a meditation on fame which parallels that in *Lycidas.* The November eclogue in the *Shepherd's Calendar* is an elegy and from it Milton borrowed a turn or two of phrase. He appears also to have been indebted to Castiglione's Latin elegy, *Alcon.*[39] Milton makes no effort to avoid these precedents; indeed, he rejoices in them. Artistically the conventionalism of the pastoral disguise serves as a decent drapery of grief, softening the outlines of the poet's emotion, depersonalizing and idealizing it, without entirely robbing it of poign-

---

[38] See Hanford, *The Pastoral Elegy and Milton's "Lycidas,"* and Norlin, *The Conventions of the Pastoral Elegy.*

[39] See Harrison, *The Latin Pastorals of Milton and Castiglione.*

ancy. The pastoral tradition justified also the introduction of thinly concealed personal digressions. The theme is apt to be as much the poet's own ambitions and disappointments as it is the praise of his dead friend. Thus Milton, in writing *Lycidas,* is, like Shelley in *Adonais,* primarily taking account of the meaning of the experience to himself. King is the poet who has been cut off in the midst of his youthful promise by the hand of fate. Of what use is high endeavor when life is subject to such accidents? The answer is Milton's first great confession of faith—in himself and his earnest way of life, in God and immortality. The rebuke administered to the corrupt clergy is an echo of his own determination not to go into the church. At the close he turns, with a chastened resolution, toward the future. It is untrue to say that the emotion in *Lycidas* is not intense. Though Milton feels the loss of King less personally than he was later to feel that of his intimate companion Diodati, he is sincerely touched by the melancholy of the event and he is even more profoundly moved by the realization of the fact of death.

As a work of art *Lycidas,* in spite of the disparagement of Johnson, who was offended by its pastoralism, has received almost universal praise.[40] Mark Pattison says that it is the high-water mark of English poetry and its full enjoyment a final fruit of literary culture. The style, though always laden with ornament and allusion, varies with the mood, rising and falling, as Milton "somewhat loudly sweeps the string" in moments of exaltation and denunciation, or bids his Muse return again to the pastoral strain

[40] For two admirable recent essays in appreciation of *Lycidas* see More, *How to Read "Lycidas,"* and Ransom, *A Poem nearly Anonymous.*

with its subdued note of tender melancholy. The analogy of music again occurs to mind as one considers the masterly way in which Milton has managed these fluctuations. No symphony was ever composed of more varied emotional elements or blended them more consummately into artistic unity. Metrically *Lycidas* is a combination of regularity and freedom. The verse is prevailingly iambic pentameter varied occasionally by the introduction of three-foot lines. The rhyme varies from the couplet form to intricate stanzaic arrangements, with a sprinkling of unrhymed lines. The poem closes with a stanza in *ottava rima*. In general Milton's formal models here are to be found in the metrical practice of contemporary Italian poetry. A more essential feature than the rhyme scheme, however, is Milton's handling of the metrical pauses and his tendency to prolong his cadences through a succession of lines in what Masson calls a series of free rhythmic paragraphs. It is in *Lycidas* that Milton's verse first takes on the characteristic qualities of rich and sonorous harmony for which we have no other word than Miltonic. These qualities, which I shall attempt to analyze later,[41] proceed fundamentally from the constitution of his mind, but the blank verse of Christopher Marlowe and the mellow cadences of Virgil have had no slight share in their making.

Lycidas bears its meaning plainly enough on its face, and there has been little room for disagreement regarding its larger features. There are, however, a few famous cruxes in particular passages. Among them is the line "Oft till the star that rose at evening bright," which is to be interpreted as referring to the evening planet appearing, rather than strictly rising, high in the heavens at dusk and setting after

[41] Chapter VI.

dark. The time during which the shepherds prolong their labors would be not all night but till a late hour. More difficult is the "two-handed engine" in line 130, which has been variously interpreted. The "uncouth swain" is Milton himself—untaught, unskilled, because the shepherd singer was traditionally supposed to be so. (Cf. Virgil, Eclogue III, lines 26–27.) The line "And old Damoetas loved to hear our song," may contain a reference to a friendly tutor. Miss Nicolson thinks this most likely to have been the famous Joseph Mead, who was on familiar terms with the students and whom Henry More refers to in a similar way as Mnemon.[42]

THE SONNETS

Milton's twenty-three sonnets fall into several chronological groups. Six of these, the sonnet "To the Nightingale" and the five Italian sonnets with the Canzone, are undoubtedly the product of his last years at the University. Sonnet VII, "How soon hath Time," was written on his twenty-fourth [43] birthday. Sonnet VIII, "Captain or Colonel or Knight at Arms," belongs to the year 1642. Sonnets IX and X, "Lady that in the prime of earliest youth" and "Daughter to that good Earl," followed in 1644. This whole group was published consecutively in the 1645 volume of the poems. The composition of the remaining thirteen fell between 1645 and 1658.[44] Four of these remained unprinted

[42] See Nicolson, *Milton's "Old Damoetas."*

[43] Assuming the soundness of Parker's argument in *Some Problems.*

[44] For a discussion of the dates of the sonnets see Stevens, *The Order of Milton's Sonnets,* Hanford, *The Arrangement and Dates of Milton's Sonnets,* and the introduction to Grierson's edition. The argument advanced by me for placing the Italian sonnets before the

until 1694, having been omitted from the 1673 volume for political reasons.

The Italian poems have already been discussed. The nightingale sonnet belongs with them in spirit and style and constitutes an introduction to the series. In it Milton, following the Chaucerian [45] tradition (though his poem is a sonnet in Petrarchan form), writes himself gracefully into the rôle of unsuccessful lovers. The later English sonnets, beginning with the one on his twenty-third birthday, reflect a complete change of attitude. The romantic note disappears entirely, the style is plain and direct, with none of the conventional phraseology which belongs to the tradition. They are the most immediately personal of all Milton's utterances, representing emotional moments in his later life experience which find no adequate expression in the prose writing in the publication of which he was during these years primarily engaged. We may believe also that they were, like the Psalms, prompted in part by a conscious desire in Milton to exercise himself in verse in preparation for the epic poem which he still intended.

Volumes have been written in discussion of Milton's sonnets, but their definitive treatment has been the work of the late Mr. J. S. Smart,[46] who has cleared away much error regarding their relation to literary tradition and has explained many obscure details of their meaning. He points out that Milton characteristically makes use of the form

Nativity Ode is challenged by Tillyard, pp. 372–3, who would date them a few years later.

[45] The poem seems to be reminiscent of Clanvowe's *The Cuckoo and the Nightingale,* a piece which Milton would have read as Chaucer's, for he used the Speght Edition in which it is included. See Magoun, *The Chaucer of Spenser and Milton.*

[46] *The Sonnets of Milton.*

at a time when its vogue has already passed. His formal model is not the English sonnet, with its tendency to close with a couplet, but the Italian originals which, on the whole, avoided such an ending. It is not true that he violates Italian precedent by failing to preserve a rhetorical pause at the exact conclusion of the octave. This is a principle of Petrarch but not of some Italian sonneteers, including Giovanni della Casa, a volume of whose poetry has survived from Milton's library.[47] His dedication of the sonnet to other themes than that of love is not an innovation, as it is so often said to be. Tasso, one of Milton's favorite authors, has a division of heroical sonnets on subjects like Milton's address to Cromwell, and even the Elizabethan tradition, though mainly so, is not by any means exclusively amatory. Yet, on the whole, Milton's sonnets strike a new note of lofty dignity conformable to his epic personality and justify Wordsworth's description:

> In his hands
> The Thing became a trumpet; whence he blew
> Soul-animating strains—alas, too few!

This applies primarily to the group in which he touches on great public events and personalities: the sonnets to Cromwell, Vane, and Fairfax, and the one on the late massacre in Piedmont. Those in which he expresses a more personal emotion—the sonnet *On his being arrived to the Age of Twenty-three,* the two poems on his blindness, and the one written in memory of his second wife—combine a poignant pathos with an earnest ethical and religious idealism. The addresses to Lawes, Skinner, Edward (not Henry) Lawrence, Lady Margaret Ley, and the unidentified vir-

[47] It is now in the New York Public Library.

tuous young Lady of Sonnet IX, also the elegy for Mrs.
Katharine Thomason, are pitched in lower key, but they
are beautifully expressive of a genial friendliness and a
warm glow of human sympathy quite at variance with the
common impression of Milton as a harsh and austere Puritan. The two sonnets on the reception of his divorce pamphlets and the twenty-line sonnet (*caudata*) *On the New
Forcers of Conscience under the Long Parliament* are a
revelation of the poet's capacity for scathing denunciation.
The whole group is a perfect record of Milton's unique
personality in all its varying moods. The workmanship
throughout is finished to the last degree [48] and each poem,
even the least of them, is a memorable and impressive work.
Samuel Johnson's disparagement of the sonnets ("of the
best it can only be said that they are not bad") is one of
the strangest literary judgments on record. The history of
their influence tells a very different story. It was Milton
rather than the Elizabethans who set the style of the English
sonnet at its revival toward the end of the eighteenth century.[49] The importance of Milton's sonnets as the chief inspiring force and model of those of Wordsworth is well
known.

THE PSALMS AND OTHER TRANSLATIONS

The task of reducing the Psalms to regular meters,
whether as a literary exercise or for the purpose of better
adapting them to congregational singing, seems to us now
of all literary endeavors the most vain and forbidding. Yet

[48] The most elaborate analysis of the technique of Milton's sonnets
is to be found in the introduction to Pattison's edition but see also the
corrective observations of Smart.
[49] See Chapter VIII.

it was little less than a passion with Milton's predecessors and contemporaries. He himself tried his hand at it on three different occasions in his life, each time with a somewhat different motive and result.

In 1624 at the age of fifteen (if one can trust the statement prefixed to the poems in the 1645 edition) he wrote paraphrases on Psalms CXIV and CXXXVI. These compositions derive a special interest from the fact that they constitute Milton's earliest preserved poetry of any sort. They may be school exercises, but it seems more likely that they were written under the encouragement of Milton's father, who was interested in the composition of psalm settings, contributing several to Ravenscroft's Psalter, which was published in 1621. There are traces in their phraseology (e. g., in the use of such epithets as "froth-becurled") of Milton's early fondness for Sylvester's translation of Du Bartas's *La Semaine*.[50] The One Hundred and Fourteenth Psalm is in Sylvester's meter and is more closely imitative of his style than the One Hundred and Thirty-sixth. Tillyard calls attention particularly to the violence of the following lines of Psalm CXIV as thoroughly representative of the manner of Sylvester's rendering:

> That glassy flood from rugged rocks can crush
> And make soft rills from fiery flint-stones gush.

In several expressions, moreover, he appears to be following Buchanan's versions of the Psalms in Horatian meters, which were much admired for their elegant Latinity and sometimes read in schools. Despite their lack of originality Milton's renderings have a freedom of rhythm and an elo-

[50] See the parallels in Dunster, *Considerations*, also Tillyard, *Milton*, pp. 8–9.

quence of language which marks them as the products of a genuine if immature poetic enthusiasm.

The second set of translations comprising Psalms LXXX to LXXXVIII, was first published in the 1673 edition of the poems with the heading "Nine of the Psalms done into Meter, wherein all but what is in a different character, are the very words of the Text, translated from the original." They are, in fact, more literal and less eloquent than the two youthful Psalms. Milton's purpose in writing them probably was to supply a version at once accurate and doctrinally sound to supplant the old Sternhold and Hopkins Psalter for congregational singing. He accordingly adopted the common service meter $(8 + 6)$. It is pointed out that Milton's rendering of the Hebrew is sometimes mistaken and evidence has been adduced to show that he resorted to the Vulgate for assistance.[51] It seems likely, however, that he was as competent as anyone in his time to interpret his originals, and the errors seem, in some cases, at least, to be due to the recollection of a phrase from some other version that was familiar to him.[52]

Finally, in 1653, on almost successive days, he turned Psalms I to VIII into a variety of metrical and stanzaic forms, no two being exactly the same. One surmises that he had resumed his task this time as a means of amusement and spiritual consolation in the early period of his blindness. The attempt to follow the Hebrew with minute fidelity is now abandoned; occasional touches reveal the degree to which Milton is reading his own experiences into the psalmist's cry to God out of the anguish of his soul.

[51] Baldwin, *Milton and the Psalms.*
[52] For a discussion of Milton's relation to earlier versions see Studley, *Milton and his Paraphrases of the Psalms.*

A single non-Scriptural translation appeared in the 1673 edition, the remarkably ingenious version of Horace's *Quis multa gracilis,* "rendered almost word for word without Rhyme according to the Latin Measure, as near as the Language will permit." [53] Other fragmentary bits (generally in blank verse) from classic and Italian authors are scattered through the prose.

[53] Commonly dated after 1645. Parker, *Some Problems,* p. 282, thinks that it belongs to Milton's earlier college years.

CHAPTER IV

PARADISE LOST

COMPOSITION AND PUBLICATION

STEPS IN THE DEVELOPMENT OF MILTON'S PLAN. The story of the evolution of *Paradise Lost* in Milton's mind is an intimate and vital part of his biography for a period of over a quarter of a century. The record of his preliminary meditation of the project is to be found chiefly in his published writings and in his preserved manuscript notes. This record, including his early deliberations as to a choice of subject, is here given chronologically and in considerable detail.

1628. *Vacation Exercise.* Milton expresses his ambition to employ the English language in some lofty subject comparable to the *Iliad* or the *Odyssey*. Addressing his mother tongue, now employed in the triviality of a mock oration, he voices his more serious poetic purposes (lines 23–52). There is no suggestion here of the theme of the fall of man, nor indeed of any specific subject. The lines are rather a survey of the whole scene and materials of epic poetry as his imagination conceived them. Though the coloring is Greek we have no difficulty in recognizing the Christian and Miltonic substance. Apollo sings "before the thundrous throne" as the angels in *Paradise Lost* hymn the praises of

177

the Almighty; the "deep transported mind" of the poet already wanders in anticipation "through upper and through middle air," and explores the mysteries of created nature. There is even a hint of the motive of rebellion. The atmosphere and broader scope of Milton's intention are already determined; regarding the specific theme and the person of an epic hero Milton has no very tangible ideas.

December, 1629. *Elegy VI.* Milton dedicates himself to the seriousness of epic as opposed to the lightness of elegiac poetry and prescribes for himself a way of life appropriate to such an ambition. For the later account in the *Apology for Smectymnuus* of the resolution thus taken on his twenty-first birthday and of the steps which led to it see Appendix B. The terms in which he describes his proposed subject matter carry us directly back to the *Vacation Exercise,* but they are considerably more specific, suggesting Virgil rather than Homer as a model. "But the poet who sings of heaven subject now to mature Jove, and of pious heroes and leaders half divine, who sings now of the sacred conferences of the high gods, now of the abysmal realm where barks a savage dog, that poet should live sparingly as did the Samian teacher and should find in herbs his simple food."

1637. *Lycidas.* The poet complains in the opening lines that the sad occasion of the death of Edward King has compelled him to write again before his time. The digressions on fame and on the corrupt clergy, and the closing line "To-morrow to fresh woods and pastures new" illustrate his discontent with his present themes, a restlessness parallel with that expressed in the *Vacation Exercise* eight years before. Milton had inherited from his predecessors, specifically Virgil and Spenser, the idea that the normal development of a great poet was from pastoral to epic. He makes capital of this conviction as applied to himself and dramatically hails the intrusions of the "epic strain" into his now outgrown Arcadianism: "Begin and somewhat loudly sweep the string"; "Return, Alpheus, that dread voice is past"; "that strain I heard was of a higher mood."

1639–40. *Mansus.* He announces the legendary history of Britain as his theme. "I will some day recall in song the things of my native land, and Arthur, who carried war even into fairyland. Or I shall tell of those great-hearted champions bound in the society of the Round Table, and (O may the Spirit be in me!) I shall break the Saxon phalanxes with British war." That his thoughts should take this direction is not surprising. The precedent of Virgil taught him to seek a national hero; Spenser and the Tudor revival of interest in British origins directed him to Arthur. Obviously, however, this theme provided no scope for the cosmic interests exhibited in the *Vacation Exercise.*

1640. *Epitaphium Damonis.* Milton implies that he has made a first attempt at the Arthurian Epic and describes his proposed subject more fully as embracing the history of the Britons from the landing of Brutus to the times of Arthur. This is the last we hear of such a poem as being actually in progress or even definitely projected. Milton gives as a reason for abandoning it his sense of the inadequacy of his style, hitherto used only to the simpler themes of pastoral, but other reasons are not far to seek. In the *History of Britain* he deals critically with the sources of historical knowledge about King Arthur, expresses the doubt "whether ever any such reigned in Britain," and speaks scornfully of those "who can accept legends for good story." In *Paradise Lost* (Book IX, lines 29 ff.) he seems to be congratulating himself on having declined to meddle with a kind of subject which requires the poet

> to dissect
> With long and tedious havoc fabl'd Knights
> In Battels feign'd.

His change from enthusiasm to distaste is remarkable but intelligible. It is to be associated with the general distrust of "antiquarianism" and the figments of monkish annalists expressed in the early ecclesiastical pamphlets in which Milton was soon to be engaged.[1] The historicity of the Arthurian legend had been challenged as early as Polydore Virgil. When James I revived the Tudor claim of descent from Arthur new forces of seventeenth century historical scholarship were brought to bear on the question. The controversy is rightly considered by Miss Brinkley a factor in determining Milton's change of attitude.[2]

1642. *Reason of Church Government*. Milton tells of the formation of his resolution to write a great English poem and makes an important statement regarding the function and purpose of poetry as he has proposed it for himself, showing, incidentally, that he is now undecided both as to the form and substance of his work. The passage is given in full in Appendix B. We may note that his tentative protagonist must be not only "one of our victorious kings" but "the pattern of a Christian hero." Arthur's unfitness for such a role must have been increasingly apparent as

[1] See Jones, *Milton and the Epic Subject*.
[2] See above, p. 116, note.

Milton's sympathies turned more strongly away from the traditions of Catholic and feudal Christianity. His feeling, also, that it is incumbent on him to vindicate literature against the disrepute into which it has fallen, leads him naturally back toward a specifically religious subject matter. He mentions Biblical along with classical models, and in the more general description of the poet's office which follows he gives emphasis to his obligation to sing directly of God's almightiness and of "what he works and what he suffers to be wrought with high Providence in his Church." All of this moves us on toward *Paradise Lost*.

1640–42. *The Cambridge Manuscript*. Shortly after his return from Italy, Milton set down a list of about a hundred possible literary subjects from Biblical and British history: some of them merely indicated, some already developed into tentative outlines.[3] All the plans are for dramas, but it is possible that there was a similar list of epic themes which

[3] The order of the materials in the Trinity MS. is as follows:

p. 35. The first three outlines of a drama on the Fall, with three additional titles under the head "other Tragedies." Among these are "Adam in Banishment" and "The Deluge."

p. 36. A brief outline for "The Deluge," numerous Biblical subjects from the Old Testament, a few of them with suggestions for treatment.

p. 37–38. Thirty-three British subjects from Holinshed, Malmesbury, Speed, etc.

p. 39. Well-developed outlines for "Abraham from Morea," "Baptistes," and "Sodom Burning."

p. 40. A continuation of "Sodom Burning" and the fourth outline for a drama on the Fall, under the heading "Adam Unparadiz'd," the titles of five New Testament subjects.

p. 41. Titles of "Scotch stories," with brief outlines of a "Phineas" and a "Christus Patiens."

Parker (*Milton's Plans for a Tragedy*) infers that Milton, after beginning with the *Paradise Lost* project, was temporarily dissatisfied has not been preserved.[4] The subject of the fall of man evidently now holds first place in his thoughts. His successive redraftings of the plan for a drama on this theme constitute the first definite step in the composition of *Paradise Lost*. Phillips reports that he actually wrote at this time a version of Satan's address to the sun (*Paradise Lost*, Book IV, lines 30–41) as the opening of such a drama. The four outlines in order of composition are as follows:

FIRST DRAFT (*canceled*) [5]	SECOND DRAFT (*canceled*) [5]
the Persons	*the Persons*
Michael	Moses
Heavenly Love	Wisdom, Justice, Mercy
Chorus of Angels	Heavenly Love
	The Evening Star Hesperus
	Chorus of Angels
Lucifer	Lucifer
Adam ⎱ with the serpent	Adam
Eve ⎰	Eve
Conscience	Conscience

with it and turned to canvass other possibilities. He thinks quite rightly that Milton's mind probably never reverted to most of these ideas. We may fairly suppose, however, that he was projecting more than one drama; the reform of the English stage being at this time uppermost in his thoughts. The Abraham, John the Baptist, and Sodom plays are almost as fully elaborated as the final draft of *Paradise Lost*. He seems even to have made an addition to the Sodom outline after completing "Adam Unparadiz'd." Though he keeps recurring to historical subjects he elaborates none of these as he does several from Scripture.

[4] Gilbert, *The Cambridge Manuscript*. The dramatic plans have been extensively studied by Schork.

[5] From the Facsimile of the Cambridge MS. edited by W. A. Wright.

Death	Labour ⎫
Labour	Sicknesse ⎪
Sicknesse ⎫	Discontent ⎬ Mutes
Discontent ⎪	Ignorance ⎪
Ignorance ⎬ Mutes	Feare ⎪
with others ⎭	Death ⎭

Faith	Faith
Hope	Hope
Charity	Charity

THIRD DRAFT

The Persons. Moses προλογίζει recounting how he as-
sum'd his true bodie, that it corrupts not because of his
[converse] with god in the mount declares the like of Enoch
and Eliah, besides the purity of the pl[ace] that certaine
pure winds, dues, and clouds praeserve it from corruption
whence [he ex]horts to the sight of god, tells they cannot
se Adam in the state of innocence by reason of thire sin.

Justice ⎫
Mercie ⎬ debating what should become of man if he fall
Wisdome⎭
Chorus of Angels sing a hymne of the creation.

Act 2
Heavenly Love
Evening starre
chorus sing the mariage song and describe Paradice.

Act 3
Lucifer contriving Adams ruine

Chorus feares for Adam and relates Lucifers rebellion and fall

Act 4

Adam }
Eve } fallen

Conscience cites them to Gods examination

Chorus bewails and tells the good Adam hath lost

Act 5

Adam and Eve, driven out of Paradice praesented by an angel with Labour griefe hatred Envie warre famine Pestilence

sicknesse
discontent } mutes to whom he gives thire names
Ignorance } likewise winter, heat Tempest etc.
Feare   } entered into the world
Death

Faith   }
Hope   } comfort him and instruct him
Charity }

Chorus breifly concludes

FOURTH DRAFT [6]

Adam Unparadised. [I] The Angel Gabriel, either descending or entering—showing, since this globe was created, his frequency as much on Earth as in Heaven—describes Paradise. Next the Chorus, showing the reason of

---

[6] Masson's modernized transcript, corrected by the MS. The act divisions, suggested by those in the third draft, have been supplied by the present writer.

his coming—to keep his watch in Paradise, after Lucifer's rebellion, by command from God—and withal expressing his desire to see and know more concerning this excellent and new creature, Man.—[II] The Angel Gabriel, as by his name signifying a Prince of Power, tracing Paradise with a more free office, passes by the station of the Chorus, and, desired by them, relates what he knew of Man, as the creation of Eve, with their love and marriage.—[III] After this, Lucifer appears, after his overthrow; bemoans himself; seeks revenge upon Man. The Chorus prepare resistance at his first approach. At last, after discourse of enmity on either side, he departs; whereat the Chorus sings of the battle and victory in Heaven against him and his accomplices, as before, after the first Act, was sung a hymn of the Creation.—[IV] Here again may appear Lucifer, relating and insulting in what he had done to the destruction of Man. Man next and Eve, having been by this time seduced by the Serpent, appears confusedly, covered with leaves. Conscience, in a shape, accuses him; Justice cites him to the place whither Jehovah called for him. In the meantime the Chorus entertains the stage and is informed by some Angel of the manner of the Fall. Here the Chorus bewails Adam's fall.—[V] Adam then and Eve return and accuse one another; but especially Adam lays the blame to his wife—is stubborn in his offence. Justice appears, reasons with him, convinces him. The Chorus admonisheth Adam, and bids him beware Lucifer's example of impenitence.—The Angel is sent to banish them out of Paradise; but, before, causes to pass before his eyes, in shapes, a masque of all the evils of this life and world. He is humbled, relents, despairs. At last appears Mercy, comforts him, promises him the Messiah; then calls in Faith, Hope, Charity; instructs him. He re-

original personification, and Adam pronounces the name of Death. The order of events in the epic is on the whole that of the fourth draft, but there are some interesting alterations. Thus, in the poem, freed from the necessity of preserving unity of place, Milton can begin with Satan on the burning lake and introduce the indispensable infernal council. The narrative of creation is likewise made to follow instead of to precede that of the war in heaven, a gain both in effectiveness and significance.

Circa 1642. Edward Phillips states that Milton showed him the opening verses of his tragedy.

1654. In the *Second Defense of the English People,* Milton makes a statement implying that he has in a sense fulfilled his expressed intention of celebrating the exploits of his own countrymen, not, indeed, the deeds of the early kings, but the more thrilling achievements wrought by Cromwell and the people of England in the Great Rebellion.

As the epic poet who adheres at all to the rules of that species of composition does not profess to describe the whole life of the hero whom he celebrates but only some particular action of his life, as the resentment of Achilles, at Troy, the return of Ulysses, or the coming of Aeneas into Italy ; so it will be sufficient, either for my justification or apology, that I have heroically celebrated at least one exploit of my countrymen ; I pass by the rest for who could recite the achievements of a whole people ?

This is to some degree a characteristic piece of Miltonic rationalization, for the immediate motivation of the defenses was something quite different, but the idea may well have served to free the poet's mind from a self-imposed obligation which might have interfered with his concentration of effort on the Biblical epic.[7]

REASONS FOR THE CHANGE FROM DRAMA TO EPIC. We do not know exactly either when or why Milton abandoned his idea of a drama on the Fall and determined to throw his materials into epic form. It is apparent from the fourth draft that Milton, when he came to visualize the drama more concretely, found himself obliged to sacrifice much of the material which belonged to the larger theme as he had first conceived it. He must have hesitated to treat the subject thus narrowly. Yet there is no reason to believe that this fact alone would have deterred him. Quiller-Couch [8] believes the closing of the theaters in 1642 to have determined his change of plan, arguing that he had intended his "Adam Unparadised" for actual performance as a revived mystery play in classical form. Milton's own earlier experience with the masque and the fact that religious allegory did not seem as remote from popular interest then as it does today are suggested by Quiller-Couch as reasons for thinking it probable that he "meant to achieve on the actual stage something of the sort that Handel afterwards achieved in opera" and that he was deterred by the edict from proceeding. There is evidence, however, that if Milton intended public performance for his work, he was looking for a kind of performance very different from any provided by the traditions, public or private, of the Jacobean stage. In the passage quoted on page 375. Milton urges the magistrates themselves to take over the problem of providing public

[7] See Grierson's discussion, *Milton and Wordsworth*, pp. 71 ff.
[8] *Milton*, pp. 134 ff.

sports and festival pastimes for the people and he invites them to consider whether even religious instruction may not be given, "not only in pulpits, but after another persuasive method, at set and solemn paneguries, in theaters, porches, or what other place or way may win most upon the people to receive at once both recreation and instruction."

These sentences do, indeed, throw light upon Milton's attitude and perhaps explain the trend of his thought toward drama after his return from Italy. But the official prohibiting of stage plays, a few months after the passage was penned, could hardly have seemed to him decisive against such ceremonies and exhibitions as he here described. One wonders, indeed, how much Milton would himself have been against the edict. The later restrictions imposed by the régime he certainly disliked, but in the passage cited he talks like a Puritan of the corruption which the youth of the nation sucks in "from the writings and interludes of libidinous poetasters," and he expressly disapproves of the pastimes which were "authorized a while since" as provocations of drunkenness and lust.

The real reason for his failure to continue either "Adam Unparadised" or any other purely artistic project during the Civil War is nobly given in his own words and there is little reason to seek another explanation. The accomplishment of such designs, he says, "lies in a power above man's to promise." He will pursue them "as far as life and free leisure will extend." But there is a prior duty, "to free the land from this impertinent yoke of prelaty, under whose inquisitorious duncery no free and splendid wit can flourish."

Milton thus foresaw in 1640 that he would, until its political issue was settled, make scanty progress with his masterpiece. He did not foresee how long drawn out the struggle would be or how deeply he himself would be involved. It seems likely that he paused from time to time in the intervals of controversy and official business to re-meditate the literary problem. His theme of the Fall of Man, already preferred before the others, would naturally have come to incorporate within itself more and more of the materials of Milton's experience and thought, and it must soon have become apparent to him that only the epic form could embrace his purposes in their full maturity. It is, therefore, in a very literal sense that we owe the epic of *Paradise Lost* to Milton's absorbing interest in the politics of his time and to his sense of civic obligation.

STAGES IN THE COMPOSITION OF THE POEM. The actual composition of the poem is generally believed to have begun in the period of leisure following the termination of Milton's literary war with Morus in 1655 or the appointment of Andrew Marvell as assistant Latin Secretary in 1657. Aubrey, on the oral authority of Edward Phillips, states that the poem was begun about two years before the king came in, i. e., about May, 1658. Phillips in his published life of Milton is less definite. It seems improbable that Milton had progressed far in the work before the stormy and dangerous moment of the Restoration intervened to again disturb him. Masson guesses that Books I and II might have been complete before this event and the poem resumed after Milton had been released from custody and become permanently domiciled in Jewin Street. He points with good reason to a passage in the invocation of Book VII:

On evil dayes though fall'n, and evil tongues;
In darkness, and with dangers compast round,

as clearly reflecting Milton's situation after the Restoration. Professor Tillyard emphasizes the relationship between the *Second Defense* and the earlier books of *Paradise Lost,* and argues for a renewal of poetic activity before 1654. The Hymn to Light at the beginning of Book III is, he says, a poetic version of part of the prose passage on Milton's blindness (quoted in Appendix B) and was probably composed about the same time. There is further an analogy between the "characters" of the Devils in Book II of the poem and those of Cromwell and his fellows in the *Defense.* It is entirely possible that Milton might have returned to these materials at a later time but Tillyard's general thesis that the first part of *Paradise Lost* is pervaded by the mood and spirit of Milton's greatest prose work has much to recommend it.

The poem is said by Aubrey to have been finished in 1663. It was certainly complete before the autumn of 1665, when Thomas Ellwood, according to a well-known anecdote recorded in his autobiography,[9] was handed the manuscript by Milton at Chalfont St. Giles. The minimum period probably covered by its composition was, therefore, some five years, with interruptions. For the recorded details of Milton's habits of dictation, etc., see above, pp. 57 ff.

PUBLICATION. *Paradise Lost* was published in 1667. The articles of agreement (now in the British Museum) between Milton and his printer, Samuel Simmons, are dated April 27;[10] the poem is entered in the Stationers' Register

[9] See above, pp. 56 ff.

[10] Text in Masson, Vol. VI, pp. 509–511. This contract is remarkable in the history of publishing for the protection it gives the author. Simmons agrees to print not more than 4,500 copies in three impressions of 1,500 copies each, to pay £5 down, a second £5 "at the end of the first impression," a third £5 "at the end of the second impression,"

August 20. The actual printing of the work presumably followed in the autumn. Between thirteen and fifteen hundred copies had been sold by April, 1669, when Milton received the second payment of five pounds due to him according to the agreement. Of this first impression only a part was actually put on sale in 1667. The printer issued subsequent installments from time to time with different title pages.[11] Accordingly, the preserved copies of the first edition bear varying dates—1667, 1668, and 1669. In some cases Milton's name is used; in at least one, simply his initials. For one of the 1668 issues Milton added the arguments to the various books, printed together at the beginning of the volume, and the prefatory note on the verse. There are minor variations in the text, especially toward the close of the poem, due to disturbance of the type during the process of printing. The bibliographical problems connected with the first edition are therefore very complicated and the data have never yet been fully assembled. See, however, Pollard, *The Bibliography of Milton*.

and a fourth £5 "at the end of the third impression." The impressions are accounted to "end" when 1,300 of the possible 1,500 copies are sold. The publisher presumably had the 200 additional copies to dispose of as he saw fit without further payment to Milton. According to the law of that period not more than 1,500 copies of any book could be printed without resetting. The contract calls for a sworn accounting of sales at demand before a Master in Chancery. No provision is made for further impressions or for a new edition. In 1680 Elizabeth Milton gave over all her rights in the copy of the second edition to Simmons for £8. What, if anything, Milton received in the first instance for the copy of the second edition is not known.

[11] Bibliographers give the number variously from six to twelve. It is easy enough to explain the use of title pages bearing new dates. But how account for the fact that there are apparently four different 1667 title pages? Masson's theory that the sale was slow will hardly do. Note that there could have been at most 200 copies available for distribution between 1669 and 1674.

The second edition appeared in 1674, the year of Milton's death. Besides making a few textual changes and distributing the arguments in their proper places throughout the poem, Milton now divided Books VII and X into two each, thereby making an epic of twelve books instead of the original ten.

The original manuscript of *Paradise Lost* is not preserved. There is, however, in the Morgan library in New York a fair copy of Book I. This transcript was formerly supposed to have been prepared not for the press but for inspection by the licenser,[12] whose "imprimatur" it bears, but the fact that it has come down to us through Jacob Tonson, who states in a preserved letter that he bought it along with the copyright of *Paradise Lost,* the presence in the margins of printer's symbols made in the process of laying off the copy for pagination, and other evidences demonstrate conclusively that the text of the 1667 edition was set from it. A comparison of the printed text with its original, besides throwing additional light on Milton's intentions regarding spelling (see Appendix E), makes possible the restoration of some authentic readings which have never yet been embodied in an edition of the poem.[13]

EXPOSITORY OUTLINE

BOOK I. Following the practice of Homer and Virgil, Milton begins with a statement of his theme (lines 1–5): the fall of man in Adam, who is at once the progenitor

[12] Thomas Tomkins, who was chaplain to Archbishop Sheldon in 1666–67. There is nothing in the MS. to confirm Richardson's story that he objected to the lines on the comet, Book I, lines 554–559.

[13] See Darbishire, *The Manuscript of Paradise Lost, Book I* and Hanford, *The Manuscript of Paradise Lost.*

and the representative of the race, the cause and type of human sin. Consideration of this subject carries the Christian inevitably on to the redemption, without which sin is unintelligible in a world governed by a wise and merciful Providence. Milton thus affirms (lines 24–25) that his purpose in the poem is to assert Providence as opposed to Fate and to "justify," i. e., to make apparent the justice of, God's dealings with men.

In the invocation to the Muse (lines 6–23) Milton follows a poetic tradition adopted from antiquity—not conventionally, but in such a way as to fill it with significance. The Heavenly Muse (i. e., Urania, originally the Muse of astronomy) is in reality that divine inspiration which revealed the truths of religion to Moses. It is also the spirit of God which dwells in the heart of every believer. Milton's invocations are, therefore, really Christian prayers.[14]

The studied and significant parallelism with ancient epic continues (lines 27–49) in the adoption of the formula "what cause?" and its answer, "the infernal serpent," the origin of whose malice, viz., pride and ungrateful rebel-

---

[14] Some commentators have identified Milton's Muse with the third person of the Trinity. (See Larson, *Milton and Servetus*, pp. 891–934 and Fletcher, *Milton's Semitic Studies*, pp. 115–125.) But Milton expressly states in *De Doctrina* that the Holy Ghost cannot be invoked. (See Kelley, *Milton and the Third Person of the Trinity*, pp. 221–234.) The poet naturally brought all manner of symbolism and association, Biblical, classic, neoplatonic, Rabbinical, into play in the invocations. Gilbert Murray (*The Classical Tradition in Poetry*, pp. 9 ff.) has shown how deeply colored his conception is with Paganism. But Milton was the very opposite of a polytheist, and he is careful to show that whatever he may call the power which speaks through him, the reality is always the same:

The meaning, not the Name I call.

If one must have a theological formula it is best to say with Kelley that Milton's prayers are addressed to God the Father, and not to the Holy Spirit in any technical sense.

lion, is here briefly alluded to, and the proper subject of the poem is begun at the logical point, the moment when Satan, recovering from the confusion of his grand defeat, raises his head from the burning lake.

Surveying with comprehensive sweep the fearful scene about him, he beholds Beëlzebub, called the Prince of Devils in Scripture. His address, couched in language of unrivaled grandeur, is expressive of the situation and of the human passions which dwell with superhuman intensity in his heart. At the root of his sense of the glory of the attempt, and of his determination to persist, is the fundamental perversion of his will. This, in turn, implies a perversion of the intellect, for his language shows that he has lost his original comprehension of God and has attributed to him motives and a being like his own. He falls into the heresy of the Manichees who held the angels to be coexistent with God, attributes his own creation to Fate, and proclaims his independent immortality. He thus manifests himself as the "father of lies," though at first our perception of his true nature is swallowed up in admiration of the heroic "virtue" which he brings with him as mark and seal of his divine origin.

Beëlzebub (lines 124–155), though he holds the same fatalistic creed as his lord, is inferior in his ability to face the situation. Satan meets his pessimism (lines 157–190) with a superb expression of resolute opposition to the will of God, and proposes the terms of the eternal warfare between good and evil (lines 162–168). His utterance reaches its highest pitch of glory when, standing at length on the burning shore, he welcomes the appalling region as his future home (lines 241–270), expressing the great principle of the supremacy of soul over its environment.

Milton's own passion for liberty is embodied in Satan's "Here at least we shall be free." In the following address to the host (lines 315 ff.) he assumes the rôle of an inspiring leader rousing his troops from lethargy by stinging words and filling them with his own great spirit.

Descriptions of the landscape of Hell and of the personal appearance of Satan and his lieutenants are interspersed artistically through the action. Thus we are given at first the general impression of the fiery gulf in which the devils lie confounded, and of the "darkness visible" of the infernal region (lines 50 ff.), then the more specific image of Satan, prone on the flood, with head uplifted, then further details progressively, as the leaders, followed by their legions, rise from the lake and take their places on the burning plain. Elaborate and suggestive similes, more abundant here than in any other portion of the poem, enrich the description at every point. The comparison drawn by Macaulay between the vast indefiniteness of Milton's pictures and the detailed realism of Dante's treatment of his corresponding material in the *Inferno* is fundamentally sound.

Having assembled the infernal host, Milton proceeds to an enumeration, following the precedent of Homer's catalogue of ships and heroes in the second book of the *Iliad*.[15] The names are drawn partly from Scripture, and

[15] McColley, "The Epic Catalogue in *Paradise Lost*," notes striking resemblances in Milton's list to the enumeration of pagan deities in Alexander Ross's *Pansebeia, A View of All Religions of the World*, 1653, showing that Milton recites the descriptions of Moloch, Chemos, Peor, Baalim and Astoroth in the reverse order in which they occur in Ross. The title of this work may also have suggested Milton's "Pandemonium." Selden's *De Diis Syriis* (1617) should also be consulted as a basic Miltonic source of knowledge supplementary to the Fathers and to Scripture. Whole chapters, freighted

have bulked large in Book I now give way to a primarily dramatic representation of the infernal council—a super-human parliamentary debate as majestic in eloquence as it is momentous in the consequences involved. Milton brings to bear upon the account a lifelong study of states-manship and oratory in ancient and modern books, sup-ported by the memory of his experience with the leaders of the Revolution. His council is a magnified image of those human deliberations on which the fates of nations hang. As often in the public affairs of men, the assembly is secretly dominated by a single master will. Individuals may voice their convictions and display their passions, each with a type of eloquence appropriate to his personal character and temper, but the ultimate policy is prede-termined. Satan, in opening the debate (lines 11 ff.), as-sumes that all are with him in the purpose of recovery and revenge. The choice which is offered is one of means —open war or covert guile. Moloch, with the character-istic impetuosity and bluntness of a mere soldier, advises an immediate attack (lines 51 ff.)—an unreasoning coun-sel of desperation delivered with a brevity and force which remind one of the oratory of Oliver Cromwell. Belial, the smooth-tongued trimmer, winding his way subtly into the argument, recommends a policy of peace to which his sloth-ful and luxurious temper predisposes him (lines 119 ff.). The two represent contrasting types of public leaders, the jingo with his instinctive advocacy of violence and the plausible but cowardly counselor of peace at any price. Mammon, the third speaker, builds upon the sentiments of Belial, which have commended themselves to the audi-ence, still smarting from their recent defeat, with a more constructive suggestion. Let them give up war and make the most of Hell, availing themselves of its resources, exploiting its hidden riches, acclimating themselves to an environment which can at least be made to satisfy the impulse to possess and to create (lines 229 ff.). Such advice, from him who afterward became the Pagan god of wealth, is greeted with a murmur of approval, and public opinion seems to be dangerously drifting in a direction contrary to the intention of Satan, when Beëlzebub, the type of subservient politician, as responsive to the purposes of his master as badness could desire, rises clad in the aspect of impressive statesmanship to stem the tide (lines 310 ff.). He introduces into the discussion a new fact, craftily held back till the progress of the debate demanded it—the existence of an undefended world peopled by creatures liable to attack—a matchless opportunity for the satisfaction of a revenge as fierce as Moloch's by means as safe as Belial's and with a possibility of profit more rich than that contemplated by Mammon. His proposal promptly voted, it remains for Satan to confirm his leadership by offering to undertake the hazardous task of carrying it out. He does so with grand heroic gesture, winning infinite renown in Hell (lines 390 ff.). The whole situation is thus moulded to his private benefit, and his personal enterprise made, under democratic sanction, to figure as a splendid act of public service. The fact implies a human lesson, teaching us, as Milton points out, to scan with suspicion the specious deeds of men—"Which glory excites, or close ambition varnished o'er with zeal."

After the assembly the devils, like the heroes of the *Aeneid,* engage in epic recreation, the lower sort in physical sports, the higher in song and poetry, the noblest of all in philosophical discourse (lines 506 ff.). Still others

undertake the geographical exploration of their new abode.
As always, their doings are patterns and types of the varied
activities of men. They initiate the chief subjects of speculation and anticipate the main trends of all secular philosophy. As angels, their intellectual flights surpass the human;
as fallen souls, they have lost the key to truth and "find no
end, in wandering mazes lost."

The narrative now turns to Satan and describes his encounter with Sin, his daughter and paramour in Heaven,
and with Death their son. Loathsome as the episode is, it
yet has its significant place in the economy of the poem,
as bringing to our attention the real ugliness of evil which
has hitherto been masked in the dazzling brightness of its
author. It is Sin, who, following her nature, disobeys the
injunction of God by opening the gates of Hell.

The journey of Satan through Chaos (lines 891 ff.), the
description of the realm of the uncreated and of the old
Anarch who personifies its blind confusion, the final contrast, as the battered voyager swims into the calm and light
which radiate from ordered nature, are among the greatest
triumphs of Milton's imagination.

Book III. The change of scene to Heaven is introduced
by a new invocation (lines 1–55)—a prayer to God under
the image of light. The passage embodies the first of the
great personal utterances which recur at intervals throughout *Paradise Lost* and constitute a lyric thread interweaving
itself with the objective narrative. The pathos of blindness,
the consoling love of beauty, the thirst for fame, the consciousness of precious inward vision vouchsafed in compensation for the deprivation of outward light are expressed
with consummate eloquence.

The celestial dialogue which follows (lines 56 ff.) is an

exposition, dignified but cold, of the theological scheme. With such purely didactic material Milton, as a poet, can do little. His visual imagination is in abeyance, and his verse for the first time loses its compelling power. The intense spirituality, moreover, which pervades Dante's thorniest statements of pure doctrine in the *Paradiso,* is entirely lacking in him. He knows, in fact, only a moral Paradise, and is a stranger to the ecstasies of a mystical Heaven. There is, however, a momentary exaltation as Christ prophesies his triumph over Death, and when Milton turns from the pronouncement of the divine decrees to phrase the angelic song of worship (lines 372 ff.), he rises again to his accustomed heights. Attention should be called to the conscious parallel between Christ's proposed sacrifice for man's salvation (lines 217 ff.) and the earlier offer of Satan to undertake his ruin. The silence of Heaven before the invitation to assume man's sin corresponds to the hesitation of the fallen spirits when the project of assaulting the new world is proposed. The pronouncement that in Christ "love hath abounded more than glory abounds" points the contrast with Satan's masked motive of ambitious pride.

Milton's more mundane and romantic imagination, revealing itself in a new abundance of poetic similes, returns to him with Satan alighting on the convex of the world and beholding for the first time the beauties of the earthly garden (lines 416 ff.). The spirit of controversial satire intrudes in the anti-catholic description of the Paradise of Fools (lines 440 ff.), and there is an undue burden of astronomical and alchemical learning in the concluding account of the encounter of Satan with the archangel of the sun (lines 654 ff.). On the whole, Book III represents a pause in the onward sweep of Milton's genius, a space devoted to the transaction of business, unpoetic, but necessary to the larger didactic and philosophic purposes of the epic.

Book IV. The opening scene, with Satan standing torn by inward passion on the top of Mt. Niphates, brings us again into the realm of drama. The remorseful soliloquy which follows (lines 32 ff.) represents a reaction from the outward confidence which Satan has assumed before his host, a revelation of the Hell within the soul. He now experiences the bitterer aspect of the truth of his own principle that "the mind is its own place." The conclusion is a new resolve to accept evil for his good. The disfiguring of his countenance, which results from his inward struggle and causes the angel to recognize him as one of the fallen spirits, is a step in the progressive change of his appearance, carefully marked by Milton as evidence of the manner in which the soul transforms the body for better or for worse to its own essence (see *Comus*, lines 453–475).

In his description of the Garden of Eden (lines 210 ff.), Milton luxuriates in detail and brings to bear a wealth of comparison from his classical and romantic reading. The picture of our first parents in their naked majesty and beauty, surrounded by the abundant delights of Paradise, is in accordance with the ornate traditions of Renaissance literature and art. An instinctive emotion of admiration and pity, the momentary assertion of his angelic nature, wells up in Satan, immediately to be checked by the recollection of his cruel purpose (lines 357 ff.). It is thus that he stultifies his better impulses and prepares himself to do what else, though damned, he would abhor.

The first word which we hear Adam speak (lines 411 ff.) is appropriately one of gratitude, the next is to recall the prohibition, the pledge of their obedience and the symbol of their moral natures. Eve, in an exquisite narrative (lines 440 ff.) of her first experiences, reveals the sweet simplicity and frankness of her soul in innocence and the intensity of her love. This is the first of the epic relations which round out that part of the story not covered in the action proper. It also serves to suggest, in the incident of her contemplating her own beauty in the mirror of the pool, Eve's weakness. Satan now speaks again (lines 505 ff.), but his dominant impulse is no longer pity but the more ignoble one of envy. He anticipates the arguments of scepticism regarding the command which he is later to use to Eve and she in turn to communicate to Adam. The warning by Uriel of the angelic guard is followed by a symphony of night and married love as Adam and Eve retire to their nuptial bower (lines 610 ff.). It is in accord both with tradition and with the special purpose of motivating the subsequent action of the poem that the pair is represented primarily in the rôle of lovers. Milton takes the occasion (lines 741 ff.) to exalt the ideal domestic relationship of man and woman in both its physical and its spiritual aspects, and to denounce the false conception of chivalric love, which his observation has taught him to be too often the mask of corruption. True love exists only in marriage and it is founded not in an unsound exaltation of woman, but in mutual esteem, with rational recognition of the superior dignity and authority of man. The hard saying "he for God only, she for God in him" implies a natural hierarchy of existence on earth, corresponding to that which Satan has attempted to break down in Heaven. But Eve, like the angels, while looking to her lord for interpretation of God's will and her own and all functions analogous to his, though more refined. Milton is expressing in this curious passage, so absurd to the modern reader, two profound anti-medieval convictions which constitute the basis of his thought: the metaphysical idea that matter is real and that there is no sharp distinction between spirit and matter, the one passing insensibly into the other; and the ethical inference that the natural functions of the body are not something shameful and unworthy. The angel passes on to a new affirmation of the freedom of the will (lines 519 ff.), and then to his long narrative of the revolt and fall of Lucifer (lines 563 ff.). This discourse, which corresponds in the epic structure to the relation of Odysseus to the king of the Phæacians and of Aeneas to Dido, besides completing the story, serves to put Adam in possession of all the information necessary for victory in his coming trial. Knowledge, to Milton, is the best weapon against sin. The philosophic assumption which underlies the narrative and indeed Milton's whole conception of his poem, is given in lines 563–77. Spiritual facts can only so be represented to human sense, but there is also perhaps a real analogy between earth and Heaven, the former being, according to the Platonic doctrine of ideas, an imperfect replica of the latter, and this analogy justifies the phrasing of divine events in material terms. The incident of Abdiel (lines 800 ff.), concluded in the next book, reveals Milton's lofty conception of the moral courage which enables the individual to stand alone in his convictions against the world.

BOOK VI. The second day's battle contains the much maligned episode of the invention and first use of artillery, which should be considered not as an isolated piece of sensationalism but as a necessary completion of the idea of the book. The technical evolutions which attend the firing of the cannon are drawn from military textbooks which Milton had attentively studied and serve to give a representative and contemporary aspect to the whole.[17] Finally (lines 628 ff.), Milton converts the conflict into a primitive battle of the Titans, as the armies desert their discipline and, abandoning civilized arms, hurl confusedly at each other whatever crude missiles come to hand. He intends to suggest that the last end of war is like its beginning—bestial, anarchic, inconclusive. The utmost refinements of scientific slaughter are but a mask of chaos and can only end in a disruption of the orderly civilization of which they are the product. The significance of the account is definitely indicated at the close of the book (lines 680 ff.), when the Almighty, beholding the confusion, declares that

> Warr wearied hath perform'd what Warr can do,
> And to disorder'd rage let loose the reines,
> With Mountains as with Weapons arm'd, which makes
> Wild work in Heav'n, and dangerous to the maine,

and sends forth the Son in majesty to put an end at once to evil and to strife. In view of the poet's controlling purpose our sense of the artistic improprieties of his narrative and of the inferiority in human interest of a struggle in which, however mighty the clash of fearful opposites, nobody can be killed and the outcome is predetermined, tends to disappear. Johnson's verdict that the "confusion of spirit and matter which pervades the whole narrative of the war in Heaven fills it with incongruity" is true, but this result is in accord with Milton's funda-

---

[17] Hanford, *Milton and the Art of War.*

mental postulates regarding the parallel of things in Heaven and things on earth, and, besides, there was nothing else to do.

BOOK VII. A new invocation (lines 1–39), with personal allusions to the poet's isolation in the alien and hostile society of the Restoration, introduces an account of the creation, a theme which Milton pursues with eagerness after the general precedent of such independent Biblical poems as Du Bartas' *La Semaine* and Tasso's *Il Mondo Creato*.[18] Adam frames a modest request for the story (lines 70 ff.), and the angel, in granting it, suggests the true object of such knowledge, "to glorify the Maker and infer thee also happier," forewarning him against vain exploration of the secret things of God. It was in such a spirit that Milton himself taught in his school the natural science of his day. The ornate and majestic paraphrase of Genesis which follows, is indeed a pæan of created nature praising its great author. The phrases of the Scriptural original are preserved intact but a wealth of detail is added. The poet enumerates the tribes of fishes, birds, and animals with an appropriate sense of their marvelous variety. The creation of man himself is more briefly handled. When the six days' labor is completed the angels sing a psalm of gratitude. Nor are they silent through the long Sabbath day of rest. The purport of their song (lines 602 ff.) suggests the significance of this book, coming, as it does, after the narrative

[18] For a discussion of the complex origins of Milton's account of the creation see below, pp. 241 ff. It is easy for research to exhaust itself upon this subject. The possibilities of Medieval and Renaissance Art (including book illustrations) as sources of Milton's imagery have been barely touched on. See Whiting, *The Golden Compasses in "Paradise Lost."*

of celestial war, in Milton's larger thought. The active formation of good follows the destruction of evil in the natural order of the universe. God is even greater in his return from this victory over inchoate matter than he was in his triumph after the defeat of the giant angels. "To create is greater than created to destroy." This idea of the superiority of the works of peace is one of Milton's noblest convictions. It lies at the heart not only of this portion of *Paradise Lost,* but of the sonnets to Cromwell and Fairfax, and it determined in no small degree the character of his own zealous activity in the Commonwealth.

BOOK VIII. Instructed regarding the origin of evil, warned by an example of the consequences of disobedience, and taught to contemplate the wonders of created nature, Adam now receives further lessons on no less vital points. His questions concerning the construction of the universe (lines 15 ff.), unlike his inquiries hitherto, trespass dangerously near the boundary which divides legitimate curiosity from the spirit of prying into matters which are no concern of man. The angel perhaps detects in Adam's suggestion of a disproportion in God's creation a tendency to pick flaws in, rather than to admire, the scheme of things. He throws out a hint of the Copernican system in partial solution of these human doubts (lines 122 ff.), but quickly turns to draw the lesson: "Solicit not thy thoughts with matters hid. . . . Be lowly wise. Think only what concerns thee and thy being."

Adam is thus warned against the folly and even the danger of random speculation and taught to focus his attention on such studies as have a direct bearing on the practical art of righteous living. We have here an abiding principle of Milton's as well as an *ad hoc* suggestion which looks forward to the motives of the Fall. Had not Eve at the beginning of this discussion retired to tend her flowers she might have received a wholesome antidote against the curious and vain desire to become as God, knowing both good and evil, which afterward proved her ruin.

Adam's narrative (lines 249 ff.), corresponding to Eve's in Book IV, is exquisite in itself and full of profound significance. The quick instinctive motion of his upward spring is the symbol of his aspiration heavenward. His first moment of consciousness is one of physical self-survey. Then he turns to inquire his origin, arriving by natural reason at the idea of a divine author with attributes of goodness and of power. Having gone thus far on his search unaided he is vouchsafed a revelation, and awakening from his trance he receives the prohibition (lines 311 ff.)—a kind of categorical imperative which confirms him as a religious and a moral being.

His next instinct (lines 357 ff.) is for some human companionship. By whimsically pretending to argue him out of it, the Deity brings home the lesson that he is a man and not a brute. He then receives God's last best gift, accepted with an outburst of passionate gratitude and a superb flash of insight into the true relations of man and woman (lines 491–499). The recalling of this episode leads Adam to confess his weakness, the one flaw in his bright armor of strength and reason. He suggests that his creation after all is not quite perfect, since it has left him undefended against the charm of beauty's powerful glance. The angel, quick to scent a dangerous philosophy, asserts the supremacy of the will, and warns Adam that he must at all costs maintain self-mastery in passion (lines 561 ff.). Then, falling again into his more genial mood, he tells (lines 618 ff.) how angels love—a strange and wonderful exposition similar in philosophic purport to the account of the relations of human and angelic activities in matters of digestion in Book V.

BOOK IX. The moment of a great change in the tone of the narrative is marked by a meditative introduction (lines 1–47) in which the poet surveys his theme, and acclaims it, in its spiritual character, not less but more heroic than those of the great epics of antiquity which dealt with wars and outward struggle. Milton has evidently seriously considered the question whether his subject, with its novelty of an unhappy outcome, can properly be brought into conformity with the established epic type. He has also weighed the other assumptions against him—his four and forty degrees of northern latitude—the common notion that genius no longer flourishes in a senile world—his own advancing age. Confident, however, of the wisdom of his choice and referring all to the aid of his celestial patroness, he pushes bravely on.

The imaginative sweep which comes and goes with Satan prevails again in the description of his sevenfold encircling of the world (lines 62 ff.). There is more bitterness and more despair in the soliloquy which precedes his imbruting himself within the serpent and it is his own word which expounds the symbolism of the act.

The coming of morning brings a new dialogue between Adam and Eve (lines 192 ff.). The latter, with an impulse housewifely but unfortunate, proposes a brief separation that they may work at their gardening without the interruptions of affectionate discourse. Adam, in his superior wisdom, deprecates such hyper-conscientiousness and warns her of the danger she runs in exposing herself unprotected to the assault of the tempter. Such an apparent slighting of her firmness hurts Eve's feelings and brings the first small cloud upon the domestic horizon. It is not quite clear whether the poet intended Adam's attitude throughout this dialogue to be regarded as irreproachable and Eve's alone the cause of trouble. One fears he did; yet, judged by Milton's general philosophy, Eve has much the best of the argument. She criticizes, as he himself would have done, the naïve idea that the mere temptation leaves a stain of dishonor on the soul, and she employs the very language of *Areopagitica* in her denunciation of a fugitive and cloistered virtue unexercised and unbreathed (lines 322–341). The trouble is that her confidence is unjustified by the event and the whole discussion may perhaps be taken as a supplement rather than a contradiction to the doctrines of Milton's prose pamphlet, a warning that the philosophy of freedom does not apply to the immature and weak. Adam himself, in his refusal to coerce her will (lines 341 ff.), acts in the spirit of Milton's statement in *Areopagitica* that children and childish men may be exhorted to abstain from the possibility of evil influence but hindered forcibly they cannot be.

The parting of Adam and his spouse is full of tender loveliness, and classical mythology is ransacked for images wherewith to express Eve's beauty. Satan, watching her, is like an Iago plotting the ruin of Desdemona or even more exactly like another Lovelace preparing for what is to all intents and purposes a seduction. His crafty approach through the insidious means of flattery is subtly conceived (lines 494 ff.). Eve is deluded in her weakness, but once confronted by the tree of prohibition she recognizes clearly the guilt involved. This is Milton's modifica-

In Milton's treatment of this, the central incident of his poem, there are, besides its dramatic vividness and keen psychology, many essential points of moral and theological doctrine. He explains in the *De Doctrina Christiana* that the fall of our first parents, properly considered, was a transgression of the whole law, all sins being included in the act—unbelief, ingratitude, disobedience, gluttony; in the man, excessive uxoriousness; in the woman, a want of proper regard for her husband, parricide, theft, invasion of the rights of others, sacrilege, deceit, fraud in the means employed to attain the object, pride, and arrogance. The eating of the apple, therefore, becomes a type or even a symbol of sin rather than a particular offense. In making Eve fall through vanity and curiosity for new experience, Adam through blind passion, Milton points to what he believes the characteristic weaknesses respectively of man and woman. Adam's act was to Milton in no sense noble or heroic. It was, indeed, less pardonable than Eve's in proportion to his superior intelligence and moral strength. There is no gainsaying the fact, however, that the poet bears a grudge against woman as the perverse occasion of man's entanglement. The book, as a whole, displays new ranges of Milton's genius—a unique power of analysis of the ways of evil in the soul. Its greatness is not inferior to that of the more celebrated picture of Satan in Books I and II.

Book X. The account of the judgment (lines 104 ff.) proceeds in strict accord with the Scriptural narrative in Genesis iii, no detail being omitted. The allegory of Sin and Death is completed as the hideous pair ascend to earth and prepare to set their seal of mastery upon created nature (lines 229 ff.). Satan returns to proclaim the triumph of his epic adventure (lines 410 ff.)—a triumph which is turned to bitterness by the metamorphosis of the demons into serpents and of their shout of applause into a hiss, the sign of scorn. This degradation of their forms is the consequence and outward symbol of the degradation of their souls. A similar though less complete alteration, carried out by angels in obedience to divine command, takes place in the realm of physical nature, now no longer pure (lines 641 ff.). The passage illustrates the habit of mingling science and theology which Milton inherited from medieval thought.

A more human note is struck in the Job-like lament of Adam (lines 720 ff.), reminiscent also of the baffled speculations of Hamlet on life and death. A fine contrast not altogether favorable to the man is drawn between the remorse of Adam and Eve. She is more concerned with his state than with her own. He exhibits the brutality of disillusionment and resorts to Euripides and Ariosto [19] for bitter reflections on the curse of the eternal feminine, but is ultimately won by the helpless pathos of her appeal. She exhibits a fertile but unsound ingenuity in her suggestion of a way by which to avoid the doom pronounced upon their offspring with an implication of stoic fortitude which wins Adam's admiration (lines 966 ff.). His own courage returns in the attempt to comfort her, and the book ends, in contrast to Book IX, with a cessation of mutual blame and an access of sincere repentance.

BOOK XI. Further celestial dialogue (lines 1–125) prepares for the decree of banishment, to be pronounced, with an accompanying remission of the penalty of imme-

---

[19] *Hippolytus,* Way's translation, 616 ff.; *Orlando Furioso,* Canto XXVII, stanzas 117, 119, 120.

diate death, by Michael, the minister of God's justice.

Adam has a presentiment of some further change by the mute signs of nature (lines 193 ff.). Eve, with pathetic irony, is made to express her willingness to submit to any fate in this beloved home of Paradise. At the news that they must leave forthwith, Adam is struck dumb, and it is Eve who utters the first spontaneous lament (lines 268 ff.). Her strong instinctive love of the flowers that she has tended, of the nuptial bower that she has adorned, is rudely violated. The angel gently reminds her that her going is not lonely. Then Adam expresses his profounder fear of a break in his communion with the Divine (lines 293 ff.). To reassure him of the continued presence of God with him and his offspring and to discipline his soul in patience, Michael leads him to a lofty hill and begins a visionary revelation of the future of the race. This prophecy (lines 432 ff.), which corresponds to the Sibyl's predictions in the sixth book of the *Aeneid* of the course of Roman history, serves to round out the larger meaning of Milton's epic by displaying the operation of hereditary sin consequent upon Adam's act, and at the same time illustrates the manner in which God's love contends with the waywardness of man, until, in the process of time, his crowning purpose, of humanity's salvation through the sacrifice of Christ, is fulfilled. The passage, which extends through the remainder of Book XI and the greater part of Book XII, is a marvelous condensation of Hebrew story, comprising grave moral lessons. The first part of the exposition appropriately ends with the Flood and the apparition of the rainbow as the first prefiguring symbol of God's restoring and redeeming grace.

Book XII. From this point, the beginning of revelation

of a second world, with its higher and more mysterious matter, the angel no longer presents the scenes to Adam's eyes but narrates them to his intelligence. As the events in the history of the chosen people shape themselves Adam sees more and more clearly the operation of a providential plan. Moses and Joshua are indicated to him as types of Christ (lines 238–248; 311–313). The corruption and dissension which follow the return from captivity with the resultant passing of David's scepter to a stranger are said to be permitted that "the Anointed King Messiah might be born Barred of his Right" (lines 359–360). At the angel's mention of the virgin birth of Christ the meaning of the mysterious words of the Deity is revealed and Adam bursts forth in joy (lines 371 ff.).

The fuller story of Christ's sacrifice (lines 386 ff.), his resurrection, his triumph over Satan, his restoration of mankind to bliss leaves the listener in doubt whether he should repent him of his sin,[20] or rejoice

Much more, that much more good thereof shall spring.

[20] An interesting controversy was started by Erskine's suggestion (*The Theme of Death in "Paradise Lost"*) that Milton changed his theological attitude toward the Fall and its results before he reached the conclusion of his poem. That his conception of it as a mingled tragedy and blessing is in perfect accord with Christian tradition was shown by Moore, *The Conclusion of "Paradise Lost."* See also Stoll, *Was Paradise Well Lost?* Lovejoy, *Milton and the Paradox of the Fortunate Fall,* cites Du Bartas, Giles Fletcher, Andreini, patristic writers, and finally a passage in the Roman liturgy for Easter as instances of the recurrent motive, "O felix culpa!" St. Augustine gives the paradox a more general form, raising the question whether evil itself may not be a source of good and the Fall therefore a part of God's purpose. The only solution of the intellectual difficulty was, says Lovejoy, to keep the theme of the Fall as a supreme misfortune separate from the theme of its happy consequences through the sacrifice of Christ.

He acknowledges the lesson that man, too, has his part in the Redemption and expresses his resolve to walk henceforth the patient moral way of obedience and slow self-conquest. In thrilling words (lines 574 ff.) the angel sets the seal of approval on Adam's new-found wisdom, bidding him add deeds to his knowledge answerable—faith, virtue, patience, temperance, and love, the soul of all the rest. So shall he build a Paradise within, far happier than the one that he has lost. This is the grand climax of the poem, the spiritual goal of Milton's art. In a brief and beautiful conclusion (lines 606 ff.) we are brought back again to the specific subject of the loss of Eden. Eve awakes from a gentle dream in which she has received the essential revelation of the great deliverance through her seed. Softened and exalted she faces a future now no longer terrible. The closing lines describe in terms of mingled hope and sadness the departure of the pair from Eden.

COSMOLOGY AND DOCTRINAL CONTENT

The physical action of *Paradise Lost,* taking place as it does in Heaven, Earth, and Hell, obliges Milton to visualize the structure of the universe and to commit himself for imaginative purposes to one of the several astronomical systems which in his day offered themselves as rival explanations of the phenomena. He inevitably adopted the Ptolemaic, as it was interpreted in his day, with the Earth fixed at the center and the heavenly bodies revolving about it, as being firmly established in poetic and theological tradition and as better adapted to imaginative representation. With the mathematical detail of this system he was thoroughly familiar, and we know that he taught the elements of astronomical calculation on the Ptolemaic basis in his school, using a revised edition of the medieval textbook by Sacrobosco.[21] But he was familiar also with the principles of the Copernican astronomy, and with the discoveries which had followed the invention of the telescope.

As a Platonist, a student of mathematics, and a friend of Galileo's, he could not escape being interested in these exciting issues. The astronomical dialogue in Book VIII not only raises the fundamental question of the celestial motions but also suggests the related hypothesis of a plurality of worlds.

> For such vast room in Nature unpossest
> By living Soule . . . is obvious to dispute.

The problem of Milton's own attitude and of the sources and extent of his knowledge has been much discussed. The arguments he uses are seventeenth century commonplaces, many of them being found in Galileo's *Dialogus,* which one would think Milton likely to have read. But a strong case has recently been made by Grant McColley for his direct indebtedness to three English pamphlets of his own time, Bishop Wilkins's *The Discovery of a New World* and *A Discourse That the Earth May Be a Planet* published together in 1640, and Alexander Rosse's *The New Planet No Planet,* 1646. Wilkins states the new ideas in language strikingly similar to Milton's own. Rosse, in his refutation, apparently suggested some of the material employed by the angel to show Adam the futility of all astronomical hypotheses. The purpose of the dialogue, according to McColley, is simply to present the moot points advanced

[21] Gilbert, *Milton's Textbook of Astronomy.*

by Wilkins as England's most vigorous exponent of the "new philosophy" and to evaluate cosmological speculation in general, rather than in any real sense to weigh the rival theories.[22] There is a certain legacy from Bacon in Milton's insistence on the fruitlessness of mere speculation, while the idea that unrestrained curiosity in God's secrets may be a dangerous symptom of irreverence and pride, is a traditional one which the poet was bound to make use of in a story of the fall of man.

The greatest effect of Milton's contact with the new astronomy was the immense stimulus which it gave to his imagination. Professor Nicolson [23] believes that it was not books but the actual experience of celestial observation which significantly colored his scientific interests and enabled him to move in worlds of space hitherto unrealized. Telescopes were common in Milton's time both in Italy and in England. Milton's references to the Italian "optic glass" and the wonders revealed by it have an unmistakable first-hand character.[24] The poet mentions the four outstanding discoveries of Galileo: sun spots,[25] the true nature of the

---

[22] See McColley, *Milton's Dialogue on Astronomy: The Principal Immediate Sources.* In an earlier study, *The Astronomy of Paradise Lost,* McColley maintains that Milton's interests in astronomy are non-technical and somewhat antiquated. The Copernican idea of the triple motion of the earth, which he shared with Du Bartas, was a discarded one. He says nothing about the Tychonic theory, which rivaled the Copernican in importance among scientists. Svendsen, *Milton and the Encyclopedias of Science,* and *Cosmological Lore in Milton,* emphasizes the medieval quality of much of Milton's knowledge.

[23] *Milton and the Telescope.* Stoll, *Criticisms Criticized: Spenser and Milton,* attacks Miss Nicolson's insistence on experience.

[24] *Paradise Lost,* I, 287–91; III, 588–90; V, 261–63; *Paradise Regained,* IV, 40–42, 56–57.

[25] *Paradise Lost,* III, 588–91.

Milky Way,[26] the topographical features of the moon,[27] and, most important of all, the planets or moons of Jupiter.[28] "The sense of cosmic perspective," says Miss Nicolson, "is as characteristic of Milton as is the so-called Miltonic style—for which, indeed, it is in part responsible," and it is characteristic also of his generation. "Shakespeare lived in a world of time, Milton in a universe of space." Space dominates *Paradise Lost*. "We begin to perceive it first through the eyes of Satan as, astounded and momentarily appalled, he gazes into the chaos which opens beyond the gates of Hell. . . . We see it through the eyes of God as he 'bent down his eye His own works and their works at once to view,' and saw in one glance the sanctities of Heaven close to him, the 'Happy Garden' upon the earth, 'Hell and the gulph between. . . .' We realize it again in the further voyages of Satan—voyages, one may suspect, which were inherited from and were to influence that group of 'voyages to the moon' in which the seventeenth century delighted." It is easy to follow Miss Nicolson in her belief that all this owes much to the sudden enlargement of the range of human vision which was the experience of the seventeenth century through the invention of the telescope, and that the imaginative interest in the universe, so characteristic of Milton's later as distinguished from his earlier work, is a heritage of the new astronomy to which he refused to commit himself as a scientific hypothesis and which he rejected as the cosmological basis for his poem. We must not, however, forget that Dante was

[26] *Paradise Lost*, V, 577–81.
[27] *Ibid.*, I, 290–91.
[28] *Ibid.*, VIII, 148–51.

able to invest his medieval universe with an equal grandeur.

For the material data which Milton found necessary to his representation of Heaven, Earth, and Hell he resorted to all manner of sources and to his own invention, employing Scriptural suggestions wherever possible and taking pains to add nothing which would be directly contradictory to Holy Writ. It is not to be thought that he offered such details as the causeway from Hell to Earth, the chain by which the visible universe depended from Heaven, or the spheres themselves which encircled the Earth and carried the planets and the fixed stars, as obligatory to the understanding. They were simply imaginative representations which have a theological rather than a scientific validity. Sometimes he is deliberately vague, as when he says that Heaven is "undetermined square or round." Often his concrete detail or measurement is useful only for the moment and defies adoption into the general scheme, as where he says that the distance from Hell to Heaven was three times the distance from the center of the Earth to the pole of the uttermost encircling sphere (*P. L.* Book I, lines 73, 74).

For these reasons, it is misleading to make a detailed plan of Milton's universe, though many have been offered. The diagram given on page 223 represents only his fundamental conceptions, which are as follows:

Infinite space is thought of as originally divided into two parts,—Heaven above, also called the Empyraean; and Chaos or uncreated matter beneath. Within this Chaos God "puts forth his virtue" and builds, first Hell at the bottom, as a receptacle for the falling angels, and then the visible universe, usually referred to as "the World," as a home for man. The latter consists of the fixed Earth as a center, with a shell of concentric spheres moving about it at varying rates of speed. Beyond this shell, of course, is Chaos. The spheres themselves are ten in number. The first seven, beginning with the one nearest the Earth, carry the planets (including the Sun and the Moon) in the following order: the Moon, Mercury, Venus, the Sun, Mars, Jupiter, and Saturn, and are named from them. The eighth, properly designated the Coelum Stellatum, carries all the fixed stars. The ninth, the Crystalline, contains no bodies. Milton thinks of it as composed of water. The tenth is the Primum Mobile, or, in Milton's expression, "the first moved." Its function is to impart motion to the rest. Milton appears to have thought of the whole apparatus as encased in a hard, opaque, protective shell which was immovable.[29] He uses the term "firmament" for the whole space of "elemental air" between Earth and the watery Crystalline Heaven. It would comprise all the first eight spheres, which are evidently not spheres in any material sense.

Milton's system, as thus outlined, is, in general, parallel to that of Dante, but there are some notable points of divergence. In the first place, Dante locates Hell in the center of the Earth itself. Milton, in adopting the other alternative provided by theological tradition, remarks (Argument to Book I) that Hell is "described here not in the center (for Heaven and Earth may be supposed as not yet made, certainly not yet accursed), but in a place of utter darkness, fitliest called Chaos." He defends this location also on the same grounds, and with reference to the

[29] See Gilbert, *The Outside Shell of Milton's World.*

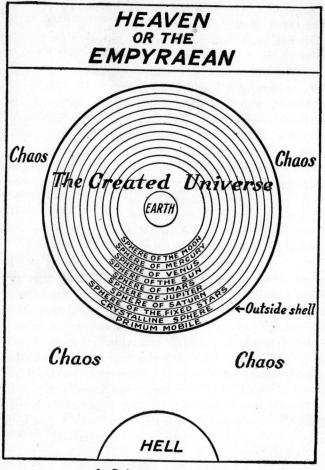

A Diagram of
Milton's Universe

opinion of Chrysostom and Luther, in the *De Doctrina Christiana,* Book I, chapter 33. In *Paradise Lost* (Book XII, line 224), however, he refers casually to a bituminous pit in Babylonia as "the mouth of Hell." Dante, secondly, makes only nine spheres, omitting the Crystalline, or identifying it with the Primum Mobile. These are, moreover, with him actual heavens in which the spirits of the blessed appear. His tenth Heaven or Heaven of Heavens is the infinite space beyond. In technical astronomical discussions the spheres ranged in number from nine to eleven. Milton, of course, omits all reference to Purgatory, with Dante a mountain on the Earth opposite to Jerusalem, and he places Paradise, which Dante locates on the top of the Purgatorial mountain, on the Tigris River in Mesopotamia. At the time of the Flood it was washed away and became a desert island in the Red Sea.

An immense amount of cosmological and other lore is given, first and last, in *Paradise Lost*. The poem is, indeed, in one aspect, a kind of cyclopedia of the popular science of Milton's time. The remarkable thing about Milton's comprehensive grasp of human knowledge is the way in which he unifies the whole and subjects it to the service of his philosophy of life. His closest precedent in this respect is Dante, and the general attitude which makes science a part of theology in the broadest sense is medieval.

The following references (the list might easily be extended) will serve as a guide to Milton's conceptions with regard to the physical construction of the universe:

Hell, II, 570–628.

Chaos, II, 890–967.

The created universe, II, 1034–1053; III, 418–735; V, 171–208; VII, 205–547.

Heaven, III, 56–79; V, 563–587; VI, passim.

The causeway from Hell to Earth, X, 272–324.

Eden and Paradise, IV, 208–287.

Physical changes after the Fall, X, 651–714.

The rival astronomical theories, VIII, 12–168.

The scale of nature and the forms of life, V, 469–490; VII, 387–547.[30]

If *Paradise Lost* is a repository of scientific and pseudo-scientific lore, it is still more a repository of theological, metaphysical, moral, and political doctrine. Milton has himself suggested a classification of this body of ideas and principles, in the headings under which he accumulated in his private notebooks the materials of his thought.[31] He had an Index Theologicus,[32] an Index Ethicus, an Index Oeconomicus (i. e., domestic), and an Index Politicus. The same fundamental scheme of thought is in his mind when he says in *Areopagitica* that liberty is religious, domestic, and civil. These divisions run into each other, and a completely logical account of the Miltonic system demands some such comprehensive and detailed analysis as is attempted by Denis Saurat in his *Milton: Man and Thinker*. For practical purposes, however, Milton's own simpler scheme will serve. Indeed, since he himself endeavored to comprehend the whole body of his thinking within the terms of Christianity, his work on the Christian Doctrine becomes the best plain guide to the intellectual fabric of *Paradise Lost* and *Paradise Regained*. It is theological, in that it deals with the nature of God and his

[30] See the works of Warren and Orchard, also the statement in Verity's edition of *Paradise Lost,* Appendix, and the articles of McColley cited above for a detailed account of Milton's universe.

[31] See Horwood, *Commonplace Book.*

[32] This portion of Milton's notes is lost.

relations to man; it is ethical, economic, and political, in that it sets forth man's duties in the private, domestic, and civic spheres, at least in so far as these duties can be formulated from Holy Writ.

To present here even the main features of Milton's system is manifestly impossible. It is also unnecessary, as they are stated or clearly implied in the poem itself. In many instances the doctrinal expositions in verse follow passages in the *De Doctrina* point by point.[33] The latter, however, are unmixed with imagery or literary fiction and they elaborate arguments, where *Paradise Lost* merely affirms conclusions. A comparison of the two works is the best test of what in the poem he regarded as matter of faith and what as data of the imagination.

Much light is thrown on the degree of literalness with which the poet took the concrete details of *Paradise Lost* (whether these details were strictly Biblical or not) by the discussion of the Scriptural representation of God in the *Christian Doctrine,* Book I, Chapter 2. He there says that actual knowledge of God passes the comprehension of man, that he is exhibited in Scripture not as he really is but in such a way as to suit our understandings. It is best, instead of forming subtle imaginations, to accept his own account of himself as if it were the literal truth. "If 'it repented Jehovah that he had made man,' let us believe that it did repent him, only taking care to remember that what is called repentance when applied to God does not arise from inadvertence." If he ascribes to himself a human image, why should we be afraid to do the same, understanding thereby "not that God is in fashion like unto men in all his parts and members, but that so far as we are concerned

[33] See the footnotes in the Bohn edition.

to know, he is of that form which he attributes to himself in sacred writings."

This idea, the so-called "theory of accommodation," fitted well with Milton's Platonism and lent support to his confidence in the authenticity of his own inspiration. He had early conceived of himself as a revealer of truth in the Platonic sense. Poetic myth was the only possible way of representing the "ideas" to human apprehension and only the poet-seer who had looked on the face of truth unveiled could so represent them. When Milton undertook to write the epic of the Fall and became thereby a successor, if not a reincarnation, of Moses, he must have taken satisfaction in the thought that the original word itself was but accommodated truth. He could not have missed and he did not miss the Platonic suggestions in the Mosaic account of the revelation on the Mount,[34] and he must have made the most of the analogy between that primary revelation and his own experience of immediate inspiration from on high. He, too, had heard the voice of God and was no less than his predecessor the author of divine fictions. His own poetic elaboration of the Biblical story might, therefore, claim a place beside the imagery of Scripture itself, as a

[34] For example, Moses' shining face and the veil which he wore when he came before the people. Though Milton nowhere mentions these attributes, he makes Moses speak like a very Plato in the proposed prologue to the drama of the Fall. (See above, p. 183.) The connection between the Greek philosopher and the Hebrew prophet was already made in Eusebius' *Praeparatio Evangelorum,* a book which we know Milton to have read. Plato is there said to be a "Moses speaking Greek." See Saint-Brisson's translation, Paris, 1846, pp. 129–131. Milton, of course, believed that the Greeks had derived their inklings of Truth from the Hebrews. The whole train of thought which made it possible for him to identify himself imaginatively with Plato, Moses, and whatsoever prophets and bards besides, flowed easily from the philosophy of poetic inspiration embodied in the *Ion.*

shadow of reality. But his imagination, however trust-worthy, was not free as it would have been on a secular subject. It must only supplement, not contradict, the Bib-lical data, and it must conform to the framework of a body of reasoned doctrine. We have, accordingly, in *Paradise Lost,* a historical fiction, divinely sanctioned, embodying not a fallible philosophy of human origin, but the verities of the Christian religion itself.

In its broad features Milton's theology is the historic Catholic system as modified by Reformation thinkers, in-cluding the fundamental doctrines of the special creation of man, his fall from grace, his salvation through the aton-ing sacrifice of Christ. The part played by Satan in the temptation, the facts of Christ's incarnation and resurrec-tion, the last judgment with the final separation of the damned from the saved—these things are the cornerstones of Milton's religion as they had been of St. Augustine's and of John Calvin's. He also accepts from traditional theology the idea of the angels as intermediaries between God and man and as appointed guardians of man's wel-fare. On the other hand, he rejects, with all the reformed theologians, the special Roman Catholic doctrines of Pur-gatory, the intercession of the saints, the papal authority, besides many practices such as confession. He departs from the Anglican Church in abandoning the idea of an ecclesiastical hierarchy and in admitting no prescriptive form of worship.

Less obvious but of equally far-reaching importance are his disagreements with orthodox Calvinism, the accepted theology of the Presbyterian Church. The first point is in regard to the doctrine of predestination and free will. Reformation theology generally had always tended to minimize man's part in salvation and to ascribe everything to the grace of God, who had determined from all eternity the rôle of the damned and the elect. Milton announces with equal vehemence the moral responsibility of the individual. He was enabled to do so by his acceptance of the doctrines of Arminius, who, without abandoning the great Protestant principle that man is dependent in all that concerns his salvation upon the grace of the spirit of God, so modified the rigorous Calvinistic statements regarding predestination, depravity, etc., as to make man responsible for his own damnation. In the Calvinistic theology the decrees of God are absolute; in the Arminian they are conditional. The divine will is still supreme, but its supremacy is moral. God is not more bound to punish than to forgive. He has elected to salvation or reprobation only those whose final faith or disbelief he foresaw. His foreknowledge is certain but it does not necessitate the event. Similarly the atonement, with the Calvinist, was for the elect alone, and for them its working was infallible. It so satisfied divine justice on their behalf that they could not fail to be saved. The Arminian, on the other hand, held that the atonement was universal. It made the salvation of all men possible, the result in each case being conditioned by faith, which lay within the will of the individual. So, finally, with the doctrine of original sin, depravity, according to the Calvinist, was complete. It admitted no possibility of spiritual good. Arminianism held that depravity was a bias which left the will free and man responsible for his own destiny through the choice of faith or unbelief. The original and inherited sin is met and neutralized by the free grace of Christ—the second Adam.

That Milton was Arminian rather than Calvinistic may

clearly be seen in his definitions of all the crucial theological terms which were in controversy. Thus predestination is defined as "the decree whereby God in pity to mankind, through foreseeing that they would fall of their own accord, predestined to eternal salvation those who should believe and continue in the faith." In other words, predestination is conditional upon the will of man.

The principle of moral freedom is central in Milton's theological thought and, as applied to Adam, it is the heart of his justification of the ways of God to man. In the *Areopagitica* Milton complains that those who deny Adam's power of choice between good and evil make him a "mere mechanical Adam" like the Adam of the puppet shows, and elsewhere in his prose writings he says that to rob man of his freedom is to impute injustice to God. One of the choruses, also, in *Samson Agonistes* raises the question of God's justice and directly attacks the Calvinist position along the lines laid down by Arminius, who contended, as we have seen, that the operation of the divine will was not necessitated from within but conditioned by the belief or unbelief of his creatures.

> Just are the ways of God,
> And justifiable to Men; . . .
>   Yet more there be who doubt his ways not just,
> As to his own edicts, found contradicting, . . .
>   As if they would confine th' interminable,
> And tie him to his own prescript,
> Who made our Laws to bind us, not himself.

In *Paradise Lost,* the justification of the divine way lies in the representation of Adam as a free agent and in the revelation of the working of God's grace which allows to him and his descendants the opportunity for a new exercise of moral choice and of consequent salvation even after the Fall. Naturally in the poem Milton does not elaborate the theological argument, but he goes out of his way again and again to insist on the fact of Adam's freedom. (See especially *P. L.* III, 96 ff., the key passage for an understanding of Milton's theological interpretation of the Fall.[35]) Conversely, Milton makes little of the sacrifice of Christ as an atonement for sin. He accepts it as a necessary condition of man's salvation but not as taking the place of man's individual choice of good. Neither personally nor as a part of his system did the idea greatly move or interest him.[36] Thus he was naturally led to treat in *Paradise Regained* of Christ's victory over Satan in the temptation rather than of his crucifixion. His acts are, in Milton's deepest feeling, not vicarious but simply patterns for humanity.

Closely related to this departure from orthodoxy is his view of Christ himself as a being divine but distinctly lower than God, and of the Holy Ghost as still inferior in importance. Without entering into intricate theological distinctions we may say that Milton is not an orthodox Trini-

[35] Kelley, *"The Theological Dogma of "Paradise Lost,"* II, 173–202, shows conclusively that the doctrinal statements in this passage, regarding predestination and its concordance with the mercy, grace, and wisdom of God are precisely in accord with the anti-Calvinistic utterances of *De Doctrina*. Lines 183–184, taken alone, are capable of Calvinistic interpretation, but in their context they too express Arminian doctrine.

[36] The student who wishes fully to understand Milton's attitude should compare *Christian Doctrine*, I, xiv–xvi and *Paradise Lost*, III, 167 ff. See also Grierson's discussion of Milton's theological attitude in *Milton and Wordsworth*, pp. 95–102, and the authoritative articles of Maurice Kelley referred to above.

tarian. He was a heretic both from the Catholic and from the Calvinistic standpoint; he did not, however, stand alone, for great theologians in this era, e. g., Servetus, Socinus, and Ochino, had advocated similar views. In *Paradise Lost* Milton conceals or modifies his anti-Trinitarian heresies, but they are discernible enough both in that poem and in *Paradise Regained,* when read in the light of the elaborate discussions in the *Christian Doctrine*.

One other point remains. It is an essential one in Milton's whole metaphysics. He denied the almost universally accepted doctrine that God created the world out of nothing. The matter which he reduced to order was as eternal as spirit. It was indeed a part of the substance of God himself. This statement receives explicit expression both in *Paradise Lost* and in the *Christian Doctrine*. The deep is boundless because God is boundless. It is not, however, "vacuous." If it is "uncreated" it is because God retires [37] from it and puts not forth his virtue, which is free to act or not (*P. L.* Book VII, lines 168 ff.). Thus Milton obliterates the sharp distinction between matter and spirit and at the same time affirms the reality of both. He insists on the corporeality of the angels, and suggests (Platonically) that Heaven itself offers a point by point analogy with Earth. As to man he is not a spirit housed in the mere senseless stock of a body and separable from it, but "a living soul," that is to say, "a body, or substance, individual, animated, sensitive, and rational." An inevitable de-

[37] Saurat in his *Milton: Man and Thinker* makes much of this expression as evidence that Milton shared with the Jewish *Zohar* the theory of "creation by retraction." Really the two ideas are quite different. In the *Zohar* God retires from the Cosmos, leaving it free; in Milton he retires from Chaos. "Retires," in this case, means merely that he does not exert his power.

duction from the definition is that at death the whole man
dies. There is no separate continued existence of the spirit,
but all sleeps together till all is revived at the Resurrection.
This, again, was a heresy which others shared. There was,
in fact, a group of advocates of such an idea, called in
Milton's time "mortalists" or "soul-sleepers." [38] With him,
however, it was, as I have suggested, no isolated oddity of
thought, but a conviction which permeated his entire philosophy. In the moral sphere it teaches him to reject
asceticism, and to allow indulgence of the flesh, insisting
only that such indulgence should be tempered by reason
and under control of the will.

This brings us more specifically to the field of Milton's
ethics. His general principles are grounded in the study of
ancient ethics, particularly Plato, Aristotle, and the Stoic
writers. From them he derived the idea of the conflict of
reason and passion in the soul of man and a conviction as
to the importance of knowledge as an instrument of virtue.
The essential fall of man occurs when passion predominates
over reason. Thus the angel instructs Adam in all that it
is essential for him to know in order to meet temptation
successfully. He fails when he allows his intelligence to
be blinded and follows the dictates of the powerful instinct
which draws him toward Eve. Thus, also, Christ foils
Satan in *Paradise Regained* by clearly surveying all the
enticements which are held out to him, analyzing them
Socratically, and detecting their fallaciousness. His discourses are intended as a model for men confronted with
a similar series of choices.

[38] Saurat holds that Milton was indebted to the first edition of
Overton's *Man's Mortality*, 1643, and was himself a contributor to
the revision of 1655. A thorough study of the heresy and Milton's participation in it has been made by Williamson.

If, however, Milton's general conception of man's moral nature is founded on the ethical wisdom of the ancients, it is in Scripture that he finds at once the sanction and the content of human virtue. God is the author of the moral law. Duty is the sole daughter of his voice. First given to Adam in the form of an arbitrary command, then to Moses as a set of specific obligations, his law is finally embodied as a spirit in the person of Christ and in that form supplements or supersedes all earlier revelations. It is no longer arbitrary but completely conformable to reason. "God and reason bid the same." It is written not alone in the Book but in the hearts of all believers, and to them is left the problem of its application. This is what Milton means by the gospel liberty (*De Doctrina Christiana,* Book I, Chapter 28), and it is on this principle of the authority of the individual conscience that he challenges the validity of man-made laws which do not have its sanction.

In the second book of the *Christian Doctrine* Milton gives a full discussion of the specific duties of man toward God, toward himself, and toward his neighbor, basing his formulation chiefly on the New Testament. Man's duties to himself are temperance, chastity, frugality, industry, fortitude, patience; among those to his neighbor are charity, meekness, veracity, faithfulness, gravity, justice, liberality, gratitude. Chapter XV opens the subject of reciprocal duties, as between parent and child, husband and wife. This includes a discussion of divorce, which falls in Milton's Commonplace Book under the head of Index Oeconomicus. There follows a brief chapter on public duties, political and ecclesiastical.

Much of this material reappears, sometimes in the form of doctrinal statement, oftener by implication, in *Paradise*

Lost. Especial emphasis is given to the subject of the proper relations of husband and wife, since these are the ones primarily involved in the story of Adam and Eve. To Milton the peace and virtue of the home were best assured if the wife remained in a proper state of subjection to her husband. Such subordination to a natural superior was, indeed, the proper law of the whole universe. Thus woman should look up to man, man to angel, inferior angel to superior angel, and all to God. It was the attempted disruption of this order which led alike to the fall of Satan and the fall of man. Milton's criticism of the system of chivalric or courtly love is that it reverses the normal situation by placing woman above man. Hence Satan assumes the rôle of Petrarchan sonneteer when he makes his initial attack on Eve.

On the question of the sources and affiliations of Milton's thought much has been written. The subject still awaits, however, definitive treatment at the hands of a competent historian of philosophy. Milton's mind had ranged through the whole realm of speculation. Ancient philosophy, Biblical and Patristic thought, Reformation theology in all its varieties, the philosophic movements and religious heterodoxies of his own day—all were familiar to him and from them he culled the elements of his own eclectic system. One distrusts the attribution of his fundamental ideas to the influence of any single source. Here are some of the men or schools whose intellectual relationship with Milton has been most strongly advocated: Bernardino Ochino,[39] Jakob Boehme,[40] the Cabalists,[41] Henry More and the

[39] Wood, *Milton's Antitrinitarian Conception*.

[40] Bailey, *Milton and Jakob Boehme*.

[41] Saurat, *Milton, Man and Thinker*, pp. 281–310; also his *Milton et le Matérialisme*.

Cambridge Platonists,[42] Giordano Bruno,[43] Michael Servetus,[44] the Quakers.[45] Not one of these is mentioned in the *De Doctrina Christiana,* which, nevertheless, lists dozens of standard theologians. It is true, however, that Milton would be likely to suppress the names of the less reputable authorities. He says in the introduction that he had not even read any of the works of heretics, so-called, "when the mistakes of those who are reckoned orthodox first taught me to agree with their opponents whenever these opponents agreed with Scripture."

With all his rationalism, however, Milton never really crosses the line which divides Christian and idealistic thought generally from naturalism in any of its ancient or modern manifestations. He could, for example, have no part in the materialistic conclusions of a Lucretius, however much one side of his intellect may have been allured by it. Accordingly, he banishes to chaos the operation of mere material force. In that realm of being, which God neglects, we have the Epicurean atoms clashing blindly against each other according to the laws of chance but powerless to evolve an ordered world without the exercise of the divine will. With regard to the radical and naturalistic thought of the sixteenth and seventeenth centuries Milton is apparently partly conscious of its menace to the idealist tradition both in the field of abstract speculation and of practical conduct. His opposition to the theological determinism of the Calvinists has behind it an opposition to the more dangerous determinism of the materialists.

[42] Marjorie Nicolson, *The Spirit World of Milton and More;* also her *Milton and the "Conjectura Cabbalistica."*

[43] Liljegren, *Milton et Giordano Bruno,* denies this influence.

[44] Martin Larson, *Milton and Servetus.*

[45] Samson, *Studies in Milton,* pp. 167 ff.

This is the source, I believe, of his distrust of uncontrolled intellectual speculation. The point of view of the Renaissance thinker who philosophized solely in order that he might philosophize had its logical result in the political realism of Machiavelli, in the ethical libertinism of free livers like the youthful Donne, and in the realistic naturalism of Hobbes; and to all this Milton was unalterably opposed. As he relegates the unguided action of force and chance to chaos so he surrenders the naturalistic point of view in conduct and belief to Satan. It has been suggested that *Paradise Lost* was intended primarily as a reply to Hobbes.[46] *Leviathan* was published in 1651, and whether or not Milton had read it he must have been aware of the stir of opposition and alarm which it caused in philosophic circles. Both politically and religiously its doctrines would have been anathema to him, and it may well be that in setting out to "justify the ways of God to man" he consciously directed his inspired utterance against this great antagonist of the faith.

Philosophically, then, Milton is a Christian idealist, though he classes himself in theology with the heretics— Arius, Socinus, Arminius, Ochino, Servetus, and who not? His religious as well as his political sympathies were on the side of the independent sects and the individual promoters of spiritual religion in the seventeenth century. In his metaphysics he shares the pantheistic tendencies of his age. His ethical thought, on the other hand, is largely

[46] By Nicolson, *Milton and Hobbes.* A bit of objective evidence is furnished by the statement of Milton's widow to Aubrey that Milton knew but did not like Hobbes, though he acknowledged him a man of parts, and that "their interests and tenets were diametrically opposite."

grounded in the study of ancient philosophy. Temperamentally, he felt a strong affinity for the Stoic doctrine, as may easily be seen by his references to the teachings of this school in *Paradise Lost* and *Paradise Regained*.[47] But he is equally drawn toward Platonism, whether in its original form or as it came to him through the more fanciful interpretation of the Neo-Platonists and the Cabala.[48] Finally, it must be remembered that Milton met many of the speculative and moral ideas which he employs already embodied in imaginative literature and that such applications are likely to have stimulated his poetic mind more powerfully than any abstract statement could do. The influence of Spenser's cosmic speculation and moral allegory is discussed on pp. 259 ff.

Political theory is not explicitly dealt with in *Paradise Lost,* yet the poem reflects in an important way Milton's long study of and experience with the problems of government. The first two books show concretely by what arts leadership is acquired and maintained in the state, how perplexing issues are threshed out in council, how great public enterprises are organized and executed. There is a certain analogy between Satan and Cromwell as military statesmen, though they are, in Milton's thought, exact opposites in their ideals and purposes, the one aiming only at destruction, the other, ultimately, at the nobler victories of peace. The infernal host, when it sends "from every rank and squared regiment the worthiest" to conference in Pan-

[47] *Paradise Lost,* II, 562–569; *Paradise Regained,* IV, 300–308. In both passages Stoicism comes last in the list of Pagan philosophies condemned and is dwelt on most fully, as if it were better worth the pains of a refutation. Satan is obviously a Stoic.

[48] See Agar, *Milton and Plato,* and Nicolson, *The Spirit World of Milton and More.*

demonium acts precisely as the Parliamentary Army had acted in the crises of the Great Rebellion. Writing to Henry Oldenburg in 1659, Milton declined to compose a history of the late troubles of England saying that they required "oblivion rather than commemoration." Yet he has in spite of himself commemorated them.

If the portrait of Satan reflects to this extent the actual phenomena of politics in a sinful and warring world, the accounts of Adam and the Patriarchs illustrate that ideal theocracy in human society toward which the thought of the Puritans aspired. Paul Elmer More has observed that the true theme of *Paradise Lost* is Paradise itself. The hope of a godly social order, needing no law but the voice of the Lord, as interpreted through his prophets, had long since departed from Milton; his efforts to guide England to a practical solution of its problems ended with *The Ready and Easy Way* in 1659. He turns now to a dream of the early world, addressing himself to the individual, rather than to mankind at large. The recovery of the moral "Paradise within thee" is the only way to freedom. When that is achieved the problems of politics will settle themselves.

One conviction which always dominated Milton's political thinking, the idea, namely, that there is a natural order of superior and inferior in the universe, the preservation of which means peace and justice, receives emphasis more than once in *Paradise Lost*. Satan and Eve attempt to break this order, with results disastrous to themselves and to others. The idea is put, like some other partial truths, in the mouth of Satan (*P. L.* V, 793), "for orders and degrees Jar not with liberty, but well consist." But it is Abdiel who voices its full meaning. (*P. L.* VI, 170 ff.)

It is no servitude, he says, to serve authority ordained by
God and nature,

> When he who rules is worthiest, and excells
> Them whom he governs. This is servitude,
> To serve th' unwise.

This represented Milton's real and final conclusion. The
fact is that he never was by temperament or experience
a democrat. He lived in isolation, knew nothing of the
common man, and naturally distrusted him. In the early
ecclesiastical pamphlets, to be sure, he expresses confidence in the "plain people" to elect ministers of the church,
and in *Areopagitica* he glories in the competent intelligence
of the English nation, but these opinions were formulated
in the course of argument and when Milton still saw no
gulf between the aims of the people and his own. Later he
became self-contradictory on the subject. In the *Tenure
of Kings and Magistrates,* for example, he asserts the right
of the people against the magistrate, but always with the
reservation that they choose good rather than ill. Similarly
in the *Defense of the English People* he advocates the
theory of popular sovereignty, yet he praises the independent army for repelling the tumultuous violence of the citi-
zens and mechanics of London. When, finally, the nation
turned against the good old cause and hailed the return of
the Stuarts, Milton was open in his denunciation of those
who preferred "bondage with ease" to "strenuous liberty,"
and he proposed in the *Ready and Easy Way* what amounts
to a self-perpetuating aristocracy as a form of government.
This brings him to the political philosophy embodied in
Paradise Lost [49] and later in *Samson Agonistes.*

[49] See Wolfe, *Milton in the Puritan Revolution.* Fink, *The Theory
of the Mixed State and the Development of Milton's Political
Thought,* stresses the consistency of Milton's political philosophy

The book sources of Milton's political thinking are easily traceable. He inherited his interest in the theory of government from the earlier Renaissance and with it his tendency to find the basis of his convictions in the writings of the ancients. The Greek and Latin historians, orators, poets, and philosophers were to him the great textbooks, next to Holy Writ, of political wisdom. His own republicanism has its roots in Roman soil. But he had also studied with diligence the records and theories of later ages, following a consistent program, some of the details of which may be gathered from his Commonplace Book. Among the outstanding modern contributors to political theory entered in the list are Jean Bodin, Buchanan, Machiavelli, Sir Thomas Smith. His controversial activity sent him scurrying to the authorities, as we have seen, but much of his political study antedates this period. For the liberalism of his own conception of government he had, of course, abundant support, as for example in Buchanan, and none of his ideas are new. A good notion of his position in the history of such speculation may be obtained from any account of political theory in the Renaissance.

THE LITERARY SOURCES

The purpose of this section is to indicate in summary fashion the chief authorities and sources which Milton probably knew and may have employed in constructing his version of the story of the Fall. The discussion here involves primarily the myth or outward narrative, the philosophical and theological elements being considered in the

which culminated in the *Ready and Easy Way*. For a broad discussion of the bases and affinities of Milton's idea of the state see the same author's notable study *The Classical Republicans*.

preceding section. The two cannot, however, be absolutely separated.

In discussing the sources of the legend, distinction should be drawn between various types of material from the point of view of Milton's attitude toward them. The Biblical references he considered as solely authoritative. Other sources had weight in his mind about in proportion to their antiquity, except that Jewish and Christian writers would be preferred to Pagan as standing nearer the fountain head of truth. Such materials had, even when manifestly fictitious, a kind of legendary authenticity, and Milton invariably preferred their detail to his own invention. He preferred it, also, when there was a choice, to more modern elaborations. There can, however, be no doubt that he had read more than one literary version of the fall of man and received from them, consciously or unconsciously, suggestions for the artistic handling of his materials.

Obviously no account of the sources of Milton's epic can be considered as exhaustive, for the poem holds in solution the whole of his immense reading. It is not, moreover, except for the Biblical and other ancient authorities, to the works which deal with the identical subject which he treats that we must look for the most vital influences, but rather to those great masterpieces of ancient and modern literature, whatever their subject, which most profoundly impressed him and with which he habitually dwelt. In other words, the essential study of the literary origins of *Paradise Lost* is the study of the formation of Milton's genius in so far as it was moulded by the minds of other men. I shall attempt to indicate here only such general influences in *Paradise Lost* as can be rather definitely pointed to in connection with some larger feature of the poem.[50]

HEBREW AND PATRISTIC AUTHORITIES. The foundation passage in Scripture for the fall of man is Genesis ii; for the war in Heaven and the fall of Satan (the Dragon) it is Revelation xii. But Milton has employed in one place or another every relevant Biblical text, and the student who would examine in full the basis of the legend in its larger outline should consult a Concordance under the heads Adam, Eve, Satan, Lucifer, etc. Scripture is also used for the subsidiary elements of the story. Thus the names and characters of the demons in Book I are largely drawn from the Old Testament. The allegory of Sin and Death in Book II is an elaboration of James i: 15. The whole account of the creation in Book IV is built upon the first chapter of Genesis. The prophecy of Michael is a résumé of Old and New Testament history. Finally, Milton is everywhere dependent on the Bible for detail. Witness the enormous number of Scriptural references cited in such editions as Todd and Verity. An outstanding example is the description of the chariot of Paternal Deity in Book VI, 749 ff., a mosaic from the first chapter of Ezekiel. The borrowings are of course intended to be recognized, and, extending as they do to the minutest turn of phrase, they put one's familiarity with Scripture to a severe test. Milton's poem is, as he doubtless expected it to be, an invitation to read and reread the Bible, and many an Old or New Testament passage which has been perhaps passed by unnoticed acquires force and meaning when we return to it from Milton's poetic interpretation.

[50] The most comprehensive account of the literary relations of *Paradise Lost* is Woodhull's *The Epic of "Paradise Lost."*

Beyond the canonical books of the Bible there was also the Apocrypha, which would in Milton's mind enjoy an only slightly diminished prestige. The Book of Enoch contained a statement as to the fall of the angels, and Milton derived from it at least the name of Satan's standard bearer, Azazael.[51] His employment of Raphael as the genial messenger of God to Adam in his innocence was suggested by the Book of Tobit, where this angel is the helpful guide and companion of the hero through his several adventures (cf. *P. L.* V, 220–222).

Milton also found in the rabbinical commentaries on the Old Testament narrative many legendary details which proved useful in elaborating and interpreting the myth. The outstanding points of contact between these embellishments of the Scriptural account of Adam and Eve and Milton's handling in *Paradise Lost* may readily be gathered from Louis Ginzberg's scholarly and comprehensive account of the rabbinical materials in his *Legends of the Jews,* Vol. I. It is said, for example, that Satan was envious of man in his conjugal relations (cf. *P. L.* Book IV, lines 504 ff.) ; that he offered to Eve as proof of the harmlessness of the forbidden fruit the fact that he himself had eaten it and had not died (cf. *P. L.* Book IX, lines 687 ff.) ; that he suggested to her God's jealousy as the real motive of the prohibition (cf. *P. L.* Book IX, lines 703 ff.).

Of Milton's knowledge of these Talmudic writings there can be no doubt, since he frequently employs them in his

[51] The Book of Enoch was inaccessible in Milton's time, but he had met the passage in question in the Byzantine chronicler Georgius Syncellus. See Saurat, *Milton, Man and Thinker,* p. 254. More extensive claims have recently been made for the influence of the Book of Enoch by McColley.

prose works.[52] He mentions, for example, in *Tetrachordon* the idea of the originally bisexual nature of Adam, a rabbinical fancy which he made no use of in *Paradise Lost*. Among the later Hebrew sources certainly known to Milton was the work of the medieval Rabbi Maimonides. There was also the Jewish history of Josephus, and the parallel work of Yosippon, called the Pseudo-Josephus, both of which he explicitly refers to.[53] From the latter he appears to have taken suggestions as to the manner in which Satan approached Eve to tempt her and the motive of jealousy which led her to forestall a possible second marriage of Adam's by giving him the apple. There also he probably found the basic ideas for the naïve details of the conversation between God and Adam (*P. L.* VIII, 403–411), where both speculate on their loneliness. Yosippon writes: "Now Adam walked about the Garden of Eden like one of the ministering angels. God said: Just as I am alone in My world, so is Adam; just as I have no companion, neither has Adam. Tomorrow the creatures will say, 'He does not propagate, he is surely our creator.' It is not good for man to be alone, I will make a helpmeet for him" (Gaster's translation, p. 17).[54] The claims which M. Saurat has made for Milton's obligations to the body of Jewish mystical philosophy known as the Zohar, though plausible, must be regarded as unproved. Fletcher has

jealousy

[52] This subject has been fully dealt with by Fletcher in his volumes, *Milton's Semitic Studies* and *Milton's Rabbinical Readings*.

[53] Fletcher, *Milton and Yosippon*.

[54] Fletcher (*Milton's Rabbinical Readings*) refers to Rashi's commentary on Genesis ii in Buxtorf's Bible as a basis for Milton's treatment of the Episode of Eve's creation. There is, however, in Rashi no such specific parallel as this one from Yosippon, which Fletcher fails to mention. See Baldwin, *Semitic Influences*.

shown that many of the ideas and motives of the Cabala might more plausibly have come to him directly from such rabbinical commentary as is to be found in Buxtorf's Hebrew Bible and from the other Hebraic authorities. They were also present in the writings of the Cambridge Platonists.

Equally important and almost equally intangible is Milton's debt to the Greek and Latin fathers of the church. We know from the Commonplace Book that he had studied them thoroughly, beginning with the Horton period, along with his reading in the early Byzantine historians. They dealt extensively, of course, with questions connected with the Biblical narrative of the Fall and supplied many features which became a permanent part of the legend as it was handed on to the Middle Ages. Some of these details they adopted from Jewish speculations which would not otherwise have been accessible to Milton. Thus the conversion of the fallen angels into demons and their identification with the false gods of the gentiles is a piece of Jewish tradition perpetuated in the Fathers. The parallel between Adam and the Messiah, and between Eve and Mary, is also patristic.[55]

A very important authority for Milton's interpretation of the fall of man, particularly with reference to the elements of sensuality involved in it, was St. Augustine, and every mature student of *Paradise Lost* should read Book XIV, chapters 11–28, of the *City of God*, where the matter is dealt with. It will be evident enough that Milton had

---

[55] In his pamphlet *Of Prelatical Episcopacy,* Columbia Edition, III, 94, Milton scolds Irenaeus for making the special relation between Eve and Mary a basis for Papistical idolatry. In *Paradise Lost* he himself adopts the idea. See Saurat, p. 255.

before him in interpreting the Fall many of the issues raised by this mighty elaborator of Catholic Christianity and that the Protestant poet is influenced even where he is in fundamental disagreement with St. Augustine and is making a point against him. The relation here is primarily philosophical and theological, but there are obvious effects also in the course of the narrative.[56] Still another patristic source of Milton's ideas is Lactantius, from whom he quotes in the Commonplace Book.[57]

It would be useless to go on enumerating the Christian commentators, Hebraists, and theologians from whose works Milton might have taken a turn of thought or even the suggestion for an incident. Their name is legion and the list would extend over centuries. Of medieval writers he naturally made little direct use. His angelology, for example, is not that of the standard Catholic authority, the Pseudo-Dionysius, *De coelesti Hierarchia*. Milton may or may not have read this work, but he would in any case have been sufficiently familiar with the system from Dante's *Divine Comedy*. With the works of many Reformation and contemporary scholars he was acquainted, including those of John Selden, who, besides being the greatest legal antiquarian of his time, was also a learned writer on Hebrew antiquities. His *De Diis Syriis* affords many illustrations of Milton's demonology.

The discussion of these authorities has carried us somewhat far afield. I return now to the question of Milton's debt to more specifically literary influences.

---

[56] See Saurat, pp. 273 ff., for a full discussion, but Saurat attributes too exclusively to St. Augustine Miltonic ideas which have a manifold source.

[57] See Hartwell, *Lactantius and Milton*.

FORMATIVE INFLUENCES ON *PARADISE LOST* IN GREEK AND ROMAN LITERATURE. Ancient epic—the *Iliad,* the *Odyssey,* and the *Aeneid*—furnishes Milton with his authoritative model of form and structure as Scripture does of substance and interpretation. The classical epic conventions were, of course, fixed by Renaissance usage and formulated in critical theory; but it is right to assume in regard to Milton's employment of them that his conscious sources are in each case the ancient originals themselves. They are the precedents to which he wishes the reader to revert, recognizing with admiration the manner in which the new material is ingeniously made to conform to the ancient mould. For the larger structural features of *Paradise Lost,* the *Aeneid,* which itself derives both from the *Iliad* and the *Odyssey,* is a sufficient illustration. The principal points of comparison are as follows: (1) the beginning of the poem with the action proper at a mid-point in the larger story of which it is a part; (2) the introduction of this larger story by way of narrative and prophecy in the course of the narrower action; (3) the alternation of scenes on earth with scenes in Heaven; (4) the alternation of dramatic dialogue with more or less extensive narrative and descriptive passages. Among the smaller features in *Paradise Lost* which have their precedent in ancient epic may be mentioned: (1) the invocation, repeated at important moments of change in the action; (2) the enumeration of the host of Satan in Book I; (3) the representation of a council of leaders in Book II and of divine personages in Book III; (4) the introduction of an allegorical episode, as that of Sin and Death, Book II; (5) epic games, Book II; descriptions of technical processes

—e. g., the building of Pandemonium, Book II, and the casting of cannon, Book VI; (7) a celestial visitant warning and advising a mortal, Book V; (8) war, episodes of single combat with challenge and reply, Book VI; (9) historical prophecy divinely inspired, Book XI ff.; (10) dreams, Books V, XII.[58]

Of the other types of ancient literature Greek drama is the most conspicuous in its structural influence on *Paradise Lost*. The way to such influence was opened by the fact that Milton's more particular theme, the fall of man, found closer parallels in classical tragedy than it did in classical epic, and that he had originally planned to cast his material in dramatic form. In the completed poem the careful motivation of the action and the revelation through dialogue and soliloquy of the inner experience of his characters certainly go back rather to dramatic than to epic precedent. The literary influences in this respect are rather vague and often they seem more Elizabethan than Greek; but there can be no doubt that in portraying, for example, the unnatural exhilaration of Adam and Eve immediately after their sin Milton is drawing upon the ancient representation of "hybris."

The remaining influence of ancient literature is largely a matter of style and allusion. We may note, however, that Milton's infernal council has a precedent in Claudian's *De Raptu Proserpinae* and that in Eve's description of her first experiences (Book V, 450 ff.) the poet draws on the myth of Narcissus and falls for a moment into the spirit of pastoral narrative, recollecting such a passage as the

[58] For specific references and additional points see Buff, *Milton's Paradise Lost, etc.*

pursuit of Daphne by Apollo in the *Metamorphoses* and employing the inevitable "quem fugis" motive adopted by Ovid from Theocritus.

NARRATIVE TREATMENTS OF THE FALL AND RELATED THEMES IN MEDIEVAL AND RENAISSANCE LITERATURE. *Paradise Lost,* as a Biblical and didactic epic, belongs to a tradition which reaches back to the early centuries of Christian Latin culture and persists in full vigor through the Renaissance. Among the earliest of these is St. Avitus' *De Mosaicae Historiae Gestis* (circa 500 A.D.), which treats of the Fall incidentally in the course of a paraphrase of Bible history and lays down the main lines of the literary elaboration of the material. It is by no means impossible that Milton should have known this work, which was printed before his time and thought well of by the Protestant humanists for its good Latinity. Christian Latin writers of similar type are mentioned among the prescribed studies at St. Paul's school in Colet's original program of instruction.[59]

Strong claims have also been made for his employment of a work of the same type as that of Avitus which develops the story of the fall of man nearly in the plot form which it assumes in *Paradise Lost.* This work is the Anglo-Saxon Genesis, attributed to Caedmon, particularly that portion known as Genesis B.[60] The narrative, in outline, is as follows:

Satan and his followers revolt and fall. They are banished to a hill of alternate cold and heat. God, to supply

[59] See Leach, *Milton as a Schoolboy.* Guizot, in *The History of Civilization,* was the first person to call attention to the parallels between Milton and Avitus. The subject is also discussed in the introduction to Barham's translation of Grotius's *Adamus Exul.*

[60] See Gurteen, *The Epic of the Fall of Man.*

their places, creates the world and places Adam and Eve in a garden of beauty and delight. Satan, in a dramatic address to the rebel angels, laments his present situation, complains of God's injustice in creating man, and plots to extend his empire by corrupting Adam and Eve. He sends an emissary to Earth, pretending to be a messenger from Heaven, tempts Adam in Eve's presence but is repulsed. Turning to Eve who is thoroughly deceived, he succeeds. Adam also falls, and a revulsion of feeling follows, with bitter lamentation and remorse.

The general parallelism here with *Paradise Lost* of course means nothing; since, as we shall see, many of the later treatments, some of which Milton certainly knew, proceed in essentially the same manner. There are, however, some rather striking similarities of detail in Satan's speeches to his followers, in the account of the journey through the abyss to Earth and in the self-reproaching dialogue of Adam and Eve after the Fall. In both poems Satan contrasts the horrible scene about him with the delights of his former home. He mentions to his followers the creation of Earth and man as a rumor (cf. *P. L.* I, 650 ff.). He flatteringly praises Eve's beauty, though not, as in Milton, before her sin. There is nothing, however, which can fairly be called conclusive of Milton's indebtedness, and the question resolves itself into one of probability dependent upon the likelihood of Milton's having actually read the Anglo-Saxon poem. It had been published in 1655 at Amsterdam by the Dutch scholar Francis Junius, just at the time when Milton was beginning the actual composition of his epic. Junius lived in England until 1651, when he received the Caedmon manuscript from Bishop Ussher, and must, Masson thinks, almost certainly have been an acquaintance of Milton's. There is, on the other hand, evidence that Milton was not well enough versed in Anglo-Saxon to make anything out of the Caedmonian *Genesis.* In his *History of Britain* (1670) he describes the "Battle of Brunanburgh," which he had before him in the Anglo-Saxon Chronicle, together with a word for word Latin translation, as being quite unintelligible because of its extravagant fancies and metaphors. "Brunanburgh" is much simpler than the Biblical poems and had Milton been through the latter, with or without Junius as interpreter, it is hard to see how he could have spoken in such perplexity.

An outstanding religious work of the Renaissance, Du Bartas' *La Première Semaine* and *La Seconde Semaine,* translated into English by Joshua Sylvester as *Du Bartas His Divine Weeks and Works* (published in parts, 1592–1598, first quarto, 1605), specializes on the creation, with much detailed description of the wonders of the universe and with incidental treatment of the Fall. Du Bartas' poem, like the first two chapters of Raleigh's *History of the World,* belongs in the tradition of hexaemeral literature which interprets the Biblical account of the creation, intermingling with simple exegesis an immense amount of philosophical and scientific material from various sources.[61] Among the writers of such commentaries were Basil, Augustine, Johannes Scotus and many other serious theologians who made this their vehicle for discussion of such standard problems as the nature of God, the processes and purposes of creation, the construction of the universe, the angels, man, the animals, etc. Milton knew Sylvester's translation of Du Bartas well and its influence on his

[61] See F. E. Robbins, *The Hexaemeral Literature,* and Arnold Williams, *Milton and the Renaissance Commentaries on Genesis.*

youthful poetic style is well established. The general tone
of the work is obviously reproduced in *Paradise Lost* and
many Miltonic scenes, motives, and ideas have their parallels in the earlier epic. Professor Taylor,[62] who believes
that Milton owed more to Sylvester's Du Bartas than to
any other work, points out verbal resemblances as well
(including one whole line word for word the same). Perhaps, as has been suggested, Milton more or less consciously undertook to outdo Sylvester, as Spenser had
undertaken to "overgo" Ariosto.[63] Another poem of Du
Bartas', *La Muse Chrétienne*, may also have been known
to Milton. Here Urania is, for the first time in literature,
hailed as the celestial patroness of divine poetry rather
than as the muse of astronomy. This conception became
traditional and Milton's invocations are directly referable
to it.[64]

Renaissance Dramatic Versions of the Fall. The
story of the fall and redemption of man was a central subject in medieval religious drama and Milton's first conception of it as literary material was deeply influenced by
this tradition. It is, to be sure, doubtful if he knew any of
these plays directly,[65] though he may well have watched

[62] *Milton's Use of Du Bartas.* Dunster (*Considerations on Milton's
Early Reading*), is mainly concerned with the influence on the early
poems, but he suggests, without giving details, that *Paradise Lost*
was deeply indebted to the same source. Dunster probably assumed
that Milton carried the recollection of Du Bartas from his childhood;
Taylor, that he continued to read and respect it.

[63] On the general indebtedness of Milton to Renaissance epic tradition see Tillyard, *The Miltonic Setting*, pp. 141 ff.

[64] See Lily B. Campbell, *The Christian Muse*, Huntington Library
Bulletin, October, 1935.

[65] He may have known them. See Gilbert, *Milton and the Mysteries.*

as a child the puppet shows of Adam and Eve to which he alludes in *Areopagitica*.[66] But the mysteries were perpetuated in a cultivated and artistic way in the Italian *Sacre Rappresentazione,* and one such drama, the *Adamo* of Giovanni Battista Andreini [67] published in 1613, appears quite certainly to have been known to Milton. It was first mentioned in connection with *Paradise Lost* in 1727 by Voltaire, who said that Milton derived his suggestion for writing it from having seen a performance of this play on his Italian journey. The relationship is apparently confirmed by similarities, not so much in *Paradise Lost* itself as in the early dramatic plans in the Cambridge manuscript, where the allegorical figures of Labor, Famine, Death, etc., which play a prominent part in Andreini, are listed among the *dramatis personae.*

In the change from dramatic to epic form the influence of the *Adamo* becomes merged with that of general tradition and its specific traces are largely obliterated. We may note, however, the symbolic character of the incidents in Adam's vision of the consequences of his sin as a survival of the original suggestion from Andreini.[68] Thus, in witnessing the murder of Cain, Adam cries:

And have I then seen Death?

And in the description of the lazar house (XI, 480 ff.) the

[66] "A mere artificial Adam like the Adam of the motions."

[67] Translated but not very faithfully by Hayley in Cowper's edition of Milton and the parallels discussed in Hayley's *Life.* Allodoli, *Milton e L'Italia* (see also the introduction to his recent edition of the *Adamo*), is rather perversely skeptical of Milton's knowledge of the work.

[68] Reinforced, however, by the traditions of Spenserian allegory. See below, p. 263. On the elements of medieval allegory in general in Milton see Ramsay, *Morality Themes in Milton's Poetry.*

as at least equally probable. This work was highly praised by such authorities as Scaliger and Casaubon, and it ranked as one of the outstanding literary contributions of Renaissance humanism. Edward Phillips in his *Theatrum Poetarum,* a work which is thought to contain reflections of Milton's own critical opinions, mentions its author as one of the most distinguished writers of the age. Milton had been introduced to Grotius himself at Paris, and there is every reason to believe that he was thoroughly familiar with his work. Indeed, the deleted caption, "Adam's Banishment," prefixed to the fourth draft of his plan for *Paradise Lost* in the Cambridge Manuscript sounds like a conscious or unconscious reproduction of Grotius' title.

We may now consider the extent of the traceable influence of the *Adamus* on *Paradise Lost.* Unlike Andreini's *Adamo,* Grotius' play is a unified and coherent tragedy, on classical lines. It begins with a long soliloquy of Satan, who proceeds from despair and defiance to a determination to ruin Adam. In Act II Adam is instructed in the creation of the world and the fall of Satan by an angel, and holds loving dialogue with Eve. In Act III Satan in his own form tempts Adam and is firmly repulsed. In Act IV he approaches Eve as a serpent, flatters her, and finally persuades her to eat the apple. Adam enters seeking Eve. He is horrified at her deed, but yields to her love and eats. In Act V Satan triumphs in monologue. Adam is tormented by phantoms of despair. Eve endeavors to console him and restrains him from suicide, offering herself as a willing sacrifice to his vengeance. Adam expresses his great love of her. Jehovah, appearing in person, pronounces judgment, and summons the Cherubim to drive them forth. They enter into exile with expression of sorrow at the loss of Eden. The first four acts are each concluded with an angelic chorus.

In general outline this is more remote from Milton's drafts than is the *Adamo*. Milton evidently chose the mystery conception of the theme, with its allegorical attendants, as a means of displaying its wider significance in the scheme of human destiny, and this broader plan persists in the completed epic. But Grotius' play stands much nearer to Milton's actual development of the more dramatic part of his material in the coherence of the plot, in the superior handling of the human motives, and in the philosophical and ethical dignity which pervades the whole. It seems probable that Milton moved farther from Andreini and nearer to Grotius as the plan developed in his mind. When he actually undertook the composition of a drama on the Fall he began not with angelic or allegorical preliminaries, as in Andreini and the preserved drafts, but with a soliloquy of Satan, as in the *Adamus Exul*. In the substance of this soliloquy, as in the whole development of the temptation, fall, repentance, and banishment of Adam and Eve, many of the Miltonic elements are common to both Grotius and Andreini. But the detail is often closer to the Latin than to the Italian treatment. Thus all three poets make much of the brilliant colors and spectacular approach of the serpent; but Milton and Grotius both discard the rabbinical notion of his human face and in general their descriptions of his labyrinthine antics are more nearly identical. In the accounts of Satan's procedure in the temptation of Eve, Grotius, like Milton, makes him suggest a fatalistic philosophy, a detail unrepresented in the *Adamo*. The despair of Adam also is less subtly and elaborately developed in Andreini than in the others and there is no parallel to the proposal of suicide as a way of anticipating the penalty, a proposal which comes in Milton only from Eve, but from each in turn in Grotius. Other similar specific resemblances between *Paradise Lost* and *Adamus Exul* are: the geographical description of Eden; Satan's contrast of his own misery with the bliss of Adam and Eve; Adam's hymn of the visible universe as God's handiwork; the angelic ministration to Adam of cosmic instruction and moral warning (Adam's question about the stars, his narrative of his first awakening, the angel's story of Lucifer's rebellion and of the creation, his emphasis on Adam's superiority to the beasts, are all included, though briefly, in the drama). In Milton's use of such motives as the flattering of Eve by her tempter, his suggestion of God's jealousy as the motive of the prohibition, the reunion of Adam and Eve after their separation, Adam's horror at her deed, the appeal to his love, the changes in nature after the Fall, the reconciliation of the pair after their estrangement, and many others, it is impossible to tell which of his two models he is more closely following.

For the other Renaissance dramas of the Fall which have been alleged as Milton's sources much less can be said. The Italian plays mentioned by Pearce, Peck, and Todd are comparatively obscure and have no outstanding features in common with Milton's which are not conventional. The much argued case for the Dutch poet Vondel's *Lucifer* and his *Adam in Banishment* is less impressive when we consider Vondel's own debt to Grotius, Du Bartas, and other writers whom Milton knew.[70] The *Lucifer* was

[70] The fullest statement of the case for Vondel's influence is that of Edmundson, *Milton and Vondel*. For a more critical review of the evidence see Verity, *Samson Agonistes*, Appendix.

printed in 1654, the *Adam* in 1664, too late in either case to have much affected Milton's original plan. The verbal similarities, when one reads Vondel in the original and not in a Miltonized translation, are inconclusive, and there is the serious question whether Milton in his blindness and with a probably limited knowledge of Dutch could easily have obtained a close familiarity with the work of his contemporary. The significant kinship between *Lucifer* and *Paradise Lost* is that which arises from the independent handling of identical materials by the two great poets of similar culture and imaginative inheritance.

ITALIAN ROMANTIC EPIC; SPENSER; THE FLETCHERS; SHAKESPEARE; MARLOWE. It would naturally be expected that Milton's enthusiasm for the Renaissance masters of romantic narrative, which must have dominated his purpose so long as he continued to cherish the idea of an Arthurian epic, would leave an important impress on the poem which he actually did compose, however alien its theme. In form the looser structure of Boiardo, Ariosto, and Spenser was of course repudiated by him. Tasso's *Gerusalemme Liberata* and its critical defense would have fortified in him the conception of a Christian epic severely classical in outline, but with the more authoritative models of Virgil and Homer before him he needed no recourse in the matter of epic structure to a derived work. The influence of the Italians is quite traceable, however, in many details of *Paradise Lost*. To mention only the outstanding instances, the humorous and satiric description of the Paradise of Fools in Book III is plainly based on Ariosto's picture of a similar limbo of ecclesiastical vanities in the moon (*Orlando Furioso,* Canto XXXIV, stanzas 70 ff.), a passage which Milton had noted in the Commonplace

Book before his Italian journey, and the infernal council
in Book II, though Milton was familiar with similar scenes
from many sources, has much in common with Tasso's
account in the fourth Canto of the *Jerusalem*.[71]

To Spenser his debt was more profound. The beginnings
of it have already been seen in *Comus,* where the adaptation
of myth and allegory to the purpose of earnest philosophical and moral idealism is dominated by the spirit of Milton's great Elizabethan predecessor. To distinguish the
Spenserian element in *Paradise Lost* is not so easy, but
a suggestion of its importance is afforded by Milton's praise
of Spenser in *Areopagitica* as a better teacher than Scotus
or Aquinas and by his remark to Dryden that Spenser was
his "original." Spenser was a better teacher partly because
he was a poet embodying his moral lessons in beautiful
imaginative forms, and partly because he was a humanist,
deriving his philosophy from ancient and not from scholastic thought. As such he stood in Milton's thought as the
truest exemplar among his own countrymen of the poetic
function and was gladly acknowledged, in spite of differences of temper, theme, and style, as a guide and master.
The relationship between *Paradise Lost* and *The Faerie
Queene* is accordingly to be sought not in resemblances of
incident or phrase but in fundamental community of poetic
aim and method. It is pointed out by Professor Greenlaw
in his illuminating discussion of this subject [72] that there
is a striking analogy between Milton's interpretation of the
moral issues involved in Adam's fall and the representation

[71] For discussions of the influence of Tasso see Pommrich, *Miltons
Verhaeltnis zu Tasso,* and for Milton's Italian relations in general
see Allodoli, *Milton e L'Italia.*

[72] *A Better Teacher than Aquinas* and *Spenser's Influence on
"Paradise Lost."*

of virtue under trial in the person of Sir Guyon (*F. Q.* Book II). The basic teaching in each case is that of temperance interpreted according to Platonic ethics as the supremacy of the rational over the passionate principle in the soul. For such doctrine in the abstract Milton needed, of course, no source but Plato and the Renaissance tradition generally, but the claim that he found in Spenser an application of Platonic idealism which made a profound impression on his mind and which stimulated and guided his own imaginative activity is one which cannot be denied.

Professor Greenlaw also finds in Spenser's cosmic speculations materials which he believes entered deeply into the substance of Milton's poetic thought. Both poets draw, to be sure, upon the common stock of ancient, medieval, and Renaissance philosophy for their conception of man and nature, and their employment of an identical scheme of the universe is in itself no proof of Milton's indebtedness. But here, again, we may safely assume that Spenser's poetic embodiment of the cosmic vision in the last two of his *Fowre Hymns* and elsewhere was an early means of rousing Milton's interest in such matters and of firing his imagination to the height of his tremendous theme. Specifically Spenser's account of the mystic garden of Adonis furnished detail for Milton's luxuriant Garden of Eden; his expressions regarding chaos as the womb and grave of nature and the employment of Demogorgon and Night as personifications of the abyss are echoed in *Paradise Lost,* Book III. Finally, there are touches in common [73] between Spenser's story of the attempt of Mutabilitie to

[73] Note besides those mentioned by Greenlaw the sceptical suggestion by Mutabilitie that nature is not really dependent upon God (*F. Q.* VII, vii, 49. Cf. *P. L.* IX, 720).

regain Heaven and Milton's of the ascent of Satan from Hell which appear to show that the later poet felt the analogy between the two episodes and remoulded his traditional materials under the influence of the philosophical myth created by his predecessor. Minor reminiscenes of Spenserian phrase and idea are, of course, common throughout Milton's poetry.[74] The following parallel, not hitherto noted, may be given as a signal illustration of the way in which a recollected scene from Spenser might guide Milton's feeling and poetic expression where one would little expect it. King Arthur (Book I, Canto IX, stanza xv) tells Redcrosse how he dreamed of the lady of his heart and aspiration, hitherto unseen. Adam, recounting to Raphael his earliest experiences (*P. L.* VIII, 452 ff.), describes his vision of Eve in the trance which had been laid upon him during her creation. The high poetic moment in both narratives is that in which the lovers waken with an intense feeling of loss, and the similarities in expression are enough to suggest the discipleship of one poet to the other; the differences measure the vast distance between them. Spenser gives a whole leisurely stanza to the expression of his idea:

> When I awoke, and found her place devoyd,
> And nought but pressed gras wher she had lyen,
> I sorrowed all so much as earst I joyd,
> And washed all her place with watry eyen.
> From that day forth I lov'd that face divyne;
> From that day forth I cast in carefull mynd,
> To seeke her out with labor and long tyne,
> And never vow to rest, till her I fynd:
> Nyne monethes I seek in vain, yet ni'll that vow unbynd.

[74] See the parallels given by Todd, Verity, and other editors.

Milton renders Adam's kindred passion in three concentrated lines:

> She disappeerd, and left me dark, I wak'd
> To find her, or for ever to deplore
> Her loss, and other pleasures all abjure:

The influence of Spenser in coloring Milton's poetic ideas and expression blends with and is often indistinguishable from that of the seventeenth century Spenserians, particularly Giles and Phineas Fletcher, whose work he had known and had felt the power of from his boyhood.[75] Though Milton owed, perhaps, nothing as fundamental to these two poets as he owed to their original, there are, nevertheless, clear traces of the influence of their imaginative conceptions on his own. This is most notable in the case of Phineas, whose infernal council in *The Apollyonists* and its Latin counterpart, *Locustae,* includes a representation of Satan as a majestic and defiant being which bears obvious points of resemblance to Milton's. The same author's allegorical figure of Hamartia in *The Purple Island* and of Sin in *The Apollyonists* is the chief imaginative prototype of the horrible creature whom Satan encounters at Hell gate (*P. L.* III). The case for Giles Fletcher is more a matter of phraseology. Grosart lists such parallels as this:

> Heav'n wakes with all his eyes,
> Whom to behold but thee, Natures desire.
>
> > *P. L.* V, 44-5.

[75] Fully discussed by Grosart, *Poems of Phineas Fletcher*, Essay, pp. 210 ff., 278 ff. See also Cory, *Spenser, the School of the Fletchers and Milton.*

Heaven awakened all his eyes
To see another sunne at midnight rise.
Christ's Victory in Heaven, stanza 78.

The theme of *Christ's Victory in Heaven* is the same as
that of Book III of *Paradise Lost,* except that Fletcher
has preserved the old allegory of the Daughters of God
while Milton has put the Heavenly debate into the mouth
of the Father and the Son. But the provision in the dramatic plans for a discussion of man's fate by Mercy, Justice, and Wisdom points to *Christ's Victory* as an influence
in Milton's elaboration of the scheme of redemption, which
is very scantily represented in Grotius and Andreini.
Broadly speaking, the Fletchers are Milton's most immediate precedents in a kind of poetry which puts a religious subject matter in terms of sensuous beauty. Some
critics are inclined to attribute to them a much larger share
in furnishing suggestion to Milton's imagination in the
actual epic of *Paradise Lost* than to the continental sources
which first led him to project a drama on this theme.
Claims, in this connection, have also been made for the
Davideis, a Biblical epic published in 1656 by Abraham
Cowley.[76]

Of the other English writers to whom Milton owed inspiration Marlowe and Shakespeare are the most conspicuous. Marlowe's style, with its grandiose sweep and its roll
of euphonious and exotic proper names, is generally recognized as having assisted in moulding Milton's own. This

[76] Kirsten, *Studien.* Milton's third wife is reported to have said
that Spenser, Shakespeare, and Cowley were his favorite poets. Todd,
I, 162. For full discussion of the relationship of *Paradise Lost* to
preceding epic literature in English see Tillyard, *The Miltonic Setting,* pp. 141 ff.

relationship is discussed in Chapter VI. A flash, moreover, of magnificent insight in the elder poet's representation of Mephistopheles,

> Why, this is Hell, nor am I out of it,

apparently finds an echo in Satan's

> Which way I fly is Hell, myself am Hell.

Compare also Faustus's speech in Scene V:

> Nay, an this be hell, I'll willingly be damned here;
> What? walking, disputing, etc.?

with *P. L.* II, 163–164:

> Is this then worst,
> Thus sitting, thus consulting, thus in Arms?

It would be difficult to find other specific parallels.

In the case of Shakespeare the relationship is more complex. Milton's eager reading of the plays is well attested, nor did their profound difference in temperament and Milton's later reservations regarding Shakespeare's art diminish the impression which they left upon his memory. How far Shakespeare permanently determined Milton's modes of conceiving dramatic characters and situations it is hard to say, but we seem to catch in the representation of Satan plotting against Adam and Eve an echo of the similar relations of Iago, Othello, and Desdemona, or in his unrepentant remorse a parallel to the soliloquy of King Claudius. Adam's revulsion against Eve is analogous to that of Antony against Cleopatra, his meditation on the burden and mystery of human life (Book XI) like Hamlet's.[77] The parallels, however, though suggestive and, I believe, significant, are intangible, and the case for Shakespeare's influence is largely a matter of specific similarities of phrase. Professor Alwin Thaler [78] has recently collected a surprising array of such resemblances and his list, when all allowances are made for accident, remains a testimony to the degree to which Milton's poetic speech was enriched by the fertile imagination of his greatest Elizabethan predecessor.

In general we may say of Milton's echoings of incident, idea, and phrase in *Paradise Lost* and elsewhere that they illustrate the essentially literary character of his inspiration, the wide range of his reading, and the extraordinarily assimilative quality of his mind. A hint which helps account for the manifold reminiscences in his work is given by the anonymous biographer in his account of Milton's occupations during the period when he was composing *Paradise Lost.* "The evenings he likewise spent in reading some choice poets, by way of refreshment after the day's toil, *and to store his fancy against the morning.*" The cry of plagiarism is, of course, absurd. Milton's own attitude is implied in a statement in *Eikonoklastes:* "Borrowing, if it be not bettered by the borrower, among good authors is accounted plagiarie." He himself certainly leaves nothing as he found it.[79] That is why the resemblances

[77] Hanford, *The Dramatic Element.* Comparison of Milton's and Shakespeare's characterization is incidentally discussed by Stoll, *Belial as an Example.* "In the matter of giving a character a point of view of his own," says Stoll, "Milton is superior."

[78] *The Shakespearean Element in Milton;* see also Taylor, *Shakspere and Milton Again.*

[79] Some of Milton's revisions in the minor poems, Trinity MS., show him altering (and improving) a borrowed phrase. Thus he changes Shakespeare's "yellow sands" in the original text of *Comus*

which I have been discussing are in general so shadowy. All is transformed to the substance of his imagination. The Miltonic accent is everywhere, and when the labors of the source hunters are done, *Paradise Lost* remains one of the most original works in English or in any literature.

to "tawny sands" and the Shakespearean adjective "unmarried" as applied to the primrose to "unwedded" in *Lycidas*.

CHAPTER V

PARADISE REGAINED AND SAMSON AGONISTES

MILTON'S last two works appeared in 1671, in a single volume bearing the following title: *Paradise Regained. A Poem. In IV Books. To which is added Samson Agonistes. The Author John Milton.* The date of entry in the Stationers' Register is September 20, 1670. The poems had been licensed on July 2 of the same year. No positive evidence of the date or order of their composition is available. The natural inference, however, that *Paradise Regained,* being, as it is, a kind of sequel to *Paradise Lost,* would have followed that work directly, is supported by Thomas Ellwood's account of the part which he himself played in suggesting it. He had returned the manuscript of *Paradise Lost* to Milton at Chalfont St. Giles toward the end of the year 1665 with the remark, "Thou hast said much of Paradise lost, but what hast thou to say of Paradise found?" When he visited the poet again some time after his return to London in 1666 Milton showed him his second poem, saying, "This is owing to you; for you put it in my head by the question you put to me at Chalfont, which before I had not thought of." Edward Phillips is uncertain of the date of *Samson* but says that *Paradise Regained* was "doubtless begun and finished and printed after the other (*Paradise Lost*) was published," i.e., August, 1667.

Notwithstanding this statement it seems likely that both had been in Milton's mind for some time. In *The Reason of Church Government* (see Appendix B) he had mentioned, as literary forms sanctioned by classical or Biblical precedent, the long epic, the brief epic (like the Book of Job), and the drama.[1] *Paradise Lost, Paradise Regained,* and *Samson Agonistes* fit this classification perfectly. It is not necessary to say that Milton definitely planned at this time to give the public a single specimen of each, but it is clear that he was considering and hesitating between various forms and models, and we may regard it as significant that, having chosen the epic on classic lines as his first great enterprise, he should, when he came to write again, have wished to experiment with the other types. As to the subjects, the Cambridge Manuscript notes written circa 1641 contain the suggestion of a drama on the life of Christ —"Christus Patiens"—and several topics from the history of Samson.[2] The theme of *Paradise Regained* was in a

---

[1] W. R. Parker, *On Milton's Early Literary Program,* points out that Milton, in this ecclesiastical pamphlet, is partly concerned to vindicate his respect for ancient literary forms by showing that Christian and even Scriptural writers employed them. (Cf. the Preface to *Samson Agonistes* and *Paradise Regained,* IV, 284 ff.) Job is cited as a "brief model" of the epic since the Bible obviously contains no "diffuse" model. Parker's observations are just, but they do not prove that Milton did not consciously or unconsciously accept the "brief epic" as a formal literary type along with the others and consider its fitness for his present or future purposes.

[2] W. R. Parker, *The Trinity Manuscript and Milton's Plans for a Tragedy,* justly questioning the definite statements which have been made by the present writer and others regarding the number of Samson dramas which Milton lists, goes too far in saying that these early entries reveal no particular concern with the subject.

sense logically necessitated by *Paradise Lost,* not that Milton had failed in the earlier poem to present Christ's part in the theological scheme of salvation, but because he wished to give the actual process in Christ, considered as a representative of humanity, of the successful meeting of temptation corresponding to the failure of Adam in a similar situation. The analogy between Adam and Samson had already been noted in *Paradise Lost,* IX, 1059–1062, and the Hebrew champion is more than once used in the prose as an instructive symbol.[3]

There is evidence that Milton not only supervised the printing of the 1671 edition with care,[4] but, perhaps, actually made an addition to *Samson Agonistes* while the work was going through the press. Lines 1527–1535 appear at the end under the heading *omissa.* The passage in the main body of the text seems coherent without them and they may well be an afterthought designed to introduce the element of irony into the situation at this point. If so, they suggest the fact that Milton's creative interest in *Samson*

His "marriage choices," his "hybris," his various triumphs as God's champion, all of which are suggested by Milton's titles, touch closely on some of Milton's deepest interests. It would be curious to know whether the original entry and the revisions were made before or after his own marriage.

[3] In *The Reason of Church Government* the story of Samson is developed as a political allegory. Samson is the king, his locks are the laws by which he rules, Dalila and the Philistines are the prelates, enemies both of the sovereign and of the state. (See Clark, *Milton's Earlier Samson.*) Even more striking is the allusion in *Areopagitica:* "Methinks I see in my mind a noble and puissant nation rousing herself like a strong man after sleep and shaking her invincible locks." From Samson as reformed England to Samson as Milton himself is but a step. The story evidently grew in significance with the poet's own developing experience and philosophy.

[4] See Appendix E.

was still active at the time of its publication in the third last year of his life.

PARADISE REGAINED

SOURCES. The poem follows step by step the incidents of the temptation as given in the Gospel of Luke (the order in Matthew is different). The earlier events of Christ's life are introduced in retrospect and the later by implication. The elaboration of detail is largely the work of Milton's own thought and imagination, but Spenser and his successor Giles Fletcher furnished suggestions of no slight importance. The major debt is to the episode of the temptation of Sir Guion (*Faerie Queene,* Book II, Canto VIII). Spenser, like Milton, makes his demon offer wealth and (in the person of Philotime) worldly power and glory. Mammon tries to reason Sir Guion into acceptance as Satan tries to reason Christ. The two moral heroes reject in similar terms the baits held out to them. Guion's moment of apparent hesitation

> Me list not (said the Elfin knight) receave
> Thing offred, till I know it be well got,

and his exhaustion after the victory illustrate his humanity and differentiate him from Milton's Christ. Yet even here there are parallels. Thus to Satan's question:

> If thou had'st food would'st thou not eat?

Christ replies:

> Thereafter as I like the giver.

And both Guion and Christ receive physical aid divinely sent. It is evident that Spenser himself is shadowing the temptation of Christ. (Mammon's habitation is called a desert, stanza 78; and Guion is said to have been tempted three days, stanza 65). Milton must have perceived this fact and adapted the usable elements in the allegory as contributing to his own interpretation of the Scriptural event. His Christ, therefore, becomes a symbol of temperance, less explicitly but not less certainly, than Spenser's Sir Guion.[5] The influence of Giles Fletcher's *Christ's Victory and Triumph,* though the poem deals directly with the temptation and was certainly known to Milton, is less significant. Fletcher had modeled his portrait of Satan more or less on Spenser's Archimago and Milton follows him in this. Hughes says [6] that Milton's conception of Christ is to be judged in the light of the epic tradition from Boccaccio and Petrarch. It represents a fusion of the faith of the reformers in a Redeemer—the Logos of St. John's Gospel —with the craving of the critics and poets of the later Renaissance for the purely exemplary epic hero. Milton had behind him also a long line of Scriptural commentary by eminent divines with whose work he was familiar. This material deserves to be carefully explored by Milton students.

In its structure the poem is beyond doubt deeply influenced by the Book of Job, which, as we have seen, Milton regarded as a model of the brief epic. Milton parallels the trial of Christ and the trial of Job in Book I, lines 146 ff. The two works have the common characteristic of

[5] Greenlaw (*A Better Teacher than Aquinas*) makes much of this relationship. To him Spenser was indeed Milton's "original."

[6] *The Christ of "Paradise Regained."* See also his edition, pp. 405 ff., and Tillyard's answer, *The Christ of "Paradise Regained"*

and assimilated until it has become part of the substance of Milton's thought and no longer recognizable as borrowing.

EXPOSITORY OUTLINE. The first seven lines of Book I link the theme of the new poem with that of *Paradise Lost*. Christ's successful foiling of the tempter is the logical counterpart of Adam's succumbing to his wiles. The invocation is made directly to the Divine Spirit, and not, as in *Paradise Lost*, to a Muse or other symbol. The starting point of the action is the hearing by Satan of the divine pronouncement at the baptism of Jesus, "This is my beloved son." A new council is summoned in middle air and Satan again appointed to the mission of seduction. The scene then changes to Heaven and God predicts to the assembled angels the victory of the new Adam in the coming conflict, as he had earlier predicted the fall of man. The angels sing a psalm of triumph. Christ now enters the wilderness and recalls in self-communion the events of his career which have brought him as he supposed to the moment of the beginning of his ministry. The intent of God in conducting him into this desert place he does not yet perceive. After forty days Satan appears disguised as an old man, proposing, in language almost as bare as that of the Scriptural account itself, the terms of the first temptation. Christ's rejection is equally brief and simple. The words "why dost thou then suggest to me distrust?" clearly reveal Milton's interpretation of the incident. Satan has, to quote the commentary of Calvin on the first temptation,[7] "made a direct attack on the faith of Christ, in the hope that, after destroying his faith, he would drive Christ to unlawful and wicked methods of

[7] Quoted by Gilbert, *The Temptation in "Paradise Regained,"* p. 4. and the curious detail supplied by Horrell. *Milton, Limbo and Suicide.*

procuring food." In the succeeding dialogue Satan, now revealed in his true person, utters a fawning and hypocritical complaint. Christ pronounces his misery deserved and interposes no objection to his proposal of further conversation. The scene ends with Satan's vanishing and the coming on of night. In this book Milton makes little effort to enrich or elaborate his theme. His language is restrained by reverence. The plain meaning speaks.

In Book II Andrew, Simon, and others who have been baptized with Christ experience perplexity and a sense of loss at his disappearance, but they give expression to the hope that God will not allow his promises to be defeated. Mary also accepts in patience the absence of her son. The scene now reverts to middle air, whither Satan returns for further deliberation with his peers. His speech to them is entirely lacking in the high spirit of defiant ardor which had informed his utterance in the first books of *Paradise Lost*. Belial, too, has lost his eloquence, though not his sensuality; his vain suggestion, "set women in his eye," is scornfully rejected. Satan's superior intelligence perceives that the simple allurement which has sufficed for Adam's weakness is here of no avail. He proposes manlier objects —honor, glory, and popular praise—as the material of his second and more elaborate attempt, preparing first, however, a more elemental appeal to appetite and natural need. This introductory approach is not, as some critics have thought, a continuation or inartistic repetition of the first temptation, which has been definitely ended and is marked off by an intervening night and day, and which, besides, as I have said, represented something quite different from a mere offer of bread. It is rather the first step in the second, which is to comprise, in the Biblical phrase, "the kingdoms of the world and the glory of them." [8] Milton proceeds, as we shall see, through a kind of scale of values, and he appropriately begins with bodily luxury, the lowest and simplest object of worldly attainment. It is proper, therefore, that the offer should take the form of a gorgeous Roman banquet with all the accompanying blandishments of sense.

Christ's preliminary dream of food is parallel to the dream of Eve in Book V of *Paradise Lost*. We are told that now, for the first time, he hungers. Satan asks, "If food were now before thee set wouldst thou not eat?" and Christ replies, "Thereafter as I like the giver." The point is that the satisfaction of a fleshly need is not in itself a sin, but may become so when a moral issue is involved. The rich repast is the offering of Satan and is accordingly rejected. Christ's victory, here, as later, is a victory of temperance, the triumph of reason over desire.

Wealth is next offered as a means to power. Jesus in reply disparages riches without virtue. Material possession is the "wise man's cumbrance if not snare." As for the scepter which wealth can buy, true kingship is the sovereignty of man over himself, and the royal crown, golden in show, is but a wreath of thorns.

In Book III, without break in the action, Satan proceeds to propose the higher object—glory—a fruit of empire as empire had been of wealth. In a noble passage Christ anatomizes the conception, expressing Milton's scorn of the brutish fame of conquerors, and setting beside it the true fame of those spiritual heroes who sought it not. The lines are linked with the digression on the "last in-

[8] See Gilbert, *The Temptation in "Paradise Regained."* A different view of Milton's handling of the temptation is that of R. D. Miller.

firmity of noble mind" in *Lycidas* and the conclusion is the same.

As an abstract object of ambition, glory is the highest Satan has to offer. He now turns, more subtly, to matters directly connected with the fulfillment of Christ's mission, and, under guise of giving him experience toward its accomplishment, he exhibits the then kingdoms of the earth before his eyes. First, Parthia, a symbol of military strength and efficiency, inviting leadership, and affording a golden opportunity for the domination of the world. Christ's reply is that all arms are vanity, an argument of human weakness rather than of strength. His own weapons are spiritual, and his time is not yet come. As for the ten tribes of Israel, their deliverance from bondage is no work of his but is in the hands of God.

At the beginning of Book IV Satan, with increasing hopelessness, sets the face of his intended victim to the west. Rome in her glory, present mistress of the world, is at his will. It is a type of grandeur and magnificence, and, as such, is refused, like the ostentation vain of arms before. Technically, this concludes the offer of the kingdoms of the earth, and at this point Satan—futilely, since they have already been rejected—proposes his condition: "All these things will I give thee, if thou wilt fall down and worship me." Milton has, however, an important and characteristic addition to make. Christ has completely vindicated his superiority to all the glory which allures the minds of the great mass of talented ambitious men. It has, indeed, been the public glamour of these things rather than the things themselves on which Satan has relied to appeal to a spirit whom he recognized from the first as above succumbing to the inglorious enticements of secret sensuality.

Even the banquet was a kind of entertainment calculated to amaze the populace by its magnificence and lavishness. There remains a type of glory which by its very nature appeals only to the few and can hardly be said to belong to the fleshly kingdoms of the world—the glory namely, of wisdom and intellectual achievement, represented best by ancient Athens. With new enthusiasm Milton makes his Satan portray this loftier ideal in all its beauty. The passage is a wonderful résumé of the supreme accomplishments of Pagan culture—its creation of the great literary forms of epic, drama, lyric; its majestic oratory; its final fruit in philosophy, "from Heaven descended to the low-roofed house of Socrates," and proceeding from his fertile suggestion to the development of all the memorable schools of thought. Here, then, is an object, the attraction of which Milton himself felt in fullest measure and which, when offered to the historical Christ as a means at once congenial to his temper and apparently harmonious with his spiritual aims, might well be supposed to prove alluring. He replies, not altogether by rejecting it, but by exalting above it the inspired literature of the Hebrews, superior at every point in spiritual truth. Without despising the claims of intellectual culture and the arts, Christ avoids the snare of pride—that last infirmity of the noble mind divinely gifted with the capability of adding to the world's precious heritage of spiritual truth and beauty.

This test concludes the second temptation. Abruptly and in anger Satan proceeds to a final desperate attempt. The new method which he adopts is that of violence—the last resource of those whom the arts of reasoning have failed. Such, at least, is Milton's curious interpretation of the third temptation. Christ is set upon a pinnacle of the temple, with the scornful word:

> There stand, if thou wilt stand; to stand upright
> Will ask thee skill . . . if not to stand,
> Cast thy self down.

And Satan, with his persistent scepticism, looks to see him fall. The answer is no act of Christ's but a miracle. To the amazement of his enemy he remains divinely supported in his "uneasy station" and it is Satan himself who falls.[9] A throng of angels now bear the Lord from on high to a flowery valley and give him the food which he has refused at Satan's hand. The Heavenly choir sing triumph and the founding of a fairer Paradise. The poem ends with the quiet return of Jesus to his mother's house.

SAMSON AGONISTES

SOURCES. Milton is dependent on Scripture (Judges, xiii–xvi) for the material of *Samson Agonistes* and in the main on that alone. There is no convincing evidence that he made any extensive use of other literary treatments of the theme. The case for his indebtedness to Vondel's *Samson,* published in 1660, a drama in classical form, dealing, like Milton's, with the last day of the hero's life, has been strongly urged by Edmundson [10] and attacked with equal vehemence by Verity [11] and others. The similarities in phrase are not very striking, and the likeness in plot

[9] See Gilbert's interpretation, *The Temptation in "Paradise Regained."*
[10] *Milton and Vondel.*
[11] *Samson Agonistes,* Appendix.

structure hardly greater than would naturally result from an independent moulding of the Biblical materials into the form of ancient tragedy. We have already seen that the specific subject of Samson's death had long been present in Milton's mind. The development of the action by a series of visits to Samson finds no parallel in Vondel.

Some minor details are said to have been taken from the history of Samson in the fifth book of Josephus. Verity points to a description of the ruins at Gaza of the "theater of Samson" in George Sandys' *Relation of Foreign Travel* as having very probably furnished Milton with hints as to the kind of structure which Samson pulled down on the heads of the Philistines. A *History of Samson,* written in 1632 by Francis Quarles, has, as Whiting points out, some striking parallels.

Aside from the Bible, the great formative influence in *Samson Agonistes* is classical tragedy. The relation here is so important as to deserve separate discussion.

RELATIONS TO GREEK DRAMA AND TO THE CLASSICAL THEORY OF TRAGEDY. On the title page of the first edition of *Samson Agonistes* Milton printed as a motto Aristotle's definition of tragedy—"the imitation of a serious action, etc., effecting through pity and fear a purification of such emotions." In his introductory note he discusses the crux of this definition, the old question as to what is meant by the catharsis of the emotions, and gives an interpretation which has commended itself to modern critics.[12] Tragedy converts the emotions to which we are subject from a source of pain to a source of pleasure by artistically embodying them in a dramatic fiction. The pity and fear stirred up in us in the theater are a homeopathic dose, purg-

[12] It is identical with that of the Italian, Minturno.

ing the mind of its unwholesome private passions. This idea and purpose are prominently in Milton's consciousness as he writes the poem. He makes Samson describe his own inner agony in terms which strongly suggest the medical figure used in the introduction, and he has the chorus indicate at the close the calming and ennobling effect which the witnessing of this great event has had on the minds of the spectators.[13] Perhaps he also recognized an analogous effect upon himself, a tempering of such bitter moods as may occasionally have come upon him in his old age. At any rate Milton took tragedy very seriously and regarded it as a significant literary form. To be such, however, it must be written in the direct tradition of classical antiquity; it must eschew the sensationalism of the modern stage and behave itself according to the body of principles laid down by Aristotle in the *Poetics,* elaborated by the critics of the Renaissance, and illustrated by the individual dramas of Aeschylus, Sophocles, and Euripides.[14] *Samson Agonistes* is offered to us as a model of what, in

[13] See Hanford, *"Samson Agonistes" and Milton in Old Age.*

[14] See Jebb, *"Samson Agonistes" and the Hellenic Drama;* Baum, *"Samson Agonistes" Again;* and Brewer, *Two Athenian Models for Samson Agonistes.* Tillyard, *Milton,* pp. 343-345, discusses the use of *peripeteia* in Samson and makes the claim that in this matter as well as in that of catharsis Milton understood Aristotle better than most of his modern commentators. "A *peripeteia* happens, not when there is a mere change of fortune, but when an intention or action brings about the opposite of what is meant. . . . The essence of the plot in *Samson* is that nearly all the actions should lead whither they had not seemed to lead. Jebb pointed out how everything in the plot narrows Samson's prospects into greater and greater chance of ignominy. . . . The *peripeteia* consists in this choice of apparent ignominy inevitably leading to triumph." In thus making his action depend on *peripeteia,* Tillyard thinks, Milton ranged his plot under the heading of complex, preferred by Aristotle to the simple form. Milton himself in the introductory

the purpose at once of interpreting the emotions appropriate to the successive moments in the action, of clarifying
the larger significance of the whole, and of rounding out
the story by allusions to Samson's past. The narration of
the messenger was a substitute for the actual representation of the catastrophe, which Milton avoided, not only
because the Greeks had done so, but because verisimilitude,
dignity, and the desire to focus attention not on the sensational event but on its dramatic significance all demanded it.

But Milton was deeply influenced by the content as well
as by the form of ancient tragedy. He found precedents
for his suffering hero in more than one tragic figure of
antiquity and he remoulded him to a considerable degree
in their great images. Aeschylus's Prometheus is akin to
Samson in the grandeur of his woe, but there is something
of a parallel with Heracles, a giant of strength like Samson, and a performer of incredible labors, but subject also
like Samson to a spiritual weakness and becoming enthralled and ultimately brought to destruction by the influence of woman. The specific Heracles drama which
here enters into comparison with Milton's is the *Trachiniæ*
of Sophocles. In other features *Samson Agonistes* is closer
akin to the *Oedipus at Colonnus,* the direct influence of
which is very apparent. Oedipus, blind and helpless by
his own error, is visited by a succession of friends and
enemies. He resists the blandishments and threats of Creon
as Samson resists those of the Philistines. His former
greatness and present misery are remembered in dialogue
and chorus. His end is a triumph, though of different sort.
Particularly noticeable as a feature derived from the very
essence of Greek tragedy is Milton's attempt to interpret
Samson's tragic error as hybris, that overconfidence which

INTERPRETATION. The outward action of *Samson Agonistes* is summarized by Milton himself in an argument prefixed to the original edition. Though he does not divide the play into acts he intimates in his prefatory note that a five-act structure is discernible. Professor Parker, though he declines to call the divisions acts and prefers an analysis of structure based on the practice of the Greeks themselves,[16] recognizes that the play falls into "five distinct parts, each an artistic whole, and all of very nearly the same length." His designation of these parts is substantially the same as the traditional act division of the editors.[17]

1. Samson alone and with the Chorus: 1–325
2. Samson and Manoa: 326–709
3. Samson and Dalilah: 710–1060
4. Samson with two instruments of force: 1061–1440
5. Samson at the Feast: 1441–1758.

This enumeration of incidents gives no indication of

Milton's Debt to Greek Tragedy in "Samson Agonistes." Parker concludes, against Jebb, that Euripides, though Milton's favorite dramatist, is not the predominant influence in *Samson*. Milton was more like Aeschylus in his attitude toward his materials, but it is Sophocles to whom he is most deeply indebted. To Parker there is no disparity between the Hellenic form and the Hebraic substance. *"Samson Agonistes* is 'Greek' in the sense that a tragedy written in the days of Aristotle might have been. . . . Because the English poet had intellectual or artistic affinities with each of his three models, he wrote—not as an imitator of one of them or two—but as a great successor of all three."

[16] A prologos, 1–114; a parados or entering chorus, 115–175; five episodes and five stasima in alternation, 176–292, 293–325, 326–651, 652–709, 710–1009, 1010–1060, 1061–1267, 1268–1299, 1300–1426, 1427–1440; an exodos, 1441–1758, and a kommos, 1660–1758. Parker, *Milton's Debt to Greek Tragedy,* p. 17.

[17] See, for example, the earlier editions of the *Handbook.*

the real dramatic movement, and *Samson Agonistes* has often been said to be deficient in this respect. Samuel Johnson declared that it had a beginning and an end but no middle. To his mind the various visits were merely episodic, accomplishing nothing in the development of plot and climax. Such a judgment does injustice to the subtlety of Milton's inward interpretation of his theme. The drama is concerned essentially with the fallen Samson's recovery of God's lost favor. This process involves his punishment and repentance and a sort of probation under new trial, a trial provided by the timidity and lack of faith of Manoa and the Chorus, by the attempted seductions of Dalilah, and by the threats of Harapha. The spiritual movement is really much richer than one at first observes.

At the opening Samson is a spectacle of tragic woe. He expresses in language which rivals the greatest utterances of Shakespeare or the Greeks the misery and debasement of his present state, and the first chorus, unheard by him, echoes and interprets his lament, with emphasis on the contrast between what he once was and what he now is. In the ensuing dialogues his attention is diverted to the causes and significance of his suffering. The memory of his fault is more bitter than the punishment wherewith it is visited. He is, however, firm in his conviction, against the intimation of the Chorus, that he was, even in his marriage choices, led by God as his chosen instrument, and he replies to their somewhat malicious

Yet Israel still serves with all his tribes

by imputing the fault to Israel's governors who neglected the opportunities which his deeds of strength made for them. The sight of Manoa wakes "another inward grief," and his words are a goad to Samson's bitter remembrance. To his implied doubt of the justice of God's dealings in apparently electing his son as the champion of Israel and then deserting him, Samson again opposes the attitude of faith. God's ways are just. Though he himself, through his own fault, has advanced the cause of Dagon and brought doubt into the feeble hearts of Israel, "propense enough before," he remains unshaken in the belief that God will not long

> Connive, or linger, thus provok'd,
> But will arise and his great name assert.

He has as yet no intimation that he is himself to become the instrument of God's purposes, but he instinctively rejects his father's proposal to treat with the Philistine lords for his release. The whole result of the mistaken attempts at comfort has been to sharpen Samson's misery. The scene culminates in a spiritual outburst, expressive no longer of the hero's physical suffering but of the agony of soul which springs from full contemplation of his sins "and sense of Heaven's desertion."

Henceforth we have recovery. By confronting his own guilt without evasion, and by resisting the temptation to doubt that God's ways are just or to fear for the ultimate triumph of his cause, Samson has won the right to be put to proof a second time. His firmness is subjected first to the insidious approaches of Dalilah, whose visit, however doubtfully motivated in itself, is essential to the idea of the drama. Her plea is specious, but Samson remains unmoved, the significance of his victory being pointed out in the choric comment,

> Yet beauty, though injurious, hath strange power,
> After offence returning, to regain
> Love once possest, nor can be easily
> Repuls't, without much inward passion felt
> And secret sting of amorous remorse.

He next confronts physical force in the person of Harapha, who collapses, like all brute menace, before the champion's indifference to fear, and the Chorus, participating for the moment in Samson's strength, sings the great ode,

> O how comely it is and how reviving
> To the Spirits of just men long opprest!
> When God into the hands of their deliverer
> Puts invincible might
> To quell the mighty of the Earth, th' oppressour,
> The brute and boist'rous force of violent men.

They are, of course, like Samson himself, still blind to what is to come, and they go on to sing of patience as the final crown of saints.

The coming of the officer creates a problem. Samson's refusal, at first, to do his bidding illustrates his uncompromising allegiance to the God of his fathers and his contempt of personal safety. The Chorus suggests the easier way of yielding, pointing out the fact that he has already served the Philistines (with the old implication that he cannot regard himself as a being set apart). Their reasoning is met with a clear distinction between compromise in things indifferent and the surrender of a point of conscience. Then, as if in answer to this final proof of Samson's single devotedness to God's service, comes again the inner prompting, "disposing to something ex-

traordinary my thoughts." He obeys it unhesitatingly and
goes forth under divine guidance as of old. Manoa, meanwhile, is busy with misguided plans for his son's release,
the moment of his success ironically coinciding with that
of Samson's death. The news of Samson's last destructive
act [18] is received by his friends with grief and horror, turning to satisfaction in the fact that Samson died

> With God not parted from him, as was feard,
> But favouring and assisting to the end,

and to exultation in this manifestation of the Almighty's
triumph over his enemies.[19]

As thus interpreted *Samson Agonistes* fits closely into

[18] In his final justification of Samson, Milton felt obliged, as St.
Augustine and other theologians had done, to clear him of the taint of
suicide.

> And now ly'st victorious
> Among thy slain *self-kill'd*
> *Not willingly,* but tangl'd in the fold
> Of dire necessity, whose law in death conjoin'd
> Thee with thy slaughter'd foes.

This final act, like his first marriage, was a result of the divine
prompting and therefore not subject to the common ethical judgment.
(Cf. Augustine, *De Civitate Dei* I, xxi: Nec Samson aliter excusatur
. . . nisi quia spiritus latenter hoc iusserat.) Grierson, who elaborates
this point, suggests that Milton might have employed a similar formula in thinking of the "crimes" of the Republican party, when, after
the Restoration, all men joined in execrating them: "these acts are
not of man but of God and God will vindicate his cause." See H. J. C.
Grierson, *A Note upon the "Samson Agonistes" of John Milton and
"Samson of Heilige Wraeck" by Joost Van Den Vondel.* (Extrait
des *Mélanges Baldensperger*), H. Champion, Paris, 1930, also his
discussion in *Milton and Wordsworth,* pp. 138 ff.

[19] Compare with this Parker's more detailed exposition, *Milton's
Debt,* pp. 30–59. Parker says that Samson's reconciliation to God was
not possible until he had proved himself master of his old weakness
by rejecting the blandishments of Dalila. Milton is not very successful
in representing an emotional conflict in Samson here, if he intended
to do so. We have to take it on faith that he was moved to anything

the scheme of Milton's major works. It is—in a different sense to be sure from *Paradise Regained* but hardly less significantly—a counterpart of *Paradise Lost*. Lines 1059–62 of the ninth book of the latter poem show that Milton was conscious of an analogy between the sin of Adam and that of Samson. The last phase of the Hebrew champion's career provides a concrete illustration of the power of a free but erring will to face its sin, maintain itself in obedience, and be restored to grace. The drama, like the epics, is an assertion of eternal Providence and a justification of the ways of God to man.

Artistically the poem needs no paraphernalia of critical or biographical interpretation to insure its effect. Its monumental dignity, its consummate expression of the anguish of the human spirit, its extraordinary subtlety of metrical and rhetorical effect—these in themselves are sufficient to make it for many readers the most impressive of Milton's works. Yet it gains from association with our picture of Milton himself in the last days of his heroic life, blind and alone amid the alien society of the Restoration, confronted with the apparent failure of the cause for which he had battled, but seeking in religious faith the assurance that God

> will not long defer
> To vindicate the glory of his name
> Against all competition, nor will long
> Endure it, doubtful whether God be Lord,
> Or Dragon.

The analogy between his own position and that of his protagonist must have been vividly present to his mind,

but wrath. Obviously this visit like that of Harapha rouses him and "determines his will" and, in so doing, advances the action.

and into the representation of Samson he has undoubtedly
put more of himself than into any other of his imaginative creations. The sense of power and dignity, the "plain
heroic magnitude of mind," the will toward championship
—are Milton.[20] So, too, is the consciousness of deprivation
in the loss of sight ("The sun to me is dark and silent as
the moon"), and the sense of physical helplessness ("In
power of others, never in my own"). In many passages
the personal note is far too clear to be mistaken. Thus, in
the great lament of the Chorus, beginning with line 608, the
phrases, "Unjust tribunals under change of times," "Their
carcasses to dogs and fowls a prey," are certainly echoes
of the Restoration, with its brutal trials of men like Sir
Henry Vane and the indignities to which the bodies of
Cromwell and Ireton were subjected. The parallel and
not less wretched fate of poverty and disease is Milton's
own. He goes so far as almost to specify the rheumatic
ills from which he suffered—"painful diseases and de-
formed"—with the bitter reflection that these afflictions,
justly the fruit of dissipation, may come also to those who,
like himself, have lived in temperance. We must beware,

[20] The Milton, at least, of other days. Tillyard thinks that the poet
had recovered his lost faith in action and is affirming it in this poem.
Paradise Regained, he says, "concerns itself with a single idea,
namely that action is to be distrusted and that what matters almost
exclusively is that inner paradise which it is in the power of every
individual to attain." In *Samson* "he makes a deed, not a thought, the
center of his drama." This may be true, but I find it hard to believe
that Milton, in spite of the fact that he did actually reënter the field
of public controversy in 1674, had any such expectation of personal
achievement for his country's good as he possessed in 1650. *Samson*
in this respect is a wish fulfillment only. The reader may turn to
Manoa's speech in lines 1489–1501 and estimate for himself the analogy and the contrast which Milton felt between his own destiny and
that of Samson.

however, of making the identification of Samson and Milton too complete. Unlike his hero Milton himself was conscious of no fault, and even where Samson's expressions of suffering are appropriate enough in their application to his own case, we must remember that all is heightened and idealized for purposes of art. The tragic gloom and flat despair of Samson, the wretchedness of pain, the distaste of life are the embodiments of an aesthetic mood which owes as much to literature as it does to personal experience. Milton doubtless realized in himself the baleful force of such emotions, but he had against them the sure guidance of religious faith and the consoling power of poetry. The very expression of them, under the shield of dramatic objectivity, must have been a kind of deliverance from sorrow, a means of securing for himself the serenity of soul which, in spite of all, he evidently possessed throughout his later days. But the fact that *Samson Agonistes* triumphantly illustrates the working of divine Providence and ends on a note of peace and consolation does not prevent it from leaving on the reader an impression mainly tragic. The facts of suffering and death are not so easily resolved by religious faith. Despite his assured belief that "all is best," Milton is too human and too great not to have experienced in full measure the tragic sense of life, and *Samson Agonistes* stands with *Oedipus* and with *King Lear* as a sublime expression of the greatness and the misery of man.[21]

[21] See Parker's able discussion of the issue long ago raised by Jebb and especially his explanation (p. 242) of the reason why, though the philosophy of the two works is the same, *Samson Agonistes* is more tragic than *Paradise Lost*. But even in the story of the Fall, as told by Milton with all "appliances and means" of regeneration, there is an element of tragedy unresolved.

CHAPTER VI

MILTON'S STYLE AND VERSIFICATION

WITH SPECIAL REFERENCE TO "PARADISE LOST"

MILTON, of all English writers, is the greatest innovator in the matter of expression. It is not merely that his style is individual as that of Shelley or Wordsworth or Browning is individual. It is, in effect, a new and unique medium forged out of various materials and marked by bold departures from the English literary usage of his own or any time. The most interesting features of Miltonic expression are those that are most clearly the result of the individual temper and the peculiar mental habit of its author; those, also, which serve most definitely to suggest his predilections and affinities.

We may note first that his style, despite his employment of a verse form identical with the Elizabethan dramatists, stands at an opposite pole from that of Shakespeare and his colleagues. Milton's language, unlike theirs, has little relish of the speech of men. Where their anomalies are colloquial and idiomatic, his are the product of a preference for the unusual and recondite, in vocabulary and construction, which leads him to archaism on the one hand, and to the substitution of foreign idiom, particularly Latin, for native on the other. Sometimes not even classical or earlier English example can be alleged. Milton is simply carving for himself, remoulding and creating with fine dis-regard for precedent. In general, Milton's style may be described as almost uniquely literary and intellectual. Freighted with learning and bookish phrase, elaborate in construction, often alien in vocabulary,[1] it achieves a uni-form effect of dignity and aloofness and becomes a perfect medium for the restrained and elevated yet intensely pas-sionate personality of its author.[2]

When we come to consider specific characteristics of Miltonic English, we are confronted with a large and dif-ficult task. The nearest approach to systematic treatment is that of David Masson in the third volume of his edition of the *Poetical Works*. The detail of this is too elaborate for presentation here, and much of it is simply a statement

---

[1] Some modification should perhaps be made in the emphasis I have placed on Milton's Latin diction. He uses a larger proportion of words of Latin derivation than Shakespeare, a smaller one than many prose writers, for example, Samuel Johnson. He is not so far from the norm of English poets as one might expect. Marsh estimated 33 per cent of Anglo-Saxon words in Milton's total vocabulary as against 60 per cent for Shakespeare and the English Bible (see the studies of Milton's diction in progress at the University of Texas under the direction of Professor E. M. Clark), but statistics in any case do not tell the story. One unusual word of whatever origin, or one word used in a sense not English, may count more than a dozen which merely happen to be derived from Latin, and it is difficult to distinguish between effects of diction and effects of syntax. Biblical phrase, archaism, allusions, and exotic names contribute as much to the remote and unusual character of Milton's style as Latinity. Much of Milton, even in *Paradise Lost,* is English pure and undefiled. It remains true, however, that his speech is not "a selection of the language used by men." Donne and Dryden come nearer to being that. Milton is in the Spenserian tradition of ornate expression, though he has given it a new turn.

[2] For the current complaint against the rhetorical character of Mil-ton's style and its allegedly bad influence on subsequent English poetry see below, p. 346.

of peculiarities of sixteenth and seventeenth century usage in general. Professor Havens [3] has given a simpler classification of the characteristics of Miltonic style which were thought in the eighteenth century to distinguish it from other poetry and which the poets of the period felt obliged to reproduce when they wrote blank verse. Though not pretending to completeness or scientific accuracy, this list is a very serviceable statement of the obvious differentia of Milton's poetic speech in his blank verse poems. It includes, besides the vaguer items of dignity, stateliness, the "organ tone," the following concrete characteristics: [4]

1. Inversion of the natural order of words and phrases:

> Them thus imploid beheld
> With pittie Heav'ns high King. . . .
>
> *P. L.* V, 219–20.

and especially the placing of a word between two others which depend upon it or on which it depends, e. g., (noun between adjectives), "temperate vapours bland"; (verb between nouns), "Firm peace recovered soon and wonted calm."

2. The omission of words not necessary to the sense:

> . . . extended wide
> In circuit, undetermind square or round
>
> *P. L.* II, 1047–48.

3. Parenthesis and apposition:

> Of Abbana and Pharphar, lucid streams
>
> *P. L.* I, 469.

[3] *The Influence of Milton,* pp. 80–88.
[4] I have slightly modified some of Havens' statements and have retained in each case only one or two of his many illustrations.

> Thir song was partial, but the harmony
> (What could it less when Spirits immortal sing?)
> Suspended Hell. . . .
>
> *P. L.* II, 552–4.

4. The use of one part of speech for another: e. g., (verb form as noun) "the great consult began"; (adjective form as adverb or as noun) "grinned horrible"; "the palpable obscure"; "dark with excessive bright."

5. Archaisms and Latinisms in vocabulary: e. g., "frore," "areed," "wons," "emprise," "nocent," "congratulant," "attrite."

6. Fondness for collocations of more or less exotic proper names:

> Of Cambalu, seat of Cathaian Can
> And Samarchand by Oxus, Temirs throne,
> To Paquin of Sinæan Kings, and thence
> To Agra and Lahor of great Mogul. . . .
>
> *P. L.* XI, 388–91.

7. Unusual compound epithets analogous to those in Homer: e. g., "night-warbling bird," "three-bolted thunder," "Heaven-banished host," "double-founted streams."

There is perhaps no practice here of which abundant examples could not be found in English literature before Milton. The unique thing is the degree to which they become in him habitual features of style—the warp and woof of his poetical expression. Spenser, of course, uses archaisms much more persistently than Milton, with whom the practice is in part at least a survival of the Spenserian tradition in poetry. Marlowe affords the closest English precedent for the magniloquent employment of proper nouns and adjectives, and Milton is indebted to him for

this device, though the classics, particularly Aeschylus'
Prometheus, are also influential. The use of Latinisms and
"ink-horn" terms in general had been a feature of English
expression since the beginnings of humanism, and was at
its height in the early seventeenth century. It was, however, most common in formal prose and was on the whole
avoided by the poets. John Donne, to be sure, makes free
use of the terminology of scholastic philosophy, but neither
he nor any other English poet before Milton habitually
resorts to a highly Latinized diction and sentence structure as a means of removing his speech from the sphere
of daily life to the lofty and sonorous realms of epic.

One feature of Miltonic style, briefly indicated by
Havens under the head of "inversion," has received fuller
treatment by a German scholar, Gustav Hübener, in his
monograph, *Die Stilistische Spannung in "Paradise Lost."*
Suspension as a trait of style is differentiated from simple
suspension as a matter of syntax through its greater arti-
ficiality and elaborateness. It is not native to English speech
and does not occur in English poetry before the Renaissance, except sporadically and in initial sentences. Nor is
it especially characteristic of Spenser. We find it first
freely used in Surrey's translation of the *Aeneid,* where it
reproduces the periodic structure of the Latin sentence,
and it reaches its height in Milton's immediate predecessors
of the early seventeenth century—Davies, Donne, the
Fletchers, Cowley. It is to their influence, reinforced by
Milton's general penchant toward the classical style in
which it originates, that the elaborate periodicity of his
construction may be ascribed. Hübener finds less of it in
the early poems, but a remarkably Latinized sentence from
Comus may be cited as an example:

> Bacchus that first from out the purple Grape
> Crush't the sweet poyson of mis-used Wine
> After the Tuscan Mariners transform'd
> Coasting the Tyrrhene shore, as the winds listed,
> On Circes Iland fell.
>
> *Comus,* 46–50.

Here the suspension is accomplished by the insertion between subject and predicate of several subordinate elements which retard the completion of the sense. The first clause itself is suspended by the inversion of the verb "crush't" and the adverbial phrase "from out the purple grape." Finally the sentence includes two bits of Latin idiom which do not contribute to the suspension, viz., "that first," with "first" probably felt as an adjective (Latin, *qui primus*), and the un-English construction "after the Tuscan mariners transformed" (Latin, *post nautas mutatos*).

In *Paradise Lost* such suspensions recur at frequent intervals. The opening sentence:

> Of Man's First Disobedience, and the Fruit
> Of that Forbidden Tree, whose mortal tast
> Brought Death into the World, and all our woe,
> With loss of Eden, till one greater Man
> Restore us, and regain the blissful Seat,
> Sing, Heav'nly Muse . . .

departs from a natural order, which is especially firmly fixed in imperative sentences, by beginning with the genitive object and inserting between it and the predicate a relative clause with various dependent elements. Hübener finds twenty-three elaborate suspensions of one sort or another in the first book, never occurring in succession but alternating with unsuspended passages. The suspensions mark moments of emphatic meaning in the steady flow of the epic narrative, as, for example, the opening of Satan's address to Beëlzebub:

> If thou beest he; But O how fall'n! how chang'd
> From him, who in the happy Realms of Light
> Cloth'd with transcendent brightnes didst outshine
> Myriads though bright: If he whom mutual league,
> United thoughts and counsels, equal hope,
> And hazard in the Glorious Enterprize,
> Joynd with me once, now misery hath joynd
> In equal ruin.
>
> *P. L.* I, 84–92.

The structural feature thus described must be accepted as an authentic character of Milton's utterance and one which contributes more perhaps than any other single element to the elevation of his poetic style. But it will not do to treat his sentences as if they were written in accordance with formal grammatical patterns. There is, indeed, a subtle and pervasive defiance of logic in much of his expression which makes such an analysis as Hübener's an only partially adequate representation of the texture of his poetic thought. The "suspension" is often more apparent than real.

The lines just quoted, for example, can from one point of view be interpreted as a periodic sentence, beginning with a conditional clause—"If thou beest he who, etc. . . . if he whom, etc. . . . now misery hath joined thee with me in equal ruin"— In actual effect, however, they are a conglomerate of more or less coördinate ideas expressed in a series of grammatical fragments. It is as if Satan exclaimed first: "Can you be Beëlzebub!" then, "How changed you are from your former angelic state," then, "Once we were joined in glorious enterprize, now we are joined in ruin." Clauses formally subordinate here have a weight which gives them the effect of independent statements, and this is characteristic. That Milton himself felt the flow of his poetry in a kind of grammatical continuum is often shown by his punctuation. Note the semicolon after "he" and the colon after "bright," where we would use commas and parentheses. Note also the colon after "ruin," where we would perhaps use a period. The next sentence— "And that strife was not inglorious"—thus becomes a continuation of this one. Often a mere comma separates sentences grammatically independent:

> thou hast given me to possess
> Life in myself for ever, by thee I live,
> Though now to death I yeild, and am his due
> All that of me can die, yet that debt paid,
> Thou wilt not leave me in the loathsom grave
> His prey.

This quotation illustrates a further characteristic element in Milton's thought structure. The use of the comma after "live" leaves the syntax of the next line ambiguous. As we read we inevitably take the clause in connection with the preceding verb, until we come to "yet that debt paid," when we are compelled to readjust our minds and take it with the following. We may, if we wish, clarify the construction by a semicolon, but such ambiguities are too numerous and too effective to warrant this procedure. Similar syntactical ambiguities are illustrated in:

> With thee conversing I forget all time,
> All seasons and thir change, all please alike.

A slightly different and perhaps less certain ambiguity is illustrated by the following:

> for see the Morn,
> All unconcern'd with our unrest, begins
> Her rosie progress smiling.

Here there is an economy of expression. Milton says both "Behold the morn," and "Morn begins her rosy progress," the single word serving both as object and subject. The fact that Milton dictated rather than wrote his mature poetry may have increased his tendency toward a free type of expression characteristic of speech. In any case, his utterance, while pursuing its undeviating larger course and revealing everywhere deliberate purpose, seems like an effect of nature as well as of art, and perfectly witnesses the truth of his own account of its inspired origin:

> If answerable style I can obtaine
> Of my Celestial Patroness, who deignes
> Her nightly visitation unimplor'd,
> And dictates to me slumbring, or inspires
> Easie my unpremeditated Verse.

Another essential quality of Miltonic style is its allusiveness. This allusiveness, in so far as it consists of a rich suggestion of matters of observation in the realm of nature and human experience, is a trait which Milton shares with many poets. In the degree, however, to which his vision is colored by the experience of other men and simple observation modified by knowledge, he is almost unique. The whole treasury of poetry and the whole storehouse of learning are at his command. He assumes that they are also at the command of his reader and accordingly he loads every rift of his verse with the ore of myth and legend, historical, literary, and scientific fact. Of no other English style is erudition so integral a part. Classical and Biblical allusion is, of course, the most abundant, constituting a kind of current coin of expression wherewith to convey a meaning rich in poetic and cultural suggestion.

But Milton writes not only as a literary connoisseur but also as a scholar, appealing in his readers to a love of ordered learning like his own. Even the echoes of ancient phrase should often be considered, not as mere borrowings, conscious or unconscious, but as allusions intended to carry with them, when recognized, the connotation of their original setting. The comprehensiveness and precision of his references and the pains he is often at to introduce some piece of essential information not really relevant to the simple purpose of expression are aspects of his general didacticism. The extraordinary thing is the way in which this object is accomplished without loss of poetic quality. The secret seems to be the degree to which the materials of learning have become associated with sensuous imagery and with moving poetical ideas. Milton is erudite, but all erudition is not for him of equal value. Winnowed, humanized, and touched with the fire of imagination, his studies have passed into vital experience and afford him as natural a body of poetical data as birds and flowers.

The scholarly habit of mind, seeking order and comprehensiveness even in the heat of poetical inspiration, is well illustrated by such a passage as the comparison of the Satanic host to various military assemblages of epic legend at the close of Book I of *Paradise Lost:*

> . . . for never since created man,
> Met such imbodied force, as nam'd with these
> Could merit more than that small infantry

Warr'd on by Cranes: though all the Giant brood
Of Phlegra with th' Heroic Race were joyn'd
That fought at Theb's and Ilium, on each side
Mixt with auxiliar Gods; and what resounds
In Fable or Romance of Uthers Son
Begirt with British and Armoric Knights;
And all who since, Baptiz'd or Infidel
Jousted in Aspramont or Montalban,
Damasco, or Marocco, or Trebisond,
Or whom Biserta sent from Afric shore
When Charlemain with all his Peerage fell
By Fontarabbia.

The passage is a miniature survey, chronologically arranged, of the great conflicts of heroic legend; a survey, indeed, of the materials of the epic poetry of the past: the wars of the gods and giants (Hesiod); the sieges of Troy and Thebes (Homer, Statius); the battles of Arthur (Geoffrey of Monmouth, etc.); the Crusades and the wars of Charlemagne (Italian chivalric epic). Such comprehensiveness goes beyond the requirements of mere illustration. So, too, does the accurate classification of the two divisions of Celtic chivalry in the phrase, "Begirt with British and Armoric knights."

A more elaborate illustration of ripe humanistic scholarship distilled to an essence and put to the service of poetry is to be found in the descriptive analysis of the culture of ancient Athens offered by Satan as a bait to Christ in *Paradise Regained* (IV, 236 ff.). An outline of it would read like the program of a set of lectures on Greek civilization: the physical environment; lyric poetry, Ionian and Doric; Homer and the tragedians; oratory; the schools of philosophy, proceeding from the fountain head of

Socrates—Academics old and new, Peripatetics, Epicureans, Stoics. Everything is compact, orderly, accurate; the essential points and distinctions are indicated with scholarly precision, yet the whole passage, vibrating as it is with Milton's intense enthusiasm for classic culture, is unquestionably poetry. Its phrases—"wielded at will that fierce democraty," "from Heaven descended to the low-roofed house of Socrates"—are as concrete in imagery as they are pregnant with suggestion. No other poet has written in precisely this way.

A striking feature of Milton's style in *Paradise Lost* is his use of the epic or expanded simile.[5] He follows in this the model of Homer, Virgil, Statius, Lucan, Spenser, Tasso, etc., and even borrows in some cases similes already employed by these epic predecessors. Where he is original the materials of his comparison are sometimes based on simple observation of nature, but oftener on myth and legend, history, travel, science, or the technical arts. These digressions are for him a welcome means of pouring forth the treasures of his mind. When once he is in the vein he does not stop with a single elaborate comparison, but proceeds from one to another. Thus the multitude of the Satanic host becomes:

> . . . like that Pygmean Race
> Beyond the Indian Mount, or Faerie Elves,

[5] See Whaler's article, *The Miltonic Simile*, referred to below, also his studies entitled *The Compounding and Distribution of Similes in "Paradise Lost," Animal Simile in "Paradise Lost," Grammatical Nexus of the Miltonic Simile*. Whaler points out the importance of Lucan's similes as a model for Milton. Mahaffy had previously remarked that Milton's learned similes resemble those of Apollonius Rhodius rather than those of Homer. *What Have the Greeks Done?*, p. 43.

Whose midnight Revels by a Forrest side
Or Fountain some belated Peasant sees,
Or dreams he sees, while over head the Moon
Sits Arbitress and neerer to the Earth
Wheels her pale course, they on their mirth
         and dance
Intent, with jocund Music charm his ear;
At once with joy and fear his heart rebounds.

The alternative comparisons thus offered are usually from widely separated provinces or literatures, particularly from classical mythology and the Bible. Thus Satan's huge bulk is compared first to the ancient giants overthrown by Zeus, then to the Scriptural Leviathan, who, however, promptly becomes the sea beast mistaken for an island of the books of travel. The key to this habit is again, in part at least, Milton's passion for scholarly completeness. He is at pains, for example, in describing the Garden of Eden to omit a reference to no parallel happy garden which has been made memorable in song or story. The result, however, is not an effect of pedantry, but one of rich and ornate profusion.

The rhetoric of the Miltonic simile has been exhaustively and very technically studied by James Whaler.[6] Some of his conclusions as to their characteristic features may here be given. Milton less often than other epic poets uses the simile merely to suspend the narrative and afford relief amid scenes of strife, pain, or crisis. He is generally controlling his expression to some specific logical purpose, whether illustration, aggrandizement, or prolepsis. The second use is particularly important in such a fable as his, and Whaler explains the preference for unusual images

[6] *The Miltonic Simile.*

over homely ones like Homer's as due to the fact that Milton is seeking to ennoble his narrative rather than merely to illustrate it. The proleptic or anticipatory use of the simile is particularly distinctive of Milton. Thus in *Paradise Lost,* X, 306–11, he likens the construction by Sin and Death of a causey across Chaos to reach the world and enslave mankind, to the bridge which Xerxes built over the Hellespont. In so doing he not only illustrates the action but to the knowing reader suggestively foreshadows later events. The Persian expedition came to nought, and the same, for all their present ostentatiousness, is to be the history of Sin and Death. Whaler demonstrates, finally, that Milton's similes are organically composed to a degree beyond those of his epic predecessors. A typically complex Miltonic simile directs each detail to some application in the fable, i. e., homologation rather than heterogeneity between terms is the rule. It requires a subtle reader to catch all the suggested points of the comparison and the student must be referred for detail to Whaler's elaborate exposition.

We may, however, illustrate what he means by analyzing the simile in *Paradise Lost,* II, 706–11.

> On th' other side
> Incenc't with indignation Satan stood
> Unterrifi'd, and like a Comet burn'd,
> That fires the length of Ophiuchus huge
> In th' Artick Sky, and from his horrid hair
> Shakes Pestilence and Warr.

Satan is like the comet in fiery radiance, in enormousness, in the fact that both are ominous of impending calamity. But there is still more. Satan is a serpent—"Ophiuchus" means "holder of serpents"; hence the comet is appropriately said to fire the length of this particular constellation. Furthermore Satan is always associated with the quarters of the North, for which reason Milton puts Ophiuchus in the arctic sky, though only with considerable astronomical freedom.

Even when Milton digresses in his similes he does not do so, as Homer and other poets do, for the sole reason of drawing a diverting picture. There is always some relevant suggestion to be found if one thinks of all the associations. Thus in the celebrated comparison of the shield of Satan to the moon Milton apparently departs from the point to tell of Galileo's telescope and even to mention the place of observation:

> from the top of Fesole,
> Or in Valdarno

and he describes what the telescope reveals:

> new Lands
> Rivers or Mountains in her spotty Globe.

But these digressions help. We are invited to see the moon through the eyes of the most quick-sighted and intelligent astronomer of modern times, under ideal atmospheric conditions, under the clear dry sky of Italy. See it thus, "with the daring imagination and furtively proud mind of a scientist" in the days of the Inquisition and you are prepared to imagine more vividly and with more emotion the shield of Satan. The fact that the moon is not smooth but ridged and channeled intimates the same of Satan's shield and "faintly suggests the most superb shield in Homer and in literature, that of Achilles." It is, then, in the completeness of its correspondences with the object that the Miltonic simile is most unique and best demonstrates the control which he exercised over his artistic imagination.

The characteristics of Milton's expression which come out so clearly in the similes are to be found in a more subtle form in his verse generally. Though little progress has thus far been made in analyzing these characteristics, attention may be directed to an exceptionally suggestive stylistic study by William Empson, entitled *Bentley and Milton*.[7] Empson points out in a succession of examples that where Bentley finds fault with Milton he almost invariably does so on a point where eighteenth century demands for logic, explicitness, singleness of meaning are violated in the interest of poetic overtones and suggestions characteristic both of Elizabethan and of modern verse. Bentley is wrong in his criticisms, certainly, but he writes honestly from the point of view of his age; and such defenders of Milton as Pearce are really no nearer to catching the poet's intention than the heavy-handed classicist whom they ridicule. Thus, for example, neither Bentley nor Pearce recognizes the secret pun which gives poetic richness to the following:

> The birds their quire apply, aires, vernal aires
> Breathing the smell of field and grove,
> Attune the trembling leaves.

Bentley objects that "air" has no plural number in Greek, Latin, or English, where "airs" signifies "tunes." Pearce defends his author on philological grounds, giving authority for taking different airs as different breezes. Both ignore the obvious lead suggested by the word "attunes." "The

[7] In *Some Versions of Pastoral.*

airs attune the leaves," says Empson, "because the air itself is as enlivening as a tune: the trees and wildflowers
that are smelt on the air match, as if they caused, as if they
were caused by, the birds and leaves that are heard on the
air; Nature because of a poem becomes a single organism."
It is doubtless possible to be oversubtle in this kind of
analysis, but it leads us nearer to the truth than the rough
judgment of T. S. Eliot [8] that the only specifically poetic
pleasure that Milton's verse affords is the pleasure of the
ear.

It is a curious fact that similes and figurative language
generally are not at all evenly distributed in Milton's blank
verse poems or even in *Paradise Lost* itself. In Books
I and II they are scattered thick as stars. Thereafter they
fall off in number, and there are long stretches of the
poem, as, for example, the theological discussion in Book
III and the dialogue between Adam and Raphael in Book
VIII, in which there are none.[9]

This phenomenon may serve to direct our attention to
the fact that Milton really has two styles, corresponding
to two different kinds of object or two qualities of poetic
inspiration. The one is abundant, highly colored, pictorial,
figurative; the other direct, closely woven, and relatively
plain. The first is the language of Milton's impassioned
visual imagination, the second, of his ethical and intellectual intensity. Many passages, to be sure, show the two
modes in combination, and both have the fundamental
Miltonic qualities already analyzed. The contrast between
them in their purity is, nevertheless, strongly marked. It
may already be discerned in *Comus,* but it is clearest in the

---

[8] *A Note on the Verse of John Milton.*
[9] See Whaler, *The Compounding and Distribution of Similes.*

later poems. In the sonnets, *Paradise Regained* and *Samson Agonistes,* the barer style predominates, though there are patches of the other, as in the description of the banquet spread for Christ, or the nightly storm followed by a serene dawn, or the choric description of Samson's descent upon the Philistines like an eagle upon tame villatic fowl. In *Paradise Lost* they are balanced fairly evenly. Hell, Chaos, the Garden, Satan lying on the burning lake or standing like Teneriffe or Atlas, visions of Cherubim gliding to their stations, the brandished sword of God fierce as a comet, passions of demons, the loves of Adam and Eve—these are the objects of a style brilliant with the wealth of Ormus or of Ind. The soberer dialogue in Hell, the correlative council in Heaven, all exposition of doctrine, Satan's or Adam's self-communion, Raphael's final thrilling exhortation, all this is couched in a language relatively plain, but full of lofty dignity and capable of both eloquence and passion. The rich and glowing splendors of Milton's visual imagination are doubtless of a more immediate appeal; the intensity of ethical and human meaning in the other at its best is equally characteristic and equally enduring.

Regarding the development of Milton's style and its relation to the tendencies of his age, much has been written. The alterations in the Trinity MS., already alluded to in the discussion of the minor poems, show something of the conscious effort which he made to achieve certain definite qualities. Mr. C. S. Lewis [10] shows that in a dozen or so of the changes in *Comus,* Milton was deliberately moving away from the dramatic and ebullient in expression toward the "gnomic and poetically chaste." Thus:

[10] *A Note on "Comus."*

> force him to return his purchas back
> Or drag him by the curles and cleave his scalp
> Down to the hips.

becomes in the revision:

> drag him by the curls to a foul death
> Curst as his life.

Other changes tell a different story. Milton often substitutes a fresher and more meaningful epithet for a conventional one, as in "opening eyelids of the Morn" for "glimmering eyelids," and "westering wheel" for "burnisht wheel." In general the language of *Paradise Lost,* especially of the first two books, is bolder and more striking than that of the minor poems. It is also, however, apt to be more condensed, more difficult, and in a sense more severe. Tillyard [11] notes that the tenderness, sensuousness of Milton's youth, while absent from the poem as a whole, are occasionally, as in the close, allowed to have place, as if to reassure us that no powers which he once possessed are lost. He points out also that the remoteness of Milton's mature manner, which has been disliked by some critics, is in conformity with the seventeenth century theory of propriety in heroic poetry. "The heightened style of *Paradise Lost* was something demanded of him as an epic poet with a rigor against which there was no possible appeal." A similar point is elaborated by Mario Praz, who finds in Milton's style, with its refinement and spiritualization of sixteenth century sensuousness through the influence of the ideal forms of the classics, a close parallel with the baroque art of Nicolas Poussin.[12]

[11] *The Miltonic Setting,* pp. 115 ff.
[12] *Milton and Poussin.*

The discussion has inevitably carried us away from the outward features of Milton's literary utterance to the qualities of intellect and emotion which determine them. We may now return to formulate as simply as possible the more obvious facts regarding his versification. It should be said at the outset that the most complete scientific description of Miltonic prosody would carry us but a little way toward an understanding of the total effect produced by his poetry. Rhythm, vocabulary, sentence structure, imagery, all unite in indistinguishable combination to form the majestic garment of Miltonic thought and feeling. Thus the "blank verse paragraph" so often mentioned in discussions of Milton's poetry is as much a matter of rhetoric as it is of verse. It is because the sense is suspended through line after line, and because Milton takes pains to avoid coincidence of the rhetorical pauses with the line end that we have the continuity of rhythm which is so characteristic a feature of his blank verse.[13]

Even, however, in prosody, strictly considered, Milton is an innovator as well as a master, although in this as in stylistic habit his originality consists in the bolder and more individual employment of practices for which precedent can be found in earlier English poetry. Thus, while the formal description of his varieties of blank verse will correspond in general with a similar description of those of Shakespeare, the examples of variation from the basic metrical pattern will be at once more numerous and more extreme.[14] The following statement aims at a simple ob-

[13] Banks, *Miltonic Rhythm,* calculates that forty per cent of the full stops in *Paradise Lost* occur medially.

[14] This is a mere impression and awaits statistical investigation. Routh's calculations, *English Iambic Meter,* tending to show that all English blank verse, including Milton's, runs about alike in the pro-

jective classification, avoiding as far as possible controversial questions of metrical theory.

BASIC RHYTHM. The standard of Milton's verse in *Paradise Lost* and *Paradise Regained* and *Samson Agonistes* (except the choruses) may be taken as the line of ten syllables and five accents in rising rhythm (i. e., iambic pentameter unrhymed). Clear examples are:

> Torments him; round he throws his baleful eyes
> > *P. L.* I, 56.

or, better yet:

> United thought and counsels, equal hope
> > *P. L.* I, 88.

As a matter of fact, lines with such even and regular iambic beat are comparatively rare—rarer in Milton's verse than in most English iambic pentameter. Yet probably a majority of lines even with him approximate it so closely that we are unconscious of a variation. Thus in the line:

> Of that Forbidden Tree whose mortal tast
> > *P. L.* I, 2.

most readers would emphasize the second syllable only slightly less than the succeeding ones which bear the metrical accent, and in the line:

> The force of those dire Arms? yet not for those
> > *P. L.* I, 94.

though the word "dire" is nearly equivalent in weight to "arms" it does not disturb in any marked way the regularity of beat.

portion of variation in the strict iambic pattern, are rendered unreliable by his eccentric reading of the lines which he chooses as examples.

VARIATIONS IN NUMBER OF SYLLABLES. As compared
with the eighteenth century writers of the couplet Milton
is very free in the admission of syllables above the standard ten. There is, as in most pentameter verse, a considerable number, though not so many as in Shakespeare's later
plays, of lines of one or rarely two extra unaccented syllables at the end (weak or feminine ending) :

> And high disdain, from sence of injur'd merit
> > *P. L.* I, 98.
> That durst dislike his reign, and me preferring
> > *P. L.* I, 102.
> > For solitude sometimes is best societie
> > > *P. L.* IX, 249.

Extra syllables may also be introduced at any point in
the line. This liberty was freely used in later Elizabethan
dramatic blank verse. Milton, however, influenced no
doubt by classical and Italian practice, apparently admitted extra-metrical syllables within the line only when
they could be brought under certain rules of elision and
contraction. These rules (omitting the elisions and con-
tractions of common speech) were formulated by Robert
Bridges in his work on *Milton's Prosody* under the following heads : [15]

1. Open vowels ; e. g. :

> Above th*e A*onian Mount, while it pursues
> > *P. L.* I, 15.
> Strange horror seise th*ee, a*nd pangs unfelt before
> > *P. L.* II, 703.

[15] For detailed application of the rules and the discussion of apparent or actual exceptions the reader is referred to the latest edition of
Mr. Bridges' work, *Milton's Prosody*, Oxford, 1921. My summary,
however, is from the simpler statement in the edition of 1894.

2. Vowels separated by the liquids l, n, r:

As one who long in pop*ulo*us City pent
P. L. IX, 445.
His Temple right against the Temp*le o*f God
P. L. I, 402.
A Pill*ar of* State; deep on his Front engraven
P. L. II, 302.

3. Final *en;* e. g., fall'n, ris'n, driv'n, etc.
4. The second person singular of verbs, e. g.; remembrest, thinkst, etc.

The rules of contraction (3 and 4) may be understood to indicate an actual suppression of the contracted syllable in pronunciation, as is clearly indicated by Milton's careful spelling in the first edition. (He prints "Heav'n," "thinkst," etc., as given above.) Not so, however, the elisions. There might be some doubt in the case of "the" before a word beginning with a vowel, where Milton actually prints "th' " [16] but a suppression of the vowel sound in "thee"

Strange horror seise *thee,* and pangs unfelt before

is unthinkable. Mr. Bridges, therefore, concludes that Milton scanned his verse one way (syllabically) and read it another. Yet Milton's elisions are not without practical consequence in the aesthetic consciousness of the modern reader. "We may say generally," says Mr. Bridges, "that Milton's system in *Paradise Lost* was an attempt to keep blank verse decasyllabic by means of fictions, or . . . it may be said that he formulated the conditions most com-

[16] For a discussion of the peculiarities of Milton's spelling, which are often of importance as indications of his reading of his lines, see the introduction to Beeching's and Grierson's editions.

mon to those syllables which were oftenest and best used for trisyllabic places; and then worked within the lines thus drawn." [17] Whatever the aesthetic validity or significance of his practice, the facts are interesting as an illustration of the artistic discipline which coexisted in his work with artistic freedom.

In *Paradise Regained* and *Samson Agonistes* Milton admits extra syllables on a somewhat freer basis, not, however, to the extent to which they are admitted in the early poems or in English pentameter verse generally.

VARIATION IN THE PLACING OF ACCENT (INVERSION OF RHYTHM). The iambic succession of unaccented-accented syllables is freely varied; very commonly at the beginning of the line:

> Róse out of Chaos: or if Sion Hill
>> *P. L.* I, 10.

This is the easiest and most normal variation of the iambic pattern and is common even with the couplet versifiers of the eighteenth century.

Similar reversal after a rhetorical or metrical pause is almost as little disturbing to the regularity of the rhythm:

> Illumine, what is low || raíse and support.
>> *P. L.* I, 23.

Elsewhere such alteration of accent is more strongly felt. Examples of Milton's daring and success are:

> Of Mán's Fírst Disobedience, and the Fruit
>> *P. L.* I, 1.

[17] In the 1921 edition, p. 18, Bridges sums up the matter thus: "As a matter, then, of rhythm it may well enough be said that Milton's elisions are trisyllabic feet; but historically and in prosody they are 'elisions,' the great-grandchildren of Homeric elision."

Which tasted works knówledge of Good and Evil
P. L. VII, 543.
Beyond all past example and fúture
P. L. X, 840.
Which of us who beholds the bright súrface
P. L. VI, 472.

The last two instances, with inversion in the final foot, are very unusual, and some misguided editors would accent the words "futúre" and "surfáce" to escape it. This question has been discussed further under the head "Phrasing."

VARIATIONS IN NUMBER OF ACCENTS. As I have said above, it is possible to scan most lines in *Paradise Lost* fairly easily as pentameters, allowing for substitution but not doing violence to the prose accent of the words. There are, however, many cases in which it is impossible to recognize the normal number of accents in any intelligent reading of the line:

To the Garden of bliss, thy seat prepared
P. L. VIII, 299.
In the Visions of God: It was a Hill
P. L. XI, 377.
Rocks, Caves, Lakes, Fens, Bogs, Dens, and shades of Death
P. L. II, 621.
Light-arm'd or heavy, sharp, smooth, swift or slow
P. L. II, 922.

These are extreme instances, in which we feel the rhythm for the moment sharply altered. The normal situation is better represented in such lines as the following, where we have a choice of renderings:

And now a stripling Cherube he appeers.

the question being the degree of stress, if any, one is to put on "he." Bridges says that there is a "theoretical stress" on such words. Actually, whatever we may do with our voice, our aesthetic sense is held by two rhythms simultaneously; and there are enough such lines almost to establish a four beat as well as a five beat pattern. If one wishes to refine on this he may consider the line:

> Immutable, immortal, infinite
>
> *P. L.* III, 373.

as capable of being read three different ways:

> Immútablé, immórtal, ínfiníte
> Immútable, immórtal, ínfiníte
> Immútable, immórtal, ínfiníte.

Obviously there is opportunity for great variety and sub-tlety, and of this opportunity Milton makes the most, the more so because the rhythm is not marked by stress alone but by other elements as well. This leads us to consider

PAUSE. The normal pentameter line tends to divide it-self into two balancing parts, but all poets, even the regular versifiers of the eighteenth century, vary the position of the break to avoid monotony. Milton does so more freely than others. Bridges shows that the metrical pause in Milton, as determined by a grammatical pause, may come at any point within the line. Extreme instances are:

> Thus with the Year
> Seasons return, but not to me returns
> Day, || or the sweet approach of Ev'n or Morn.
>
> (1 + 9)
>
> And Bush with frizl'd hair implicit: || last
> Rose as in Dance the stately Trees
>
> (9 + 1)

There are sometimes two breaks in a line, the "variety and severity" of the breaks being, according to Bridges, a distinction of Milton's verse.

> Hail Son of God, || Saviour of Men, || thy Name
> $(4+4+2)$
> Regions of sorrow, || doleful shades, || where peace
> $(5+3+2)$

Here again the situation is more complex than any simple and definite statement like the foregoing can do justice to. Pause is a means both of logical expression and of emphasis. It is a factor, partly metrical, partly grammatical and rhetorical. The same is true of stress. In the use of both, a compromise has to be effected between the demands of prose meaning and of poetic rhythm. We see the problem here particularly clearly at the ends of lines. From the metrical point of view each line is a unit and requires some kind of demarcation at the end. From the grammatical or rhetorical point of view it is often so closely connected with the following line that any break at all is illogical. Note, for example, the lines:

> not to me *returns*
> *Day,* or the sweet approach of Ev'n or Morn.

Readers will differ in what they do here. They may make a slight pause after "returns" or, better, slightly strengthen the metrical stress of the second syllable of the word, or lengthen that syllable, or do both. The eye plays a part, too, making us aware of the line structure, even against a vocal interpretation which does not recognize it at all. There is some external evidence [18] that Milton himself, however

[18] See Diekhoff, *Terminal Pause in Milton's Verse.*

much he may have thought in "verse paragraphs," regarded the line as a more or less isolated unit to be indicated as such by some sort of breath, pause, or lingering at the end.

The question of metrical versus grammatical and rhetorical pause applies also to the breaks within the line. In the line:

> Regions of sorrow, || doleful shades, || where peace
> And rest can never dwell

the two internal breaks would be of equal strength in prose rhetoric or the second might be greater. But verse rhythm requires the second to be less.

Whenever we take a Miltonic verse and scrutinize it in this way, we realize that the sources of its beauty are beyond our powers of analysis, and that the reader is called on to exercise a delicacy of artistic judgment like that of a singer or the performer of a piece of instrumental music. Exactly what the author or composer would himself have done, we should be glad to know; but there is no unalterably right way of interpretation. The matter becomes even more complex when we add the factors of pitch, texture or quality, and tempo. The latter point, which has already been touched on, requires much study. English verse has been roughly defined as "speech in which stresses occur at apparently equal intervals of time," [19] with the explanation that the time intervals are "not exactly equal but only nearly enough equal to seem so to the ear." The analogy with music is very close, the stresses being comparable to the beats in music, and the units of time or feet, to the measures. And verse is perhaps best scanned by using musical notation. Expression in reading, insofar as it in-

[19] Stewart, *The Technique of English Verse*, p. 2.

volves the time factor, is like rhythmic interpretation in music. Perfectly regular and accurate playing is monotonous and unexpressive. The interpreting musician lengthens one measure or series of measures, quickens others. His beat is constantly changing, yet there is always an approximation of regularity. Such is also the case with the good reader of poetry.

PHRASING. There is, finally, in Milton, as in all poetry, the problem of phrasing or the grouping of syllables into units of pronunciation. Pause, stress, and tempo are all factors here. The phrasal units may sometimes correspond more or less exactly to the metrical feet, as in the monosyllabic line:

And swims | or sinks, | or wades, | or creeps, | or flyes.

Oftener they do not. Thus in the line:

Of Man's | First Dis | obe | dience and | the Fruit

"disobedience" is a unit of pronunciation which occupies parts of three feet. Some students of Milton's verse, impressed by the power and importance of the phrasal units, have tried to apply complicated systems of scansion, making use of all the varieties of feet recognized by the Greek and Roman rhetoricians. To do this is to lose sight of the simpler and more regular verse patterns which, though modified, are not destroyed by the irregularities of phrasing. The smallest groups consist of single words like "disobedience" or of two or three short words like "and the fruit." But there are larger groupings which embrace the smaller, with varying degrees of pause between them. Again the situation is analogous with that of music. Skill in reading Milton aloud is largely a matter of making the most of the phrasing and the verse patterns at the same time. As in the case of stress, there is a kind of overlapping of phrasal patterns which is perceived by the mind though it cannot be fully rendered by the voice. How, for example, shall we plot the larger phrasal pattern of:

> Outshon the wealth of Ormus and of Ind?

We see the possibility of saying:

> Outshon the wealth | of Ormus and of Ind

and also of saying:

> Outshon the wealth of Ormus | and of Ind

perhaps, even of saying:

> Outshon | the wealth of Ormus and of Ind

and finally of treating the whole line as a unit:

> Outshon the wealth of Ormus and of Ind.

It would certainly be difficult to indicate all this vocally, but the alternative groupings are nevertheless felt. A simpler case is illustrated by the line given as an example of the coincidence of phrasal units with metrical feet:

> And swims or sinks, | or wades, | or creeps, | or flyes.

Certainly the impression of monotony is part of the effect wanted, and good reading requires a pause after each verb. But "swims or sinks" go more closely together than the others, a fact emphasized by the omission of the comma in the original edition, and this can be recognized in reading by making the pause briefer after "swims" or by using a slightly different inflection of the voice.

The natural accent in the phrase considered as prose may run counter to the regular beat of the iambic verse. In conspicuous cases we may say (see page 316) that the type of foot is changed. Thus we may say that "Of Man's" is an iamb, but "first dis-" is an "inverted foot" or a trochee. But the reader feels the iambic beat, and it is an open question how much he is to recognize it in pronunciation. The same is true of the "missing beats" in a foot like " | ience and | the fruit". The phrase, "and the fruit," is a unit with one prose accent. But "and" invites metrical emphasis in the iambic pattern. This brings us back to the subject of five and four beat rhythms, already sufficiently discussed. I am thinking here, however, not of two more or less regular patterns but of an entirely irregular prose accent crossing the verse accent. Notable examples are the following:

Prose accent:

> Búrnt áfter them to the bóttomless pít.

Verse accent:

> Burnt áfter thém to the bóttomless pít.

Prose accent:

> Síng Héav'nly Múse

Verse accent:

> Síng Heav'nly Múse.

RHYMED VERSE. GREEK METERS IN SAMSON AGONISTES. I have omitted in this discussion Milton's rhymed verse and the choruses in *Samson Agonistes*. Rhyme has the effect of marking the line end, even where the sense is run on. It is an ornament, also, which serves to distinguish verse from prose in an obvious and easy way. The stylistic heightening and the bold effects of rhythm in Milton's blank verse are in part due to the need which he felt of supplying the deficiency of rhyme by other means. The choruses of *Samson Agonistes* have irregular line lengths and sometimes rhyme. The variations from the iambic pattern are so great that one is inclined to abandon the attempt to recognize a theoretical conformity to this English pattern and consider them frankly as a reproduction of Greek and Roman rhythms.

Milton himself has given ground for so doing. He says in the preface: "The measure of verse used in the Chorus is of all sorts, called by the Greeks monostrophic, or rather Apolelymenon, without regard had to strophe, antistrophe, or Epode—which were a kind of stanzas framed only for the music, then used with the Chorus that sung; not essential to the poem, and therefore not material; or, being divided into stanzas, they may be called alloeostropha." At first reading, this would seem to refer only to the stanzaic arrangement, and to warn the reader not to look for the kind of regularity which he knew to exist in the Greek odes (i. e. identity of strophe and strophe, antistrophe and antistrophe). But Milton means to imply also that the individual verses are not in conformity with the specific patterns found in ancient odes. This becomes very clear if we compare the statement prefixed to the *Ode to Rous,* where the distinction is made between pattern verses and free verses. "The ode consists of three strophes, an equal number of antistrophes, and an epode at its close. These divisions, though they do not precisely correspond, either in number of verses or in sections (cola) that are everywhere unchangeable, we have made in the way mentioned above, having in view the convenience of the reader, rather than an arrangement by which they might be sung according to the ancient measures. In other respects this poetic form should perhaps be more correctly called monostrophic. The meters in part follow a definite scheme, in part are used freely (apolelymenon). The Phalaecian verses twice admit a spondee in the third foot, a substitution which Catullus makes at will in the second foot."

The inference from this statement is that even when writing a Latin ode (in 1647) Milton was unwilling to bind himself invariably to the recognized ancient types, but that he knew perfectly well what some of them (i. e. at least those used by Horace and Catullus) were, and what liberties were allowed within them. His own inventions are simply in the way of further modifications such as the ancients themselves might have made. The Greek choruses, which must have seemed to him more irregular than they do to modern metrists, would have given him even stronger precedent than the occasional variations admitted by the Romans.[20] He would certainly have scanned the verses of the *Ode to Rous* in the Greek way; and he perhaps invites the reader to do the same with the choruses of Samson. The meter would be that of the freest form known to the ancients, the logaoedic, which is a trochaic measure with

[20] The study of the more complicated Greek choral rhythms is said by Williamowitz not to have progressed in Milton's time beyond the point of noting the correspondence of strophe and strophe, antistrophe and antistrophe. It is hard to say exactly how Milton would have read them, except that he would be sure to have observed that the types used by the Romans occurred. He must also have seen that the prevailing rhythms were trochaic in the formal sung Choruses.

dactyls and other substitutions. When the lines begin with the upbeat the movement is often very similar to the logaoedic patterns. For example:

> Thīs, | thīs, | ĭs hē;
>   Sōftlў | ă whīle,
> Lēt ŭs | nŏt brēak | ĭn ūp | ŏn hīm;
> Ō chānge | bĕyŏnd | rĕpōrt | thŏught | ŏr bĕlīef!
> Căn thĭs | bĕ hēe | thăt hĕ | rōĭc, | thăt Rĕ | nōwned,
> Īrres | īstĭblĕ | Sāmsŏn? | whŏm | ŭnārm'd.

But though these lines begin with trochees, spondees, or dactyls they seem to end in almost every case with iambs, and from this point on in the choruses the general movement is more clearly iambic, though with occasional lines which definitely suggest the ancient rhythms:

> Ūsĕlĕss thĕ | fōrgĕrў
> Ādămăn | tēan | Prōof.

The genius of the language and the traditions of English verse were too strong to admit of Milton's giving us real Greek verse, even in *Samson,* without doing violence to his instincts. He must have considered and rejected the attempts which had been made by Harvey, Sidney, and others to introduce the principles of classic meter consistently into English verse.

CHAPTER VII

MILTON'S FAME AND INFLUENCE

THE SEVENTEENTH CENTURY

THOUGH Milton lived his last days in quietness and published his great poems with no accompaniment of public demonstration, he had at his death already taken his place among the notables of England. As a man of learning, as a Latin and English poet, as the writer of the *Defense against Salmasius,* and as a last survivor of the Commonwealth government, he was naturally an object of public interest, and, to royalists, of scandal. He was visited in his London obscurity by distinguished foreigners. John Dryden asked his leave to turn *Paradise Lost* into an opera, and conversed with him on literary matters, receiving the scornful answer, "Yes, Mr. Dryden, you may tag my verses." Numerous biographies were written and published in the first quarter century after his death.

Though Milton would have acquired no such prompt notoriety on the strength of his English poetry alone, and though the taste and temper of the Restoration were all against a proper understanding of his work, there is evidence that *Paradise Lost* was both read and admired from the first, not alone by the few men of Milton's own circle who, like Andrew Marvell, shared his moral and political ideas, but even occasionally by the wits of the new age.[1]

[1] Richardson has an account of Sir John Denham's enthusiasm for *Paradise Lost,* "wet from the press." He sent it to Dryden, who remarked "This man cuts us all out and the ancients too." On the authenticity of the anecdote see Banks, *Sir John Denham and "Paradise Lost,"* Baldwin's *Sir John Denham and "Paradise Lost,"* and Banks's edition of Denham, pp. 32–33.

Professor Havens estimates that some four thousand copies of *Paradise Lost* were in circulation by 1680, enough to supply the "fit audience though few" whom Milton thought he had a right to expect in any age. The leader in critical admiration and the true founder of Milton's literary reputation was John Dryden, who returned to his work again and again in his prose discussions. The idea of Milton's unpopularity in the Restoration period was greatly exaggerated by eighteenth century writers, in contrast to the universal admiration of their own age.[2]

It remains true, however, that the changes in the moral tone of the nation which attended the Revolution of 1688 made possible a rapid widening of the circle of Milton's admirers. Jacob Tonson, into whose hands the copyright of *Paradise Lost* had fallen, published five successive editions of the poem in the decade from 1688 to 1698, one of them (that of 1695) with elaborate learned annotations by Patrick Hume. This is the first really scholarly edition of Milton or, indeed, of any English poet. Latin translations were made of *Paradise Lost* and other Miltonic poems. Even the prose works began to be read again with sympathy as the anti-Puritan reaction came to an end and the Stuart régime was finally overthrown.

[2] See Havens, *Seventeenth Century Notices of Milton,* also Good's *Studies in the Milton Tradition* to which I am greatly indebted for data regarding the early editions, biographies, and critiques of Milton. The popularity of the minor poems is more problematical, but we have the records of Wotton's admiration, and Henry Vaughn, whose early poems are said to show Milton's influence, apparently refers to him in 1655 as one of the irreverent poets who are, nevertheless, among the principal and most learned writers of English verse. See Guiney, *Milton, and Henry Vaughn.*

There is a copy of *Lycidas* bearing the signature of Izaak Walton.

school of Pope; and as this tendency asserted itself more powerfully, Milton became more and more acclaimed as a champion of the inwardness and freedom of true poetry. Finally, Milton's style and versification were fascinating by their very contrast with prevailing literary modes. He was a quarry of poetical phrase for everybody, even for Pope, and a direct model for the vast school of blank versifiers who maintained what might be called the other poetical tradition of the eighteenth century. Taken as a whole, the Miltonism of the eighteenth century is an extraordinarily varied and complex phenomenon. I shall here attempt to set forth only a few of its outstanding phases.

THE EIGHTEENTH CENTURY ESTIMATE OF MILTON. Critical admiration of Milton was somewhat tempered in the early period by the judgment that his poems failed to conform to the neo-classical rules of poetry. Dryden, in spite of his sense of Milton's greatness, was forced to admit that *Paradise Lost* was no "true epic," and this was a common verdict. The tendency, however, of Milton devotees among the classicists was naturally to frame a defense which would justify him according to the accepted standards of their school. It was in this spirit that Addison wrote his famous series of papers on Milton in the *Spectator*. Both he and Steele had previously, by casual notices and quotations, commended Milton to public notice. In the critique Addison, besides exhibiting its individual beauties, analyzes *Paradise Lost* according to the ancient theory and dares to compare it on equal terms with the deified works of Homer and Virgil. The effect of this praise from the most respected critic of the time was to enhance the reputation of Milton in all quarters. It has even been said that Addison's essays created the vogue of *Paradise Lost*, though this appears to be not altogether true. Certainly, however, the papers became at once the standard piece of Milton criticism. They were published separately in 1719 and have been reissued and reread down to the present day. Translated into French (1727),[4] German (1740), and Italian (1742), they became, along with an essay by Voltaire (*Essaie sur la poésie epique*, 1727), the means of introducing Milton's English works widely for the first time to a continental audience.[5]

Of course Addison did not claim that Milton's poem was wholly regular; and in one paper he points out its defects, employing the same rules of judgment that he had used in praising him. Thus Milton's "fable" is defective, being that of tragedy rather than of epic. Some of his incidents have not "probability enough for an epic poem." His digressions and his allusions to heathen fables in a Christian poem "sin against the canon of unity." To other critics even these

[4] Although the first French translation of the *Spectator* was completed in 1718, Addison's essays on Milton remained untranslated until 1727, when N. F. Dupré de Saint-Maur included them as a preface to his translation of *Paradise Lost*. The earlier translator had omitted them because of the lack of a current French rendering of the poem.

[5] For the continental fame of Milton see the studies by Telleen, Robertson, Pizzo, and the more specialized investigations listed by Stevens, *Reference Guide*, pp. 279–286. A translation of *Paradise Lost* into German by Ernst Gottlieb Berge had appeared in 1682. This is said to have been the first rendering into a modern foreign language. Still unexplored is the career of *Paradise Lost* in Russia. A translation was made by the poet Petrov, about 1772, and there is abundant critical discussion. See André Lirondelle, *Shakespeare in Russia*, pp. 24, 27, 63, 74, 168. A prose version published in cheap editions, with colored pictures, is said to have been circulated all over Russia, and "greedily read by the peasants, who have no idea that it is a poem but enjoy it as a tale of fantastic adventure and miraculous events." Maurice Baring, *Landmarks in Russian Literature*, 1910, p. 113.

reservations were unacceptable. They said that Milton was not to be tried by the neo-classical code. He had invented a new type of poem, the divine epic, superior to anything in antiquity. If he was irregular they would exult in his irregularity. "The fine arts," said Thomas Leland (1764), "have no rules but genius to direct them."

This attitude falls in with the increasing tendency to exalt imagination and emotion in poetry above the "correctness" which had been the ideal of the school of Pope. Thus Joseph Warton, in his *Essay on the Writings and Genius of Pope* (1756), places Milton, because of his sublimity and passion, in the first rank of poets with Shakespeare and Spenser and far above the accepted writers of his own day. As the romantic currents of the eighteenth century became stronger, the feeling that Milton represented the true ideal from which poetry had since declined became increasingly dominant. The new interest in nature, the taste for color and romance, political liberalism, developing humanitarian sentiment, and finally the movement toward a greater earnestness and spirituality in religion were all favorable to a more generous appreciation of Milton's essential qualities.

The most interesting evidences of this are to be found in the warmth and insight which pervade the poetical tributes to his genius scattered thick through the literature of the period. The modern feeling of admiration for Milton's heroic personality and of astonishment at the boldness and sublimity of his imagination finds expression much earlier and more completely in verse than it does in prose. The list of fully sympathetic poetical utterances about Milton is headed by Andrew Marvell's verses prefixed to the 1674 edition of *Paradise Lost*. His praise, though tinged with religious sobriety, sets the style for the more extravagant utterances of later times.

> That majesty which through thy work doth reign
> Draws the devout, deterring the profane;
> And things divine thou treat'st of in such state
> As them preserves, and thee, inviolate.
> At once delight and horror on us seize,
> Thou sing'st with so much gravity and ease,
> And above human flight dost soar aloft,
> With plumes so strong, so equal, and so soft;
> A bird named from that paradise you sing
> So never flags, but always keeps on wing.

Dryden's famous epigram, already referred to, placed under Milton's portrait in the folio of 1688, goes much further than its author was willing to do in the cooler and more critical element of prose:

> Three poets, in three distant ages born,
> Greece, Italy, and England did adorn.
> The first in loftiness of thought surpassed;
> The next in majesty: in thought the last.
> The force of nature could no further go;
> To make a third, she joined the other two.

Pope, Addison, and many others expressed their admiration in verse with similar absence of reservation. Milton's blindness is often mentioned in these tributes, especially by those men who inclined to make poetic inspiration a quality of the soul, and his own claim to a compensatory inward vision accepted and elaborated. It remained for Thomas Gray [6] to express this more romantic feeling of his time in language worthy of the theme:

[6] In *The Progress of Poesy.*

Nor second he that rode sublime
Upon the seraph-wings of extasy,
The secrets of the abyss to spy.
He passed the flaming bounds of Place and Time:
The living throne, the sapphire-blaze,
Where angels tremble when they gaze,
He saw; but blasted with excess of light,
Clos'd his eyes in endless night.

This widening conception is an index of the acceptance of the whole of Milton. His appeal, originally felt almost exclusively in *Paradise Lost,* came gradually to embrace his other works as well; and the minor poems, as we shall see, became a part of his direct influence on the history of poetry itself.[7] An odd development of Miltonic enthusiasm of the later eighteenth century was the continuous popularity of *Comus* in adapted versions on the stage.[8]

The general trend met something of opposition in the most important single pronouncement on Milton after Addison's critique, namely, that contained in the celebrated biography by Samuel Johnson in the *Lives of the Poets* (1779). Johnson joined the general chorus in praise of *Paradise Lost,* "a poem which, considered with respect to design, may claim the first place, and with respect to performance, the second, among the productions of the human mind." On the whole, however, his treatment of Milton is reactionary. Johnson loathed Milton's politics, and he disparaged his personal character at every point. He was

[7] The minor poems were not entirely neglected before 1740. See Sherburn, *The Early Popularity of Milton's Minor Poems.*

[8] Thaler, *Milton in the Theater,* records public performances in practically every year from 1738 to 1800. The University of Michigan Library contains nineteen separate editions of either Dalton or Coleman revisions.

evidently annoyed, also, by the admiration of his contemporaries for the minor poems, and he denied all merit whatever to *Lycidas* and the Sonnets. His churlishness provoked
a storm of reply from those who accepted Milton's liberalism as completely as they did his art. Cowper, who had a
passionate reverence for Milton and once saw him in a
vision, expressed the desire to thrash the old Tory till his
pension should jingle in his pocket.

One phase of eighteenth century critical discussion of
Milton concerned his versification. The issue as to the
respective merits of blank verse and rhyme was one of
long standing. Milton himself, in the foreword to *Paradise
Lost,* had thrown out a challenge against the prevailing
practice of the Restoration poets. But rhyme and regularity
had already triumphed, and it was part of the work of
eighteenth century Milton critics to justify his verse on
aesthetic grounds. The defense of his subtler harmonies,
and of the technique by which they were secured, was timid
at first, but finally emphatic enough. An outstanding pronouncement in favor of the Miltonic freedom against the
tyranny of the couplet was that of Edward Young in his
Conjectures on Original Composition (1759). Young declared that Pope's rhyming of Homer had "put Achilles in
petticoats a second time." "How much nobler had it been,"
he continues, "if his numbers had rolled on in full flow,
through various modulations of masculine melody, into
those grandeurs of solemn sound which are indispensably
demanded by the native dignity of heroic song. . . . Blank
verse is verse unfallen, uncursed; verse reclaimed, re-
enthroned in the true language of the gods."

MILTON'S INFLUENCE ON EIGHTEENTH CENTURY
POETRY. The general admiration for Milton which was felt

by eighteenth century writers and the acceptance of *Paradise Lost* as a classic, as worthy of imitation as the ancients themselves,[9] resulted in far-reaching influence on eighteenth century poetry. Blank verse was written in large quantities throughout the period, and practically all of it, as Professor Havens has shown,[10] is Miltonic. Except in drama, there was, indeed, no other model. And the Miltonic manner, as distinct from his spirit and inspiration, was not difficult to catch. His use of Latinisms, his inversions of natural word order, his collocations of sonorous proper names, and many other conspicuous external traits furnished a ready means of stylistic ornamentation which an age largely destitute of poetic originality was all too ready to adopt. It served to cover the bareness of whole acres of descriptive and didactic poetry; it enabled epic poets to conceal their lack of inspiration from themselves. One of the earliest wearers of the Miltonic garment was John Phillips in the burlesque poem, *The Splendid Shilling* (1701). Such employment of the high phraseology of *Paradise Lost* on trivial themes to secure an effect of the absurd was very popular. But it was not only the minor men or the parodists who submitted themselves to the spell of Milton. Pope himself, though he used only couplets, plundered the general treasury of phrase to good effect, while Thomson, Young, and Cowper, who maintained in blank verse the more solemn and inward tradition of poetry

[9] Crane, *Imitation of Spenser and Milton,* points out that the attitude underlying the use of Spenser and Milton was, or might be, in close harmony with the neo-classic conception of poetic imitation.

[10] *The Influence of Milton on English Poetry.* This learned and important work is my chief source of information regarding the poetic imitation of Milton.

before its culmination in Wordsworth, were much more profoundly influenced.

Thomson was genuinely stirred by the Miltonic sweep and grandeur. His own imaginative and vaguely religious sense of the majesty of nature found support in the work of his greater predecessor. His style was moulded in a remarkable degree out of the Miltonic materials, and sometimes he succeeded in achieving a kindred eloquence. In general, however, the sword of Achilles was far too mighty for him to use successfully and as a result he fell into all manner of extravagance and absurdity. The grandiose expressions, which were natural and fitting in their application to the remote and lofty matters with which Milton dealt, became a grotesque affectation when employed, as they often were by Thomson and others, as a means of elevating the commonplace. *The Seasons* (1726–1730) was the first serious and thoroughgoing attempt to offset the absence of rhyme by resorting to the ornamentation of Miltonic phrase, and it set the pattern for much subsequent blank verse. It had also an effect in establishing the artificial diction which is the curse of eighteenth century poetry generally. Cowper's superior taste enabled him to avoid the excessive Miltonism of Thomson, but his intimate familiarity with, and profound admiration for, *Paradise Lost* left a strong mark on his own blank verse. "One feature or another of Milton's style and diction," says Havens, "occurs in almost every paragraph of *The Task*."

The discussion of Miltonic imitation has thus far concerned *Paradise Lost* alone. Of his other works only the lyrics, *L'Allegro* and *Il Penseroso,* exerted any considerable influence on eighteenth century poetry, and this influence came late. Lyricism was dead in the first half of the period. Its revival after 1740 among men of romantic inclinations took place in part under the influence of these two exquisite companion pieces. Their combination of freshness and poetic enthusiasm with precision of workmanship and restraint of mood made them, as Havens remarks, particularly adapted to a transition stage between classicism and romanticism. Both Collins and Gray were inspired by them and adopted their personifications, their tone, and, to some extent, their rhythms. A more thorough-going imitator was Thomas Warton the younger, whose favorite octosyllabic verse, with its pleasing and mildly romantic descriptions of English rural landscape, reflects the charm of *L'Allegro* and *Il Penseroso* and employs their phraseology at every turn. Through these men *L'Allegro* and *Il Penseroso* were made widely popular, and their influence was carried on into the great lyric movement of the early nineteenth century. *Il Penseroso* is sometimes held accountable for the eighteenth century passion for poetic melancholy. This is hardly true, for the work of the "Graveyard School" antedated the vogue of Milton's minor poems, and its lugubriousness is of a different type. The tone of *Il Penseroso* fell in, however, with this sentiment, and devotion to the melancholy Muse is at least in part Miltonic.

MILTON SCHOLARSHIP IN THE EIGHTEENTH CENTURY. The Miltonic activity of the eighteenth century was not confined to poetic imitation and to the attempt to establish his rank according to classic or romantic principles of criticism. The work of scholarly interpretation was also vigorously undertaken by a distinguished line of editors and commentators.[11] This activity consisted in: (1) the elaboration of Milton's biography on the basis of earlier records and of the personal material in the prose and poetry; (2) the explanation and illustration of details in the poems; (3) the discovery of sources and analogues for *Paradise Lost* and in less degree for the other poems. These contributions were generally included in one or another of the innumerable editions of Milton's works. They are, of course, closely connected with the critical discussions already mentioned. The learned editorial labors of Patrick Hume in 1695 were followed in 1732 by Richard Bentley's more sensational but less worthy attempt to constitute a critical text of *Paradise Lost* according to the methods which, as a classical scholar, he had been accustomed to apply to ancient authors. Bentley made the unwarranted assumption that Milton's work had been corrupted by an editor who, taking advantage of the poet's blindness, had interpolated passages and made minor changes to the detriment of the meter and the meaning. In his attempt to restore the poem to its original form, Bentley, guided solely by his idea of what Milton ought to have said, exhibits the most extraordinary bad taste and judgment. He was roughly answered in his own time by Pearce and others, and such ineptitudes as his rewriting of the close of *Paradise Lost*:

> They hand in hand with social steps their way
> Through Eden took with Heavenly comfort cheered.

have furnished a perennial theme of ridicule for later writers. It has remained for William Empson [12] to declare

[11] An elaborate study of the early editions is that of Oras, *Milton's Editors and Commentators from Patrick Hume to Henry Todd.*
[12] *Bentley and Milton.*

Bentley superior both in sincerity and in discernment to those critics who have found no aesthetic difficulties in Milton's poetry and who praise him for the wrong reasons. Of Bentley's vast body of emendations but two have been adopted in the received text, while some five or ten additional ones are held by J. W. Mackail to be all but certain.[13]

The two Jonathan Richardsons, father and son, published in 1734 *Explanatory Notes and Remarks on "Paradise Lost,"* including also, as usual, a new life of the poet. The elder Richardson had inherited traditions of the Restoration period and contributed some valuable personal detail regarding Milton. The son, who was a competent classical scholar, contributed useful explanations of the learned allusions. Both were sympathetic and intelligent, and their work became a standard commentary. An elaborate commentary on the complete works, together with a biographical study, was issued in 1740 by Francis Peck under the title *New Memoirs of the Life and Poetical Works of John Milton*. Peck devoted considerable attention to Milton's style and language and to his methods of composition as illustrated by his manuscript corrections. The first variorum edition of *Paradise Lost* was that of Thomas Newton, published with a new life, the best that had been written up to that time, in 1749. This became the basis of a complete variorum of the poetical works by Henry Todd, published in 1801 and revised in 1809. Todd collects in his preliminary account of Milton's life and in his extensive notes to, and discussions of, the poems, the fruits of the scholarly and critical activities of the whole century. He also contributes much material of his own. He adduces a host of literary parallels from classical and mod-

---

[13] *Bentley's Milton.*

ern authors, takes account of the valuable materials afforded by the Cambridge Manuscript, prints the records of the nuncupative will proceedings, and deals extensively with Milton's sources and analogues. His work was not superseded until Masson's three-volume edition of the poems in 1890, and it still remains a mine of information for Milton students.

The exploration, often with the implication of plagiarism, of Milton's literary borrowings was a favorite amusement of both eighteenth and nineteenth century scholars. The most sensational incident in this connection was William Lauder's claim in his *Essay on Milton's Imitation of the Moderns* (1749) to have found the originals of *Paradise Lost* in the Latin drama *Adamus Exul* of Hugo Grotius and in other out-of-the-way neo-Latin poems. It was afterwards shown that the remarkable closeness of Lauder's parallels was due to the fact that he had interpolated among them passages from a Latin translation of Milton's poem by William Hog. If Lauder had contented himself with the *Adamus Exul* as he found it, he would have been on solid ground with Hayley,[14] who, following a suggestion of Voltaire, pointed out the similarities between *Paradise Lost* and the *Adamo* of Andreini, and with Dunster, who brought forward Sylvester's *Du Bartas* as a primary formative influence in Milton's style. The plausibility of these relationships and of the later claims in favor of Caedmon and Vondel has been discussed in Chapter IV.

THE NINETEENTH AND TWENTIETH CENTURIES

There is no evidence of a narrowing of the circle of Milton's readers in the first quarter of the nineteenth cen-

[14] *Life of Milton*, pp. 233 ff.

tury. New editions appeared in increasing numbers, and literary critics continued to pay tribute to his greatness. The discovery, in 1823, of the manuscript of the *Christian Doctrine* was an event of national interest. Bishop Sumner was commissioned by the King to publish and translate it; [15] Macaulay's essay, which owed its fame as much to its subject as to its intrinsic brilliancy, was written as a review of Milton's treatise, and it was made the subject of a popular study by the American Unitarian, William Ellery Channing, in 1826.

It was, however, among the poets who came in the wake of the French Revolution that Milton was the most dynamic force. He was so already in the late eighteenth century to William Blake, in whose image-haunted brain he took his place among the prophets, visiting his waking dreams in person and contributing largely to the materials of his imagination in poetry and art. Over ninety of Blake's paintings and engravings are on Miltonic subjects. [16] His Urizen in the epic poem *Vala* is a wild counterpart of Satan, and Milton himself, standing for the ideal poet, is the titular hero of another work. Blake's own fantastic cosmology and the philosophic ideas embodied in it are somehow indebted, whether by agreement or opposition, to the Miltonic system, but it surpasses the powers of human reason to make clear the relationship between them. [17]

In the *Marriage of Heaven and Hell* Blake says that Satan represents desire, and the Messiah, reason or the restrainer. He then goes on to invert Milton's ethical code by proclaiming the Messiah rather than Satan the Evil

15 He published the text and translation in two volumes in 1825.
16 Havens, *Milton's Influence*, p. 217.
17 See Saurat, *Blake and Milton*, 1920, for an attempt to do so.

One, adding in a note that the reason why Milton wrote in fetters when he wrote of angels and God, and at liberty when of devils and Hell, is because he was a true poet and of the Devil's party without knowing it. This Rousseauistic proposition represents something new in Milton interpretation. It is really quite different in its implications from Dryden's statement that Satan is the hero of *Paradise Lost,* for Dryden is thinking in terms of epic technique, while Blake is declaring that passion and rebellion, typified in Satan, are the vital motives of Milton's poetic inspiration. In so doing, he keenly anticipates the trend of a good deal of subsequent criticism. An identical point of view pervades Sir Walter Raleigh's brilliant book on Milton, which may fairly be said to represent the standard opinion of the romantic school. The theological and moral system under which Milton disciplined himself, its validity no longer felt, was thought to be a contradiction to his actual experience. Hence the ideals and aims which he thought he was achieving have been discredited as not representing the real values of his work, with the inference that Milton's poetry can no longer be admired as a whole or on his own terms. Matthew Arnold finds the obsoleteness of Milton's theology a barrier to modern acceptance of *Paradise Lost* and recommends that it be read in fragments. In general, the dramatic portrayal of Satan in Books I and II is held to outrank in creative power all the rest of the poem.

Shelley and Byron, without analyzing the situation as Blake had done, rejected or ignored Milton's Puritanism, while making the most of those elements in him which coincided with their own revolutionary ideas. Thus Shelley found Milton's Satan, as a moral being, infinitely superior to his God, who bore the familiar earmarks of the tyrant.

His own Prometheus he recognized to be a kindred figure, superior, however, because his activities were directed to man's good instead of to his destruction. Byron gave a more direct literary application to the Satan worship of the time by making Lucifer, in the drama of *Cain,* a champion of man's thirst for intellectual emancipation. The new age of spiritual rebellion thus adopted Milton as its ally against his will. Their sympathies led them naturally to exalt his personal career. Thus Shelley ranges him in *Adonais* with the other poet-heroes who have had the world against them.

> . . . He died
> Who was the sire of an immortal strain,
> Blind, old, and lonely, when his country's pride
> The priest, the slave, and the liberticide
> Trampled and mocked with many a loathed rite
> Of lust and blood.

Wordsworth had a juster sense of Milton's true quality and he was profoundly influenced by his spirit and art. His own combination of a temperate love of liberty with an intense moral earnestness was akin to Milton's and predisposed him to admiration. His sonnet, "Milton, thou should'st be living at this hour," illustrates how deeply he had assimilated the ethical idealism of his master. It was, indeed, the reading of Milton's sonnets which inspired his own masterpieces in this form. There is also a Miltonic quality in Wordsworth's more exalted utterances in blank verse, and though he does not, like Thomson, ape Milton's stylistic peculiarities in an obvious manner, echoes of Miltonic phrase are frequent in his work.

Keats, too, was a Miltonist, but on lines quite different from either Shelley or Wordsworth. His feeling for Milton's poetry was primarily aesthetic. The richness of Milton's expression, "poetical luxury," as Keats called it, was naturally attractive to his temperament, but he learned to admire the restraint and dignity which elevated Milton above his own earlier masters. Keats's enthusiastic study of *Paradise Lost* just after he had written *Endymion* is rightly held to have been of great influence in disciplining and ennobling his later work. His *Hyperion* represents an attempt to compose a blank verse epic on the Miltonic plane. In both conception and style, the poem owes much to *Paradise Lost*. It was abandoned, because Keats felt himself to be doing violence to his genius in adopting a poetical mode which was, after all, alien to his own. Taken as a whole, the romantic period, though its view of Milton was colored by its own emotions, stood close to him in imaginative sympathy and was better able than the eighteenth century to value his true poetic quality.

The decline which may be traced in the popular vogue of Milton through the later nineteenth century and early twentieth century is to be attributed in part to the rise of a modern romantic literature, which rendered him less necessary as a rallying point for poetical enthusiasm, in part to his increasing remoteness in an age no longer thoroughly disciplined in classical knowledge and thought,—an age, also, for which his theological system has become largely obsolete. Milton is no longer in the degree he was for over a century after his death a theme of heated controversy. He has become a classic, and as such is abandoned to the limited audience of those who are equipped to read him. For poets, his supreme mastery of the language of the gods, though no longer a thing to imitate, has been and will long continue to be an inspiration. There is, however, a current rebellion against his leadership in this respect. Mr. T. S. Eliot and others compare Milton's style unfavorably with that of Donne and Dryden. Milton had a "habit of exploiting language as a kind of musical medium outside himself." There is in his verse "no suggestion of any complex and varying currents of feeling and sensation." He "made the language stiff and tortuous, even distorted, unusable in that form by poets, but Dryden made it miraculously flexible." Milton's predominance in various forms from Thomson through Gray, Cowper, Wordsworth, Keats, and Tennyson, is a fact deplored. He "broke the tradition" of English poetic diction, and the significance of the modern movement in poetry lies in its reconstruction of that tradition "by the reopening of communication with the seventeenth century of Shakespeare, Donne, Middleton, Tourneur and so on." All this, however, is very much a matter of taste and opinion. Readers who persist in thinking Milton a good poet will find the recent anti-Miltonians ably answered by Logan Pearsall Smith.[18]

Meanwhile, the scholarly study of Milton's life and work has been carried to a point far beyond that reached by the activity of the eighteenth century. The collected edition of the poetry and prose published by John Mitford in 1851 was for many years the standard collection of the works, while the Bohn edition of the prose, with its translations of the Latin pamphlets, has been the most available means of access to these materials. The Columbia Edition, completed in 1938, supersedes all others as the official corpus of Mil-

[18] See *Milton and his Modern Critics*. Smith's list of Milton detractors includes Ezra Pound, Middleton Murray, Herbert Reed, Bonamy Dobree, F. L. Lucas, Frank Leavis, and T. S. Eliot.

ton's writings. It adds a number of hitherto uncollected
works, some of them published from MS. for the first time.
It contains all that could be wished in the way of textual
apparatus and though it does not attempt the heroic task
of furnishing a complete editorial equipment in the form
of annotations and introductions, it supplies much data
beyond the strict requirement of an edition of the text itself. All the Latin, even that of the Commonplace Book,
the Correspondence, and the Marginalia is translated. There
is an excellent subject index. It is likely to remain the standard collection for an indefinite time. The learned annotating
of the poetry is most completely represented in Verity's editions. There is no modern variorum of Milton like the Fur-
ness Shakespeare and the Johns Hopkins Spenser. Milton
offers greater difficulties in this respect than either of these
authors. The series of individual editions of the prose published by the Yale and continued by the Cornell Press have
unfortunately not been carried to completion. The paraphernalia of Milton study has also been enriched by the publication of dictionaries of his language and of his geographical,
historical, and Biblical allusions and by a concordance of the
Latin poems. There is still no large-scale allusion book, but
Professor Parker's *Milton's Contemporary Reputation* covers the subject to 1674 and the studies of Havens and Good
provide a great deal of such material for the eighteenth century.

An indispensable bibliographical aid to the study of Milton was provided by Stevens in his *Reference Guide,* published in 1930. This, however, includes only materials published since 1800. Fletcher's supplement carries the subject
down to 1930. The making of a complete and up-to-date

bibliography remains a great desideratum. It is especially desirable since there has been much detailed work done of late on problems connected with the early publication of Milton's works.

The modern study of Milton as a man and poet rests on David Masson's monumental *Life of Milton in Connection with the History of his Times,* the first volume of which appeared in 1859 and the last in 1894. Masson's indefatigable labors in the records and pamphlets of the Puritan period, and his minute attention to every detail in the remotest degree related to Milton, have made his work, though of oppressive magnitude, the one indispensable body of biographical information. Later biographers, like Mark Pattison, whose brief life of Milton is still among the best, have constructed their interpretations of Milton largely out of the materials furnished by Masson. They have largely ignored the work of Alfred Stern, published in two volumes in 1877–1879, which nevertheless contains some things not found in its greater English rival. Smaller general biographies continue to be written with varying emphases and from different points of view. Hilaire Belloc, as a Catholic, has little sympathy for the Miltonic religious, political, or social ideals, but is full of admiration for his creative power. His aesthetic judgments are vigorous and unconventional. Rose Macaulay's brief life, based on a sound scholarship in seventeenth century literature and history, is more conservative. Dora Raymond [19] chooses to forget that Milton was a poet and to retell in considerable detail the story of his public and political career. Documentary research, which slackened for a time, has been very active in the last decade, as the notes and bibliography to

[19] *Oliver's Secretary.*

the present volume sufficiently demonstrate, and though no one has yet endeavored to rival Masson, the accumulation of new data begins to warrant such an undertaking.

The recent interpreters of Milton have made an effort to see him clearly in his intellectual, as earlier students had done in his literary and political relationships. With the decline of active prejudice against his theology there has come a higher valuation of his original contribution as a humane and philosophical thinker. It has come to be clearly seen that the modern mind need not be alienated from Milton by the fact that he expressed his thought in a terminology which has now become obsolete. The problems of human life and destiny are really the same in all ages and anyone who has grappled with experience as sincerely and powerfully as Milton did will have a message for whoever takes the trouble to learn his language. Milton's "system" gives order to his convictions and it is possible to convert it, after a fashion, into more modern terms. Thus M. Denis Saurat [20] treats Milton's theology according to the formulae of nineteenth century metaphysics, as a means of "disentangling from theological rubbish the permanent and human interest in his thought." He finds in Milton a complete ontology, cosmology, psychology, ethics, religion, and politics, with many original features in them. His God becomes in Saurat's treatment "The Absolute." Christ is "intelligence triumphant over passion." This attempt to re-systematize Milton's system is perhaps carried too far, but it does serve to bring out his stripe of thought. Milton was passionately convinced that the universe was a unit, that man was the author of his own destiny, that human nature and the human race were on their way toward good.

[20] *Milton, Man and Thinker.*

the Puritan epoch in the cold light of historical realism, equips Milton not only with an extraordinary measure of Renaissance egotism but with a Machiavellian ruthlessness which stands in strange contrast to the Puritan profession. On a doubtful evidential basis he makes him resort to a piece of pure dishonesty in his refutation of *Eikon Basilike*. Another continental scholar, Heinrich Mutschmann,[22] employing the Adlerian psychology, finds the secret of Milton's personality in an inferiority complex, based on a congenital physical weakness. Mutschmann's supposition that Milton was an albino is wholly fantastic, but there is food for thought in his analysis. The present writer,[23] and more recently, Tillyard,[24] have traced in detail Milton's psychological development as revealed in his work, and H. J. C. Grierson,[25] with a broader and more balanced view than Liljegren or Mutschmann and a thorough understanding of the phenomenon of Puritanism, has given perhaps the richest and most humane account of Milton's character in its strength and weakness against the background of his time.

Grierson's latest volume [26] deals with Milton and Wordsworth, the two great English poets who, in time of public agitation, endeavored to guide their countrymen by the light of truth. Both began with "a vision of human nature

---

[22] *Milton und das Licht.* See also the controversy which has followed this strange study in *Anglia, Englische Studien, Neophilologus,* etc., since 1920. A full bibliography will be found in Stevens' *Reference Guide.*

[23] *The Youth of Milton.*

[24] *Milton.*

[25] *Cross Currents.*

[26] *Milton and Wordsworth.*

born again" and both were disillusioned. But Milton's final pronouncements are the expression of a conclusion reached by conscious deduction from his experiences, whereas Wordsworth's deepest convictions were reached intuitionally. "We have passed, indeed are still passing," says Grierson, "through a period in which it is hard to judge *Paradise Lost* aright. When we have escaped from the wish either to defend or criticize his cosmology and history and theology we shall see it as a great utterance of a great soul in a great but troubled age."

Grierson makes less of the disappointment of Milton's domestic life, more of his reaction to political events. When England deserted the cause to which he had given a large part of his life, Milton was not only left without a practical outlet for his energies, but he lost the deep conviction that men could be quickly won to the support of his ideal order of society. He might conceivably have experienced a spiritual rebirth. Instead of this, he became defensive. His vision was impaired and he was left passionate and embittered, grimly contemplating the ruin of his hopes. In the great poems he is still fighting the lost battle in his mind. In proclaiming the freedom and responsibility of man and the loss of that freedom through weakness, the greatest of sins, Milton is accounting for defeat. In showing how liberty was restored

> By one man's firm obedience fully tried
> Through all temptation

he is limiting regeneration to the individual and postponing the day of New Heavens, New Earth till the Millennium. In showing, finally, how he who has fallen through weakness may yet recover his lost strength and wreak vengeance on God's enemies, the mighty of the earth, he is resigning such a triumph for himself. In all this Milton is argumentative and didactic, not prophetic.

To the present writer, Grierson's interpretation of Milton, while containing much that is suggestive, fails to take full account of the vitality of the poet's idealism and of the coherence of his program from youth to old age. We may recognize the spiritual flaws in his nature, the harshness, the defect of love; we may admit that he can be unpleasantly argumentative, and that the motive of justification is at times a liability on his art; but we cannot say that he is in his later days less a prophet than before or that what he has gained is not more than what he has lost.

Milton's extraordinary power of remaining a matter of more than literary and academic concern to men continues to be illustrated at every turn of religious, political, and cultural ideology. The exact degree and moment of Milton's deviation from orthodox theology, the nature and limitations of his doctrine of liberty, have been studied intensively and debated with warmth.[27] Unencumbered by political bias or psychological theory, W. O. Haller has demonstrated how closely Milton's ideas, attitudes, and even imagery follow the traditions of Puritan expression.[28] He turned from the pulpit to poetry as a medium for the exercise of his gift of interpreting the word of God because he was "church-outed by the prelates;" he turned from poetry to pamphleteering be-

[27] Sewell, *A Study of Milton's "Christian Doctrine"*; Kelley, *This Great Argument*; Woodhouse, *Puritanism and Liberty*; Barker, *Milton and the Puritan Dilemma*; Wolfe, *Milton in the Puritan Revolution*; Grierson, "Milton and Liberty."
[28] *The Rise of Puritanism*; "The Puritan Art of Love."

cause a lively expectation of Utopia momentarily inspired him with hope of practical achievement. His poems, considered in one aspect, are Puritan sermons. This view is in opposition to the more personal interpretations of Saurat and Grierson.

Finally, C. S. Lewis,[29] writing from the point of view of a sophisticated orthodoxy, protests on the one hand against irrelevant erudition and on the other against the modernistic criticism. Milton is to be understood only by those who enter into and accept at face value both his literary and his religious tradition. So understood he may be judged. Milton's poetic talent failed him in the outline of sacred history in the last two books and in his presentation of God. But those who blame these defects on his subject matter do so out of ignorance or hatred of the theme itself. Its truth and passion were never, in essence, assailed until rebellion and pride came, in the romantic age, to be admired for their own sake. "On this side the adverse criticism of Milton is not so much a literary phenomenon as the shadow cast upon literature by revolutionary politics, antinomian ethics, and the worship of Man by Man." We seem here to be getting "back to Milton," but actually, I believe, are as much as ever in the eddies of contemporary thought.

[29] *Preface to "Paradise Lost."*

APPENDIX A

MILTON AND THE UNIVERSITIES

MILTON'S attitude toward the universities was uniformly unfriendly. Though he may, as his early biographers declare, have "performed all his exercises with very good applause" and departed "loved and admired by all," he was obviously neither a happy conformist to the Cambridge routine while he was a student nor a loyal alumnus afterward. The story begins, so far as we have evidence, with the quarrel with Chappell, in Milton's second academic year (1627). In the first Latin elegy, written at this time, Milton expresses not only resentment at the indignities to which he has been personally subjected, but also a general disrelish for the place itself. The fields of Cambridge are "bare of pleasant shade." The votaries of Phoebus fare ill there. He does not care to go back.

This reaction may well have been but momentary. It is not long, however, before we hear him complaining to his St. Paul's tutor, Gill, of the shallowness of the student body. (See above, page 17.) The terms in which he does so suggest that he has been arming himself with the traditional humanistic arguments and specifically with the Baconian indictment of scholasticism. There is also, however, a trace of personal animosity and defense. We must remember that Milton, though a scholar and poet at heart, still intended to enter the church and regarded his university studies as preparation for a kind of ministry conform-

355

able to the best ideals of the Reformation. Before his time there had been at Cambridge a strong Puritan movement which would have won his approval, and one of the "spiritual brotherhood," Thomas Goodwin, was still preaching there.[1] But the repressive influences were already beginning to be felt, and there must have been little encouragement for Milton's idealism in the prevailing atmosphere after the beginning of the rise of Laud. He says nothing directly of the religious issue as it was reflected in official Cambridge, but concentrates his attention on the student body. His fellow aspirants for orders, he says, care nothing for solid studies, but only for such theological scraps as will enable them to succeed in the flashy occupation of the typical churchman. He is afraid that the clergy will "relapse into the sacerdotal ignorance of a former age."

The academic exercises, which, though they cannot be precisely dated, belong in general to the latter part of Milton's university career, show the poet fully confirmed in his anti-scholastic point of view and already a master of the rhetoric of humanistic reform. (See above, pages 72 ff.) The practice of disputation, he calls an "enforced vanity." His petty fellows have, for the most part, "no right reason, no sound judgment, but only pride in a certain overboiling and truly laughable foam of words." The system wholly neglects what should be its chief concern: geography, history, science, sound philosophy, and religious truth. Milton stands with Colet in his devotion to Plato as opposed to Aristotle, with Erasmus in his scorn of the barbarous inanity of the schools. On Mount Parnassus there is no room for these unlovely studies, "horrid with brambles and thorns, overgrown with thistles and thick nettles."

[1] See Haller, *The Rise of Puritanism*, pp. 293 ff.

Having thus said his say in open consistory, putting erring elders in their place, bearing witness to the truth even amid the pomp and circumstance of university ceremonial, Milton leaves Cambridge, a Master of Arts, in 1632. It is an open question whether he was offered a fellowship, and on what grounds he rejected one, if it was available. His later remark that the fellows of his college signified "how much it would content them if I should stay" may refer only to the personal expressions of individuals. Haller's idea that Milton's bitterness had its real origin in the thwarting of a life program which involved the acceptance of a fellowship and the peaceful entry upon a liberal ministry is suggestive but has no real support. Milton would, I believe, have been more explicit if the facts were as Mr. Haller believes them to be. My own view is that he had not in 1632 developed the conviction that he was "church-outed by the prelates." The question of whether a Puritan could preach under the Anglican régime was already before him when Young was "church-outed" in 1620. Yet Milton still assumed that he was to enter the ministry when he wrote the *Letter to a Friend* at Horton. I do not doubt the sincerity of Milton's intention, but the decision was one which had been made for him rather than by him. The idea of entering the church ran counter to his temperament and interests, and came to seem increasingly remote until the course of public events and his own growing independence enabled him to reverse it.

During his years at Horton and in Italy, we have no expressions of irritation at the universities. The Platonism of *Comus,* the denunciation of the clergy in *Lycidas,* the announcement of his intention to make his own preparation deep and thorough (*Letter to a Friend,* above, page

23), replace direct attack on the academic "feast of sow thistles and brambles" which had so disgusted him. Perhaps he turned to Oxford in the interim [2] and found there, at least books and a humane librarian.

But when the Civil Wars begin Milton turns again on the universities, without discrimination and more violently than before. They were already enlisted in the Royal cause and the cry had gone up for their purgation. Cambridge, says Milton in 1642, "vomits now out of a sickness, but ere it will be well with her, she must vomit by a strong physic." Though the issue has now become a political one, Milton takes his stand on the old indictment, declaring that "the gentry of England, fed with the scragged and thorny lectures of monkish and miserable sophistry, are trained for the service of Prelaty, instead of the service of God." Their lack of genuine humanistic culture is evidenced in

[2] He was incorporated A.M. in 1635.

Oxford was easier of access from Horton, and he had connections there. His acquaintance with Rous may or may not have begun at the time. Later, in a letter to Oldenburg (June 25, 1656), Milton demurs at his friend's expressions of satisfaction in scholarly retirement at Oxford on the old ground of absence of fit associates in study.

"I see not what advantage you can have in that retirement except in an access to a multitude of books: the associates in study whom you have found there, were I believe rather made students by their own natural inclinations, than by the discipline of the place. But perhaps I am less partial to the place because it detains you, whose absence I regret. You rightly observe, that there are too many there who pollute all learning, divine and human, by their frivolous subtleties and barren disputations; and who seem to do nothing to deserve the salary which they receive."

The letter does not suggest a pleasant feeling about the institution, but Rous had died in 1652, and any distinction that Milton's personal experience may have prompted him to make had doubtless long since been obliterated.

their inability "to speak or write in a pure style, much less to distinguish the ideas and various kinds of style." They are equally unlettered in Latin and Greek, while in the Hebrew text—which is so necessary to be understood—except for some few of them, "their lips are utterly uncircumcised."

From now on much of Milton's constructive thinking on the subject of education is conditioned by his disapproval of the university methods and the case that he had built up out of his unhappy personal experience at Cambridge. His own program in the pamphlet *Of Education* is for a complete and generous discipline as far removed as possible from that to which he had been subjected. There are to be no scraggy thorns of sophistry in Milton's school, and that school, with others like it, is intended not to prepare for the universities but to replace them. Milton is at no pains whatsoever to be moderate or judicious. He shows no interest in such evidences as there were of progress within the universities; he even passes over in silence the "godly thorough reformation" effected there after 1652 by Cromwell. As late as 1659, in the argument against a hireling clergy, he is still belaboring the system as vehemently as ever. The theological studies are "Such as tend least of all to the edification or capacity of the people, but rather perplex and leaven pure doctrine with scholastic trash than enable any minister to the better preaching of the gospel." He argues that the ministers do not need either the elaborate intellectual equipment of the trained scholastic theologian or the expensive private libraries which they employ to maintain their intellectual pride. Thinking of his own proposals in *Of Education,* he goes on to declare that "all the learning, either human or divine, necessary to a minister may as easily and less chargeably be had in any private house."

That Milton's one-sided view, however he may have rationalized it, is ultimately based on personal dislikes is obvious from the character of his allusions to his fellow students in their sports and relaxations. The violent disapproval expressed in the first Prolusion (see above, page 18) shows signs of softening in *Lycidas,* if indeed the lines:

> Rough satyrs danced
> And fauns with cloven heel

are based on Cambridge memories, but the description of the student comedies in the *Apology for Smectymnuus* (1642) is eloquent of an attitude which is, to say the least, uncharitable. "There while they acted and overacted, among other young scholars, I was a spectator; they thought themselves gallant men, and I thought them fools; they made sport and I laughed; they mispronounced, and I misliked; and, to make up the atticism, they were out, and I hissed." One suspects that unnamed individuals are in Milton's mind, and we may, if we please, think of Thomas Randolph as one of the likeliest offenders.

So much then for Milton's case against his Alma Mater. It is small wonder that contemporary scholars who happen to be Cambridge alumni are inclined to evade the subject. Thus Mr. Arthur Gray's statement that Milton, nursed on the self-same hill with Lycidas, "had a kindness for his college and university which time and after-prejudice outwore," is, as we have seen, far from the truth, and J. B. Mullinger hardly covers the case when he writes:

"Beyond the culture of his classical taste, there is little reason in supposing that Cambridge did much toward moulding his character." Milton's classical taste was already formed before he entered the university, and his experience there, if it did not mould his character, did do much, for better and worse, to determine or to confirm his attitudes.

In order to get the full picture and to do justice to the positive as well as the negative side of the Cambridge influence, it is necessary to go beyond Milton's own direct statements and consider certain contributions which may plausibly be attributed to his Cambridge environment but which he was too churlish to acknowledge explicitly. It is unlikely that he spent six years in one of the great intellectual centers of his country only to build up a set of opinions based wholly on resentment. He speaks in general terms of the encouragement of tutors and fellows, and admits the presence of "two or three" likeminded with himself. We have the beautiful Latin poems and the occasionally serene Prolusions as evidence of his more profitable activity. These things were certainly not written without applause from some quarter. The meed of silence accorded to his second tutor, Tovey, may indicate that he was not unhelpful. An unnamed Fellow, who asked Milton to supply him with verses for an academic oration, took unwittingly the very best way of bringing out the poet's talents.

Of even greater importance was his inevitable contact with the new ideas which were forcing their way into the traditional framework of Cambridge thought. Joseph Mead, the most distinguished man in the university, was a Platonist and a dabbler in Cabbalistic lore. The spirit which was to result in the later activity of Henry More and the latitudinarians was already in the air, and Milton, though he never so much as mentions the Cambridge Platonists, individually or as a group, was obviously stimulated by it.

It seems likely, also, that he would have heard echoes of a major controversy which had agitated the university just before his time. Richard Montagu of King's College in his *New Gagg for a Goose* (1624) and his *Apello Caesarem* (1625), had repudiated the teachings of Calvinism and demonstrated the presence of Arminianism in the sixteenth article of the Church of England. It was his aim to show that the "errors" attributed by Calvinist or Romanist to Protestantism were not errors at all but the outcome of a deliberate suspension of judgment with respect to certain opinions. The doctrines of predestination, transubstantiation, etc. were not to be included within the limits of recognized orthodoxy and with respect to them considerable latitude was to be allowed. These radical ideas deeply affected the currents of thought at Cambridge,[8] and Milton could not have escaped being impressed by them. His own later Arminianism, maintained against the doctrines of the very group with which he was at first politically allied, may have its roots in the discussion which raged around Montagu's pronouncements.

Nor could he have failed to know of the attempted innovations which followed the death of Bacon in 1626. The chancellor had left instructions in his will for the founding of two lectureships in natural philosophy, one at Cambridge

[8] "It may be fairly questioned whether in the first half of the seventeenth century—that age of pamphleteering,—any similar production excited such ardent controversy." Mullinger, III, 31.

and one at Oxford. This bequest could not be carried into effect, and the lectureship in history established in 1627 by Bacon's disciple, Lord Brooke, was promptly terminated by Laud and the High Church party. The effects of this agitation on Milton may, however, be read in his advocacy of both scientific and historical study in the third Prolusion and in the deliberate effort which he afterwards made to remedy the deficiency of his own education in these respects. There was, finally, a movement to replace the dialectic method of Aristotle with that of Ramus. Milton's *Ars Logica* shows that he was an adherent of the Moderns in this regard. Of the reverberations stirred up at Cambridge by Hakewill's *Apology* we have no evidence, but Milton's championship of the more progressive point of view in his academic verses, *Naturam non pati Senium* (above, page 73), certainly implies that the issues had been under discussion.

Haller emphasizes the close association of these more liberal ideas of study with the activities of the higher type of reforming preacher, and he points out the fact that Milton advocates wide learning not as an end in itself, but as a means of attaining the eloquence necessary to him who would move the wills of men to righteousness. This, however, is simply to say that Milton shares the emotions and speaks the language of his time and place. His interests, his instincts, and his conscious purposes were doubtless mixed. He was a scholar and a humanistic poet as well as a young idealist vaguely hoping to reform the world. In all three rôles his nature demanded sustenance, and this eager desire to realize his capabilities enabled him to learn much more from Cambridge than he was willing to give

manner is, was not unstudied in those authors which are most commended. Whereof some were grave orators and historians, whose matter methought I loved indeed, but as my age then was, so I understood them; others were the smooth elegiac poets, whereof the schools are not scarce, whom both for the pleasing sound of their numerous writing, which in imitation I found most easy, and most agreeable to nature's part in me, and for their matter, which what it is there be few who know not, I was so allured to read, that no recreation came to me better welcome. For that it was then those years with me which are excused, though they be least severe, I may be saved the labour to remember ye. Whence having observed them to account it the chief glory of their wit, in that they were able to judge, to praise, and by that could esteem themselves worthiest to love those high perfections, which under one or other name they took to celebrate, I thought to myself by every instinct and presage of nature, which is not wont to be false, that what emboldened them to this task, might with such diligence as they used embolden me; and that what judgment, wit, or elegance was my share, would herein best appear, and best value itself, by how much more wisely, and with more love of virtue I should choose (let rude ears be absent) the object of not unlike praises. For albeit these thoughts to some will seem virtuous and commendable, to others only pardonable, to a third sort perhaps idle; yet the mentioning of them now will end in serious.

Nor blame it, readers, in those years to propose to themselves such a reward, as the noblest dispositions above other things in this life have sometimes preferred: whereof not to be sensible when good and fair in one person meet, argues both a gross and shallow judgment, and withal an ungentle and swainish breast. For by the firm settling of these persuasions, I became, to my best memory, so much a proficient, that if I found those authors anywhere speaking unworthy things of themselves or unchaste of those names which before they had extolled, this effect it wrought on me, from that time forward their art I still applauded, but the men I deplored; and above them all preferred the two famous renowners of Beatrice and Laura, who never write but honor of them to whom they devote their verse, displaying sublime and pure thoughts, without transgression. And long it was not after when I was confirmed in this opinion, that he who would not be frustrate of his hope to write well hereafter in laudable things, ought himself to be a true poem; that is a composition and pattern of the best and honorablest things; not presuming to sing praises of heroic men, or famous cities, unless he have in himself the experience and practice of all that which is praiseworthy.

Next (for hear me out now, readers, that I may tell ye whither my younger feet wandered), I betook me to those fables and romances, which recount in solemn cantos the deeds of knighthood founded by our victorious kings, and from hence in renown all over Christendom. There I read it in the oath of every knight that he should defend to the expense of his best blood, if so befell him, the honour and chastity of virgin or matron; from whence even then I learned what a noble virtue chastity must be, to the defence of which so many worthies, by such a dear adventure of themselves, had sworn. And if I found in the story afterward, any of them, by word or deed, breaking that oath, I judged it the same fault of the poet, as that which is attributed to Homer, to have written indecent things of the gods. Only this my mind gave me, that every free and gentle spirit, without that oath, ought to be born a knight, nor needed to expect the gilt spur, or the laying of a sword upon his shoulder to stir him both by his counsel and his arms, to secure and protect the weakness of any attempted chastity. So that even these books, which to many others have been the fuel of wantonness and loose living, I cannot think how, unless by divine indulgence, proved to me so many incitements, as you have heard, to the love and steadfast observation of that virtue which abhors the society of the bordellos.

Thus from the laureate fraternity of poets, riper years and the ceaseless round of studies led me to the shady spaces of philosophy; but chiefly to the divine volumes of Plato and his equal Xenophon: where if I should tell ye what I learned of chastity and love, I mean of that which is truly so, whose charming cup is only virtue, which she bears in her hand to those who are worthy (the rest are cheated with a thick intoxicating potion, which a certain sorceress, the abuser of love's name carries about) and how the first and chiefest office of love ends in the soul, producing those two happy twins of her divine generation, knowledge and virtue. With such abstracted sublimities as these, it might be worth your listening, readers, as I may one day hope to have ye in a still time, when there shall be no chiding.

Last of all, not in time, but as perfection is last, that care was ever had of me, with my earliest capacity, not to be negligently trained in the precepts of the Christian religion: this that I have hitherto related, hath been to shew, that though Christianity had been but slightly taught me, yet a certain reservedness of natural disposition, and moral discipline, learnt out of the noblest philosophy, was enough to keep me in disdain of far less incontinence than this of the bordello. But having had the doctrine of holy scripture unfolding those chaste and high mysteries, with timeliest care infused, that "the body is for the Lord and the Lord for in body"; thus also I argued to myself, that if unchastity in a woman, whom St. Paul terms the glory of man, be such a scandal and dishonour, then certainly in a man, who is both the image and glory of God, it must, though commonly not so thought, be much more deflowering and dishonourable; in that he sins both against his own body, which is the perfecter sex, and his own glory, which is in the woman; and, that which is worst, against the image and glory of God, which is in him-

self. Nor did I slumber over that place expressing such high
rewards of ever accompanying the Lamb, with those celestial
songs to others inapprehensible, but not to those who were
not defiled with women, which doubtless means fornication;
for marriage must not be called a defilement.

In the first paragraph Milton indicates with some precision the moment of a new kind of emotional response,
characteristic of adolescence, to the stimulus of reading.
The smooth and glowing love poetry of Ovid and his fellows has spoken powerfully to his imagination and has
roused in him the impulse of imitation. The result is
clearly written in his own Latin elegies, particularly the
First, Fifth, and Seventh, with their strong accent of
sensuous feeling and their only partly chastened Ovidian
tone. The time to which he refers would be about his
nineteenth year. At a later period he evidently felt the
need of regarding the activities of this epoch with some
indulgence. He implies, however, that even then his zest
for the elegists was attended with an idealistic reaction
which soon led to his deserting them for higher objects.
Becoming an adept in rejecting the grosser enticements of
the flesh he finds in Dante and Petrarch with their exaltation of woman and their refinement of the sentiment of
love the embodiment of his new aspirations. The Italian
Sonnets, closely imitated from Petrarch, may, though their
precise date is uncertain, be taken as the immediate fruits
of Milton's second literary discipleship. A more decided
advance in point of view is indicated in the next sentence:
"And long it was not after when I was confirmed in this
opinion, that he who would not be frustrate of his hope to
write well hereafter in laudable things, ought himself to be

a true poem." The key to this is furnished by the Sixth Elegy, in which Milton takes farewell of the mood of lax indulgence in favor of an earnest asceticism. The formula given in this work for the discipline of an epic poet is so closely parallel to that in the *Apology* as to make it clear that in the quoted passage Milton is looking back to and thinking in terms of his meditation of 1629. We may assume that he is recording a more or less definite resolution regarding his life work, a resolution which we may associate with his coming of age in the same month in which the Latin poem was written. The poem *On the Nativity* followed immediately after, in earnest of his future devotion to the highest themes.

Passing over more transient moods and influences which may have intervened, Milton next sets forth his enthusiasm for the literature of chivalry. He is referring, I think, not to his earliest acquaintance with the stories of knighthood in Geoffrey or Malory, but to a period of more serious occupation with them as they were interpreted and moralized by the poets of the Renaissance. Above all he is thinking of the "solemn cantos" of the "sage and serious" Spenser, who becomes henceforth a dominant influence in his poetic aspirations. The time is the Horton period or slightly earlier; Milton's present interests are leading him toward the selection of an Arthurian subject for his projected epic. The time, however, is not ripe and he lingers a while in the easier paths of pastoral poetry. Meanwhile he is mingling with his zeal for romantic poetry the study of philosophy. The character of his reference and his bracketing of Plato and Xenophon show very clearly that it is the high doctrine of love and virtue as set forth in the *Symposium* that chiefly attracts him. Such "abstracted sublimities" fit well with the concrete embodiments in Spenser, who had already assimilated them. But in thus turning toward the Renaissance star of Platonic love Milton also turns to its counterpart of Christian chastity, dwelling with special eagerness on the image of the heavenly nuptials of the pure as given in the fourteenth chapter of Revelation. The outcome of these elevated yet fervid imaginings is *Comus,* in which the correlative influences of Spenserian, Platonic, and Apocalyptic allegory are clearly to be traced. The idea of the mystic marriage of the pure soul with God, which is the theme of the Attendant Spirit's Epilogue, is touched on again in *Lycidas* (1637) and, with much sensuous elaboration, in the *Epitaph of Damon* (1640). The "unexpressive nuptial song" mentioned in the two elegies carries us directly to that place in scripture (*Rev.* xiv) over which Milton said he did not sleep. In the *Comus* passage the imagery is exclusively Spenserian and Platonic, though the emotion is Christian.

The fervor of Milton's philosophic studies during the Horton period and the degree to which they colored his personal relations and his aspirations as a poet are reflected in the letter to Charles Diodati (quoted above, p. 21). Here under the aegis of the Platonic philosophy the emotion of friendship expands to its loftiest significance, fusing itself with the poet's ethical aspirations and with his impassioned dream of fame. The passage prepares us for the outburst four years later in the *Epitaphium Damonis* and the two utterances together represent the culmination of the glowing idealism of Milton's early manhood.

But precisely what does he mean when in 1642, after

the return from Italy, he proposes to entertain his readers with the abstracted sublimities of love and virtue. It is a curious fact that Heavenly Love appears as a character in each of the first three dramatic plans for *Paradise Lost,* composed about this time.[2] In the poem itself as Milton finally constructed it some twenty years later the Platonic raptures have taken on something of a Puritan sobriety. The praise of chastity has become the praise of wedded love. The heavenly marriage finds its counterpart on earth and the mystic raptures of the Garden of Adonis are transferred to the more human joys of the Garden of Eden. Yet even in *Paradise Lost* we have the strange account of the loves of angels (*P. L.* VIII, 611 ff.) and the whole poem may stand as Milton's fulfillment of his promise to write of "that love which is truly so," whose "first and chiefest office ends in the soul, producing those two happy twins of her divine generation, knowledge and virtue."

In writing the passage from the *Apology* Milton's vision is wholly retrospective and it embraces only one element in his experience, but that element is to be recognized as primary in its claims on his attention during the period of his youth and in its domination of his more intense and personal poetic expression. Meanwhile, however, his cultural interests were broadening and his purposes in art and life were defining themselves more sharply. The political thought of the ancient orators and historians, and

[2] The motive of love and chastity is to be found also in the other dramatic plans, notably in "Sodom Burning," where in an inserted passage Milton outlines a scene in which the angels, pitying the beauty of the Sodomites, "dispute of love and how it differs from lust seeking to win them." At the final destruction of the city the "Angel appears all girt with flame which he saith are the flames of true love."

the public problems of his own day, though they exercise as yet but little influence in his creative works, are gaining increasing hold on his attention. His conception of virtue is broadening to include justice and morality in the body politic, and the idea of his own service to his countrymen as one of spiritual and intellectual leadership is acquiring a patriotic and indeed a religious fervor. The explicit record of these interests takes the form of a description of the function of the poet in a personal digression in *The Reason of Church Government,* written some months earlier than the statement in the *Apology* but better representing the mature aims which are finally to dominate Milton's poetic art. The passage, omitting the beginning, which has already been given, is as follows:

Time serves not now, and perhaps I might seem too profuse to give any certain account of what the mind at home, in the spacious circuits of her musing, hath liberty to propose to herself, though of highest hope and hardest attempting; whether that epic form whereof the two poems of Homer, and those other two of Virgil and Tasso, are a diffuse, and the book of Job a brief model: or whether the rules of Aristotle herein are strictly to be kept, or nature to be followed, which in them that know art, and use judgment, is no transgression, but an enriching of art: and lastly, what king or knight, before the conquest, might be chosen in whom to lay the pattern of a Christian hero. And as Tasso gave to a prince of Italy his choice whether he would command him to write of Godfrey's expedition against the Infidels, or Belisarius against the Goths, or Charlemain against the Lombards; if to the instinct of nature and the emboldening of art aught may be trusted, and that there be nothing adverse in our climate, or the fate of this age, it haply would be no rashness, from an equal diligence and inclination, to present the like offer in our own ancient stories; or whether those dramatic constitutions, wherein Sophocles and Euripides reign, shall be found more doctrinal and exemplary to a nation. The Scripture also affords us a divine pastoral drama in the Song of Solomon, consisting of two persons, and a double chorus, as Origen rightly judges. And the Apocalypse of St. John is the majestic image of a high and stately tragedy, shutting up and inter-mingling her solemn scenes and acts with a sevenfold chorus of hallelujahs and harping symphonies: and this my opinion the grave authority of Pareus, commenting on that book, is sufficient to confirm. Or if occasion shall lead, to imitate those magnific odes and hymns, wherein Pindarus and Callimachus are in most things worthy, some others in their frame judicious, in their matter most an end faulty. But those frequent songs throughout the law and prophets beyond all these, not in their divine argument alone, but in the very critical art of composition, may be easily made appear over all the kinds of lyric poesy to be incomparable. These abilities, wheresoever they be found, are the inspired gift of God, rarely bestowed, but yet to some (though most abuse) in every nation; and are of power, beside the office of a pulpit, to imbreed and cherish in a great people the seeds of virtue and public civility, to allay the perturbations of the mind, and set the affections in right tune; to celebrate in glorious and lofty hymns the throne and equipage of God's almightiness, and what He works, and what He suffers to be wrought with high providence in His church; to sing victorious agonies of martyrs and saints, the deeds and triumphs of just and pious nations, doing valiantly through faith against the enemies of Christ; to deplore the general relapses of kingdoms and states from justice and God's true worship. Lastly, whatsoever in religion is holy and sublime, in virtue amiable or grave, what-soever hath passion or admiration in all the changes of that which is called fortune from without, or the wily subtleties and refluxes of man's thoughts from within; all these things with a solid and treatable smoothness to paint out and describe. Teaching over the whole book of sanctity and virtue, through all the instances of example, with such delight to those especially of soft and delicious temper, who will not so much as look upon truth herself, unless they see her elegantly dressed; that whereas the paths of honesty and good life appear now rugged and difficult, though they be indeed easy and pleasant, they will then appear to all men both easy and pleasant, though they were rugged and difficult indeed. And what a benefit this would be to our youth and gentry, may be soon guessed by what we know of the corruption and bane which they suck in daily from the writings and interludes of libidinous and ignorant poetasters, who having scarce ever heard of that which is the main consistence of a true poem, the choice of such persons as they ought to introduce, and what is moral and decent to each one; do for the most part lay up vicious principles in sweet pills to be swallowed down, and make the taste of virtuous documents harsh and sour. But because the spirit of man cannot demean itself lively in this body, without some recreating intermission of labor and serious things, it were happy for the commonwealth, if our magistrates, as in those famous governments of old, would take into their care, not only the deciding of our contentious law-cases and brawls, but the managing of our public sports and festival pastimes; that they might be, not such as were authorized a while since, the provocations of drunkenness and lust, but such as may inure and harden our bodies by martial exercises to all warlike skill and performance; and may civilize, adorn, and make discreet our minds by the learned and affable meeting of frequent academies, and the procurement of wise and artful recitations, sweetened with eloquent and graceful enticements to the love and practice of justice, temperance, and fortitude, instructing and bettering the nation at all opportunities, that the call of wisdom and virtue may be heard everywhere, as Solomon saith: "She crieth without, she uttereth her voice in the streets, in the top of high places, in the chief concourse, and in the openings of the gates." Whether this may not be, not only in pulpits, but after another persuasive method, at set and solemn paneguries, in theatres, porches, or what other place or way may win most upon the people to receive at once both recreation and instruction, let them in authority consult. The thing which I had to say and those intentions which have lived within me ever since I could conceive myself anything worth to my country, I return to crave excuse that urgent reason hath plucked from me, by an abortive and foredated discovery. And the accomplishment of them lies not but in a power above man's to promise; but that none hath by more studious ways endeavored, and with more unwearied spirit that none shall, that I dare almost aver of myself, as far as life and free leisure will extend; and that the land had once enfranchised herself from this impertinent yoke of prelaty, under whose inquisitorious and tyrannical duncery, no free and splendid wit can flourish. Neither do I think it shame to covenant with any knowing reader, that for some few years yet I may go on trust with him toward the payment of what I am now indebted, as being a work not to be raised from the heat of youth, or the vapors of wine; like that which flows at waste from the pen of some vulgar amorist, or the trencher fury of a rhyming parasite; nor to be obtained by the invocation of dame memory and her siren daughters, but by devout prayer to that eternal Spirit, who can enrich with all utterance and knowledge, and sends out his seraphim, with the hallowed fire of his altar, to touch and purify the lips of whom he pleases: to this must be added industrious and select reading, steady observation, insight into all seemly and generous arts and affairs; till which in some measure be compassed, at mine own peril and cost, I refuse not to sustain this expectation from as many as are not loth to hazard so much credulity upon the best pledges that I can give them.[3]

The function which Milton here proposes to himself is essentially a public one, analogous on the one hand to that of the prophets of Israel and on the other to that of the orators and statesmen of Greece and Rome. In the imagination of such a task his ambitions take the form of a loftier enthusiasm than the desire to rival an Ovid or even a Spenser, and though he is still questioning "what king or knight before the conquest might be chosen in whom to lay the pattern of a Christian hero," it is easy to see that such a theme will fail to satisfy his more comprehensive purposes. His passion for individual perfection henceforth clothes itself in zeal for public righteousness, and though he still cherishes for himself and for those who can receive it the esoteric doctrine of chastity and true love, his vision is more often directed toward outward objects and events. Both the personal and the public emotions and ideals are embodied in his later writings. Indeed, the two have become largely one.

But though Milton's purposes are already marked and established and the fundamental processes of his development from youth to maturity seem to be consummated, it required his later experience of life to complete the formation of his poetic mind. His participation in the struggles of the Commonwealth provided him with new materials of art. The disappointment of his hopes and the bitterness of personal affliction deepened his religious emotions

[3] For a discussion of this passage and for a complete collection of references in Milton's work illustrative of his conception of the poet's function see Langdon, *Milton's Theory of Poetry*.

and led him to seek again in the world of imagination the
satisfactions which were denied to him in life. His blindness, especially, had an important effect on his inner life
and was interpreted by him as an added evidence of the
all but sacred character of his inspiration. In this connection I now quote a further prose passage, from the
Second Defense of the English People (1654), which,
set beside the great personal passages in *Paradise Lost,* may
stand as the final chapter in Milton's spiritual autobiography. It is in answer to the charge that his affliction was a
judgment on him for his sins.

I wish that I could with equal facility refute what this barbarous opponent has said of my blindness; but I cannot do
it; and I must submit to the affliction. It is not so wretched
to be blind, as it is not to be capable of enduring blindness.
But why should I not endure a misfortune which it behooves
every one to be prepared to endure if it should happen; which
may, in the common course of things, happen to any man;
and which has been known to happen to the most distinguished
and virtuous persons in history. Shall I mention those wise and
ancient bards, whose misfortunes the gods are said to have
compensated by superior endowments, and whom men so much
revered, that they chose rather to impute their want of sight
to the injustice of heaven than to their own want of innocence
or virtue? What is reported of the Augur Tiresias is well
known, of whom Apollonius sung thus in his Argonauts:

> To men he dar'd the will divine disclose,
> Nor fear'd what Jove might in his wrath impose.
> The gods assigned him age, without decay,
> But snatched the blessing of his sight away.

But God himself is truth, in propagating which, as men
display a greater integrity and zeal, they approach nearer
to the similitude of God, and possess a greater portion of his

love. We cannot suppose the Deity envious of truth, or unwilling that it should be freely communicated to mankind.
The loss of sight, therefore, which this inspired sage, who
was so eager in promoting knowledge among men, sustained,
cannot be considered as a judicial punishment. Or shall I
mention those worthies who were as distinguished for wisdom in the cabinet, as for valour in the field? And first,
Timoleon of Corinth, who delivered his city and all Sicily
from the yoke of slavery; than whom there never lived in
any age, a more virtuous man, or a more incorrupt statesman: next Appius Claudius, whose discreet counsels in the
senate, though they could not restore sight to his own eyes,
saved Italy from the formidable inroads of Pyrrhus: then
Caecilius Metellus the high priest, who lost his sight, while
he saved, not only the city, but the palladium, the protection
of the city, and the most sacred relics, from the destruction
of the flames. On other occasions Providence has indeed given
conspicuous proofs of its regard for such singular exertions
of patriotism and virtue; what, therefore, happened to so
great and so good a man, I can hardly place in the catalogue
of misfortunes. Why should I mention others of later times,
as Dandolo of Venice, the incomparable Doge; or Boemar
Zisca, the bravest of generals, and the champion of the cross;
or Jerome Zanchius, and some other theologians of the highest
reputation? For it is evident that the patriarch Isaac, than
whom no man ever enjoyed more of the divine regard, lived
blind for many years; and perhaps also his son Jacob, who
was equally an object of the divine benevolence. And in short,
did not our Saviour himself clearly declare that poor man
whom he restored to sight had not been born blind, either on
account of his own sins or those of his progenitors? And with
respect to myself, though I have accurately examined my conduct, and scrutinized my soul, I call thee, O God, the searcher
of hearts, to witness, that I am not conscious, either in the
more early or in the later periods of my life, of having com-

glory, ought to be an object of superior admiration and esteem; I resolved, therefore, to make the short interval of sight,
which was left me to enjoy, as beneficial as possible to the
public interest. Thus it is clear by what motives I was governed in the measures which I took, and the losses which I
sustained. Let then the calumniators of the divine goodness
cease to revile, or to make me the object of their superstitious
imaginations. Let them consider, that my situation, such as it
is, is neither an object of my shame or my regret, that my
resolutions are too firm to be shaken, that I am not depressed
by any sense of the divine displeasure; that, on the other hand,
in the most momentous periods, I have had full experience of
the divine favour and protection; and that, in the solace and
the strength which have been infused into me from above, I
have been enabled to do the will of God; that I may oftener
think on what he has bestowed, than on what he has withheld; that, in short, I am unwilling to exchange my consciousness of rectitude with that of any other person; and that I
feel the recollection a treasured store of tranquillity and delight. But, if the choice were necessary, I would, sir, prefer
my blindness to yours; yours is a cloud spread over the mind,
which darkens both the light of reason and of conscience;
mine keeps from my view only the coloured surfaces of things,
while it leaves me at liberty to contemplate the beauty and
stability of virtue and of truth. How many things are there
besides which I would not willingly see; how many which I
must see against my will; and how few which I feel any anx-
iety to see! There is, as the apostle has remarked, a way of
strength through weakness. Let me then be the most feeble
creature alive, as long as that feebleness serves to invigorate
the energies of my rational and immortal spirit; as long as in
that obscurity, in which I am enveloped, the light of the divine
presence more clearly shines. Then, in proportion as I am
weak, I shall be invincibly strong; and in proportion as I am
blind, I shall more clearly see. O! that I may thus be perfected

found place in *Paradise Regained.* Their absence suggests
the completeness with which Milton had transcended his
doubts, his fears, his hopes. Both poems are in one sense
all Milton. The poet is well aware of the spiritual forces
which are ranged against him, and he is still the conscious
champion of righteousness and truth. But his self-portraiture is now wholly merged in his creative art. Christ
speaks for him in *Paradise Regained,* serenely rejecting the
specious enticements of physical comfort, riches, fame, and
worldly wisdom. The Savior's meditation on his childhood
with its ambitious dreams and his interpretation of the true
nature of his spiritual office are clearly a reflection of Milton's own deepest thoughts of self. *Samson* is, as I have
already said, autobiographical in all its implications. It expresses Milton's great desire for a vindication of his life
endeavor as a chosen one of God and it gives relieving
utterance to the despondency against which religion armed
him. The drama, however, would not be recognized as a
subjective expression were we not aware from other
sources of the personal experience which animates it. It
proves by its triumphant art how completely the poet had
fulfilled his purposes. Here in his best and final word there
is no confession, no pleading with the reader for acceptance; there is not even recourse to the half-pagan presences
which have hitherto peopled his poetic reverie. The emotion which has attached itself to these symbols is as ardent
as ever; but Milton is at last able to dispense with them in
favor of the uncompromising monotheism of the Old Testament.

APPENDIX C

THE MILTON PORTRAITS

MILTON'S daughter, Deborah Clarke, informed George Vertue in 1721 that the poet's widow had two portraits of her husband, one when a schoolboy, the other at the age of about twenty. The first of these, a well-executed oil painting by Cornelius Janssen, was purchased by the republican and Milton-lover, Thomas Hollis, from Mrs. Milton's estate and is now in the John Pierpont Morgan library in New York. This portrait has been beautifully reproduced in color as the frontispiece of the Columbia Milton. It is a somewhat prim but yet engaging half length representation of the boy Milton, clad in aristocratic Elizabethan doublet, with a countenance expressive of the sweet sobriety of childhood. The face is fair, the hair an unmistakable auburn. The picture is dated 1618 and inscribed "John Milton. Aetat. 10."

The second picture, referred to by Aubrey (page 16 above) as a better likeness than the frontispieces of his books and said by Mrs. Milton to have been given her by her husband "to show what he was in his youth," was destroyed in the eighteenth century by its owner, Speaker Onslow, because he was annoyed by the requests of visitors to see it. A copy had, however, been made and is now at Nuneham. (See the reproduction opposite the title page of this volume.) The original was also used by Vertue for an engraving, published in 1731 and frequently reproduced.

A third authentic contemporary likeness of Milton is represented by the engraving prefixed to the first edition of Milton's *History of Britain*. A Latin inscription declares the engraving to have been done from life by William Faithorne. It gives the deeply lined face of the mature Milton familiar from numerous engravings and busts based on it. The very similar Bayfordbury drawing and the Hobart painting are connected with this engraving, all three being perhaps copies from one original.

Save for the distorted engraving by Marshall prefixed to the 1645 edition of the Poems, which Milton himself ridiculed in the Greek lines below it, these three represent all the unquestionable contemporary likenesses. Catalogues have been published of two considerable collections of Milton prints, portraits, etc., one by George C. Williamson, the other, somewhat more extensive, by Beverley Chew.

APPENDIX D

MILTON'S PRIVATE LIBRARY

MANY references in Milton's works show him to have been a persistent and enthusiastic book collector, and the building of his private library must be regarded as no insignificant aspect of his biography. He speaks (see page 22) of expeditions from Horton to London to buy books. He promises in 1634 to meet his friend Gill on Monday "among the book sellers." He asks Diodati in 1637 to send him a copy of Justinian's *History of Venice*. Phillips says that he shipped a parcel of curious and rare books home from Italy, particularly "a chest or two of choice music books." And late in the fifties, long after he could read books with his own eyes, we find him eagerly negotiating purchases with continental friends.[1] He hesitated to buy the best Bleau Atlas at thirty florins, protesting that "with the present rage for typographical luxury, the furniture of a library costs hardly less than that of a villa." But he did undertake to purchase the stately and expensive volumes of the *Corpus Byzantinae Historiae* as they were issued from the Royal Press at Paris.[2]

Just how extensive Milton's private collection became before it was dissipated is impossible to determine. He had access to the libraries at Cambridge and Oxford, but

[1] *Familiar Letters,* passim.
[2] *Epist. XXI* to Bigot, 1658.

it seems probable that the greater part of his wide reading was done at home, and it is safe to say that he owned copies of the authors from whom he cites more or less continuously: the Classics, English literature, the standard historians as listed in the *Commonplace Book,* the Church Fathers, the Protestant divines, the great Italians. He owned the manuscript of Sir Walter Raleigh's *Cabinet Council,* as we learn from his preface to his edition of that work, and it has recently been shown that he possessed a copy of the *Heptaplomeres* of Jean Bodin, a notoriously heretical work clandestinely circulated in manuscript and very difficult to obtain. If the presence of these rarities is at all characteristic Milton's library must have been interesting indeed.

The following books, once owned by Milton, bear his unquestionably genuine autograph.[3]

1. Holy Bible, authorized version, 1612, containing entries of the births and deaths of Milton's family. Now in the British Museum.
2. Euripidis Tragoediae, Gr. et Lat. Beckii, with autograph and notes. Now in the Bodleian.
3. Lycophronis Alexandra, with autograph and notes. In the library of Mr. and Mrs. Adrian Van Sinderen of Brooklyn.
4. Pindari Olympia, etc., Salmurii, 1620, with notes. Now in the library of Harvard University.

[3] See Sotheby, pp. 124 ff., and especially *The Columbia Milton,* Vol. XVIII, pp. 557 ff., where all the books which have been attributed to Milton's library are more accurately discussed, and the greater part of their marginalia reproduced. Both lists err on the side of inclusiveness. The present writer has omitted all the items of whose authenticity he has not personally convinced himself. It is not his intention to deny the claims of others.

5. Arati Phaenomena, etc., 1559, with autograph and notes. Now in the British Museum.

6. Heraclidis Pontici Allegoriae in Homeri Fabulas de Diis, Gr. et Lat., Gesnero interprete, 1544, with autograph.

7. Rime e Prose di Giovanni della Casa, 1563, with autograph and notes. Now in the New York Public Library.

8. Gildas, De Excidio et Conquestu Britanniae Epistola, with autograph notes. Now in the library of Harvard University.

The purchase dates of most of these volumes, as written on the fly leaf in Milton's hand, range from 1629 to 1637. Some of them, particularly the Pindar and the Euripides, are heavily annotated by Milton in the most learned fashion and at several periods in his life. A sonnet from another edition has been copied by one of the known amanuenses on a blank half page of the della Casa volume. There is an emendation in the text of Lycophron which Milton offers not as a restoration but as an improvement on the original. The line reads "Τρίτωνος ἠμάλαψε κάρχαρος κύων." Milton's comment is "utinam esset καρχαρόδους hoc enim grandior." These are the faint traces of John Milton's keen and passionate occupation with his authors in his days at Horton and in the quiet intervals of his later life.

There is evidence to show that Milton's library was partly dissipated before his death. The student may choose between the allegation of Elizabeth Fisher (see p. 67) that his children "made away with some of his books" and the statement of Toland, that Milton himself contracted his library "both because the heirs he left could not make a right use of it, and that he thought he might sell it more to their advantage than they would be able to do themselves." In any case, however, we have the statement of

the anonymous biographer, that Milton left "a fair collection." The chances are that this was promptly scattered
at his decease. Mrs. Milton retained, at least, the Bible and
"two books of paradise," which, together with "some old
pictures," "Mr. Milton's pictures and coat of arms," "a
tobacco box," etc. are listed in the inventory of her posses-
sions. An unsigned letter in the library of the Marquis of
Bath states that Mr. Milton's books "have been looked
over by one Mr. Skinner, a scholar and a bold young man,
who has culled out what he thought fit." This is Daniel
Skinner, Milton's last amanuensis, who had possession of
Milton's theological treatise and of his copies of the state
letters in manuscript. Edward Phillips, who inherited the
notes for the Latin Dictionary, may also have had his
share of books.

APPENDIX E

MILTON AND HIS PRINTERS

THE text of Milton involves no such difficulties as that of Shakespeare, but it offers problems enough for the amusement and edification of students and the puzzlement of editors. The poet was nothing if not fastidious, and there is plenty of evidence of a struggle on his part to get his work before the public as he wanted it to be, down to the most minute detail—a struggle which was continuously defeated by human perversity and carelessness, and by the accident of Milton's being blind. The difficulty of the modern editor of Milton is two-fold. He is not sure whether, in a given instance of variation between one edition and another published in the poet's lifetime, he has to do with a Miltonic revision or a printer's error. And he does not know how far Milton himself determined and set store by the minutiae of spelling and punctuation. Perhaps, too, he is uncertain whether these minutiae are worth intruding upon the attention of the modern reader. For these reasons he does not know which edition to follow or how far to normalize the text. Solutions range all the way from facsimile reproductions of this or that edition to complete eclectic modernizations. The question of decision regarding readings is further complicated by the existence of some of Milton's manuscripts. A study of the situation raises some interesting questions of interpretation and takes us behind the scenes in Milton's literary workshop. Only a few outstanding points can be mentioned here. The interested student may be referred to the introductions to various modern editions, particularly Grierson's, Beeching's, Wright's, and that recently published by the Columbia University Press. (See Bibliography.)

Milton's first printed work was the poem *On Shakespeare,* which appeared in the second folio of Shakespeare's plays and (with the initials I. M.) in a 1640 edition of Shakespeare's *Poems* before it was reprinted in the 1645 and 1673 editions of Milton's *Poems.* The variations in these texts raise the question of whether Milton corrected his proofs and of how far he revised his already printed work. The 1645 and 1673 texts are, except for a few spellings, identical. The 1640 and 1645 texts have more considerable but still minor variations. The title is altered from "An Epitaph on the admirable Dramaticke Poet William Shakespeare" to "On Shakespear 1630." This, of course, was determined by Milton himself. So too, probably, was "needs" for "neede" in line 1 and "needs't" for "needs" in line 6, this last change being a return to the reading of the second folio. Between the second folio and the 1645 there are several important variations. "Such dull witness of thy name" becomes "such weak witness of thy name," certainly a Miltonic revision to secure alliteration. But also,

> Each *part*
> Hath from the leaves of thy unvalu'd Book
> Those Delphick lines with deep impression took.

appears in 1640, as it does in 1645 and 1673, as "each

heart," etc., and this surely is simply a correction. "Part" must be a misreading by the compositor due to a resemblance between "h" and "p" in script. We may infer that Milton did *not* see the proof of the poem as it was printed in the second folio, and that he here experienced his first motion of disgust with printers and their ways.[1]

He must have been even more deeply disillusioned when he saw *Lycidas* in the memorial volume to Edward King, for here a whole line is omitted and there are many obvious misprints. In this case we have to guide us as to Milton's intentions the original manuscript, the above mentioned text in the memorial volume (1638), copies of the latter with marginal corrections in Milton's hand, the text in the collected poems of 1645 and 1673. The most interesting specific questions for the modern editor are whether to print "he knew himself to sing" or "he well knew himself to sing" and whether to paragraph at line 22 or at line 24. Both research and good sense are requisite to a wise decision. Milton wrote "he well knew" twice in the MS. and let it stand. The first printed text reads "he knew"; the copy with Miltonic corrections inserts a "well" marginally; the 1645 and 1673 editions, which supposedly represent Milton's carefully made official version of his work, print, again, "he knew." Plenty of opportunity here

---

[1] The problems raised by the varying texts of this poem are neatly dealt with by Garrod, *Milton's Lines on Shakespeare,* where, however, "part" is accepted as representing Milton's original intention. One of the copies of the second folio has "star-ypointed" for "star-ypointing," a more correct form, historically speaking. But Milton probably wrote "star-ypointing." See Robert W. Smith, *The Variant Issues of Shakespeare's Second Folio and Milton's First Published Poem.* Bethlehem, Pa.: Lehigh University, 1928.

for theory! The present writer decides, against the arguments of Diekhoff and the authority of Percy Simpson, for
"he well knew," assuming that Milton overlooked the
omission in proof-reading the 1645 edition. (This was
set from the 1638, but not, presumably, from the extant
corrected copy.) Regarding the paragraph there is no real
question, if the editor takes the trouble to investigate the
facts or to think of the meaning. Milton's MS. paragraphed
at line 24. The 1638 edition made no division. The 1645 and
the 1673 paragraph at line 24. This, however, apparently violates logic, since the lines:

> For we were nursed upon the self-same hill
> Fed the same flocks, by fountain, shade, and rill,

introduce the pastoral description of the common life of
Milton and King at Cambridge. Some modern editors
have therefore succumbed to the temptation to paragraph
at line 22. They should have considered the more subtle
relationships of the thought, adjusting their minds to what
was plainly Milton's intention.

The other minor poems offer equally interesting problems. We can here consider only the certain evidence that
in the 1673 text a blundering hand attempted to improve
Milton's meaning. The poet had furnished the publisher
with a printed copy of the 1645 text, in the margins of
which he must have written a few corrections and revisions
(e. g., "concent," the reading of the MS., for "content" in
the poem "At a Solemn Music") and to which he had
added many MS. pages of new material. What must he
have thought and said if the following unauthorized alterations ever came to his attention:

She was pincht and pull'd she sed,
And he by Friars Lanthorn led
Tells how the drudging goblin swet.
L'Allegro, Ed. 1645.

And by the Friar's Lanthorn led.
Ed. 1673.

To meditate my rural minstrelsie
Comus, Ed. 1645.

To meditate upon my rural minstrelsie
Ed. 1673.

And hearken, if I may, her business here
Comus, Ed. 1645.

And hearken if I may her business heare
(Errata, Ed. 1673.)

The corrector simply did not understand Miltonic idiom, Latin or English. "She" and "he" are "illa" and "ille," meaning "one in the company, a woman," "another in the company, a man." "She was pinched and pulled, she said . . . and tells" is grammatically impossible. In the next instance the corrector would have been saved had he remembered "Musam meditare avena" in Virgil. To "meditate the muse" is one thing, to meditate upon it quite another, even if no question of rhythm were involved. The third reading is more open to doubt, but again the corrector apparently could not accept the archaic turn in the transitive use of "hearken." Milton had written the passage in the MS. precisely as it was printed in 1645. The fact that this change is made in the Errata is puzzling enough. Perhaps Milton commissioned Edward Phillips or Daniel Skinner or some less educated amanuensis to see the edition through the press. The modern editor who wishes to give us Milton's true copy should base his text on the 1645 edition, except for the added material and for occasional readings from the 1673 edition which obviously represent revision.

In the case of *Paradise Lost* the text problem is a very simple one, unless one wishes to confront the question of restoring Milton's own spelling and punctuation, in which case it becomes insoluble. The edition of 1667 was very carefully printed. Corrections were made by Milton himself in an errata sheet and an argument was added in later issues of this edition. The edition of 1674 was set from a printed copy of the 1667, and contains few variations of importance except those made by Milton himself in the process of revision. He divided Books VIII and X into two each, adding a few transitional lines; he distributed the arguments, prefixing them to the various books instead of massing them at the end, and he made some other textual alterations.

The best check we have on Milton's original intentions regarding spelling, punctuation, etc. and on the extent to which they were followed by the printers is the preserved manuscript of Book I, from which the 1667 text was set.[2] This is in the hand of an amanuensis. That the poet did care for spelling in certain particulars is proved, first by the corrections in the MS., as for example "there" to "thir," "voyce" to "voice," "entralls" to "entrails," "Heavn" to "Heav'n," "the" to "th'," "hee" to "he," secondly by the following items in the errata of the 1667 edition: Book I, l. 760, "for hundreds read hunderds"; II, 414, for "we" read "wee"; VI, 184, for "blessed" read "blest." He evi-

[2] See above, p. 193.

dently was attempting to secure a correct and musical reading of his verse. It was his evident intention to spell such
words as "blessed" with the "ed" when it was to be read
as a dissyllable, with "t" when it was to be read as a mono-
syllable, to print "th'" for "the" when the syllable count
required elision, to spell "mee," "wee," "hee" when the
pronoun bore the accent. The latter objective he never succeeded in having consistently carried out even in the manuscript. There is one such alteration in the 1674 edition
which appears to show that he had the proof read aloud to
him:

> if ought propos'd
> And judg'd of public moment, could deterre
> Mee [1667, me] from attempting.

It is easy to imagine a careless reader missing the slight
(but, for both rhythm and meaning, important) emphasis
on the pronoun. Milton's ear would have detected the
blunder and attempted to save posterity from repeating
it by ordering the revised spelling. But elsewhere in this
text many emphatic "hee's," "wee's," etc., are altered to
"he," "we," etc. The problem of working out Milton's
intentions from the available data has been carefully studied
by Miss Darbishire.[3] Her conclusion is that the printed
page of the first edition is nearer than the manuscript to
what Milton would have written if he could. Percy Simpson[4] concurs in this opinion. On Miss Darbishire's own
evidence, however, it is apparent that Milton did not correct the proofs nearly as carefully as he corrected his fair
copy, and that the Miltonic improvements in the 1667 edi-

---

[3] *The MS. of "Paradise Lost."*

[4] *Proof-Reading in the Sixteenth, Seventeenth and Eighteenth
Centuries.* London, 1935. p. 35.

tion are more than counterbalanced by the instances in which the printer deviated from the text in a direction contrary to what may be inferred to have been Milton's wishes. According to the calculation of Mr. Donald Stillman [5] there are 695 odd variations between the manuscript of Book I and the 1667 text. Of these the manuscript reading is clearly to be preferred in 104 cases, the first edition in only 45. In the rest of the variations Milton was indifferent or helpless both as to his scribe's practices and as to those of the printer. The 1674 edition, though correct in other respects, is even farther from the standard of spelling, punctuation, and capitalization which the poet had endeavored to set up.

Modern editors either follow the second edition minutely, or modernize the text throughout, or preserve spellings which they think are characteristic and significant. If they adopt the last mentioned practice they are largely at the mercy of their own whim. A study of the parts of the Trinity MS. which are in Milton's own hand would give his characteristic spellings for an earlier period of his career, but even these are not consistent. It remains for some enterprising editor to make a text based on the manuscript and the 1667 edition but incorporating the clearly Miltonic revisions in the 1674 and carrying out as consistently as possible all the practices which have been determined as representing Milton's fixed intentions.

There is one passage in which both the original editions and all the modern ones following them alter a punctuation of the manuscript to the detriment of the sense. They put a semicolon after "fire" and a comma after "hue" in Book I, lines 229–30, where the MS. has the reverse. Milton

[5] In an unpublished paper. See MLN, May, 1939, p. 353.

intended the simile to apply to the whole phenomenon of "solid fire" and not simply to the color. These are minute points, but Milton, who valued finesse and reverenced his own exact meaning beyond all other poets, would have been concerned about them.

Of the individuals with whom Milton had to deal in the publication of his poems the most interesting was Humphrey Moseley, publisher of the edition of 1645. Moseley was a man of real taste, who obviously took pride in the character of the books issued under his imprint and who rightly regarded himself as a promoter of excellence in English poetry. "It is the love I have to our language," he writes in a signed preface to the Milton volume, "that hath made me diligent to collect and set forth such pieces, both in prose and verse, as may renew the wonted honour and esteem of our English tongue." Masson notes his avoidance of controversial literature and lists among the poets whose copy he acquired either by original publication or by subsequent purchase such distinguished names as Donne, Suckling, Crashaw, Carew, Waller, Denham, Davenant, Cowley, and Henry Vaughan. Moseley died in 1661, and the second edition of the *Poems* was printed for Thomas Dring. The first, second, and third editions of *Paradise Lost* were issued by Samuel Simmons, the first of *Paradise Regained* and *Samson Agonistes* by John Starkey. Neither of these men occupies a position comparable to that of Moseley. Jacob Tonson, however, who ultimately acquired the right to publish *Paradise Lost* and made a fortune from it, was a worthy eighteenth century successor of Milton's first commercial publisher.

The prose works offer fewer textual problems than the poetry, but their printing history is interesting. The first three tracts, *Of Reformation, Of Prelatical Episcopacy,* and *Animadversions* were published anonymously by Thomas Underhill. The unnamed printers, as Parker has shown,[6] were Richard Oulton and Gregory Dexter. *The Reason of Church Government* and *An Apology,* which bore Milton's name, were entrusted to another bookseller, John Rothwell, and another printer, E[dward] G[riffin]. All five tracts were unlicensed and unregistered, a fact easily explained by the lax administration of the law from the beginning of the Long Parliament until the passing of the Ordinance for Printing, June 14, 1643. When Milton was ready to issue the *Doctrine and Discipline* there was greater difficulty. The book obviously could not be licensed, and Milton was presumably obliged to seek bolder publishers and printers. The imprint bears the initials of Thomas Paine and Matthew Simmons. The latter printed also *The Judgment of Martin Bucer,* a duly licensed publication, in 1644 and *Eikonoklastes* in 1649. He may have printed *Tetrachordon* and *Colasterion.* By 1650 Milton had deserted him, perhaps because of his carelessness in printing *Eikonoklastes.*[7] Samuel Simmons, to whom seventeen years later he gave the copy of *Paradise Lost,* was his successor, perhaps his son.[8]

Of Milton's later prose publications *The History of Britain,* which appeared in 1670, is notable as containing the Faithorne engraving. The text of this edition has been shown to exist in several "states," representing successive strata of correction made while the work was going through the press.[9] Some copies, usually without the por-

---

[6] *Contributions Toward a Milton Bibliography.*

[7] See Parker, *Milton, Rothwell and Simmons.*

[8] Masson, Vol. VI, p. 509.

[9] See Fletcher, *Milton's History of Britain.*

APPENDIX F

MILTON IN ITALY

NO episode in Milton's life is more appealing to the biographer than the tour which he made to the Continent
in 1638 and 1639. Its obvious importance prompted Masson
to a very full treatment of the facts and background, and
some additions have been made to our knowledge since his
time. There remains, however, much to do before the experience can be appraised in its total effect on the poet's
personality and achievement. Even Allodoli's monograph [1]
accomplishes less than we might have expected of it in view
of the author's opportunities for research in Italian libraries.
The present essay undertakes only to present some considerations which might well be the object of further study. The
coöperative effort of English and Italian scholarship is required for a really fruitful investigation of this great moment
in the cultural relationship between the two nations.

There is little direct evidence why Milton decided at just
the time he did to "visit foreign parts and particularly Italy."
The tradition of the Continental tour as the capstone of
English education was and continued to be strong. But the
new travel was different from the old. What Italy now had
to offer, while not so rich actually, was at least more varied
and more accessible to Englishmen than in the earlier Rennaissance. Some measure of assimilation and knowledge is

[1] *Giovanni Milton e l'Italia.*

necessary before any but the pioneers of culture can make fruitful use of a foreign civilization, and such conditions were not fulfilled in England before the 1600's. The prestige of Italy, long in the making, was still strong enough to prevent the idea of its degeneration and decay from deterring Englishmen from going there for serious study. Addison in the eighteenth century could point triumphantly to the destitution of the Campagna as demonstrating what an aversion mankind has to arbitrary government, and thereby help deflect travellers toward France. Milton's earlier remark about the decline of wit with liberty was more than counterbalanced by an interest in and enthusiasm for things Italian. From the point of view of numbers, Italian travel was at its height in his time. Sandys and others speak frequently of the number of foreigners with whom the streets of Italian cities were "pestered." In many respects Italy was for Englishmen in the seventeenth century what France was to become in the eighteenth, a school of sophistication in all the arts.[2]

The list of outstanding Englishmen who profited by Italy is in itself an indication of what was sought. Inigo Jones studied architecture and drama there for several years and purchased works of art for the Earls of Pembroke and Arundel. Thomas Carew, as secretary to Sir Dudley Carleton in 1613–15, became versed in Italian literature. So also did Suckling and Crashaw at a later time. Sir Kenelm Digby spent two years in Florence in 1622–3. Giovanni Coperario, the teacher of Henry Lawes, received his musical education in Italy earlier. Robert Boyle's travels in 1638 closely paralleled Milton's. Another earnest traveller was Evelyn,

[2] See Howard, Clare M., *English Travellers of the Renaissance*, New York, 1913, chapter VII.

who bought "rare tables of veins and nerves" at Padua in 1646. This enumeration omits the mere vacationists, the patrons, the teachers, and the professional writers of travel literature like Moryson, Coryate, Howell, and Sandys.

To return to Milton's personal motivations, we should remember, first, that although he had given up or all but given up the church as a career, he was determined not only to be a scholar and a poet but to exercise an influence by his writings parallel to that of the pulpit. The political-religious motive for going to Italy was an important one. Milton, as a prospective statesman of Protestant reform, naturally wanted to see Catholicism at home—to witness, as Luther had done before him, the magnificence and the corruption of the Roman Church. Once on the scene, he behaved like one of God's spies. He visited a Jesuit college, made the acquaintance of a Cardinal, received favors from a future Papal nuncio,[3] allowed himself to be guided by a hermit, contracted his most lasting Italian friendship with one of the Florentine literati who had remained firmly Catholic in spite of the liberalism of the group. He discussed religion everywhere, but not in such a way as to shut the doors of information. Certainly the Church and its workings was one of the great things for an Englishman to witness abroad. He might be expected to return confirmed but no longer naïve in his loyalty to the Protestant cause.

The issues were sharpened for Milton by his acquaintance with the Diodati family and their refugee tradition. Perhaps he was looking for vestiges of Italian Protestantism in his trip to Lucca, its place of origin. In any case the visit to

[3] Lukas Holsten, himself a convert, represented the Papacy at the conversion of Queen Christina.

Giovanni Diodati at Geneva put him in contact with the freshest memories of this exciting chapter in Reformation history.[4] In this connection one should remember that his English mentor, Wotton, had undertaken to formulate, with Paolo Sarpi and Diodati himself, a Protestant movement in Venice.

To point out this aspect of Milton's interest is not to deny the more obvious cultural objectives.[5] Milton went to Italy, of course, to improve his knowledge of the Italian language and literature, in which he had already made great progress, to see the remains of classical antiquity, and to meet the personalities who, he thought, still carried on the tradition of the Renaissance. Important in this group were the Vatican librarian, Lukas Holsten, a humanist of the old school, the learned Florentines of the Svogliati Academy, and the venerable patron of Tasso, Giovanni Battista Manso.

The visit to Galileo is the most dramatic and suggestive of all his contacts. Here, as in his earlier meeting with Grotius, Milton is seeking membership, not in the conservative older humanistic group nor in the newer body of dilettanti and mere hangers-on of scholarship, but in the seventeenth century Republic of Letters itself, in its greatest and most modern aspect. He must have known the difference.

[4] See below, p. 418.

[5] Milton's description of the animating idea of liberal study in the third Prolusion suggests a formula for foreign travel: "to study all the countries of the world set out in the map and to visit them in your imagination, to scan the places trodden by the heroes of old, to traverse, too, the regions glorified in the tales of famous poets, now to cross the stormy Adriatic, now to approach unhurt the flames of Etna; next to observe the manners of men and the national governments that have been fairly ordered and thence to investigate the nature of all living things."

Milton's allusion to the visit in *Areopagitica* is our sole evidence that it actually took place. He is speaking of the discouragement which restraint of publication brings to learned men, contrasting Italy in this respect with England.

"I could recount what I have seen and heard in other countries, where this kind of inquisition tyrannizes, when I have sat among their learned men (for that honor I had) and been counted happy to be born in such a place of philosophic freedom as they supposed England was, while themselves did nothing but bemoan the servile condition into which learning amongst them was brought: that this was it which had damped the glory of Italian wits; that nothing had been there written now these many years but flattery and fustian. There it was that I found and visited the famous Galileo grown old, a prisoner to the Inquisition for thinking in astronomy otherwise than the Franciscan and Dominican licencers thought."

This recollection and the later allusions to Galileo's telescope suggest the character and accent of Milton's most important kind of activity in Italy. He went to see people more than things and to discuss with them the interests— cultural, political, religious—which were of the deepest concern to him and them. He took the opportunities which offered themselves to any Englishman qualified to hold converse with the noted scholars and thinkers of the age. But he enjoyed also and made use of special privileges.

The whole subject of Milton's personal relationships on the Continent remains to be worked out. It would be especially interesting to know just how he made his various contacts, what introductions he had, what messages he carried. It was the journeyings and correspondence of men like him that held the widely scattered intellectual group together.

We know that Milton carried letters to Lord Scudamore, the English ambassador at Paris, and that he was introduced by Scudamore to Grotius and by Lukas Holsten to Cardinal Barberini. The rest is still a matter of guesswork.

It is most tempting to speculate on how Milton got access to Galileo. A real problem exists here, though Liljegren's opinion that such a visit never actually took place has been rejected by Milton and Galileo scholars alike.[6] Interviews with the blind philosopher were no common treat for Englishmen at this time. He was restricted to his house, with the provision that he might attend church a block away, and visits by foreigners and especially by heretics were strictly interdicted. There was, however, clandestine communication with the outside world. Who were the friends who facilitated the meeting? Directly, perhaps, Carlo Dati,[7] who had been Galileo's pupil. But there is a possibility that the Parisian intellectuals who were trying to help Galileo in very practical ways, may have directed Milton to him, or even used the poet as a courier. Grotius was one of these, but the principal conspirator against the restrictions of the Inquisition was a person unmentioned by Milton biographers, but whom it is plausible to suppose he knew. I refer to Elie Diodati, a Parliamentary Advocate at Paris, who had translated some of Galileo's writings into Latin and visited him more than once in Italy.[8] In 1638, the year of Milton's visit,

[6] See Marjorie Nicolson, *Milton and the Telescope,* pp. 9–10.

[7] See G. Andreini, *La vita e l'opera di Carlo Dati,* Florence, 1913. In his letter to Milton written in 1648, Dati sends greetings from Galilei, presumably the astronomer's son.

[8] See Schotel, G.D.J., *Jean Diodati,* Gravenshage, 1844, pp. 106 ff., for an account of Elie Diodati. His relations with Galileo are indicated by J. J. Fahie in *Galileo, His Life and Works,* London and

he had translated from the Italian and secured publication of
the *Dialogus*. On August 14 of that year Galileo wrote telling him that the Holy Office had learned of certain negotiations between Diodati and the States General of Holland
for the purchase of Galileo's invention for the determination
of longitude, and he thanked Diodati for having induced
their agent Hortensio to postpone a journey to see him at
Florence. Diodati must have made use of any trustworthy
persons to carry messages, and Milton certainly would have
been trustworthy. Diodati was related to the English family
of that name, being a cousin several times removed of
Dr. Theodore, Charles' father, in London, and of Theodore's
brother, Giovanni, whom Milton was to meet in Geneva.
This refugee clan kept in close touch with one another
throughout Europe, and Milton is not likely to have passed
by so conspicuous and congenial a member of it as Elie.[9]

One other contact must be mentioned as associated with
a very interesting phase of Milton's life in Italy. The minutes
of the Svogliati for March 24, 1639, record the reading
by Giovanni Battista Doni of a scene from one of his tragedies. At this meeting of the academy Milton was also a

New York, 1903. The detail of this activity may be followed in the
National Edition of Galileo's works. The interrelations of the group
of intellectuals to which Galileo and Diodati belonged—Campanella,
Gassendi, DuPuy, etc.—are best studied in the correspondence of
Peiresc. See Philippe Tamizey de Larroque, *Lettres de Peiresc*, IV,
pp. 338 ff.

[9] Actual contact of Elie with the English family cannot be demonstrated. But both he and they visited Geneva, and Giovanni visited
England. Elie knew Lord Herbert of Cherbury and transmitted
copies of his *De Veritate Religionis Christianae* to Gassendi, Peiresc,
and Campanella. See Gassendi, *Opera*, 1727, III, pp. 337 ff.; Joseph
Bougerel, *Vie de Pierre Gassendi*, Paris, 1737; and Peiresc, *loc. cit.*

performer. He mentions Doni to Lukas Holsten in a letter written six days later as being then in Rome but soon to return to Florence as Professor of Greek.

This Doni [10] was one of the ablest and most creative persons whom Milton could have met in Italy. A Florentine patrician, born in 1594, he studied literature, philosophy, and mathematics at Rome, jurisprudence in France, Oriental languages and Hebrew at Pisa, where he became laureate in 1621. The election of Maffeo Barberini as Pope Urban VIII brought him to Rome in close friendship with Cardinal Francesco, whom he accompanied to France and Spain. At the time of Milton's visit he was secretary of the Academy Basiliana founded by Francesco for the study of Greek, but, as we have seen, he had also assumed a professorship of Greek at Florence.[11] He compiled a corpus of ancient inscriptions, projected a great work on libraries, and wrote many treatises on linguistic, literary, and historical subjects.

Most important in the present connection are his contributions to music and the drama, for here is where Milton would have learned something very much to his purpose and from a most distinguished and authoritative source. Doni was one of the theorists of the operatic development which took place in the seventeenth century. Following the tradition of a famous earlier group of Florentine scholars

[10] See A. M. Bandini, *De Vita et Scriptis J. B. Doni,* Florence, 1635. Dati prints letters of Doni in *Prose Fiorentine.*

[11] Masson is confused about Doni, apparently not understanding that he could hold the Florentine professorship while still in residence at Rome. As a matter of fact it was not until he left Rome in 1646 that he gave it up and was succeeded in 1647 by Dati, who had been his pupil.

and composers, including the father of Galileo, he promoted
a revival of what he believed to have been Greek practice,
advocating a return to ancient simplicity against the virtu-
osity of the madrigal style. The choruses of Greek tragedy
provided a model for the monody sung in recitativo, with
primary importance given to the words. But it was the
belief of the time that all of Greek drama and not only the
choruses were sung. The effort to reproduce these supposed
music-dramas of antiquity, influencing and influenced by
the native Italian developments in musical and dramatic
entertainment, resulted in the invention of modern opera.[12]
Doni himself set the *Troades* of Seneca to music for performance at the Barberini theater, and Milton, as is well
known, was present at the brilliant performance of the pastoral opera, *Chi soffre, speri,* in the same place.[13] The reference to Doni in the letter to Holsten makes no mention of his

[12] See Finney, G. L., "Chorus in *Samson Agonistes.*"

[13] For the facts about this notable performance see Belloni, Antonio, *Il Seicento,* Milan, 1930, p. 134; Smart, J. S., "Milton in
Rome," *Modern Language Review,* VIII (1913) p. 91; *Nuovo Anto-
logia,* LXIII (1927) p. 523; *Revista Musicale,* XIV (1907) p. 473.
The text was by Guilio Rospigliosi (then a member of Cardinal
Francesco's household, afterwards Pope Clement IX), the music
by Virgilio Mazzocchi and Marco Marazzuoli, the stage design by
Bernini. Of this last, Bernini's biographer, Baldinucci, remarks: "ne
vivra sempre la fama nel mondo." Milton calls the entertainment
an "ἀκρόαμα *musicum,*" which would be about the nearest classical
word he could get for a musical drama of this kind. According to an
eyewitness description, it was Antonio and not Francesco who
greeted everybody at the door. Francesco went about from bench
to bench. One young man who became noisy was thrown out by Antonio. Milton could not have heard Leonora sing on this occasion.
There were no women performers at the Barberini entertainments.
On the Barberini as patrons of melodrama see Solerti, Angelo, *Le
Origini del Melodrama,* Turin, 1903.

musical theories or of his service to the Barberini, but in view of Milton's deep interest it is hard to believe that the poet did not, either then or later, seek an occasion to talk with him and read his works. The poet's own contribution to the issue between the madrigal and the recitativo style is in the sonnet which he addressed to Henry Lawes in 1646. It finds precedent in Campion's comments on the art of "wedding notes and music lovingly together," [14] and in what other poets were saying about Lawes himself. But the Italians had long been philosophizing on this subject. A sixteenth century example is Caccini's statement that no value should be placed upon music which makes it impossible to understand the words. Musicians who disregard meaning "destroy the unity and meter, sometimes lengthening the syllables, sometimes shortening them in order to suit the counterpoint—a real mangling of the poetry." [15]

Milton's concern with Italian music and his acquaintance with the Italian theater is a subject on which Masson gives us little. The suggestion has been made [16] that Milton was already aware of the new developments before he left England, and that *Comus* was written under the influence of the "dramma per musica." Henry Lawes, the pupil of Coperario,

[14] Cf. *L'Allegro,* 135–136:

> Lap me in soft Lydian airs
> Married to immortal verse.

and *At a Solemn Music,* 2–3:

> Sphere-born harmonious sisters, Voice and Verse.

[15] Quoted in Enid Welsford, *The Court Masque,* p. 104.

[16] Finney, G. L., *"Comus,* Dramma per Musica." Mrs. Finney has made a strong case for the specific influence on Milton of *La Catena d'Adone,* a melodrama based on Marino's *Adone,* written by Tronsarelli and Mazzocchi and produced and published (in score) at Rome in 1626.

is sure to have communicated what he knew of Italian music to his friend and to have sent him abroad well primed to acquire more. The chests of choice music books which Milton sent home from Venice included, according to Phillips: Orazio Vecchi, composer of *Amphiparnaso,* a "commedia harmonica," not in the *stilo rappresentativo,* but an attempt at conceiving dialogue in madrigal form; Luca Marenzio, who is said to have concentrated on musical expression of the words and to have defended this principle; Gesualdo, a real innovator in harmony, who set poems by Tasso to music; and finally, Monteverde. Milton's interest in the last named composer opens up interesting possibilities. He says he spent a whole month in Venice where Monteverde was director of St. Mark's choir. Two public theaters, the first in Italy, had been established there for the performance of melodramas, and operas of Monteverde were being given in the year of Milton's visit.[17] The poet was a good enough musician to know the quality of what was set before him, if indeed he had the opportunity to witness such a work as the *Arianna,* and to report it with enthusiasm to his father and to Lawes.

This brings us to the old question of the dramatic plans in the Cambridge MS. and their relation to Italian sources. Warburton writing to Birch [18] argued against the influence of Andreini, saying that Milton was first inclined to make an opera of the material when Sir John Denham and others contrived to get operas performed after the closing of the theaters. It seems more likely that the poet, enamored of what he had seen in Italy and full of enthusiasm for trans-

[17] See Belloni, *Il Seicento,* pp. 420 ff.
[18] Todd, *Poetical Works,* 1809, II, p. 214.

planting it to England, wrote out this and the other plans very soon after his return. The program of entertainment to be promoted by the government in *Reason of Church Government* (1642), written, certainly, before the closing of the theaters, includes, besides martial exercises, the "learned and affable meetings of frequent academies," and "set and solemn panurgies in theaters, porches" and other public places. Drama is not specifically mentioned, but "panurgies" is perhaps general enough to include some kinds. Of all the plans the early scenarios of *Paradise Lost* seem most operatic. The subject was common enough in Italy and there is at least one instance of a full musical treatment.[19] The *Adamo* of Andreini, which still stands as the most plausible Italian influence on Milton's original conception, belonged to the older tradition of the *Sacra Rappresentazione* but was influenced also by contemporary melodrama in the choruses and ballets.[20] I find no evidence that it was produced in Milton's time, but the poet could have bought the book, with its many illustrations taken from the actual performance, and easily imagined, on the basis of entertainments which he actually had seen, what it would have been like.

Mrs. G. L. Finney has argued [21] convincingly that *Sam-*

[19] See *The Monthly Magazine*, 198 (1810) pp. 145–147, which prints the Latin text of an oratorio on the Fall, said to have been "copied from an ancient manuscript, found some years ago, in the library of Marquis Scati at Milan," where it was "performed for the first time when Milton was there." There is a succession of brief lyric scenes: Adam contemplating creation; Lucifer rousing his followers; the loves of Adam and Eve with Satan envying; distressful premonitions of Eve, with Adam comforting; the temptation and fall; Satan glorying; Adam and Eve despairing and repentant.

[20] See Winifred Smith, *Italian Actors of the Renaissance,* 1930.

[21] "Chorus in *Samson Agonistes.*"

son Agonistes is also in part a fruit of Milton's Italian experience. The chorus had come to be disapproved of in Italy, as in France and England, for strictly literary plays; but its use in melodrama was defended by men like Doni as part of the program of classical revival. The seventeenth century did not, Mrs. Finney points out, distinguish sharply between pastoral and tragedy. Music dramas full of triviality reflect classical standards, and even oratorio [22] was felt to be subject to Aristotelian technique. "La Tragedia" appears frequently as the prologue for music dramas, for example Rinuccini's *Euridice*. When Milton speaks in the prefatory note to *Samson* of the chorus as still in use among the Italians it is melodrama and oratorio that he is referring to. At least one oratorio having the Samson story as a theme was in print.[23] One is bound to conclude that the case for Milton's having learned much from those who were contributing to Italy's last great original achievement in the arts is a strong, though at present a rather intangible, one.[24]

[22] For the popularity of oratorio see Alaleona, *Studi su la storia dell Oratorio musicale in Italia,* Turin, 1903, cited by G. L. Finney, "Chorus in *Samson Agonistes.*"

[23] *Il Sansone, dialogo per musica,* by Pietro dell Isola, 1638. Mrs. Finney describes another Samson (unpublished) by Benedetto Ferrari, who like Monteverde was writing for the new Venetian opera houses at the time of Milton's visit.

[24] One wonders whether what Milton learned in Italy may not have had some influence on the future course of theatrical development in England. He must have imparted his ideas and plans to Lawes, perhaps proposing collaboration. Lawes later supplied the music for Davenant's *First Day's Entertainment at Rutland House,* described on the title page *(1657)* as being "by declamation and music, after the manner of the ancients." The quoted phrase suggests the descriptions of ἀκρόαμα in ancient writers, as well as the theory and practice of the Italians. It says something more than, "This is not a play," to the learned critic who, like Milton, objected to the English

Of Milton's actual itinerary there is at present little to add to his own statement as interpreted by Masson. It may, however, be pointed out that we are reasonably well informed only about his brief visit to Naples and his life in Florence, four or five months at most out of sixteen. He was in Rome for an equal period, but the record of his experiences and contacts there is obviously very incomplete. For the visits to Paris and Geneva there is some data. The period in Venice is a complete blank, except that we know that he must have been there in the spring of 1639. Allowing for the longer residences and for the time consumed in getting from place to place by carriage or on horseback, we have at least three months left to account for, whether in France, Italy, or Switzerland. The possibility of dating his visits to Pisa, Siena, Lucca, Bologna, Ferrara, Verona, Milan, etc., depends on the discovery of continental records. It was suggested to me by Count Sforza that local antiquarianism in Italy might be expected to help in this, even after the destruction wrought by war. Certainly the surviving correspondence of all persons Milton is known to have met and the minutes of academies he might have been received in should be thoroughly searched. Without such material we

stage partly because it had deserted the classical tradition. (See above, p. 408.) These ideas were current both inside and outside of Puritan circles and they carried over to the Restoration. When Dryden asked permission to make an "opera" out of *Paradise Lost*, he perhaps knew he was returning to Milton's original idea. Those who recorded the incident presumably did *not* know. Milton is still protesting in *Samson* and in the prefatory note to *Paradise Lost*. He could not, of course, be satisfied with Davenant's and Dryden's reading of the high doctrine of the poet's function which Milton himself had taught in his school out of Aristotle, Horace, and "the Italian commentaries of Castelvetro, Tasso, and Mazzoni, and the others."

can reconstruct his adventures only conjecturally. The general conditions of Italian travel and the customary experiences of Englishmen in the places Milton visited are described in the travel literature of the time. We know, for example, that Milton's trip would have cost him something like £400,[25] and that much of his journey would have been on horseback. If the account of Moryson is to be trusted, he would have found the tables in the inns at Florence "spread with white cloths, strewed with flowers and fig leaves, with ingestors or glasses of divers colored wines set upon them and delicate fruits which would invite a man to eat and drink who otherwise hath no appetite, being all open to the sight of passengers as they ride by the highway, through their great unglazed windows."

We know also that his luggage would have been ransacked at almost every city for dutiable articles unless he gave the officials a suitable tip. We can imagine him being impressed, as Moryson was, with the condition of the peasantry, "whom the Italians use like oxen and asses for their work," and with the merry life of the courtesans, "feasted at home by their lovers and honored by all men with respectful salutations." Sandys says there were 30,000 of the latter in Naples to a population of 300,000. The remarks which won Milton the reputation among the Italians of being something of a prude may have been directed against this shamelessness.

The guide books tell us, finally, what sights he would have been confronted with in every city and what galleries he would have found open. Thus at Florence there were the Duke's wild beasts, the Pitti Palace, and the Pratolino garden with its water tricks. In Venice he could have visited

[25] See Howard, *op. cit.*, p. 156.

the Doges' palace and seen the masterworks of Titian and Veronese on the walls. That the echoes of such common experiences in Milton's later writings are few proves little. Vallombrosa and Fiesole return to furnish beautiful similes in *Paradise Lost,* and there is a casual mention of Italian mountebanks in the *Pro se Defensio.* Miss Nicolson has argued plausibly that a visit to the Phlegraean Fields furnished materials for the account of Hell and Pandemonium.[26] The description of imperial Rome in *Paradise Regained,* more visual in its imagery than the parallel portrayal of Athens, perhaps adds reality to Milton's statement that he spent time "viewing the antiquities of that city." But that is about all that remains to attest his interest in the more obvious aspects of Italian travel. However much these things may have impressed him at the time, he did not often store them up for use.

> Me, of these
> Nor skilled nor studious higher argument
> Remains.

His capacity for discarding "tinsel trappings" is illustrated in the reference to his visit to the Viceroy's palace in Naples, which includes no mention of what so much impressed other English travellers : the "royal and most lovely household stuff," the "large and most sweet gardens and delicate walks paved with divers colored and engraved marbles," the two banqueting houses, the "secret fountains and delicate cages of birds," the astonishing array of implements of war.

The effects of the Italian journey on Milton's mind were

[26] "Milton and the Phlegraean Fields"

nevertheless extensive and profound, including such significant minutiae as the adopting of the italic "e" in his handwriting and the Roman pronunciation of Latin words, but
also, more intangibly, what seems to me a new maturity of
purpose and a richer conception of the art of poetry.[27] The
reasons he gives for returning to England without extending his visit to Sicily and Greece are suggestive of what was
happening to him. He had come to feel himself a man and
wanted to begin his work. The long period of preparation,
which years of study at Horton would never have completed,
was over. He had become an accepted citizen of the world of
intellect and culture. He had measured the difference between the tradition of his own and other peoples and matched
his abilities with those of famous men. He had experienced
the stimulation of new and sophisticated ideas in art. It is
not surprising that the impediments to action should suddenly have been lifted from his mind.

The great program with which he returned to his native
land had two related aspects. He proposed a cultural and
spiritual reform of England, in which he as poet and publicist should play a leading part. The literary plans in the
Trinity MS, the exhortation to the magistrates to provide

[27] The influence of Italian poetry on Milton of course antedates
the Continental journey, but his interest in and knowledge of recent
and contemporary authors must have been greatly extended by his
contacts in Italy. The case for Marino is a strong one. See Nethercot
in *Modern Language Review*, XXV, p. 154, and Kastner, *The Works
of William Drummond*, I, xxxii, where the claim is made that Edward Phillips in his comparison of Drummond with the Italians is
recording his uncle's estimates. Chiabrera, who died in the first year
of Milton's visit, is discussed in the correspondence with Carlo Dati.
This poet, beside his Anacreontic lyrics written for music, collab-
orated with Caccini and others in melodrama.

worthy entertainment for the people in *Reason of Church Government,* and the actual writing of the first pamphlets show the direction of his mind. And in all this we can clearly trace the influence of his experiences abroad: the theaters and academies, Manso, Doni, Italian literature and literary theory, on the one hand; Grotius, Galileo, Giovanni Diodati, and the traditions of Italian and Geneva Protestantism against the actual background of the Counter Reformation on the other.

Of the two sets of influence the latter is perhaps the more speculative, but it is certainly not to be neglected. The deepest emotion of Milton's youth was his friendship with Charles Diodati. The most comprehensive political ideal of his maturity was the achievement in Europe of Christian unity under the leadership of Reformed England. In Paris, Italy, and Geneva he had had brought home to him the significance of the whole movement which had made the Diodatis exiles,[28] which had governed the political activity of Wotton, which commanded the intellectual energies of Grotius, which accounted for the frustration of Galileo. It

[28] Milton must have been thoroughly acquainted with the saga of the Italian refugees. The various families, Diodati, Calandrini, Burlamaqui, Turrentini, had intermarried, and they all had a rallying point in Geneva, where the continuous tradition of the Italian church shows a succession of pastors from the Lucchese group to 1689. It is now known that Milton's friend Charles Diodati studied theology in this nursery of his clan in 1630. (See Dorian, "Charles Diodati at Geneva.") Elie Diodati was there in that year and again in 1634. Milton's early intimacy with the London family extended beyond Charles himself. See his letter of September 2, 1637. He also knew a Calandrini in London, and a Turrentini in Geneva. The Italian girl, Emilia, of the sonnets, has never been identified, but the conviction lingers that she must have been of the same background. However much Anglicized or Gallicized the different members of the

was inevitable with him that his personal loyalties should help motivate and determine his devotion to a public cause. His own peculiar stripe of Protestant theology may owe something to the Italian reformers.[29] Peter Martyr of Vermigli, Bernardino Ochino of Siena, Fausto Socino, Paolo Sarpi, Giacomo Contio (Acontius), Marsiglio of Padua, Tremellio of Ferrara, Matteo Gribaldi, Aonio Paleario, Castellio were familiar names in Reformation history. Some of these men were Christian humanists rather than Lutherans or Calvinists pure and simple. Generally speaking, Milton was of this tradition. Socinus was the arch heretic of the age and Milton came nearer to holding with him than with his enemies. Ochino has been claimed as the source of Milton's anti-trinitarian conception. He wrote also a dialogue on polygamy and divorce, translated into English in 1567.[30] Acontius undertook in his book of the Stratagems of Satan [31] to show how few were the essential doctrines of Christianity. This work was revived by the Independents and appeared in English in 1648, with an epistle by John Goodwin and Milton's fellow worker for Protestant unity, John Durie. Lord Falkland with his latitudinarian motto:

clan may have become, they could hardly have forgotten or ceased talking about such a burning ancestral experience as that recorded in the family memoirs now in the Geneva library. (Facsimiles in the possession of Donald C. Dorian of Rutgers University.)

[29] See M. Young, *The Life and Times of Aonio Paleario,* or *A History of the Italian Reformers in the Sixteenth Century,* London, 1860.

[30] See L. A. Wood, *The Form and Origin of Milton's Anti-trinitarian Conception,* London, Ontario, 1911.

[31] Edited by Charles D. O'Malley, *Occasional Papers,* English Series No. 5, Parts I and II, California State Library, San Francisco, 1940. Ramus, Chillingworth, Ames, Hartlib, and Comenius are mentioned by O'Malley as having been influenced by Acontius.

BIBLIOGRAPHY[1]

Editions

The Poetical Works of John Milton

Edited by H. J. Todd. First edition, London, 1801; six volumes. Second edition, much enlarged, London, 1809; seven volumes.

Todd's Variorum Edition is the readiest means of access to the results of eighteenth century critical and scholarly work on Milton.

The Prose Works of John Milton

Edited by J. A. St. John. London, 1848–1853. (Bohn Library); five volumes.

Translations only of Latin works, including *De Doctrina Christiana*. Prefaces and notes.

The Works of John Milton in Prose and Verse

Edited by John Mitford. London, 1851; eight volumes.

Complete except for the *De Doctrina Christiana* and minor items. Latin texts of prose; no translations. Index, no notes.

---

[1] The abbreviations of references to periodicals are as follows:
ELH A Journal of English Literary History
ES Englische Studien
JEGP Journal of English and Germanic Philology
MLN Modern Language Notes
MLR Modern Language Review
MP Modern Philology
PQ Philological Quarterly
PMLA Publications of the Modern Language Association of America
RES Review of English Studies
RLC Revue de littérature comparée
SP Studies in Philology
TLS Times Literary Supplement

The Poetical Works of John Milton

Edited by David Masson. London, 1874; three volumes.

Elaborate introductions, notes, and essays.

"Arcades" and *Comus,* "Ode on the Morning of Christ's Nativity," etc.; "L'Allegro," "Il Penseroso," "Lycidas," *Paradise Lost, Samson Agonistes.*

Edited by A. W. Verity. Cambridge, 1891–1912 (Pitt Press Series); eleven volumes. Revised edition of *Paradise Lost* in one volume, 1910.

The most learnedly annotated of all modern editions.

The Complete Poetical Works of John Milton

Edited by William Vaughn Moody. Boston, 1899 (The Cambridge Poets). New Edition with revision of the translations by E. K. Rand, 1924.

Brilliant introductions but occasionally inaccurate.

The Poetical Works of John Milton

Edited by W. A. Wright, Cambridge, 1903.

Gives variant readings in full; the best modernized text.

The Poems of John Milton

Edited by H. J. C. Grierson. London, 1925.

All the poems arranged chronologically; attempts to preserve significant features of the original text.

Poems in English by John Milton, with Illustrations by William Blake. London, 1926.

The Student's Milton

Edited by Frank Allen Patterson, New York, 1930.

Complete poems and the bulk of the prose in a single volume. The text of the poems is that of the original editions, with careful collations. A new translation of the Latin poems by Nelson G. McCrea. A revision of this valuable edition appeared in 1933, with annotations to both the poetry and the prose.

The Works of John Milton

Edited by various hands under the general editorship of Frank A. Patterson. New York, 1931–1938 (The Columbia Edition). Eighteen volumes in twenty-one.

This edition is more inclusive than any hitherto. The texts are based on a complete collation of all the MSS and early prints. The eighteenth volume contains the hitherto uncollected writings, marginalia, and many items which have been ascribed to Milton on more or less doubtful authority. Additions are to be found in "A First Supplement to the Columbia Milton," by T. O. Mabbott and J. Milton French. *Notes and Queries*, CLXXVII (1939), 329–330.

An Index to the Columbia Edition of the Works of John Milton

Edited by Frank L. Patterson, assisted by French R. Fogle. New York, 1940. Two volumes.

The Poems of John Milton

Edited with Introduction and Notes by James Holly Hanford. New York, 1936.

The poems are chronologically arranged, the texts given in modern spelling but with the characteristic features of the original punctuation preserved.

Milton. Paradise Lost

Edited by Merritt Y. Hughes. New York, 1935.

Milton. Paradise Regained, the Minor Poems and Samson Agonistes.

Edited by Merritt Y. Hughes. New York, 1937.

Professor Hughes's editions contain excellent introductions and notes.

Milton on Himself. Milton's utterances upon himself and his works.

Edited with Introduction and Notes by John S. Diekhoff. Oxford University Press, 1939.

The Poetical Works of John Milton

Edited after the original texts by H. C. Beeching. London, 1938.

A new edition with translations of the Italian, Latin, and Greek poems from the Columbia University edition and A Reader's Guide by William Skeat.

The English Poems of John Milton

Oxford University Press, 1940.

A re-issue of the World Classics Edition with Introduction by Charles Williams.

The Complete Poetical Works of John Milton

A new text edited with Introduction and Notes by Harris F. Fletcher. Boston, 1941.

John Milton's Complete Poetical Works Reproduced in Photographic Facsimile.

A critical text compiled and edited by Harris F. Fletcher. Cambridge, 1943. Volume I (Minor Poems).

BIBLIOGRAPHICAL AND REFERENCE WORKS

Bradshaw, John. A Concordance to the Poetical Works of John Milton. London, 1894.

Bush, Douglas. Mythology and the Renaissance Tradition. University of Minnesota Press, 1932.

Cooper, Lane. A Concordance of the Latin, Greek, and Italian Poems of John Milton. Halle, 1923.

Craig, Hardin, and others. "Recent Literature of the English Renaissance." *Studies in Philology,* April issues from 1923 to date.

This very comprehensive annual bibliography regularly contains a section devoted to Milton.

Fletcher, Harris. Contributions to a Milton Bibliography. University of Illinois Studies, Urbana, 1931.

Lockwood, Laura. Lexicon to the English Poetical Works of John Milton. New York, 1907.

Madan, F. F. "Milton, Salmasius, and DuGard." *The Library,* Fourth Series, IV (1923), 119-145.

Osgood, C. G. The Classical Mythology of Milton's English Poems. New York, 1900. Reprinted, Oxford, 1925.

A dictionary of Milton's mythological allusions.

Parker, William R. "Contributions toward a Milton Bibliography." *The Library,* Fourth Series, XVI (1935).

Parker, William R. "John Milton, Scrivener, 1590–1632." *MLN* LIX (1944), 532–537.

Parker, William R. "Milton, Rothwell, and Simmons." *The Library,* Fourth Series, XVIII (1937), 89–103.

Pollard, A. W. "The Bibliography of Milton." *The Library,* N. S., X (1909), 1–33.

Stevens, David H. Reference Guide to Milton from 1800 to

the Present Day. The University of Chicago Press, 1930.

Thomson, E. N. S. John Milton. A Topical Bibliography. Yale University Press, 1916.

BIOGRAPHIES

Belloc, Hilaire. Milton. Philadelphia, 1935.

Darbishire, Helen. The Early Lives of Milton. London, 1932.

Garnett, Richard. Life of John Milton. London, 1890.

Lockwood, Laura E. ed. *Of Education; Areopagitica; The Commonwealth,* by John Milton; with Early Biographies of Milton. Boston, 1911 (The Riverside Literature Series).

Macaulay, Rose. Milton. London, 1933 (Great Lives).

Masson, David. The Life of Milton. London, 1859–1894. First volume revised, 1881. Seven volumes including index.

The standard authority on Milton and the political, ecclesiastical, and literary background of his career.

Pattison, Mark. Milton. London, 1879 (The English Men of Letters Series).

Raleigh, Sir Walter A. Milton. New York and London, 1900.

Raymond, Dora B. Oliver's Secretary. New York, 1932.

Stern, A. Milton und seine Zeit. Leipzig, 1877–1879.

A parallel work to Masson.

Tillyard, E. M. W. Milton. New York, 1930.

Trent, William P. John Milton: a Short Study of His Life and Works. New York, 1899.

BIOGRAPHICAL STUDIES

Allodoli, Ettore. Giovanni Milton e l'Italia. Prato, 1907.

Barker, Arthur. "Milton's School-Masters." *MLR,* XXXII (1937), 517–536.

Brennecke, Ernest Jr. John Milton the Elder and his Music. Columbia University Press, 1938.

Contains a complete survey of the extant musical compositions of Milton's father and prints many of them for the first time.

Brown, Eleanor. Milton's Blindness. Columbia University Press, 1934.

Brunner, Hildegarde. Miltons persönliche und ideele Welt in ihrer Beziehung zum Aristokratismus. Bonn, 1933.

Dobrée, Bonamy. "Milton and Dryden: A Comparison and Contrast in Poetic Ideas and Poetic Method." *ELH*, III (1936), 83–100.

Fink, Zera S. "Milton and the Theory of Climatic Influence." *Modern Language Quarterly*, II (1941), 67–80.

French, J. Milton. "The Autographs of John Milton." *ELH*, IV (1937), 300–380.

French, J. Milton. "John Milton, Scrivener, the Temples of Stowe, and Sir John Lenthall." *Huntington Library Quarterly*, IV (1941), 303–308.

French, J. Milton. "Milton as a Historian." *PMLA*, L (1935), 469–479.

French, J. Milton. Milton in Chancery; New Chapters in the Lives of the Poet and His Father. New York, 1939.

French, J. Milton. "Milton, Needham, and *Mercurius Politicus*." *SP*, XXXIII (1936), 236–252.

French, J. Milton. "Milton's Annotated Copy of Gildas." *Harvard Studies and Notes*, XX (1938), 76–80.

French, J. Milton. "Milton's Supplicats." *Huntington Library Quarterly*, V (1942), 349–359.

French, J. Milton. "The Powell-Milton Bond." *Harvard Studies and Notes*, XX (1938), 61–73.

Hanford, James H. "The Chronology of Milton's Private Studies." *PMLA*, XXXVI (1921), 251–314.

Hanford, James H. "Creative Personality: the Case of John Milton." *The Johns Hopkins Alumni Magazine*, XV (June, 1927), 328–352.

Hanford, James H. "Dr. Paget's Library." *Bulletin of the Medical Library Association*, XXXIII (1945), 91–99.

Hanford, James H. "John Milton Forswears Physic." *Bulletin of the Medical Library Association*, XXXII (1944), 23–34.

Hanford, James H. "The Rosenbach Milton Documents." *PMLA*, XXXVIII (1923), 290–296.

Hanford, James H. "The Youth of Milton." *Studies in Shakespeare, Milton, and Donne*. New York, 1925, pp. 89–163.

Leach, A. F. "Milton as Schoolboy and Schoolmaster." *Proceedings of the British Academy*, 1908, pp. 295–318.

Liljegren, S. B. Studies in Milton. Lund, 1918.

Martin, Burns. "The Date of Milton's First Marriage." *SP*, XXV (1928), 457–462.

Morand, Paul P. De Comus à Satan, l'ouvre poétique de John Milton expliquée par sa vie. Paris, 1939.

Morand, Paul P. The Effects of His Political Life upon John Milton. Paris, 1939.

Nicolson, Marjorie. "Milton and the Telescope." *ELH*, II (1935), 1–32.

Nicolson, Marjorie H. "Milton's 'Old Damoetas.'" *MLN*, XLI (1926), 293–300.

Parker, William R. "Milton and Edward Phillips." *TLS*, Feb. 28, 1942.

Parker, William R. Milton's Contemporary Reputation, an Essay, together with *A Tentative List of Printed Allusions to Milton, 1641–1674*, and facsimile reproductions of five contemporary pamphlets written in answer to Milton. Ohio State University Press, 1940.

Parker, William R. "Milton's Last Sonnet: Addressed to First or Second Wife?" *RES*, XXI (1945), 235–238.

Parker, William R. "Milton's Unknown Friend." *TLS*, May 16, 1936.

Parker, William R. "On Milton's Early Literary Program." *MP*, XXXIII (1935), 49–53.

Parker, William R. "The Trinity Manuscript and Milton's Plans for a Tragedy." *JEGP*, XXXIV (1935), 225–232.

Parsons, Edward S. "Concerning *The Earliest Life of Milton*." *ELH*, IX (1942), 106–117.

428   BIBLIOGRAPHY

Pompen, F. R. "Recent Theories about Milton's Personality." *Neophilologus,* VII (1921–2), 272–279.

Potter, G. R. "Milton and Roger Williams." *Rhode Island Historical Society,* XIII (1920), 113.

Powell, Chilton L. English Domestic Relations, 1487–1653. Columbia University Press, 1917.

Powell, Chilton L. "Milton Agonistes." *Sewanee Review,* XXXIV (1926), 169–183.

Rand, E. K. "Milton in Rustication." *SP,* XIX (1922), 109–135.

Saurat, Denis. Milton: Man and Thinker. New York, 1925. Second edition, revised, 1944.

Saurat, Denis. "Two Notes on Milton." *RES,* XII (1936).

Sewell, Arthur. "Milton and the Mosaic Law." *MLR,* XXX (1935), 12–18.

Smart, J. S. "Milton in Rome." *MLR,* VIII (1913), 91.

Sotheby, Samuel Leigh. Ramblings in the Elucidation of the Autograph of Milton. London, 1861.

Thompson, E. N. S. "Milton's Part in *Theatrum Poetarum.*" *MLN,* XXXVI (1921), 18–21.

Wolfe, Don M. "Lilburne's Note on Milton." *MLN,* LVI (1941), 360–363.

Wolff, Samuel L. "Milton's *Advocatum nescio quem:* Milton, Salmasius, and John Clark." *Modern Language Quarterly,* II (1941), 559–600.

Wright, B. A. "Milton's First Marriage." *MLR,* XXVI (1931), 383–400, and XXVII (1932), 6–23.

THE PROSE WORKS

Ainsworth, Oliver M. "Milton as a Writer on Education." *Transactions of the Wisconsin Academy of Sciences, Arts, and Letters,* XXI (1924), 41–50.

Ainsworth, Oliver M., ed. Milton on Education; the Tractate *Of Education,* edited with an Introduction and Notes; with

Supplementary Extracts from other Writings of Milton. Yale University Press, 1930.

Allison, William T., ed. *The Tenure of Kings and Magistrates.* New York, 1911 (Yale Studies in English).

Barker, Arthur. "Christian Liberty in Milton's Divorce Pamphlets." *MLR,* XXXV (1940), 153–161.

Cawley, Robert R. Milton's Literary Craftsmanship: a study of *A Brief History of Moscovia:* with an edition of the text. Princeton University Press, 1941.

Clark, Evert M., ed. *The Readie and Easie Way to Establish a Free Commonwealth.* Yale University Press, 1915.

Dowden, Edward. Puritan and Anglican: Studies in Literature. New York, 1900.

Fink, Zera S. "The Development of Milton's Political Thought." *PMLA,* LVII (1942), 705–736.

Firth, C. H. "Milton as an Historian." *Proceedings of the British Academy,* 1907–1908, 227–257.

Fletcher, Harris. "Milton's *History of Britain.*" *JEGP,* XXXV (1936), 405 ff.

Fletcher, Harris. The Use of the Bible in Milton's Prose. University of Illinois Press, 1929.

French, J. Milton. "That Late Villain Milton; History of the Publications of Milton's Letters of State." *PMLA,* LV (1940), 102–118.

French, J. Milton. "The Burning of Milton's *Defensio* in France." *MLN,* LVI (1941), 275–277.

Gilman, Wilbur M. Milton's Rhetoric: Studies in His Defense of Liberty. University of Missouri Press, 1939.

Glicksman, Harry. "The Editions of Milton's *History of Britain.*" *PMLA,* XXXV (1920), 116–122.

Hale, Will T., ed. *Of Reformation Touching Church Discipline in England.* Yale University Press, 1916.

Hales, J. W., ed. Milton's *Areopagitica.* Revised edition. Oxford University Press, 1882.

Haller, William O. "Before *Areopagitica.*" *PMLA,* XLII (1927), 875–900.

Haller, William O. Tracts on Liberty in the Puritan Revolution. 3 vols., Columbia University Press, 1934.

Hanford, James H. "The Date of Milton's *De Doctrina Christiana.*" *SP,* XVII (1920), 309–319.

Hanford, James H. "Milton and Ochino." *MLN,* XXXVI (1921), 121–122.

Hardeland, Gertrud. Miltons Anschauungen von Staat, Kirche, Toleranz. Halle, 1934.

Horwood, Alfred J., ed. A Commonplace Book of John Milton. London, 1876 (Camden Society). Revised edition, 1877; Manuscript Reproduction, 1876.

Jones, Richard. The Background of the *Battle of the Books. Washington University Studies, Humanistic Series,* VII (1920), No. 2.

Kelley, Maurice. "Milton's Debt to Wolleb's *Compendium Theologiae Christianae.*" *PMLA,* L (1935), 156–165.

Kelley, Maurice. This Great Argument: a Study of Milton's *De Doctrina Christiana* as a Gloss upon *Paradise Lost.* (Princeton Studies in English XXII.) Princeton University Press and Oxford University Press, 1941.

Lowenhaupt, Warren H. "The Writing of Milton's *Eikonoklastes.*" *SP,* XX (1923), 29–51.

Mabbott, Thomas O. "On Milton's Letters." *TLS,* February 16, 1928, 112.

Mirsky, Prince D. S. *A Brief History of Moscovia* by John Milton. London, 1929.

Neumann, J. H. "Milton's Prose Vocabulary." *PMLA,* LX (1945), 102–120.

Parks, George B. "Occasion of Milton's *Moscovia.*" *SP,* XL (1943), 399–404.

Rice, Warner G. "A Note on Areopagitica." *JEGP,* XL (1941), 474–481.

Scott-Craig, T. S. K. "Milton's Use of Wolleb and Ames."

MLN, LV (1940), 403–407. Review of Sewell's study on Milton's *Christian Doctrine.*

Sewell, Arthur. "Milton's *De Doctrina Christiana.*" *Essays and Studies,* XIX (1934), 40–65.

Sewell, Arthur. A Study of Milton's Christian Doctrine. Oxford University Press, 1939.

Smart, John S. "Milton and the King's Prayer." *RES,* I (1925), 385–391.

Smith, G. C. Moore. "A Note on Milton's *Art of Logic.*" *RES,* XIII (1937), 335–340.

Thompson, E. N. S. "Milton's *Of Education.*" *SP,* XV (1918), 159–175.

Vogt, Karl F. Milton als Publizist. Würzburg, 1933.

Watson, Foster. "A Suggested Source of Milton's Tractate *Of Education.*" *Nineteenth Century,* LXVI (1909), 607–617.

Whiting, George W. "A Late Seventeenth Century Milton Plagiarism." *SP,* XXXI (1934), 37–50.

Whiting, George W. "Milton and Lord Brooke on the Church." *MLN,* LI (1936), 161–166.

Whiting, George W. "The Satire in *Eikonoklastes.*" *Notes and Queries,* CLXX (1936), 435–458.

Whiting, George W. "The Sources of *Eikonoklastes:* A Resurvey." *SP,* XXXII (1935), 74–103.

Whiting, George W. "Woodward's Debt to Milton in 1644." *SP,* XXXIII (1936), 228–235.

Wolfe, D. M. Milton in the Puritan Revolution. New York, 1941.

Wolfe, D. M. "Milton, Lilburne, and the People." *MP,* XXXI (1934), 253–272.

THE MINOR POEMS

Babb, Lawrence. "The Background of Il Penseroso." *SP,* XXXVII (1940), 257–273.

Badt, Bertha. "Miltons *Comus* und Peeles *Old Wives Tale.*"

Archiv für das Studium der Neueren Sprachen und Literaturen, N.S., CXXIII (1909), 305–309.

Baldwin, E. C. "Milton and the Psalms." *MP,* XVII (1919), 457–463.

Barker, Arthur. "The Pattern of Milton's Nativity Ode." *University of Toronto Quarterly,* X (1941), 167–181.

Bense, J. F. " 'Meliboeus old' in Milton's *Comus." Neophilologus,* I (1916), 62–64.

Bridge, Sir Frederick. *The Masque of Comus*—the Original Music by Henry Lawes and Other Contemporary Composers. London, 1908.

Brie, F. "Das Märchen von Childe Rowland und sein Nachleben." *Palaestra,* CXLVIII (1925), 118–143.

Cook, Albert S. Notes on Milton's "Ode on the Morning of Christ's Nativity." *Transactions of the Connecticut Academy,* XV (1909), 307–368.

Damon, S. F. "Milton and Marston." *PMLA,* XLII (1927), 873–875.

de Filippis, Michele. "Milton and Manso: Cups or Books?" *PMLA,* LI (1936), 745–756.

Diekhoff, John S. "The Text of *Comus." PMLA,* LII (1937), 705–727.

Dorian, D. C. "Milton's 'Two-Handed Engine.' " *PMLA,* XLV (1930), 204–215.

Egerton, Lady Alix. Milton's *Comus,* being the Bridgewater Manuscript, with Notes and a Short Family Memoir. London, 1910.

Evans, G. Blakemore. "Two New Manuscript Versions of Milton's Hobson Poems." *MLN,* LVII (1942), 192–194.

Fletcher, G. B. A. "Milton's Latin Poems." *MP,* XXXVII (1940), 343–350.

Garrod, H. W. "Milton's Lines on Shakespeare." *Essays and Studies by Members of the English Association,* XII (1926), 1–23.

Hall, E. A. *"Comus, Old Wives Tale,* and Drury's *Alvredus."*

Manly Anniversary Studies, 104–144. University of Chicago Press, 1923.

Hanford, James H. "The Arrangement and Dates of Milton's Sonnets." *MP,* XVIII (1921), 475–483.

Hanford, James H. "The Evening Star in Milton." *MLN,* XXXVII (1922), 444–445.

Hanford, James H. "The Pastoral Elegy and Milton's *Lycidas.*" *PMLA,* XXV (1910), 403–447.

Harrison, T. P. "The Latin Pastorals of Milton and Castiglione." *PMLA,* L (1935), 480–493.

LeComte, Edward S. "New Light on the 'Haemony' Passage in *Comus.*" *PQ,* XXI (1942), 283–298.

Lewis, C. S. "A Note on *Comus.*" *RES,* VIII (1932), 170–176.

Lockwood, Laura E. "Milton's Corrections to the *Minor Poems.*" *MLN,* XXV (1910), 201–205.

Lowes, J. L. *"L'Allegro and The Passionate Shepheard." MLR,* VI (1911), 206–209.

MacKellar, Walter. ed. The Latin Poems of John Milton. Cornell University Press, 1930.

Milton's Minor Poems. London, 1924. [The Douglas Replicas]
    A photographic facsimile of the 1645 edition of the poems.

Milton's Poems, 1645. Oxford, 1924. A type-facsimile.

More, Paul Elmer. "How to Read *Lycidas.*" *The American Review,* VII (1936), 140–158.

Mutschmann, H. "That Two-Handed Engine at the Door." *TLS* (April 25, 1936), 356.
    Discussion follows throughout July and August.

Norlin, G. "The Conventions of Pastoral Elegy." *American Journal of Philology,* XXXII (1911), 294–312.

Padelford, F. M. "An Unnoted Source of *L'Allegro.*" *MLN,* XXII (1907), 200.

Parker, William R. "Milton's Hobson Poems: Some Neglected Early Texts." *MLR,* XXXI (1936), 395–402.

Parker, W. R. "Some Problems in the Chronology of Milton's Early Poems." *RES,* XI (1935), 276–283.

Pattison, Mark, ed. The Sonnets of John Milton. New York, 1883.

Potter, George R. "Milton's Early Poems, the School of Donne, and the Elizabethan Sonneteers." *PQ*, VI (1927), 396–400.

Ransom, John Crowe. "A Poem Nearly Anonymous." *The World's Body*. New York, 1938. 1–28.

Sensabaugh, George F. "Milieu of *Comus*." *SP*, XLI (1944), 238–249.

Singleton, Ralph H. "Milton's *Comus* and the *Comus* of Erycius Pluteanus." *PMLA*, LVIII (1943), 949–957.

Skeat, W. W., translator. Epitaphium Damonis. Cambridge University Press, 1933.

Smart, John S. "The Italian Singer in Milton's Sonnets." *The Musical Antiquary* (January, 1913), 91–97.

Smart, John S. The Sonnets of John Milton. Glasgow, 1921.

Spencer, Theodore. "Shakespeare and Milton." *MLN*, LIII (1938), 366–367.

Stevens, David H. "The Bridgewater Manuscript of *Comus*." *MP*, XXIV (1926–1927), 315–320.

Stevens, David H. "The Order of Milton's Sonnets." *MP*, XVII (1919), 25–33.

Studley, Marian H. "Milton and his Paraphrases of the Psalms." *PQ*, IV (1925), 364–372.

Thaler, Alvin. "Milton in the Theater." *SP*, XVII (1920), 269–308.

Visiak, E. H., ed. Milton's *Lament for Damon* and his other Latin Poems, with a translation by Walter Skeat. Oxford University Press, 1935.

Visiak, E. H., ed. *The Mask of Comus*. London, 1937.
    Contains the five Lawes airs edited by Hubert J. Foss.

Watson, Sara R. "Milton's Ideal Day: Its Development as a Pastoral Theme." *PMLA*, LVII (1942), 404–420.

Woodhouse, A. S. P. "The Argument of Milton's *Comus*." *University of Toronto Quarterly*, XI (1941), 46–71.

Wright, William Aldis, ed. Facsimile of the Manuscript of Milton's Minor Poems. Cambridge University Press, 1899.

PARADISE LOST

Allodoli, Ettore, ed. Giambattista Andreini: *L'Adamo*. Carabba, 1913.

Anon. "Ormuz and Amurath." *TLS,* March 30, 1933.

Bailey, Margaret L. Milton and Jakob Boehme; a Study of German Mysticism in Seventeenth-Century England. Oxford University Press, 1914.

Baldwin, E. C. "Some Extra-Biblical Semitic Influences upon Milton's Story of the Fall of Man." *JEGP,* XXVIII (1929), 366–401.

Baldwin, T. W. "Sir John Denham and *Paradise Lost.*" *MLN,* XLII (1927), 508–509.

Banks, Theodore H. Denham's Poetical Works. Yale University Press, 1928.

Banks, Theodore H. "Sir John Denham and *Paradise Lost.*" *MLN,* XLI (1926), 51–54.

Barham, F. *The Adamus Exul* of Grotius, or the Prototype of *Paradise Lost.* Translated. London, 1839.

Bowra, C. M. From Virgil to Milton. London, 1945.

Buff, F. Miltons *Paradise Lost* in seinem Verhaeltnis zur *Aeneide, Ilias,* und *Odyssee.* Munich, 1904.

Bundy, Murray W. "Milton's View of Education in *Paradise Lost.*" *JEGP,* XXI (1922), 127–152.

Bush, Douglas. Paradise Lost in Our Time. Cornell University Press, 1945.

Darbishire, Helen. The Manuscript of *Paradise Lost,* Book I. Oxford University Press, 1931.

Darbishire, Helen. "Printing of the First Edition of *Paradise Lost.*" *RES,* XVII (1941), 415–427.

Diekhoff, John S. "Eve, the Devil, and Areopagitica." *Modern Language Quarterly,* V (1944), 429–434.

Diekhoff, John S. "The Function of the Prologues in *Paradise Lost.*" *PMLA,* LVII (1942), 697–704.

Dunster, Charles. Considerations on Milton's Early Reading and the Prima Stamina of his *Paradise Lost.* London, 1800.

Dworsky, Beza R. "Milton and the Rabbinical Bible." *TLS,* April 25, 1935, and May 9, 1935.

Edmundson, G. Milton and Vondel. London, 1885.

Empson, William. "Milton and Bentley." *Some Versions of Pastoral.* London, 1935.

Erskine, John. "The Theme of Death in *Paradise Lost.*" *PMLA,* XXXII (1917), 573–582.

Fletcher, Harris. "Milton and Yosippon." *SP,* XXI (1924), 496–501.

Fletcher, Harris. Milton's Rabbinical Readings. University of Illinois Press, 1930.

Fletcher, Harris. Milton's Semitic Studies and Some Manifestations of Them in His Poetry. University of Chicago Press, 1926.

Gilbert, Allan H. "The Cambridge Manuscript and Milton's Plans for an Epic." *SP,* XVI (1919), 172–176.

Gilbert, Allan H. "Milton and Galileo." *SP,* XIX (1922), 152–185.

Gilbert, Allan H. "Milton and the Mysteries." *SP,* XVII (1920), 147–169.

Gilbert, Allan H. "Milton's Textbook of Astronomy." *PMLA,* XXXVIII (1923), 297–307.

Gilbert, Allan H. "The Outside Shell of Milton's World." *SP,* XX (1923), 444–447.

Gilbert, Allan H. "The Theological Basis of Satan's Rebellion and the Function of Abdiel in *Paradise Lost.*" *MP,* XL (1942), 19–42.

Greenlaw, Edwin. "A Better Teacher than Aquinas." *SP,* XIV (1917), 196–217.

Greenlaw, Edwin. "Spenser's Influence on *Paradise Lost.*" *SP,* XVII (1920), 320–359.

Gurteen, S. Humphreys. The Epic of the Fall of Man. New York, 1896.

Hamilton, G. R. Hero or Fool? A Study of Milton's Satan. London, 1944.

Hanford, James H. "The Dramatic Element in *Paradise Lost.*" *SP,* XIV (1917), 178–195.

Hanford, James H. "The Manuscript of *Paradise Lost.*" *MP,* XXV (1928), 313–317.

Hanford, James H. "Milton and the Art of War." *SP,* XVIII (1921), 232–266.

Herford, Charles. "Dante and Milton." *The Post-War Mind of Germany.* Oxford University Press, 1927.

Horrell, Joseph. "Milton, Limbo, and Suicide." *RES,* XVIII (1942), 413–427.

Kelley, Maurice. "Milton and the Third Person of the Trinity." *SP,* XXXII (1935), 221–234.

Kelley, Maurice. "Milton's Use of 'Begot' in *Paradise Lost,* V, 603." *SP,* XXXVIII (1941), 252–265.

Kelley, Maurice. "The Theological Dogma of *Paradise Lost,* III, 173–202." *PMLA,* LII (1937), 75–79.

Kirsten, R. Studien ueber das Verhaeltnis von Cowley und Milton. Leipzig, 1899.

Lovejoy, O. "Milton and the Paradox of the Fortunate Fall." *ELH,* IV (1937), 161–179.

McColley, Grant. "The Book of Enoch and *Paradise Lost.*" *The Harvard Theological Review,* XXX (1938), 21–39.

McColley, Grant. "Milton's Dialogue on Astronomy: The Principal Immediate Sources." *PMLA,* LII (1937), 728–762.

McColley, Grant. "The Epic Catalogue of *Paradise Lost.*" *ELH,* IV (1937), 180–191.

McColley, Grant. "Milton's Technique of Source Adaptation." *SP,* XXXV (1938), 61–110.

Moore, Cecil A. "The Conclusion of *Paradise Lost.*" *PMLA*, XXXVI (1921), 1–34.

Nicolson, Marjorie. "Milton and the *Conjectura Cabbalistica.*" *PQ*, VI (1927), 1–18.

Nicolson, Marjorie. "Milton and Hobbes." *SP*, XXIII (1926), 405–433.

Nicolson, Marjorie. "Milton's Hell and the Phlegraean Fields." *The University of Toronto Quarterly*, VII (1938), 500–513.

Nicolson, Marjorie. "The 'New Astronomy' and English Literary Imagination." *SP*, XXXII (1935), 428–463.

Nicolson, Marjorie. "The Spirit World of Milton and More." *SP*, XXII (1925), 433–452.

Nicolson, Marjorie. "The Telescope and Imagination." *MP*, XXXII (1935), 233–260.

Orchard, Thomas N. The Astronomy of *Paradise Lost*. London, 1896. Revised, 1913.

Pershing, J. H. "Different States of the First Edition of *Paradise Lost.*" *The Library*, Fourth Series, XXII (1941), 34–66.

Schork, Walther. Die Dramenpläne Miltons. Quackenbruck, 1934.

Stoll, Elmer E. "Belial as an Example." *MLN*, XLVIII (1933), 419–427.

Stoll, Elmer E. "Criticisms Criticized: Spenser and Milton." *JEGP*, XLI (1942), 451–477.

Stoll, Elmer E. From Shakespeare to Joyce. New York, 1944.

Stoll, Elmer E. "Give the Devil His Due: a Reply to Mr. Lewis." *RES*, XX (1944), 108–124.

Stoll, Elmer E. Poets and Playwrights. University of Minnesota Press, 1930.

Svendsen, Kester, "Cosmological Lore in Milton." *ELH*, IX (1942), 198–223.

Svendsen, Kester. "Milton and the Encyclopedias of Science." *SP*, XXXIX (1942), 303–325.

Svendsen, Kester. "Milton and Medical Lore." *Bulletin of the History of Medicine*, XIII (1943), 161–184.

Taylor, George C. Milton's Use of Du Bartas. Cambridge, 1934.

Tillyard, E. M. W. "The Causeway from Hell to the World in the Tenth Book of *Paradise Lost*." *SP*, XXXVIII (1941), 266–270.

Warren, William F. The Universe as Pictured in Milton's *Paradise Lost*. New York, 1915.

Whaler, James. "Animal Simile in *Paradise Lost*." *PMLA*, XLVII (1932), 534–553.

Whiting, George W. "The Golden Compasses in *Paradise Lost*." *Notes and Queries*, CLXXII (1937), 294–295.

Williams, Arnold. "Milton and the Renaissance Commentaries on *Genesis*." *MP*, XXXVII (1940), 263–278.

Williams, Arnold. "Renaissance Commentaries on *Genesis* and Some Elements of the Theology of *Paradise Lost*." *PMLA*, LVI (1941), 151–164.

Woodhull, Marianna. The Epic of *Paradise Lost*. New York, 1907.

Wuelcker, R. P. "Caedmon und Milton." *Anglia*, IV (1881), 401–405.

PARADISE REGAINED AND SAMSON AGONISTES

Banks, Theodore H. "The Banquet Scene in *Paradise Regained*." *PMLA*, LV (1940), 773–776.

Baum, Paull F. "*Samson Agonistes* Again." *PMLA*, XXXVI (1921), 354–371.

Boughner, Daniel C. "Milton's Harapha and Renaissance Comedy." *ELH*, XI (1944), 297.

Brewer, W. "Two Athenian Models for *Samson Agonistes*." *PMLA*, XLII (1927), 910–920.

Brown, Macmillan. The *Samson Agonistes* of Milton. New Zealand and London, 1905.

Clark, E. M. "Milton's Conception of Samson." *University of Texas Studies in English*, VIII (1928), 88–99.

Clark, E. M. "Milton's Earlier Samson." *University of Texas Studies in English*, VII (1927), 144–154.

Curry, Walter C. *"Samson Agonistes* Yet Again." *Sewanee Review,* XXXII (1924), 336–352.

Dowden, Edward. *"Paradise Regained." Milton Memorial Lectures.* Oxford University Press, 1909.

Fink, Zera S. "The Political Implications of *Paradise Regained." JEGP,* XL (1941), 482–488.

Finney, Gretchen L. "Chorus in *Samson Agonistes." PMLA,* LVIII (1943), 649–664.

Gilbert, Allan H. "The Temptation in *Paradise Regained." JEGP,* XV (1916), 599–611.

Grierson, H. J. C. "A Note upon the *Samson Agonistes* of John Milton and *Samson of Heilige Wraeck* by Joost van den Vondel." *Mélanges Baldensperger,* Paris, 1930.

Hanford, James H. *"Samson Agonistes* and Milton in Old Age." *Studies in Shakespeare, Milton, and Donne.* New York, 1925, 167–189.

Hughes, Merritt Y. "The Christ of *Paradise Regained* and the Renaissance Heroic Tradition." *SP,* XXXV (1938), 254–277.

Jebb, Richard C. *Samson Agonistes* and the Hellenic Drama. *Proceedings of the British Academy,* 1907–1908, pp. 341–348.

Knowlton, Edgar C. "Causality in *Samson Agonistes." MLN,* XXXVII (1922), 333–339.

Lewis, C. S. A Preface to Paradise Lost. Oxford University Press, 1942.

McColley, Grant. *Paradise Lost:* an Account of Its Growth and Major Origins, with a Discussion of Milton's Use of Sources and Literary Patterns. Chicago, 1940.

Menzies, W. "Milton: The Last Poems." *Essays and Studies by Members of the English Association,* XXIV (1939).

Miller, R. D. "Milton's Conception of the Temptation as Portrayed in *Paradise Regained." MLN,* XV (1900), 202–205.

Parker, William R. Milton's Debt to Greek Tragedy in *Samson Agonistes.* The Johns Hopkins University Press, 1937.

Raleigh, Sir Walter. "Milton's Last Poems." *Living Age,* CCLX (1909), 251–253.

Rice, Warner G. *"Paradise Regained." Papers of the Michigan Academy of Science, Arts and Letters,* XXII (1937), 493–503.

Tillyard, E. M. W. "The Christ of *Paradise Regained* and the Renaissance Heroic Tradition." *SP,* XXXVI (1938), 247–252.

GENERAL CRITICISM AND BACKGROUNDS

Barker, Arthur. Milton and the Puritan Dilemma, 1641–1660. University of Toronto Press, 1942.

Brinkley, Roberta F. Arthurian Legend in the Seventeenth Century. The Johns Hopkins University Press, 1932.

Brooks, Phillips. "Milton as an Educator." *Journal of Education,* LXVIII (1908), 533–535.

Bush, Douglas. The Renaissance and English Humanism. University of Toronto Press, 1939. Reprinted 1941.

Chambers, R. W. "Poets and their Critics: Langland and Milton." London, 1941. (Warton Lecture on English Poetry.) Reprinted from *Proceedings of the British Academy,* XXVII.

Cory, Herbert E. Spenser, the School of the Fletchers and Milton. *University of California Publications,* 1912.

Diekhoff, John S. "Critical Activity of the Poetic Mind: John Milton." *PMLA,* LV (1940), 748–772.

Dowden, Edward. The Idealism of Milton. *Transcripts and Studies.* London, 1888.

Eliot, T. S. "A Note on the Verse of John Milton." *Essays and Studies by Members of the English Association,* XXI (1935), 32–40.

Fink, Zera S. The Classical Republicans: an essay in the recovery of a pattern of thought in Seventeenth Century England. Northwestern University Press, 1945. (Northwestern University Studies in Humanities No. 9.)

Grierson, H. J. C. Cross Currents in English Literature of the Seventeenth Century. London, 1929.

Grierson, H. J. C. "Milton and Liberty." *MLR,* XXXIX (1944), 97–107.

Grierson, H. J. C. Milton and Wordsworth: Poets and Prophets. Cambridge University Press, 1937.

Grosart, A. B. The Poems of Phineas Fletcher. Fuller Worthies Library, 1869.

Guerle, E. de. Milton, sa vie et ses œuvres. Paris, 1868.

Haller, William, and Davies, Godfrey, editors. The Leveller Tracts, 1647–1653. Columbia University Press, 1944.

Haller, William and Malleville. "The Puritan Art of Love." *Huntington Library Quarterly,* V (1942), 235–272.

Haller, William. The Rise of Puritanism. Columbia University Press, 1938.

Hanford, James H. "Milton and the Return to Humanism," *SP,* XVI (1919), 126–147.

Hanford, James H. "The Shakespearian Element in Milton." *PMLA,* XL (1925), 645–691.

Hanford, James H. "The Temptation Motive in Milton." *SP,* XV (1918), 176–194.

Hartwell, Kathleen Lactantius and Milton. Cambridge, Mass., 1929.

Herford, Charles H. "Dante and Milton." *The Post-War Mind of Germany and Other European Studies.* Oxford University Press, 1924.

Hughes, Merritt Y. "Milton as a Revolutionary." *ELH,* X (1943), 87.

Kellett, E. E. "Milton and Dante." *Reconsiderations.* Cambridge, 1928.

Kellett, E. E. "Milton as a Mediaevalist." *Reconsiderations.* Cambridge, 1928.

Knight, G. Wilson. Chariot of Wrath: the Message of John Milton to Democracy at War. London, 1942.

Langdon, Ida. Milton's Theory of Poetry and Fine Art. Yale University Press, 1924.

Larson, Martin A. "Milton and Servetus: a Study in the Sources of Milton's Theology." *PMLA*, XLI (1926), 891–934.

Laurie, S. S. Educational Opinion since the Renaissance. Cambridge, 1903.

Liljegren, S. B. "La Pensée de Milton et Giordano Bruno." *RLC*, III (1923), 516–540.

Liljegren, S. B. "Miltonic Philosophy in the Light of Recent Research." *Scandinavian Scientific Review*, II (1923), 114–123.

Magoun, F. P. "The Chaucer of Spenser and Milton." *MP*, XXV (1927), 129–136.

Mahaffy, J. P. What Have the Greeks Done for Modern Civilization? New York, 1909.

McLachlan, H. The Religious Opinions of Milton, Locke and Newton. Manchester University Press, 1941.

Osgood, Charles G. Poetry as a Means of Grace. Princeton University Press, 1941.

Pommerich, E. Miltons Verhaeltnis zu Torquato Tasso. Halle, 1902.

Quiller-Couch, Arthur. "Milton." *Studies in Literature*. Second Series. Cambridge University Press, 1922.

Ramsay, Robert L. "Morality Themes in Milton's Poetry." *SP*, XV (1918), 123–158.

Ross, Malcolm M. Milton's Royalism: a Study of the Conflict of Symbol and Idea in the Poems. Cornell University Press, 1943.

Sampson, Alden. Studies in Milton. New York, 1913.

Samuel, I. "Milton's References to Plato and Socrates." *SP*, XLI (1944), 50–64.

Saurat, Denis. La pensée de Milton. Paris, 1920.

Saurat, Denis. "Les sources anglaises de la pensée de Milton." *Revue germanique*, XII (1921), 353–370.

Saurat, Denis. Milton et le matérialisme chrétien en Angleterre. Paris, 1928.

Schirmer, Walter F. Antike, Renaissance und Puritanismus. Munich, 1928.

Smith, Logan P. Milton and His Modern Critics. Oxford University Press, 1940.

Stern, A. John Milton und der Calvinismus. Gotha, 1872.

Stevens, David H. Milton Papers. University of Chicago Press, 1927.

Stoll, Elmer E. "Milton a Romantic." *RES*, VIII (1932), 425–436.

Stoll, Elmer E. "Milton Classical and Romantic." *PQ*, XXIII (1944), 222–247.

Stoll, Elmer E. "Milton, Puritan of the Seventeenth Century." *Poets and Playwrights*. University of Minnesota Press, 1930.

Taine, H. "Milton: son génie et ses œuvres." *Revue des deux mondes*, IX (1857), 818–854.

Taylor, George C. "Shakspere and Milton Again." *SP*, XXIII (1926), 189–199.

Thompson, E. N. S. Essays on Milton. Yale University Press, 1914.

Thompson, E. N. S. "Milton's Knowledge of Geography." *SP*, XVI (1919), 148–171.

Tillyard, E. M. W. The Miltonic Setting; Past and Present. Cambridge University Press, 1938.

Visiak, E. H. Milton Agonistes: a Metaphysical Criticism. London, 1923.

Whiting, George W. Milton's Literary Milieu. University of North Carolina Press, 1939.

Wilde, Hans-Oskar. Milton's Geistesgeschichtliche Bedeutung. Heidelberg, 1933.

Willey, Basil. The Seventeenth Century Background: Studies in the thought of the age in relation to poetry and religion. London, 1934.

Williamson, George. "Milton and the Mortalist Heresy." *SP*, XXXII (1935).

Wolfe, Don M. Leveller Manifestoes of the Puritan Revolution. New York, 1944.

Wolfe, Don M. "Milton and Hobbes: a Contrast in Social Temper." *SP*, XLI (1944), 410–426.

Wood, L. A. The Form and Origin of Milton's Antitrinitarian Conception. London, 1911.

Woodhouse, A. S. P. "Approach to Milton: a Note on Practical Criticism." *Royal Society of Canada, Proceedings and Transactions*, XXXVIII, Sec. ii (1944), 201–213.

Woodhouse, A. S. P. Puritanism and Liberty; Being the Army Debates (1647–1649) from the Clarke Manuscripts, with Supplementary Documents. London, 1938.

MILTON'S STYLE AND VERSIFICATION

Banks, Theodore H., Jr. "Miltonic Rhythm: a Study of the Relation of the Full Stops to the Rhythm of *Paradise Lost*." *PMLA*, XLII (1927), 140–145.

Binyon, Lawrence. "A Note on Milton's Imagery and Rhythm." *Seventeenth Century Studies Presented to Sir Herbert Grierson*. Oxford University Press, 1938.

Bridges, Robert. Milton's Prosody. Revised Edition. Oxford University Press, 1921.

Diekhoff, John. "Terminal Pause in Milton's Verse." *SP*, XXXII (1935), 235–239.

Hamer, E. The Meters of English Poetry. Methuen, 1930.

Hazlitt, William C. "On Milton's Versification." *The Round Table*. London, 1817.

Hübener, Gustav. Die Stilistische Spannung in Miltons *Paradise Lost*. Halle, 1913.

Morton, Edward P. The Technique of English Non-dramatic Blank Verse. Chicago, 1910.

Praz, Mario. "Milton and Poussin." *Seventeenth Century Studies Presented to Sir Herbert Grierson*. Oxford University Press, 1938, 192–210.

Routh, James. "English Iambic Meter." *PMLA*, XL (1925), 921–932.

Smith, J. C. "Feminine Endings in Milton's Blank Verse." *TLS*, December 5, 1936, 1016.

Snell, Ada L. F. "An Objective Study of the Syllabic Quantity in English Verse." *PMLA*, XXXIII (1918), 396–408.

Spaeth, S. Milton's Knowledge of Music. Weimar, 1913.

Symonds, John A. "The Blank Verse of Milton." *Fortnightly Review*, XXII (1874), 767–781.

Whaler, James. "Grammatical Nexus of the Miltonic Simile." *JEGP*, XXX (1931), 327–334.

Whaler, James. "The Compounding and Distribution of Simile in *Paradise Lost.*" *MP*, XXVIII (1931), 313–327.

Whaler, James. "The Miltonic Simile." *PMLA*, XLVI (1931), 1034–1074.

MILTON'S FAME AND INFLUENCE

Adams, Charles F. "Knowledge of Milton in Early New England." *Nation*, LXXXVII (1908), 599–600.

Crane, Ronald S. "Imitation of Spenser and Milton in the Early Eighteenth Century; a New Document." *SP*, XV (1918), 195–206.

Good, John W. Studies in the Milton Tradition. *University of Illinois Studies in Language and Literature*, I (1915), 1–310.

Graf, Arturo. L'Anglomania el l'influsso inglese in Italia, nel secolo XVIII. Turin, 1911.

Guiney, Louise I., "Milton and Henry Vaughan," *Quarterly Review*, CCXX (1914), 353–364.

Havens, Raymond D. The Influence of Milton on English Poetry. Harvard University Press, 1922.

Havens, Raymond D. "The Early Reputation of *Paradise Lost.*" *ES*, XL (1909), 187–199.

Havens, Raymond D. "Seventeenth Century Notices of Milton." *ES*, XL (1909), 175–186.

Howard, Leon. "The Influence of Milton on Colonial American Poetry." *Huntington Library Bulletin*, No. 9 (April, 1936), 63–89.

Ibershoff, C. H. "Bodmer and Milton Once More." *PMLA*, XLIII (1928), 1055–1061.

Ibershoff, C. H. "Bodmer as a Literary Borrower." *PQ*, I (1922), 110–116.

Larson, Martin A. "The Influence of Milton's Divorce Tracts on Farquhar's *Beaux' Stratagem*." *PMLA*, XXXIX (1924). 174–178.

Mackail, J. W. "Bentley's Milton." *Proceedings of the British Academy*, 1924.

"Milton's Impress on the Provincial Literature of New England." *Report of the Massachusetts Historical Society*, February, 1909.

Oras, Ants. Milton's Editors and Commentators from Patrick Hume to Henry John Todd. Oxford University Press, 1931.

Peers, E. Allison. "Milton in Spain." *SP*, XXIII (1926), 169–183.

Pizzo, E. Miltons *Verlorenes Paradies* im deutschen Urteile des 18. Jahrhunderts. *Literar.-Hist. Forschungen*. Berlin, 1914.

Richards, Alfred E. "Milton's Popularity in the Eighteenth Century." *MLN*, XLI (1926), 322.

Robertson, John G. "Milton's Fame on the Continent." *Proceedings of the British Academy*, 1907–1908, 319–340.

Sanderlin, George. "The Influence of Milton and Wordsworth on the Early Victorian Sonnet." *ELH*, V (1938), 225–251.

Saurat, Denis. Blake and Milton. London, 1935.

Sherburn, George. "The Early Popularity of Milton's *Minor Poems*." *MP*, XVII (1920), 259–278; 515–540.

Telleen, John. M. Milton dans la littérature française. Paris, 1904.

Williams, Charles. "The New Milton." *The London Mercury*, July, 1937, 255–261.

INDEX

Throughout the Index Milton's name has been omitted from entries.

449